A MINGLED YARN

A MINGLED YARN

The web of our life is of a mingled yarn.
All's Well that Ends Well, IV, iii, 85.

Recollections

DILLWYN MILES

Gwasg Dinefwr Press

Copyright © 2000 Dillwyn Miles

The right of Dillwyn Miles to be identified as the Author of the Work has been asserted by him in accordance with the Copyright, Designs and Patents Act 1988.

All rights reserved. No part of this publication may be reproduced, stored in a retrieval system or transmitted, in any form or by any means without the prior permission of the publisher, nor be otherwise circulated in any form of binding or cover other than that in which it is published and without similar condition being imposed on the subsequent purchaser.

A CIP catalogue record for this book is available from the British Library.

ISBN 0 9519926 8 6

Published and printed in Wales by
Gwasg Dinefwr Press
Rawlings Road, Llandybie
Carmarthenshire, SA18 3YD

*In gratitude to
Joyce,
Anthony and Marilyn.
Andrew and Tamsin, Emily and Max
and Judith*

CONTENTS

The Wind and the Rain	9
To War in Jerusalem	61
Syria and the Lebanon	130
'When a man should marry . . .'	146
Back to Blighty	178
Palestine House	188
Newport Castle	202
On the Council	215
The Most Interesting Job . . .	231
The Herald Bard	262
In Anecdotage	300
Envoi	335
Chronology	336

THE WIND AND THE RAIN

When that I was and a tiny little boy,
With a hey, ho, and the wind and the rain;
A foolish thing was but a toy.
For the rain it raineth every day.
                                    Twelfth Night V, i

WHETHER IT IS THE BURNING of the Kaiser or the ride in the family waggonette that takes pride of place in my memory, I cannot tell. The Kaiser, looking more like a scarecrow than an imperial tyrant, was propped up against the pine end wall of the Midland Bank on Newport Square, and when it was lit and its straw stuffing burned furiously, a great cry went up from the people who had gathered to celebrate the end of the war that was to end all wars, as Lloyd George had said, and no one would doubt his word. My mother had taken me there and she lifted me high to see the flames consume the wicked despot who had kept her husband away from her for the best part of the last four years. David Morgan, our milkman, saw her effort to hold aloft a chubby two and a half year old and took me from her and sat me on his shoulders until the fire became a glow, and the people sang a hymn of thanksgiving

The memory of the waggonette may even be earlier. It was when we went to the annual horse and cattle show at Fishguard. The rest of the family sat on the facing side seats of the carriage, but I was wedged between my grandfather and Uncle Tom on the driver's seat, half-hidden by the rug that covered our legs. I drove the horses with loud gee-ups and tugs at the loose ends of the reins, until the swaggering rhythm of their shining haunches sent me to sleep. Perhaps I remember it best because I heard Grandma describe the occasion so many times and laugh at my innocent belief that I was really driving the horses, when she recalled the happiest of times in the half century of bliss that she and Grandpa had spent together.

It was such a long time ago, and yet seemed like yesterday, she would say, since that old gypsy woman, having had her palm crossed with silver, had told her that she would meet a tall, handsome gentleman whose other love was horses, and that however much she might try to escape him, he would pursue her until she became his wife. This prediction came true when she saw William Lewis, striding six foot and three inches tall, and carrying a riding whip, as the old gypsy had said, at Newport Fair. She spurned his advances, or pretended to do so, even when he rode over the hills on moonlit nights and threw gravel at her bedroom window but, in the end, his persistence won the day, and so it was that on the fifth day of December in 1876, Anne Phillips, of Fountain Hill, and William Lewis of Hendre, pledged their troth in the single-chambered church of Saint Dogmael in the parish of Meline in the county of Pembroke. Their son was born, and named Thomas Phillips, and baptised in the same church in the following year, but six years were to pass before Anne gave birth to their only other child, a daughter named after her grandmothers, Anne Mariah, but always known, like her maternal grandam, as Nancy. She was to become my mother.

    William Lewis had been born during the Rebecca Riots, in October 1843, at Hendre in the parish of Meline. Hendre lay at the foot of the Presely Hills, on the northern side, its land watered by a brook that ran through Cwm Hendre. The drive to the house was lined with bluebells in spring, and as it ran downward and was overhung with laburnum, the house came into view from the bottom upward, but one did not have to go far to see it all, for it was low and long, with a wing at the rear. He was the youngest son of a cadet branch of a family that traced to Cuhelyn Fardd, who wrote verse and held power in north Pembrokeshire when the Normans came. He would not talk about the glory that had gone, but he would have much to say about life as he found it, and in particular about the hunting and the shooting that were the main pastimes of his younger days. His horsemanship was a legend, and so was his marksmanship. Many a time I heard the story told of how he had shot a hare through a colleague's legs, but I never understood how it had been done. It was something that no other man had accomplished and it placed him on a pedestal among his peers. Tall and proud of bearing, and the most handsome of men, he wore a tweed jacket, buttoned high, that had pockets for everything and, above all, for cartridges and powder and shot. On his head, most times, was a stalking cap, but when he went to a horse show or a race meeting, he would don his broad-brimmed Baden Powell, which gave him further distinction. More as a companion than out of need, he carried a tall stick with a curved head that was shaped a bit like a shepherd's crook, or his blackthorn thumb stick which had more than a hundred knots. People calling at the house were sometimes shown other walking sticks from his collection. There were curiosities like his 'Harry Lauder', a contorted hazel, and sword sticks, and one made of polished mahogany that could be unscrewed to produce an elongated brandy bottle, while in its silver mounted top was secreted a small glass of the type Russians use to knock back their vodka. Then there was the pair that he had bought from an old tramp for a silver crown, each having carved upon it entwined snakes, bees and damselflies and butterflies, a cock pheasant and cherries, and oak leaves and acorns, a thistle, a shamrock, a red rose and a leek, all painted in natural colours, and an imperial crown and VR for *Victoria Regina*.

His father, Thomas Lewis of Hendre, lies buried in the graveyard beside the little grey chapel at Brynberian. He was known as 'the Grand Old Man of Hendre', yet his tombstone records that he died in his sixty-sixth year. That he should be buried in Nonconformist ground, while his forefathers lie in the churchyard at Meline, may indicate a touch of that dissent that caused an earlier William Lewis to be 'excommunicated for contumacy.' Thomas was known for his wisdom and regarded as a leader of the community. On one occasion he had undertaken to vouch for the appearance of two litigants, charged and counter charged with assault, at the Assizes at Haverfordwest. As they would have to make an early start, he invited them both to spend the night at Hendre, the one to arrive a little before nightfall, and the other after dark. When the latter came to the door, my ancestor informed him that the house was full of family and guests and apologised for having to ask him to share a bedroom with one of the guests. The man agreed and went to bed quietly in the dark, as requested, so as not to disturb his bedfellow, already asleep. When they awoke the next morning, the two litigants found themselves face to face and, as they had both slept in the same bedroom there was little purpose in pursuing their case at the Assizes.

The Battle of Balaclava was about to be fought when my grandmother was born, on 14 July 1854. She went to school at Nevern, where she learned the three Rs and played fivestones perilously on the cutwater triangles each side of Nevern Bridge. More than once, she had been made to wear the dreaded WELSH NOT, a small board inscribed WN that was handed by one child to another heard speaking Welsh, either in the classroom or on the playground. He or she who wore it at the end of the day was beaten with a stick. She was taught the spelling of English words by building up syllables phonetically until the word was complete, all in one breath and at a speed that baffled the listener, especially when the word was a long one. She would demonstrate the method to me by repeating how she had learned to spell 'valetudinarian':

v a, va; l e, le: vale; t u, tu: valetu;
d i, di: valetudi; n a, na: valetudina;
r i, ri: valetudinari; a n, an: valetudinarian.

The house in which she was born is now a ruin, save for a pine end with its big chimney beneath which, on winter's nights, the family would gather round the fire. There had been twelve children born to Thomas Phillips and his wife, Nancy. Two boys, both named Benjamin, had died in infancy, and of two Margarets one was short-lived and the other had survived only to the age of nine, so that Grandmother was left with a sister, Mary, and six brothers: John, the eldest, had married Helen Owen of Hescwm, and Owen had found a wife, Elizabeth Thomas, in Glamorgan. The other brothers had become mariners: Joshua had died in America; Tommy had succumbed to the yellow fever in Cuba, and David had perished somewhere in Australia, no one knew where. Then there was James, her favourite brother, who was a master mariner. The walls are now heaps of stones, lichen covered and part hidden by autumn bracken of so many hues that a pheasant lying among it would escape the eye of the fowler. A rowan tree grew out of the kitchen floor, and three ash trees in the parlour, for its carpet was now thick soil. The little temple that had enshrined the daily comings and goings, the thoughts and the ambitions, the happiness and the sorrow of a whole family of people, had been reduced to rubble, for mother earth had reclaimed her own. The flesh and blood that tenanted the dwelling had also reverted, earth to earth, and all that remained was the blood that ran in my veins. I walked into the walled garden and plucked a plum from the tree from which Grandmother had eaten, a century and a half before, and ate it.

Grandmother sometimes spoke of strange characters she had known, or of whom she had heard tell. She often did so in a subdued voice, as though they were within earshot and ready to wreak some dreadful vengeance upon her for even mentioning their names. Such a one was Shemi'r Halen who was said to break the hind legs of cattle to avenge the slightest provocation. She spoke with disquiet also of *y rheibwyr*, the bewitchers, of whom there were some still living in the locality, and woe betide anyone who gave them offence, though they would cause discomfiture, like casting a spell on milk so that it would not turn into butter, rather than cause bodily harm. Persons bewitched would go to see *y dadrheibwr*, the exorcist, who would remove the spell in return for a fee. Dr Joseph Harries of Werndew was a man gifted with such powers and was resorted to by sufferers.

It was written on the inside page of the Miles family Bible that my father, Joshua, had been 'born on April 24th at 9.40 a.m in the year of our Lord Jesus Christ 1868' at Heol Fach, Ystradfodwg, the third son of James Miles and his wife, Anne, daughter of John Griffiths of Penycwm, Llanelli. He was one of six sons and there were three daughters, one of whom, Elizabeth, died in infancy, and another, Elizabeth Anne, failed to see her twentieth birthday. His paternal grandfather, Joshua Miles, was the son of Miles Miles of Llandyfaelog, and on his mother's side, he was a kinsman of Dr Henry Lewis, Member of Parliament for

Llanelli, and of Lord Elwyn-Jones, the Lord Chancellor. When James Miles was appointed Manager of the Maerdy Colliery, he and his family moved to Maerdy, to live at Maerdy House. The family had its roots in Pembrokeshire since Miles ap Thomas, son of Thomas ap Gwilym ap Griffith ap Gwilym ap Gruffydd Fychan of Llaneigon in the county of Brecknock, was inducted rector of Meline on 5 June 1583. In the following year he built Penpedwast, in that parish, 'that was previously a hamlet of two or three houses, as his mansion', on land that he leased from George Owen of Henllys, lord of Cemais.

It may have been an attraction to the land of his fathers, or merely the fashion of the time to spend one's holidays at the seaside, that brought my father to Pembrokeshire, and it was while he was on a visit that he met my mother, and on 13 October 1903 he, being thirty-five years of age, married her, aged twenty-one years, at Ebenezer Congregational Church at Newport. They do not appear to have bothered having a honeymoon for, three days later, they were in business at the Castle Hotel which father had purchased from Captain William Davies for £800, which he had paid in gold sovereigns. He had followed his father's profession before he got married, and he returned to the mines during the Great War, and stayed on when the war was over. The General Strike of 1926 and the plight of the miners was a matter of great concern to him and by 1930 he had left the coal field, never to return. No one knew how heavily he lost on account of the strike: one simply heard of instances, as of rows of houses that he owned at Maerdy that no longer yielded any rent, as the tenants were all unemployed, and their maintenance had exceeded their value.

One of the few contacts he had with his younger days was the Vicar of Nevern, the Reverend Lewis Roderick, and his wife, who had taught him at school, and sometimes he would take me with him to the vicarage, which was a long walk for a small boy. We would leave the high road at Llwyngwair Lodge, a round pink-washed house looking like the Staffordshire pottery ornament on Grandmother's mantel shelf, and walk along the back drive leading to the Llwyngwair stables. The carriage-rutted road was screened by rhododendron bushes and clumps of bamboo until we came to a gap where there was a pond, across the mirror face of which moor hens darted to the safety of the encircling phragmytes and bulrushes. The road was divided from the park land in front of the big house by the kind of iron fence that one only saw on the estates of the gentry. Before we reached the clock-towered stables, the lane did a dogleg and we passed under a canopy of dark holm oaks of cathedral proportions beyond which, in the treetops, a colony of herons built their nests. We then found ourselves shuffling ankle deep in sand as we walked through Sandy Lane, and father explained to me that the land around us was once under the sea. The carriageway then crossed an open water meadow and joined the high road by Nevern Bridge. The vicarage stood among giant beech trees, a garden's width from the brook Caman, which ran past the squat-towered church. As soon as we were in his study, the vicar would call his daughter to take charge of me, and I remember being taken to the garden, where we ate grapes off a vine which, I later discovered, had been given to the poet Ioan Tegid, then vicar, by Lady Llanover when he attended the Abergavenny Eisteddfod in 1848.

My mother had been married for thirteen years before I was born, on 25 May 1916. There was considerable rejoicing, therefore, when I appeared as, otherwise the lineage would come to an end in the male line and, presumably to please both sides of the family, I was given the names of my two grandfathers, William and James, and the further name of Dillwyn, by which I have been known. It is a name that I have never liked, but it has had the advantage of giving me a name and surname so distinctive that I have never heard of another person bearing the same.

I learned to walk by clinging to the back hair of our tolerant Airedale dog, called Dash, which would take me at a patient pace round the paved courtyard at the back of our house, and up and down the long garden path. In the courtyard was a wash house, with a mangle that I feared lest I should get my fingers flattened between its rollers, and a large boiler built into one corner, in which water was boiled on laundry days. There was also an outer house which contained cast-off and unwanted things that became treasures for a curious boy. In particular, it housed my father's ancient bicycle that he kept, but never rode, because it had a peculiar braking device that had been invented by his uncle Josiah, who was better known for his invention of medical instruments, for which he received the commendation of the Royal Society.

The garden had several apple trees, one of which produced *afalau pren glas* (apples of the green tree). When ripe, the apple was golden except for a few streaks of red running down one side, and its taste, like that of a Cox's Orange Pippin, was quite distinctive. There were gooseberry and currant bushes and, at the far end of the garden, a large rhubarb bed, and a weigelia, that mother always called 'the apple blossom tree'. When the gardener came to prepare the beds and plant the potatoes and sow the seeds, I was allowed to sit on a stone bench while he had his mug of tea, and given a glass of milk and a slice of bread and butter spread thick with black currant jam. The garden fence was planted with elms, among which grew privet bushes and some elder, which I viewed with suspicion, for I once ate my fill of the berries until I became violently ill. An emetic and a good night's sleep restored my health, however, but I never again touched elderberries, except when transformed into a rich purple wine.

My childhood was softly and jealously guarded by three ancient crones, each of whom I called Anta, my attempt to say Aunt, followed by her surname. When I came to read Shakespeare's *Macbeth*, my three witches bore the wrinkled leathern countenances of these three old women. They showered me with affection and an enveloping protectiveness that was almost frightening at times. Anta Harries wore a woven shawl over her shoulders and a long dark skirt that was pinned up in front to reveal a red flannel petticoat beneath which her brass tipped clogs peeped rhythmically as she walked. In her garden, winter heliotrope produced vanilla-scented dull-lilac flowers soon after Christmas, and a thick, tangled Jew's mallow, covered in dandelion-like flowers, grew beside her back door. Anta John changed her black straw hat for one of straw in its natural colour when summer came, and wore a cream shawl and a chequered apron over a black skirt that was down to the floor. Her face was deeply furrowed, and her yellow front teeth were crossed, so that she spoke with a slight lisp. Anta Davies wore black bombazine, with a long fringed shawl and a black bonnet. She sat in a chair covered in dark green velvet, with a white lace antimacassar, except when she got up to make herself a cup of tea or prepare a meal. She always gave me a warm welcome and a hug, and said she wished I were her 'little black haired boy'. She had inherited a small fortune from her father, who was a farmer, but had succumbed to the charms of one of the farm servants who, the day after they were married, had disappeared with most of her money and had never been seen, or heard of, again.

Mrs Rayner was yet another crone, but I had little to do with her. She was crabbed and hunched and hated children. She was English, they said, although it was murmured that she was the widow of a German. She lived alone, until her sister and husband came to share the house with her. They had not been there long, however, before they both died, the one in the morning and the other in the afternoon of the same day, and left her their money, which led to more murmured speculation and innuendo.

Lizzie Williams, the midwife, also lived nearby: when I went to record an interview her about old times, she gave me a description of my birth. She and her husband, Jim, a woodsman, had three carrot-haired children: a boy named Beynon and, considerably older, twin girls, Olwen and Morfudd, so alike that only those who were near to them knew which was which. Once, when a conjurer gave a performance at the Memorial Hall, one of his most daring acts was to cut off the head of a girl who sat in a kind of Turkish bath, and convey it in what looked like a hat box to another Turkish bath. The effect was lost on those who recognised the decapitated head of Olwen when it appeared again as that of Morfudd.

Then there was old Eben Richards, who was known to me as 'Unka', my effort at Uncle. Unka had sailed the seas, times over, and was now left with a greasy sailor's hat, a pair of ebony elephants and a ship in a bottle to remind him of his voyaging. He mixed his own tobacco, which gave its aroma to the house, and the nicotine had stained his patriarchal beard so that the white hairs were yellow and the grey ones green. Next to him, but set back on a bank, was a house that was the one-man woollen factory of Daniel y Gwehydd, Daniel the Weaver. On the ground floor was a large spinning wheel, at which he sat and span before taking the wool upstairs, where the loom was. I spent hours watching the shuttle dart to and fro as it produced woollen material of various patterns. Most times it would be white with a narrow black, or grey, line suitable for making shirts and drawers for men, or else red, with wide black lines, to make petticoats.

Along the road stood the Farmers Arms which, with its four floors and bay windows and solid portico, was one of the most imposing buildings in the town. It had formerly belonged to my grandparents, and my mother had been born there. Opposite the Farmers, vying with it in height and grandeur, stood Abertawe House, which Grandma's favourite brother, Captain James Phillips, had built. He had married Anne, the eldest daughter of Evan Lewis of Blaenmeini, who was grandfather's brother, and their son and daughter, Howard and Muriel, therefore were both uncle and aunt and cousins of mine. James Phillips had named his house after his ship, the SS *Abertawe* on which he once took Grandma from Swansea to Liverpool, where she attended the Liverpool International Exhibition when it was opened by Queen Victoria in May 1886.

Alongside the Farmers Arms was David Rees the Butcher's shop, and each year, in the shop window would appear a white enamel tray full of small pears which he sold at four for a penny. Captain Thomas lived at Cemais House, next to the butcher's. He was a retired master mariner, who had sailed round Cape Horn more than once, and was now stiff and slow of movement. Beside Cemais House was a gate that opened on to a field in which a great Boy Scouts' Jamboree was once held. It was, in fact, a paddock that adjoined the Cotham Lodge stables, a long building, with hayloft over, and a blank windowless wall that backed on to the main road. Between the gate and the stables was a gabled cottage, with bushes of fuchsia each side of the door, where the Backshells lived. Backshell, as his wife always called him, was a baker, and he and his wife and children had pale faces as though they had been moulded out of the dough he kneaded each night. Mrs. Backshell's father, John Davies, who lived with them, held the tenancy as he was the gardener at Cotham Lodge, and was known to everybody as John Cotham.

Cotham Lodge was built in 1789 by James Bowen, who was mayor the previous year. Before succeeding his father at Llwyngwair in 1810 he and his wife had lived at Cotham, in Bristol, after which they named Cotham Lodge. The house was shielded from the common gaze by a high stone wall and all that was visible by the passer-by was a tall pine-end with the two windows of the maids' bedrooms on the third floor. Mature, and stately, beech trees shed their mast on the highway each autumn and, in the grounds there also grew a sweet chestnut, a monkey puzzle tree, clutches of bamboo, rhododendrons, and some Scots pines. The east wall was covered with jasmine and, beside it, an old magnolia never failed to display a fine show of white purple-stained cups each year. The house was approached through a door set in an arch in the wall, beneath a canopy of ivy and white clematis, and a pair of doors further along the wall that opened only to allow a carriage or, later, a motor car, to come and go. The wall continued up Cotham Hill as a stone hedge bank, planted with quickset, and behind it was the kitchen garden which had great beds of asparagus and celery and globe artichokes, and among the apples and pears, a row of medlar trees bore downy brown fruit that could only be eaten when they were half rotten. Four tall walnut trees grew inside the hedge bank and each autumn, among the fallen leaves on the roadside, hid glossy green plum-like fruit from which one would strip the husk to get at the crinkly shelled nut and its milky-fresh kernel.

Across the road from the garden stood Cotham Wood, a copse of perhaps a dozen pines and the like number of broad-leaved trees, with an under-storey thick with elder and holly, blackthorn and bramble, but to me it was vast as the forests of the Amazon, and in it I was the lone explorer. It was separated from the road by a trimmed hedge of beech that provided a home for the cockchafers of the neighbourhood. I would catch one of these monster scarab beetles and place it, with some beech leaves, in a matchbox and take it to school to the wonder of the other boys who, in the main, would never have seen one. In the copse sprang a stream that ran no more than thirty paces before it was forced through a cast-iron pipe set in a stone built alcove that provided cover for townspeople when they brought their two gallon cans to fetch water.

Next to Cotham Lodge was a field that belonged to 'Old' Doctor Havard which he had converted into a vegetable garden to supply his household. His gardener, Dafi'r Doctor, would pluck a young carrot from the ground and brush the earth off it with his horny hand and give it a final polish on his moleskin trousers before giving it to me to eat. After the doctor had died, his widow gave the field to the town as a site for a hall to be built in memory of those who had given their lives in the 1914-18 war. A ceremony was held for the laying of the foundation stone, or rather two foundation stones, one each side of where the front door was to be: one bore the initials D.H. and was laid by the 'young' Doctor David Havard, and the other was inscribed J.O.V. for J. O. Vaughan who was the mayor at the time and was largely responsible for having the hall built. It was originally meant to be of corrugated iron zinc but it was then felt that it would be a more befitting memorial if it were built of stone. While the foundations of the hall were being dug, a medieval pottery kiln was uncovered, containing several yellow-green vessels, drawings of which were made by a visiting young archaeologist, Mortimer Wheeler.

The hall was opened, in 1923, by the Mayor, Frederick Withington, of Bicester, in the presence of his father-in-law, Sir Marteine Lloyd, and a host of townspeople. The nimblest among the boys, including my brother, Herbert, climbed on to the cannon that had been brought to stand in front of the hall as a reminder of the horrors of war. Sir Marteine addressed the crowd in broken Welsh, and there were speeches by the Mayor and by Alderman J. O. Vaughan and others before we all went into the hall for the first time.

My brother was born on Ffair Fach day, 16 October 1918, less than a month before the Great War ended. He was named Herbert because Captain Herbert Davies, Fern Cottage, was feared missing at sea and his distraught mother implored that he should be named after her son. He was also called Thomas, after mother's brother, Uncle Tom, and Lewis, to perpetuate her unmarried name.

We had a quiet upbringing and although father was away from home most of the time, mother was able to control us with no discernible effort, and I have no recollection of ever being threatened with a stick: chastisement came in the form of stern words. I was in receipt of such a chiding one evening, sitting in the parlour, when there was a knock at the door. I sat contemplating Constable's *Haywain*, that hung on one side of the fireplace, while mother was away, hoping that her reprimand would be over when she returned, but when she sat down again in the leather armchair, she went on: 'There you are! If you don't behave yourself you'll be like that man who was at the door. The son of a minister of the gospel, and a minister himself at one time, with his own chapel in London, but he couldn't behave himself. And look at him now: a tramp, going from door to door, selling boot laces!' The unfortunate was none other than the poet Dewi Emrys who had, indeed, been in charge of Finsbury Park Congregational Church until he had joined the Army in 1917 to escape his critics. He became a cadet officer but had been cashiered, and his career had slid ever downward, yet all the time he was a poet, winning chairs, and crowns, that he sometimes pawned.

Grandmother knew that the end was near when her William no longer called for his pipe. The night before he died Herbert and I were put in Uncle Tom's bed while he and mother kept vigil. We slept soundly for we were too young and no understanding of death. On the day of the funeral, the first day of April, 1922, the snow was thick on the ground that there were fears that the horses would not be able to draw the hearse and the mourners' carriages. The rector came, as he had come to the house before, but this time he was wearing his surplice, and there were ministers from all the chapels, for death knew not denomination. Relatives from the more distant parts had arrived early so that they could take one last look at his face before the lid was put on the coffin, and tell Grandma how well he looked, how handsome still, and so much at peace. Those living nearer had already rendered this service during the three days and three nights he had lain in the parlour, with candles at each end of the coffin. After prayers and a Bible reading and a hymn, the coffin was carried out of the house and put in the hearse, the roof of which was by now covered with floral tributes, but Grandma's wreath, and our own were placed on the coffin. The hearse slithered slightly as the horses took the strain, but the snow was already melting and those that followed on foot were able to walk in the tracks of the vehicles. Herbert and I were not allowed to go to the church service or the committal in the churchyard, and were told that we would have a treat after the funeral. The treat came when J. O. Vaughan brought his T-Ford car to take mother to the polling station, as it was County Council election day and he was up for re-election, and we had our first ride in a motor vehicle.

Grandma was inconsolable, praying that the good Lord would take her that night so that she could be united with her husband for ever and ever. Nothing would ease the pain of her grief, except that I should be allowed to stay with her, to comfort her, for a little while. The 'little while' lasted twelve years.

The entrance hall at Grandma's house was covered with red, yellow and black tiles upon which stood an oak coffer that her grandmother had passed on to her. An oak staircase led up from the hall and on the first landing was a door to the loft at the back of the house, where I played with my toys, chief among which was a model of a German zeppelin, or browsed in an old Harrod's catalogue, a huge tome in which there were all the treasures of the world, it seemed. From harvest time onward the loft was seized with the smell of small apples.

In the living room an oak Welsh dresser, polished with beeswax and dragon's blood, was laden with lustre jugs and rows of willow pattern plates each stamped 'Dillwyn' on the back as they had been made at the Swansea pottery of that name. Beside it, hanging on the wall, was a long cased clock that struck the hours, from which hung a love-spoon with a ring and three pea-sized balls running loose in a hollow in its handle all carved from the one piece of wood. On the mantel shelf, at each end, were tall ornaments of duck-egg blue glass from the bowls of which dangled three-sided glass prisms that were shot with colours of the rainbow. They had been brought from Japan by Uncle James, and there were other ornaments that were gifts and mementoes from remote parts of the world. Over the mantelpiece were Alken hunting prints showing phases of the chase. On each side of the fireplace, in arched recesses, were cupboards on which rested Chinese bowls and a hookah that had never been puffed, and books. A picture of the Duke of York, who became King George V, in full naval uniform, and his bride, Princess May of Teck, who became Queen Mary, occupied the wall near the window and by the door, under more hunting prints, was a high-backed settle, or *sgiw*.

The fire in the parlour was lit on few occasions apart from the twelve days of Christmas. Normally, the rounded cast iron grate lay concealed behind a Pembroke table covered by a heavy damask cloth upon which rested the massive family Bible and the family album, together with a photograph of Grandfather in his Baden Powell hat, set in a silver frame. The Bible was the biggest book that I had ever seen. Its walnut coloured leather cover had an intricate brass work medallion on its front, and corner pieces to match. Its spine was inscribed Y BEIBL CYSSEGRLAN, which implied even greater sanctity than the English 'Holy Bible'. Here and there among its pages were plates showing Biblical animals and plants: a fierce lion, an innocent Jacob's lamb, the cinnamon-hued hoopoe, pink hyssop, the rose of Sharon and lily of the field. There was a bookmark of pink ribbon, now faded to the colour of flesh, and fragile to the touch, upon which, in a child's cross-stitch, my great-grandmother had woven, COFIWCH FI, 'Remember me'. Upon a blank page, lined in gold, were recorded the name, date and time of birth of each member of the family, and the day and hour of their departing. The album had heavy, cushioned covers, and pages of laminated card with windows in which the photographs, mostly portraits, some of them daguerreotype, were displayed. When the fire was lit, the Pembroke table was moved to one side of the fireplace, on the other side of which was a small table, also covered with a cloth so as to conceal its legs in accordance with the fashion of the time, and on it was a large glass case of flowers made of sea shells. Yet another table, in front of the window, had a dark green flower pot embossed in gold, holding a large zygocactus that gave forth purple flowers at Christmas time, cascading to the floor. Among the pictures on the walls were a painting of great-uncle James's vessel the SS *Abertawe*, and another of Vesuvius in eruption, beneath which a small earthenware pot occupied a place of honour as it had been brought from Pompeii. A pair of china dogs stood guard on the mantelpiece, and two recumbent roan greyhounds, and a pair of black cows that could be used as milk jugs. In the centre was a Staffordshire pottery house with a roof of royal blue. As I grew older the parlour became my study, and it was there, beside a spitting log fire, that I made my acquaintance with Dickens and Thackeray and Macaulay, Hardy and Scott, Tolstoi, Maupassant and Rabindranath Tagore.

At the rear of the house was the old kitchen which had a massive open chimney, the traditional *simne fawr*, on one side of which was a large built-in boiler that was used for boiling water, with a handful of bran thrown into it, with which to remove the bristles from a dead pig. Killing the pig was a ritual. The poor creature would be dragged out of its sty and laid on a form where the butcher cut its throat, and it would squeal until the last drop of blood had been pumped out of its body. The scalding water was brought out in cans and the bristles scraped off with the can lids. When the skin was clean, the carcass was brought indoors and hung from a beam in the outer kitchen, where it was disembowelled. A woman, who came for the purpose, took away the entrails and washed them under a spout of running water, cutting them into small pieces which she turned inside out, and washed, several times. They were then placed in salt water, in a special earthenware jar, with the water being renewed daily for nine days before they could be served as chitterlings, fried with an abundance of onion, to provide the finest feast in all the world. The kidneys and the liver and the lights were fried, with onions, for supper. The butcher returned the following day to cut up the pig, into forelegs and flitches and gammons, but before doing so he would take slices off the back, which provided the delicacy that evening and were shared with neighbours. The forelegs, flitches and gammons were massaged with salt and saltpetre over a period of three weeks before they were hung from the kitchen rafters to provide rashers of bacon for breakfast, and hunks to put in the *cawl*, for the next twelve months.

On long summer evenings, after I had gone to bed, I would lie listening to the *crex crex* call of the corncrake in the hayfield opposite my window. The distant call would sound like someone winding a watch and, as it got nearer, it would fill one's ears and appear to be almost within one's reach. People said that the corncrake could cast its voice, like a ventriloquist, and that you could never catch, or even see, one on that account. And you could not always tell whether it was one bird or two in the same meadow. At other times, a nightjar would begin its churring trill that would rise and fall unbroken for minutes at a time, and would then peter out as though its battery had run down.

In the yard beside the house were the stables, a coach house which held a dust-laden coach, a cart house with two carts, a pigsty, a midden and a barn. One corner of the barn had been paled off as a hay pen and in it the bales cut from the haystack, each the thickness of the hay knife, were kept ready to be carried to the stables. Some would be fed, along with freshly cut dwarf gorse, into the chaff-cutter, the wheel of which had two blades that chopped the doubly fragrant mixture into a creel. The barn was also used as a tack room, its walls hung with sets of harness for carriages long unused, and with spare bridles, snaffles, collars, belly bands, breechings, cruppers, saddles, traces, martin gales and reins of many lengths.

A lilac hedge screened the garden from the yard, and in its midst grew a forked laburnum tree that was a profusion of golden chains at Whitsuntide. Behind the hedge was the cabbage patch, and a row of dahlias of many colours. The seed bed was sown with leeks, carrots, parsnips, beetroot, shallots, the same each year, and each year self-seeded summer savoury grew, like little bonsai trees, among them. There were rows of peas and broad beans and runner beans, and the south facing slope was planted with early potatoes. Around the garden were flower borders and low shrubs among which I marvelled at the sessile flowers of the Butcher's Broom, which Grandma called 'the Crown of Thorns', but loved best the scarlet blossoms of the Japonica Quince. A row of ancient apple trees produced small red cheeked apples, while chunky green cookers hung from an espalier in the middle of the garden, beneath which grew a clump of Tenby daffodils, their small trumpets the early harbingers of spring.

Behind a paling of slate flagstones, and lying between the garden and a fast-flowing stream, was a tiny wilderness into which I hacked a way through dense undergrowth, so low that no adult could creep through, and built a little hut into which I would retreat on warm days. I also made a tree house high in a sycamore from which I surveyed the world around me, and watched the red apples ripen. The stream tinkled past a row of plum trees that grew in the garden hedge, and an errant hop vine that twined and twirled and bore clusters of frilled fruit as though to show that it could flourish in adversity. It then followed the east side of Phaeton Field until it came to a bank of wild cherries, where green lizards lazed in the sun, and foxgloves formed regiments on the overspill of rabbit burrows. The stream had no name, so I called it *Gafren,* the little goat, because of its sprightly prance.

Another stream ran down the far side of the field, which I dubbed *Duad,* the dark one, as it flowed most of its way beneath a canopy of blackthorn until it emerged beside a bed of yellow iris, and disappeared again into a ditch under a thicket of brambles and turned right to follow the bottom of Phaeton Field until it joined the Gafren beneath the roots of a white willow, forming a large pool in which my cousins, Evan and Binnie Vaughan and I used to bathe, safe from the eyes of the world, or so we thought, until their governess came one day and chased us through an adjoining field. The field was waist high with thistles and our little naked bodies became pin-cushioned with their prickly spines, as we made our escape. From this confluence onward, the river flowed down Cwm Dewi, but not before it received the overflow of Ffynnon Dewi, a holy well of the patron saint that once had slaked the thirst of pilgrims calling at Capel Dewi, a chapel of ease that had stood in one of our fields, on their way from Strata Florida to St David's. I hardly ever saw a footprint in Cwm Dewi, save those of Ianto the Poacher, who came with his gun in search of woodcock or snipe.

The field was called Phaeton Field because, at its top corner, beside the thatched haystack and a chicken shed, stood some horse-drawn vehicles, made redundant by the advent of the motor car, among which my favourite was the phaeton, which now was mine to drive galloping horses to the ends of the earth. There was also a barouche, somewhat decayed, that reminded me of the Wells Fargo coach that was chased by Red Indians round the ring of Lord John Sanger's Circus in a great crackle of gunfire and clouds of smoke as the finale to the evening's performance. Beside it I built my own circus ring, of short sticks and thatcher's twine and, as ringmaster, I stood in the centre cracking a silver mounted carriage whip at imaginary horses and camels and elephants, and, I would also be bareback rider, mahout, lion tamer, lasso spinning cowboy, clown or tumbler, in turn.

The day the circus came to town was the most exciting of the year for me. The elephants would be walked the eight miles from Fishguard and Goodwick Railway Station during the night, silent and without a trace of their passing except for great heaps of manure every so often along the road. At the first light of dawn I would settle myself on a hedge top above Pontnewydd Hill, which was then steep and narrow, and watch up to seventy gaily painted waggons move cautiously down Feidr Hill until the skids were removed at the bottom, before they would take a sharp run at the hill below me. The lighter waggons would be drawn by a pair or four horses, the heavier ones by teams of six or eight, many of them piebald or skewbald, and others bay, grey, sorrel, palomino and, occasionally the handsomely spotted Appaloosa. They would reach the hilltop wild-eyed, with nostrils curled and exuding clouds of breath in the morning air. I would sometimes play truant in order to watch the circus 'big top' being erected and preparations made for the performances, and I would also absent myself from school on one other day in the year, which was hay-making day.

On a sunny morning in June, as the dew was lifting, the mowers would arrive, each bearing his scythe like a figure of Father Time and, after sharpening their blades with long, rounded whetstones that hung from their belts, the leader would open his swath, and each man would follow, taking his time from him, so that they moved across the field in one steady rhythmic row. Every now and again, they would all stop together to sharpen their scythes again, and exchange a few words as they straightened their backs before each would take hold of his snead and proceed with measured stroke, leaving the cut hay in green windrows behind them. When the days of the scythe-men were over, a neighbouring farmer brought his mowing machine, drawn by a pair of shire horses. There were three fields to be cut and the machine would go round and round in each, leaving shining ribbons of hay, mingled with red and white clover, buttercups, eyebright and yellow rattle. After a few days, depending on the weather, the swaths were turned and teased with hand rakes so that the hay would dry the quicker. In the meantime, a round bed of hawthorn and blackthorn branches and gorse was prepared in the haggard, and upon this the hay would be built in a round stack. On harvesting day, friends and neighbours came, the men with their pitchforks and the women, in wide-brimmed hats, carrying hand-rakes. Some of the women would set off to rake the hay into ridges and then into hay cocks, ready for the men to pitch on to a cart fitted with a hay-frame, over which the carter would spread his load. The other women followed the cart, raking the wisps of hay that were left behind. The laden cart made for the haggard where two more men pitched the hay to a man who stood on top of the haystack to shape it, and when it grew too high for him to be reached, a ladder was placed against the stack upon which another man would stand and pass up each laden pitchfork.

Every now and again the beer jar would be taken round, either by an old man who was too old for any hard work, or by a boy, and each helper would have a mug of beer. This would be a low gravity ale that could be drunk as a thirst quencher, and there would be lemonade for the children, or home-made ginger beer. When meal times arrived, women brought the food in large baskets and we would all settle comfortably into hay cocks to eat the sandwiches or bread and cheese and, when day was done, we would all gather in the house and sit at the long table for the harvest supper. The evening would end, as the day had been, full of fun and banter and laughter, which made each hay making a joyous and memorable occasion.

In return for the help we received, Uncle Tom would give a hand with the hay, and sometimes I would go with him and make myself useful, carrying the beer, or leading the cart horse as the hay cart was being loaded. One of these places was The Court, as the rectory was known, where William Hughes and his wife, Kate, looked after the rector and farmed the glebe. William had once put his hand in a corn bin into which, unbeknown to him, a polecat had fallen. The creature had bitten the tip of his thumb so that its teeth met, and I kept looking at his thumbnail to see if it still had a hole in it. The rector, Canon D. G. Phillips, a small, retiring man who held himself above and apart from his parishioners, was seldom seen, other than in church, or as he walked quietly as a shadow to and from the town, when I would meet him and receive no more than a smile when I doffed my cap.

I walked the mile and a half to school each day, and often on dark nights. There is hardly a night so dark that one cannot see the lighter shade of the human face when one met a person on the open road, but I would recognise approaching footsteps, such as the heavy clog tread of farmer William Salmon, or the mincing gait of David Thomas, the grocer, heavily built though he was, returning from his round collecting orders in Dinas and, at the same time, the local news, as he was the local correspondent for *The County Echo*. Even so, one would always bid the passer by a good night, and often exchange a few words before proceeding each on his way. One particularly dark night, as I walked up the long hill to The Court, I heard footsteps that I could not identify coming towards me. They were, I thought, those of a young man, light of foot and walking briskly. When we were almost abreast I could see the white of his shirt collar, but no face. I gave utterance to a loud 'Goodnight' but the apparition only mumbled something in reply. I was very frightened, and my one concern was to increase the distance between us without making my acceleration noticeable. I was not sure whether I had seen a man or a ghost, until I discovered that the rector's son, who was a Major in the Indian Army, was home on leave and had brought with him an Indian servant. I had never seen a coloured man before.

Grandma's neighbours were the Vaughans. James Oliver Vaughan was an alderman of the town and of the Pembrokeshire County Council, and a member of the Rural District Council, and of almost every committee there was, He was married to my Aunt Bess, the younger daughter of Evan Lewis, my grandfather's elder brother, and they had two sons, Evan, born in the same year as me, and Benjamin, always known as Binnie, and a daughter, Margaret. When the boys were small Aunt Bess used to say that Evan would one day be the manager of Lloyd's Bank, and she did not have in mind the branch of that bank at Newport, or even the one at Haverfordwest where her brother, T. Y. Lewis, was the manager, but the Bank itself. Evan retired as the Deputy General Manager of Lloyd's Bank Limited, and would, in all likelihood have become General Manager had the holder of that office been old enough to retire earlier. Binnie, she said, would be a bishop. He became Bishop of Mandeville and Bishop of British Honduras before returning to this country as Bishop of Swansea and Brecon, and many were of the opinion that he should have been appointed Archbishop of Wales.

Before the Vaughans came there, the house was occupied by the Reverend Ebenezer Richards, the retired vicar of Llanfyrnach, with his wife Marian, and four sons, Lloyd, Ivor, Granville and Geraint, and a daughter, Mary. The children called Grandma 'Lish', a toddler's version of Mrs Lewis, and after they had left, the friendship continued and Lloyd, in particular, called regularly to see her for as long as she lived. Lloyd was short and nimble, prematurely bald and with a curved nose, and kind eyes that were never without a twinkle, indicating that some new story was composing itself in his mind. It was intended that he should be a doctor but ill-health had prevented the completion of his course, and he had taken up writing. He published *A Romance of Prescelly*, which was followed by *On*

Pembroke Hills, with drawings by Roy Saunders, and a novel, *Unofficial Sanction*, but he was better known as a storyteller and I have never known anyone who settled himself down with such obvious relish to tell a tale.

It was usually on a Sunday evening, after church, that he would walk up the lane to Grandma's house and each time he came they greeted each other as though they had not met for a twelvemonth. No sooner was he seated than she would bring him a glass of her best elderberry wine, and settle down to be entertained. He would sometimes begin with what had happened in church that evening, and relate in a mock serious manner how the sexton had omitted to ring a full peal, or how Admiral Alderson, in taking the collection, insisted on thanking everyone who put anything on the plate so effusively that his false teeth all but shot out each time. Or it may be that Ianto and his sons had been fighting, in drink, the previous night leaving pools of blood on the highway. Sometimes he would talk about a church that he and his mother had recently visited and had found a squint, or a square font, that they had not noticed before, or he would talk about a remote *cromlech*, or an incised stone used as a gatepost, or a large cross of stone walls he had found on Carn Ffoi and regarded as a great mystery, but was probably no more than a device for herding sheep on the open mountain. It was the talk of such things that aroused in me an interest in antiquities. At other times, he would relate a story about Twm Weunbwll, a notoriously individualistic farmer of Llanfyrnach who visited Cardigan every Saturday carrying an old water-can full of gold sovereigns to his solicitor's office for safe keeping, as he did not trust a bank. Among the many tales told about him was one in which he had refused to allow land surveyors to enter his property, but when they returned with a blue warrant, he let them into a field in which he had already placed a bull, and as the bull chased them round the field, he sat on the five-bar gate shouting: 'Show *him* the blue paper!' Many years later, when I was having dinner with a director of the Esso Petroleum Company, he told me a story in almost identical terms, except that he had heard it, as a boy, of an old character in Yorkshire.

More often, Lloyd would do an imitation of Old Daniel narrating one of his tall tales, which he later did on radio. I would frequently see Daniel standing outside his home, formerly the Parrog Arms, leaning on his stick, fresh faced and bearded at the jowls, and with his blue eyes set across the sea on the distant horizon. He would ask me into the house and I would follow him as he shuffled along a garden path into the back kitchen where he would ensconce himself by the fire into which he would spit before he began. He knew me as a willing listener and I never tired of hearing his stories, though I had heard them times over and knew that they were the most incredible collection of tall tales that I was ever likely to hear, and I never ceased to express the expected admiration or surprise or even mock disbelief, which would cause him to asseverate: 'It's as true, my boy, as you are sitting there', and seal it with spittle that made the fire hiss.

Parrog Arms stood where the road from the town ends and, from there on, motor vehicles have to drive across the beach, when the tide permits. A footpath along the top of the quay wall enables pedestrians to walk dry shod and continues past the houses on the sea front. It then traverses a well worn track, cut in the rock, which also floods at high tide, when pedestrians have to make a detour through some fields. It carries on to Cwm Betws, where there was once an inn, called The Mariners, and beyond to Cwm Dewi, more usually known as Cwm, in which a hewn stone building was erected in 1884 to house a lifeboat, called *The Clevedon* as it was given to the Royal National Lifeboat Institution by a lady from that town in Somerset. After leaving Cwm the path climbs so steeply towards Pen Catman that steps had to be cut into the rock, and the rock surface had to be striated so as to give purchase, especially during wet weather. At the top of the path was a corner seat, backed by tall slate slabs behind which two grass snakes, of enormous size, were once discovered and promptly killed, and we never sat there again without looking behind the slate slabs first. The seat commanded a panoramic view of the bay and the wide tidal estuary of the river Nevern, and of the town and the northern slopes of Carn Ingli. At low tide the river meandered between the seaweed covered rocks and the wide expanse of Traeth Mawr, but at the flood the whole area became an extension of the bay. With a westerly wind on a rising tide one had a feeling that one was about to ride the waves as they ran up the estuary. Dolphins and porpoises ploughed through the bay, and the movement of salmon was closely watched by the fishermen as they mended their nets, laid out on the grassy slope.

Seine fishing was the method of fishing at Newport and local tradition maintained that it was brought from the Seine by the monks of St Dogmael's Abbey, unaware that it was really the name of the net they used. There were two crews of seine fishermen when I was a boy, and great was the rivalry between them. Each set out from Cwm at the right stage of the tide in their black-tarred purpose-built boats. The captain of one was John Selby, and the other was commanded by Evan Davies who, having been a rabbit-catcher, was better known as 'Ianto Gwningod'. They were married to two sisters but that did nothing to calm the conflict and contention that ruled their lives. Selby had two sons in his crew, and Ianto had three who, for some inexplicable reason, were known by their mother's name, as Will Dinah and Tom Dinah and Dannie Dinah. They fished along the sea edge on Traeth Mawr and each took its turn to draw the *ergyd*, or station, allotted to it. *Y Llygad* (The Eye), at the point where the river entered the sea, was the most prized, and next to it lay *Y Dor* (The Belly) and then *Tyn Segur* (Vacant trawl), and there were two other stations taken in rotation. The crew would arrive as the high tide had ebbed enough to reveal the 'whiskers' of *Y Garreg Fach* and would change into old clothes before setting out to row the nineteen-foot boat to its appointed station. After one end had been anchored on the beach, the three hundred yard long net would be paid out from the starboard side of the boat in a huge half moon. It would then be drawn in, with three men at each end, until they came to *y rhwyd got*, the finer meshed net in the middle, in which the salmon, along with any other fish, would be gathered and dispatched with a truncheon, known as a 'priest'.

Beside the corner seat above Cwm was a stone stile that led to Pen Catman, a sloping headland where rabbits had close-cropped the grass so that thrift and bird's-foot trefoil, vernal squill and wild thyme had a monopoly of the whole area, to the edge of the cliffs. On Sunday evenings in the summer, people would walk this far after the service and sit in groups, looking out to sea, and sometimes they would be joined by parties of coal-miners who came annually for their holiday. In no time, someone would strike a note and the whole crowd would break into song, and hymn after hymn would fill the air as the sea became a lake of liquid gold and seabirds flew by silently to their roosts on the cliff ledges. The singing would go on, far into the night, with nothing to be seen on the headland save the glow of cigarettes, like so many fireflies.

A flight of steps cut into the rock, and a handrail of iron piping, led down from Pen Catman to a small sandy beach that had been set aside as the Ladies' Bathing Place. The coast path followed the cliff edge so closely that there was nothing to prevent the unwary from falling a hundred feet on to the wave-cut platform of Traeth Samuel where, at one time, slates were quarried and loaded on to little ships that took them across the sea: the *Saviour* of Newport took eleven thousand to Bristol in 1566. The point between Traeth Samuel and Chwarel Ffeiradon, 'the priests' quarry', grown high with gorse and bracken, stands over *Y Gath*, or Cat Rock, where grey seals haul out at low water, and cormorants and shags hang out their wings to dry in prehistoric poses. Above Chwarel Ffeiradon, where there had been a recent cliff-fall, was a small nook on the cliff edge, hidden from the path by a luxuriant growth of gorse, agrimony, bracken and field scabious, which I made my own. There, to the sound of the sea and the mewing of buzzards that nested on a ledge below, I read Theodore Watts-Dunton's *Aylwin* sitting, as young Henry Aylwin 'was sitting on the edge of the cliff that skirts the old churchyard of Raxton-on-Sea' until a landslide made him a cripple. I read of his love for Winifred Wynne and of his separation from her through a Gnostic curse, of his pursuit of her and, with the help of the gipsy girl, Sinfi Lovell, of their happy reunion in Snowdonia. The strange story was to haunt me, and I have many a time found myself repeating the book's *avant-propos:*

> Quoth Ja'afar, bowing low his head: 'Bold is the donkey driver, O Ka'dee! and bold the ka'dee who dares say what he will believe, what disbelieve – not knowing in any wise the mind of Allah – not knowing in any wise his own heart, and what it shall some day suffer.'

The coast path passed above the wide open beach of Brodan before descending zigzaggedly to the pebbly cove of Aber Rhigian. I never saw anyone else slither down this path, although I knew that it was sometimes used by the coast guard on patrol. On moonlit nights in winter I would walk, leaning into the wind, to a point above the beach and look down upon the sea, a boiling cauldron, below me. One night I saw something being hurled shoreward by the waves and the next morning found that it was a cask marked 'Ministry of Defence'. It contained some precious liquid and silent men came to take it away, and I received a cheque for thirty-five shillings with a letter of thanks for having reported the find.

There was nowhere as beautiful and unspoilt as Cwm Rhigian. The floor of the valley was a green bog, full of soft rush and sedge, marsh horsetail and water dropwort, with clumps of alder and goat willow breaking its level surface. On its western side, a large copse of hazel had grown tall to form a canopy from which emerged a limpid stream, edged with yellow iris, where gold-ringed dragonflies and blue damselflies hovered, eyed by brown trout in the pools below.

The little valley belonged to John Hughes, or John Rhigian as he was known. He was the unwitting lord of the valley that was Shangri La to me. He lived alone and was seldom seen except when driving his cart to market and, on Sundays, walking reverently to church in his homespun Sunday suit and wearing a bowler hat that had faded green with time. When the weather was doubtful, he wore an old mackintosh that seemed to be made of two materials, for one half was darker than the other. His head was always bent low and, in passing, he would exchange the time of day by lifting only his eyes. One had to speak to him face to face to behold the depth of his pale blue eyes, and to observe that his upper lip and chin were clean shaven within a well-trimmed beard. He was best met outside his cottage, that was hidden behind unkempt bushes of snowberry and fuchsia and an overgrown cabbage rose. He appeared to be unaware of the beauty of the valley which he owned and which he once offered to sell to me – 'but to no one else, d'you understand' – for a hundred pounds.

Although he was not able to read a book or a newspaper, he read the Bible as though by instinct, and there was hardly a verse that was unfamiliar to him.

There were not many of us at his funeral, but we had all been enriched by knowing him. There were no flowers: these were best left where they belonged – the primrose, the foxglove, the bog bean and the ragged robin, the yellow iris and the meadow sweet that had always been his, in Cwm Rhigian.

Few trod the narrow lane leading down to West Dairy and only the occasional passage of a horse and cart kept it from becoming a green lane. A cottage that stood at the top of the lane had long vanished and there remained only the walls of a pigsty, and a bullace tree, the fruit of which fell into the trough of the hungry pigs when ripe, but only those that we boys had not been able to reach while still half green and furry on the tooth. In the hedgebank on the sunny side of the lane there grew a crab-apple and a young oak, a coppiced ash and some blackthorn, the fruits of which Grandma gathered each year to make into sloe wine the colour of rubies. Low in the hedge, a clump of burdock gave the annual crop of clingers with which to tease the girls in school. The hedgerow on the shaded side was overhung with brambles and a wild growth.

At the end of the lane was a five-bar gate and, beside it, the ruins of a homestead that had been derelict so long that no one was old enough to say: 'I remember old so-and-so living there,' but the barn and the byre and the stable that belonged to it remained in use, and it was there that I last saw John A'Hearne. John had forsaken the banks of the Slaney when young and had spent a long life tramping the roads of west Wales, one of a brigade of itinerants, mostly Irish, who followed a defined circuit and left their secret signs on gates and hedgerows to indicate to others of the fraternity the kind of hospitality they were likely to receive in various houses, whether the lady of the house was kind, or the dog fierce. Of their number was Jim Herrington, who was the best known because some photographer had taken a picture of him that was sold in the shops as a colour postcard. He had been shipwrecked in the Irish Sea and was saved by clinging to a spar. 'But the round plank did turn,' he told Grandma as he called for his regular dole of bread and cheese and a can of tea. During the Great War he had joined the Royal Welch Fusiliers, but he was not ashamed to show the letter 'D' tattooed on his body to indicate that he had been a deserter. For more than forty years he had trodden the roads of west Wales in his iron-shod clogs. He called at public houses, but would never take a drink from a working man and, when his time came, he was found dead in the coach-house at the back of the Royal Oak at Fishguard. As though he knew that the end was near, he had called at the Post Office in that town and bought six penny stamps and had asked the postmaster to send them to an innkeeper at Maenclochog who had let him have a couple of pints on the slate. Seamus, of the tangled beard and long grey coat, spoke to no one nor begged, and nobody knew how he managed to survive and walk so jauntily. Paddy, on the other hand, was friendly and full of wit and charm. It was said of him that he knocked at the door of a house and, holding out a button, asked the housewife: 'Would yer be so kind as to sew a shirt on this button?'

John A'Hearne was the best loved of them all, although some of the children were afraid of him, especially when he had got himself into a rip-roaring state with the drink, brandishing his stick at the world in general and at mockng children in particular. Most times, though, he would shower one with greetings and benedictions, and it was in such a mood, mumbling to himself a song of old Ireland, that I saw him knee-deep among the watercress, taking handfuls from the bed of the stream 'for her ladyship up there in the castle.' He knew that Lady Lloyd was in residence from the flag flying from the castle flagpole, and he also knew that she would show her appreciation of his gesture with a shilling or two.

The iron latch of the five-bar gate slammed like the crack of a rifle as John reached West Dairy that evening, and the old man, weighed down with his pack, and with a heavy coat that someone had given him slung over his shoulder, rolled into the yard in fiery argument with himself. His trousers were tied below the knees with binder twine and, in his drunken state, his spindly legs wove like knitting needles towards the door of the stable, where he proposed to spend the night. The upper half of the door was open and, after some fumbling, he found and lifted the latch of the lower half and threw himself on to a heap of hay beside the manger. He then sat up and struggled to remove his pack, loudly cursing all created things as he did so. His watery eyes slowly focused on me, standing in the doorway by now, and all of a sudden his voice became soft and plaintive. 'Holy Mary. T'anks be to God you're here, m'boy,' he maundered. 'Take off my old boots so that I can die without them on.' I unlaced the leather thongs and as I placed his boots beside him, he held my hand and asked: 'Fetch me a bucket, would ya!' I looked around and found one used for watering the horses. 'Bless you, m'boy,' he said contentedly. 'Glory be to God for a bucket. Glory be to God for a bucket.' He then subsided into the soft hay and I closed the door upon him.

I went to the stable early the next morning and, fearing that I might find him dead, I gingerly opened the top half of the door, but all I saw was a smooth depression in the hay as though a fox had lain there.

The lane, beyond the yard, had a surface of smooth rock, with deep ruts cut by carts and haywains over the centuries, but as it was no longer traversed by such vehicles, the gorse bushes had grown rank so that their spiky fingers all but met in the middle of the lane. It was there, one evening, that I met Eleanor coming towards me. I had always regarded her as one would a wild rose on top of a hedge, beyond one's reach; a thing of beauty to behold, but not to touch. We spoke for longer than we had ever spoken before, and I found that there was more between us than I had thought. Our eyes met and I held her in my arms and, in the golden fragrance of the evening, I kissed her. It was the first passionate kiss of my life and, from that moment, a new restlessness possessed me, for I was a boy in love.

Sunday morning had its own distinctive air, and there was no need to be told that it was a day of rest. Although we were not a religious family, there were things that were done and things that were not done, among the former being attendance at chapel morning and evening, and Sunday school in the afternoon, and among the latter was a bar on whistling and on cutting sticks. My mother's family was Church of England, or Church in Wales following its disestablishment in 1920, but my father's people had become dissenters at some stage and belonged to the Congregational, or Independent, church.

Sunday School classes for the young ones were held in the vestry on Sunday afternoon, each group with its own teacher. The toddlers were in the charge of Sarah Harries, who was the fattest woman I had ever seen, and had a face that could only be compared to that of a hippopotamus, but who was as kind as a mother. She always wore black, and was short of breath. She taught the Bible according to her own belief, which was simple and absolute, and with her crooked finger she would point to the shining coloured map of Palestine that hung permanently on the vestry wall and say: 'There is Bethlehem, where Jesus was born' or 'This is Nazareth where his father had a carpenter's shop' or 'That is the Sea of Galilee where He stilled the storm.' And then, with a special pride, as though she knew the place intimately, she would point to Jerusalem and say: 'And that is the Holy City. Its streets are paved with gold.'

I had the choice of church or chapel and chose the latter, not for any devotional tendency but because my contemporaries at school went to Ebenezer Congregational Chapel, and I went with them. There were seven of us who were confirmed together, on the evening of the first Wednesday in 1931: Picton Thomas and his younger brother, Willie, Idris Isaac, Jim Mendus, Jack James, Llewelyn Evans and me. And although we were not all of us as venturesome as Picton, we were stamped with his reputation, and Sunday was a day that taxed his energy and imagination more than any other. Sometimes, on a fine summer evening, we would go for a smoke. This required careful planning as it was necessary to arrange that, between us, we would have succeeded in saving tuppence from our church collection money in order to buy a packet of Woodbines, and then there would be a casting of lots to decide who should go to Mrs Lindstrum's shop, that stood by the lime kilns, to buy the cigarettes. She was the wife of one of the Russian Finns sent, during the Great War, to cut down the trees at Llwyngwair, and hers was the only shop open on Sunday and no one objected because she was said to be Jewish, and could do what she liked on Sundays. As we proposed to commit a sinful act, we would walk far over the cliffs until we came to a clandestine place, a derelict sheepfold that was surrounded by tall gorse bushes. Here we shared the cigarettes, drawing lots for a half if there should be more than five of us, and then held our breath until the first one was lit. We puffed and inhaled until we were giddy, and then made our way home, brimful of guilt and chewing grass madly to get rid of the smell of smoke on our breath. Once, when there had been a fall in the cliff and we had to step over a newly-formed chasm, a boy who later became a Baptist minister said: 'Careful, boys. Don't forget, He's been watching us!'

We began to wonder whether He was watching us one evening in chapel It was rather gloomy as the lamps had not been lit, for it was still summer, and the Reverend Ben Morris, stood ready to give out the first hymn as we walked in. He had taken his large white handkerchief from the hidden pocket at the back of his frock coat to wipe his brow, and given his huge moustache a final sweep, and now held his pince-nez in his left hand as he watched us file in to the front row in the gallery, doubtless wondering why we were not making for the parental pews as usual. We were conscious of his gaze as we squeezed, seven of us, into a pew meant for five adults, endeavouring to evade the chiding glances of those whose heaven was sure. We were instantly aware that Mrs Margaret Mathias was in the pew behind us and she would think nothing of twisting our ears or rap our heads with her knuckles if we misbehaved. We therefore instinctively leant forward so as to be beyond her reach, resting our chins on the wide gallery ledge. Towards the end of the second hymn, the Reverend Ben mounted the stairs to the high canopied pulpit and, having seen that everyone was ready to give ear to his word, he gave forth his text. Earlier, when we had bent our heads in prayer, Picton had snatched a little yellow rose from my lapel and was now picking off the petals, one by one, and placing them on the ledge before us. As the Reverend Ben was working himself in a great *hwyl* towards the climax of his sermon, Willie, not to be outdone, pretended to blow at the laid-out petals, whereupon Jack gave him a thump on his back, which caused him to release more air than he intended, and more violently. The petals shot off the ledge and descended like a shower of yellow snowflakes on the unsuspecting worshippers below. The Reverend Ben halted half-way through a word and diverted his eloquence to describing the fiery future that awaited wicked boys who did not show the required respect for the House of God. He had hardly uttered the words when there was a blinding flash of lightning, followed by a crack of thunder that sounded as if the chapel had been rent asunder. In the silence that followed, Ben mopped his brow and murmured: 'I need say no more.' And those who had any doubt about his power to call down the wrath of the Lord, doubted no longer.

The chapel vestry was above the caretaker's house, a sort of 'upper chamber', I used to think, without being disrespectful. It was approached by a flight of stone steps, with a vestibule at the top in which men would turn down the turn-ups of their trousers, having rolled them up against the mud of country lanes or long grass in crossing fields, and the ladies would adjust their hats or shake the rain off their umbrellas. These, and other simple acts, were performed with the kind of solemnity that a Moslem observes as he removes his sandals before entering a mosque. Inside the vestry heavy pitch pine benches were arranged in rows on either side. The men sat together on the left, and the women on the right, so that families who shared the same pew in the chapel were divided in the vestry. On the wall hung Curwen's Modulator with the aid of which the Reverend Ben tutored us in tonic sol-fa to the extent that even the most unmusical, such as I, obtained the Intermediate Certificate of the Tonic Sol-fa College. He would take a long pointer and point up and down the modulator, over and over again, leading with his rich baritone voice: *d.d.r.m.* or *d.m.f.s.* or *d.d.d.d.r.m.r.d.* Thus did we learn the hymn tunes 'Boston' and 'French' and 'The Old Hundredth' by their notes, and I progressed so well that my mother bought me a small flute with which I gave the only recital of my life at a church concert. We were never introduced to the intricacies of staff notation which has remained for me no clearer then the hieroglyphs of the Pharaohs.

When we were about eight years of age, we were transferred from the vestry to the chapel where the classes were held in scattered pews, and we progressed from one class to the next as we advanced in age. By the time I was thirteen, along with the other boys of that age, I was in a class taught by J. M. Evans, an elderly gentleman who had retired from a drapery business in Aberdare. He was a handsome man, well-versed in the Bible and fond of open discussion. 'Eternity,' he said one Sunday, 'is time without end. It goes on and on and on for ever. There is no end to it, and our souls will also go on for ever.' 'If it has no end, when did it begin?' I enquired,. 'It did not begin,' he retorted smartly, 'it's been going on for ever.' 'Then where have we been – our souls, I mean – until now?' My question pole-axed him. He stared at me, as though he could not believe that anyone could query such an incontrovertible fact. He mumbled something and moved on to another topic. I was not to know that my simple question was going to haunt me for the rest of my life, and to change my whole attitude to religious belief.

One of the great events of the year was the *Pwnc* festival, when chapels of the same denomination came together on Whit-Monday to vie with each other in performance. *Pwnc* is a primitive practice, going back to the days before people could read. The word appears to derive from the Latin *punctus* which can mean 'a brief clause' or 'a short section', but for us it meant the recitation of a chapter from the Bible in a monotone, not dissimilar to a Gregorian chant. Preparations began on the Sunday after Easter, when the ordinary routine of the Sunday school was interrupted so as to concentrate on the chapter chosen for study that year, and its intoning by individual classes according to age and sex. The opening verses would be recited in a measured drone by the Sunday school as a whole. Every eye would be on the leader, who would be one of the elders, waiting for him to 'strike' with a slight uplift of the Bible, when he would bellow forth, and we would all bellow forth: *Yn y dechreuad oedd y gair* . . . (In the beginning was the word . . .), or whatever the opening verse would be. The infant girls' class followed, with a soft rippling torrent of words that could hardly be understood, except that we knew them, and then the small boys, unabashed and loud for all to hear. The teenage girls rushed through their verses in a merged whisper, and their male counterparts, with voices breaking in various degrees, introduced a jarring dissonance. After the middle-aged groups of both sexes had performed unremarkably, the old ladies brought a high-pitched clarity that comes of long practice and, finally, the old men gave ponderous, emphatic tones, before the whole assembly resumed its resonant burthen to dispatch the final verses. The performance would have reached a state of near perfection by Whit-Monday, when the *Pwnc* festival took place in one of the participating chapels. After each recital, the minister of the chapel concerned would catechize his well-rehearsed congregation, as though in obedience to Tertullian's injunction, in about 200 AD, that Pentecost, was the time to conduct a catechism.

The place of my choice was Brynberian, one of the earliest Independent chapels in west Wales. It was said that when the site of the chapel was dedicated, the well-known divine invited to do so chose to preach on the evils of cockfighting which, unfortunately, was the favourite sport of the local squire who had donated the land. He immediately withdrew his offer and the chapel had to be built on the adjoining common land. The green sward beside the graveyard was kept cropped as a lawn by sheep and geese and was surrounded by laburnum, or 'golden chain' trees, as Grandma called them. The old woman who looked after the chapel lived in a tiny pink cottage nearby, its door hidden by a Jews' mallow, and a snow berry hedge half blocked the path to it. The stable, adjoining the chapel, smelt strongly of horse urine, and the manure heap outside gave it a homely feeling. Wild strawberries grew between the tombstones in the graveyard, and over unkempt graves.

Below Ebenezer Chapel was the Board School, as the older generation still called it, which had been built in 1874 and had been enlarged forty years later so as to accommodate up to two hundred pupils, though the number did not exceed a hundred and twenty in my time. I cannot remember when I first entered its green double-doors but I have a clear recollection of Miss Ellis's infants' class in which I had been placed. Miss Ellis was an elderly lady whose face had been contorted on one side by Bell's palsy, so that she seemed to speak through the side of her mouth, and there was hair growing out of an old beauty spot on her cheek. A tall abacus, with brightly coloured beads, was the first thing that caught my eye as I walked into her classroom, and four rows of miniature desks that faced a fireplace, that was almost hidden behind a galvanised fireguard, and Miss Ellis's desk that towered above the others. Wall charts of shining oilcloth were hung round the room, most of them illustrating Welsh nursery rhymes like *Hen Fenyw Fach Cydweli*, with pictures of the old Kidwelly woman selling black treacle toffee, 'ten pieces for a penny, but eleven for me,' or *Beti Bwt*, showing Beti, as round as a dumpling, washing clothes down by the river but when she went to fetch soap, the clothes were washed away. One chart showed the Welsh alphabet, each letter, capital and small, with an appropriate illustration, from *A a Afal*, which had a picture of a rosy red apple, to *Y y Ychain* showing a pair of oxen. It was only decades later that I discovered that the chart had been devised by Cadrawd, whose sons, Colonel Llewelyn Evans and Michael Gareth Llewelyn, the author, claimed to be distant relatives of mine, and that it also contained early, bardic and ogham alphabets. Then there was a many-sheeted chart that had to be brought down with the aid of the window pole and placed over the back of an easel so that its sheets could be turned over and rolled back to reveal words like 'cat' and phrases such as 'The cat is on the mat', which we copied on to our slates with much screeching of slate pencils, and thus began to learn and to read the language of Shakespeare.

I had no reason to think that I was in any way brighter than the next until we got to Standard IV and I was the first to finish the arithmetic tests, and had the best marks for English grammar and composition. This expertise brought its rewards, for Selby, who sat next to me, had an inexhaustible supply of sweets bought with pennies that he earned by carrying water for elderly ladies, and he would ply me with wine gums and jelly babies as long as I allowed him to copy my work. It also brought the envy of those of lesser talent, and of their parents, even to the extent of casting doubt on my paternity, presumably attributing it to a man they considered a better scholar than my father. Most of the children completed their education at the school and few, before my time, had proceeded to a secondary school. During the last few months at school, four of us were chosen to sit the entrance examination to Fishguard County School, and when the results appeared in the local newspapers I was pleasantly surprised to see my name third on the list.

Fishguard County School was set on a hill and, like the Biblical city, it could not be hidden, despite efforts made to do so by planting a belt of Scots pines around it when it was built at the end of the nineteenth century. The building was adequate at the time, with its central hall and clusters of classrooms at each end so that to the eye of a seagull it looked rather like a dumbbell. To one corner, a two-storey building had been added to provide the accommodation for a physics laboratory, on the ground floor, and a large classroom above. On our first day at the school, on the fifth of September 1928, the new boys had good reason for trepidation for we had been warned in the most frightening terms of the ceremony of initiation, which turned out to be nothing worse than being upended by the bigger boys and having our heads 'ducked' in a pail of water.

Our headmaster, Owen Gledhill, was a fine Yorkshireman who had been there since 1895, but had absorbed little of the Welsh culture beyond painting the walls of the Sixth Form, with friezes of dragons and daffodils. He had designed a school badge emblazoned with a herring between two curved leeks, reflecting Fishguard's long held fame for its herring industry. At assembly, held in the school hall each morning, he would often deliver a homily on behaviour and good manners, and miscreants were summoned to the platform to receive their punishment which consisted of a number of lashes delivered on the hand with a piece of rubber tubing, that hardly hurt, I was told. When he retired, I was asked to prepare and edit an album in which members of the staff and pupils could record their tributes to him. I painted a portrait of him looking out through one of the assembly hall windows, which was a habit of his.

In the first two years, handsomely bound books were given as school prizes. I also won prizes, consisting of star-like medals, at the County Urdd Eisteddfod for poetry, calligraphy and art, and I was one of a party that went, in 1932, to the Urdd National Eisteddfod at Machynlleth, where we joined hundreds of children from all parts of Wales, and marched in procession past the Wynnstay Hotel, where David Lloyd George and Ifan ab Owen Edwards, the founder of *Urdd Gobaith Cymru*, stood on the porch and waved to us as we trundled by in a seemingly endless column.

I had heard a good deal about D. J. Williams, the English master, before I set foot in the school. Jim Mendus, who had been there a year already, had warned me that I should 'watch out for Old Bill,' for so was he known among the boys. 'If you upset him,' said Jim, 'you'll get a clout that will drop you to the floor.' I therefore kept clear of D.J. at first, which was not difficult as he taught from the second year onward, and I cannot remember having any converse with him before a day in the following February.

Snow began to fall halfway through the morning that day and by lunch time it was a depth upon the ground, and blown by the wind into drifts in places. It clung to the telephone lines and froze, so that they hung so low that one could reach them, and many snapped, or dragged the poles down. We were told that the road to Newport was blocked and that arrangements had been made for those of us who were from that area to be accommodated at the homes of members of the staff. Willie 'Bach' Thomas and I were billeted with our Welsh master, J. J. Evans, and his wife, who was expecting the arrival of their daughter, Mari, and their little son, called Pryderi. We stayed there for five nights before gangs of road men had cleared a way through the snow along which we could walk the seven miles home. Three of the masters came to escort us, of whom one was D.J. We had to walk along the ditches down Fishguard Hill, as its gradient of one in seven shone like glass. A path cleared along the main road was narrow and in places the snow drifts were so high that it was as if we were walking through a canyon. We got to the Glan Hotel at Dinas by about noon and were given some hot soup to fortify us for the rest of the way. Two of the masters came no further, but D.J. insisted on accompanying the remaining few of us to Newport. He got into conversation with me as we trudged through the snow and asked about my family and background, and appeared to be interested to hear about customs and events in our neighbourhood. He had some food at our house before setting out on the return journey, and we became firm friends from that snow-ridden day onward.

The following September I found myself sitting at his feet, learning English grammar with difficulty, but getting good marks for essays. One day, he told us to write a story that had no end to it and I remembered my grandmother's tale about Tomi'r Parcau, who was rather slow paying his bills, going to John James the Cobbler one day to order a pair of boots. 'But when are you going to pay me for the last pair?' John asked him. 'I'll pay you when the sow has the next litter,' replied Tomi. 'And when will that be?' enquired the cobbler. 'Oh,' said Tomi, 'I'll be taking her to the boar tomorrow – and then . . .' D.J. was impressed and gave me full marks which, he said, was the first time he had ever done so.

He frequently complimented me on my handwriting, which he said was 'like copperplate,' whereas his was 'like crows' feet,' and he asked me one day whether I could find time to copy something for him. This was one of his short stories, *Ben Ty'n Grug a'i Filgi* and it was the first of a number of stories that I copied and which were gathered together and published under the title *Hen Wynebau* (Old Faces), which was hailed as the finest book of Welsh short stories ever produced.

Often, when the lesson was over, D.J. would produce copies of *Y Ddraig Goch* and *The Welsh Nationalist* and give them to those who promised to read them. Later, he brought bundles of these papers which he asked some of us to distribute in our localities. He also gave me a copy of his booklet *AE a Chymru*. AE was the pseudonym of George Russell, the Irish poet and economist and editor of *The*

Irish Statesman, whose book, *The National Being*, had inspired D.J. to write a series of articles for *Y Faner* and these were now published as a booklet. We learned that D.J. had been a member of *Plaid Genedlaethol Cymru*, the Welsh Nationalist Party, since it foundation in 1926. He asked me, one day, if I would arrange a meeting at Newport so that he could speak on Welsh affairs, and I managed to persuade a representative gathering to assemble at the Beehive Café, which was owned by E. R. Gronow, whom I knew would be interested in the subject. D.J. gave an interesting talk on the situation in Wales and ended with a statement of the case for self-government, which led to a lengthy discussion that caused D.J. to miss the last bus and he had to borrow my bicycle to ride home to Fishguard. I knew that he was accustomed to riding a bicycle at night as he had told me of the time he had ridden home from Oxford, when told that his father was dangerously ill. He was unsure of the way and, every now and again, he had to get off the bike, take the oil lamp off its bracket and, as he was so short-sighted and the lamp gave such a glimmer of light, he had to climb each finger post in order to read the place-names.

He then asked me to arrange other meetings, for him to speak on *Rhamant Hanes Cymru* (The Romance of Welsh History), but the concluding message was the same. He had, by now, bought himself a new bicycle, and he invited me to join him. Some times it would be eleven o'clock at night before we returned to my home, often soaked to the skin and, after a cup of tea, or maybe a glass of mulled wine, he would set off for Fishguard. By the beginning of 1935, having been to a number of meetings with D.J., I felt sufficiently confident to establish a branch of *Plaid Genedlaethol Cymru* at Newport. The Reverend D. P. George, a native of Dinas who had returned after ministering in the valleys of Glamorgan for many years, was appointed chairman, Nest Gwili Jenkins, treasurer, and I, secretary. We were not able to interest sufficient numbers to sustain the branch for long, as the minute book which I deposited in the County Record Office may indicate.

During an English lesson in Form VI, one day, D.J. drew our attention to a summer school that was to be held at Llandysul in the following August and four of us agreed to go there. When we arrived, on our bicycles, we found that we were in time for the annual meeting of Plaid Genedlaethol Cymru for which D.J. had enrolled us as delegates and had, furthermore, paid for our accommodation, which consisted of a mattress on the floor of one of the classrooms in the Grammar School. Any misgivings that some of us may have had at finding ourselves there were dispelled when we found that we were in the company of some of the leading Welsh scholars of the time, such as Saunders Lewis, Professor W. J. Gruffydd, Gwenallt, Dyfnallt, Kate Roberts and Arthur Wade Wade-Evans, and others who were to make their name in Wales, and to become lifelong friends, like Alun and Aneirin Talfan Davies, Geraint Dyfnallt Owen, Ike Davies, Kitchener Davies, Islwyn Williams, Hywel D. Roberts, Norah Isaac and Efelyn Williams. One afternoon, Aneirin, Geraint Dyfnallt, Efelyn and I were asked to go to a cattle show at nearby Cwrtnewydd to distribute leaflets and to spread the message. On our return journey, Efelyn happened to mention that she had recently been admitted a member of the Gorsedd of Bards of the Isle of Britain by examination, and suggested that I should take the examinations. I was already involved in the preparations for the first visit of the Royal National Eisteddfod of Wales to Pembrokeshire at Fishguard in 1936 and particularly in the erection of the Gorsedd Circle on Penslade in readiness for the Proclamation ceremony. The local Gorsedd Committee had invited each of the surrounding parishes to provide a stone pillar to erect the Circle and, as Clerk of the Parish Council, I was deputed to find one for the parish of Newport and have it conveyed to Penslade where it stands in the Circle with the name 'Trefdraeth' engraved upon it.

No National Eisteddfod can be held without being proclaimed at least a year and a day in advance of the festival by the Gorsedd of Bards. The Gorsedd is an academy of Welsh poets, writers, musicians and artists, which meets, in colourful pageantry for the Proclamation ceremony and for ceremonial occasions during the festival. Candidates are admitted into the Ovate Order, wearing a green robe, or the Order of Bards, Musicians and Literati, in the blue robe, according to qualification. The Druidic Order, in the white robe, is confined to those who are honoured by the Gorsedd for their outstanding contribution to Welsh life and letters. I sat the Gorsedd examinations and despite having to compose a *cywydd* to the dawn and an *englyn* to a summer's day while rain was beating the devil's tattoo on the windows, I succeeded in pleasing the examiners to the extent that they placed me in the first grade of the Bardic Order.

On the Sunday evening before the Eisteddfod opened, my friends and I were ambling along on the Parrog when a car pulled up beside us and the driver asked where he and his passenger could obtain a meal. I recognised the driver, from photographs I had seen, as Cynan and, beside him, sat the Eisteddfod conductor Caerwyn. I had long admired Cynan's poems, such as *Nico* (the goldfinch), written while he was a soldier in Salonika during the First War, and *I'r Duw Nid Adwaenir* (To the Unknown God), that broke all the rules of Welsh prosody but won him the Chair at the Pontypool Eisteddfod in 1924, and I was thrilled to meet him. I learned later that he had set out the previous day and had planned to break the journey at the Feathers Hotel at Aberaeron. He had written to reserve accommodation for Caerwyn and himself but had not received a reply to his letter, and he had therefore sent a telegram, but there was still no reply by the time he left his home, at Menai Bridge, on the Saturday morning. After he had left, however, a telegram arrived reading: 'Room booked for two. Olive.' His wife, Nel, was greatly disturbed when she read it, and her fury mounted daily, until he returned at the end of the week and explained to her that the landlord of the Feathers was a Mr Olive.

It was no easy matter trying to find somewhere to eat on a Sunday evening in Wales in those days. I was anxious to be of assistance and took them to Fishguard, but without success. I then told them that there was only one place where they could be assured of a decent meal, but that it was an inn, and they may not wish to go to a public house, especially on a Sunday. They looked at each other and decided that, under the circumstances and as there was no alternative, they would go to the inn. I took them to the Sailors Safety at Pwllgwaelod where Arthur Duigenan greeted them in the grand manner, saying that any friends of mine would be warmly welcomed. They made me join them for the meal and I soon found that, instead of being the abstinent teetotallers that I had anticipated, they enjoined the liquid refreshment that Duigenan supplied as though the Queen's writ did not run at Pwllgwaelod. We had a splendid meal and fine wine and, after dinner, Cynan and Duigenan exchanged stories to a late hour.

The Sailors Safety was a popular venue throughout Eisteddfod week, visited by leading Eisteddfodwyr and journalists, such as Hannen Swaffer, 'the dour dean of Fleet Street', and J. C. Griffith Jones of the *News Chronicle*, and we even had a *noson lawen* there, which lasted until dawn. Another *noson lawen* was held, on another night, at Ffynnonddofn, a farmhouse above Newport Sands, which was the first of many such 'merry nights' held in some country house during the Eisteddfod week, over which Cynan 'presided', and story telling and singing to the harp, nourished by some home-brewed ale, provided a form of entertainment that had changed little since medieval times.

The Eisteddfod was opened, on the Monday morning, by the Lord Lieutenant of the county of Pembroke, Sir Evan Davies Jones, Bart., in the presence of the Member of Parliament, Major Gwilym Lloyd George, later Viscount Tenby, and other notables, in a large pavilion erected in Lota Park. Sir Evan was a native of Fishguard who became a civil engineer and worked on the Severn Tunnel and the Manchester Ship Canal and, in 1919, was appointed Controller of Mines.

I was told to appear at the Church Hall at Fishguard by seven o'clock on the Tuesday morning complete with my blue bardic robe and, by eight o'clock, we were all assembled on Fishguard Square ready to move in procession to the Gorsedd Circle on Penslade. The procession was led by the Herald Bard, Captain Geoffrey Crawshay, mounted on a lively horse. Behind him came the Horn of Plenty, borne on a kind of bier by four red-robed men, and there followed those few of us who were to be admitted, robed in green and in blue but without the head wear, which we carried over our arms, and then came the fully robed orders, green and blue and white, followed by the high officers but, on this occasion, with no archdruid, for Gwili had died during his term of office. In his place, the Reverend J. J. Williams was installed and he, then, admitted the new members. I was given the bardic name 'Dillwyn ap Cemais'.

Among those who were on the Eisteddfod field during the week were Ivor Novello, Sibyl Thorndike, Sir Walford Davies, Lord Davies of Llandinam, Lord Howard de Walden, George Lansbury and David Lloyd George, as well as the leading Welsh poets and literary figures and notables of the day. Conspicuous among them was the red-bearded artist Augustus John who was accompanied by a young couple. It later transpired that Augustus had brought the young lady, Caitlin Macnamara, with him and that the young man, Dylan Thomas, had followed in a car driven by the artist, Alfred Janes. On the return journey, Janes's vehicle broke down and Dylan transferred to Augustus's car. They stopped for refreshment at the Ivy Bush at Carmarthren and afterwards an argument took place in the hotel car park, when Augustus knocked Dylan to the ground and drove off with Caitlin.

A month after the Eisteddfod, D. J. Williams, Saunders Lewis and the Reverend Lewis Valentine, in protest against the Air Ministry's proposal to establish an RAF bombing school at Penyberth, on the Lleyn Peninsula, set fire to some buildings on the site. They had retired to Saunders Lewis's car while the fire was burning and spent the time discussing D.J.'s story *Dros y Bryniau Tywyll Niwlog* which was based, he said, on a story that I had told him about a visit by the hymnologist William Williams, Pantycelyn, to Llwyngwair, where he was said to have written the hymn, 'O'er the gloomy hills of darkness.' They then went to the police station at Pwllheli and reported their action to a disbelieving policeman. They were eventually charged with arson and malicious damage to the value of £2,355, and were tried at the Assizes at Caernarfon, where the jury failed to agree. The case was taken to the Old Bailey where they were sentenced to nine months' imprisonment in the second division at Wormwood Scrubs.

There was every indication that, on his release from prison, D.J. would not be reinstated, especially as Saunders Lewis had been dismissed from his post as lecturer at Swansea University. Some of the parents were opposed to his reinstatement, and among the governors there were those who were plotting his dismissal. I prepared a petition, addressed to the Governors, and got as many former pupils as I could find to sign it, and I was told that the Governors were impressed to find that his old pupils thought sufficiently highly of him to plead his cause. He was reinstated as English master, which greatly pleased him, but when J. J. Evans was appointed headmaster of St David's Grammar School, he was overjoyed when he was appointed to take his place as Welsh master.

On Sunday evening, the twelfth of June 1932, my mother and brother had been to supper at Grandma's house. I had seen little of them as I was preparing for the Central Welsh Board School Certificate examinations, which were to begin in less than a fortnight's time. I went to bed after they had left and must have gone to sleep immediately, for I was awakened by my brother calling through the open window of my bedroom. On returning home, Mother had found Father dead and, when the doctor came, he tried to console her by saying that there was nothing she could have done had she been in the house, as he had died of heart failure. The next few days were taken up with the funeral arrangements and informing distant relatives of his death.

Among those who came to the funeral was my cousin Arthur Miles, who was the science master at the Ferndale Grammar School, and he invited me to stay at his home in Maerdy. I felt myself a stranger in the environment into which my paternal ancestors had strayed from the green pastures of Pembrokeshire for the previous three generations, lured by the promise of black diamonds. The hundred years or so in which they had been apart had created a barrier between them and my mother's people, who had not come to terms with the industrial age. Here I was in the Rhondda valley, once tree lined so closely, it was said, that a squirrel could leap from branch to branch all the way to Cardiff, where now a cat could walk along the housetops. Here I was in Maerdy, 'Little Moscow', where industry throve and the people sang, but now blighted by the General Strike that was to mould and impoverish the lives of a generation.

I was awakened the next morning, it being New Year's Day, by children singing. I went to the bay window of my bedroom, which commanded a sweeping view of coal tips, each snow-capped like a diminutive Kilimanjaro, where men were scraping the slack slopes searching for nuggets of coal. The children stood round a neighbour's door bringing the New Year's greeting in the hope of obtaining the traditional *calennig*. They shivered in the snow as they sang, so that there was an unwanted tremolo in their voices. Their clothes were worn thin and tattered, but clean. Their faces drawn and pallid, and their large eyes, spoke of hunger. When they came to our door, my cousins treated them well, and I gave them a penny each from my meagre pocket money.

My father was one of nine children, and Arthur was the elder son of the eldest brother. The only surviving brother, James, lived at Trealaw with his wife, Sal, and another Aunt Sal, widow of another brother, William Henry, lived at Ton Pentre. Arthur took me to see them, and so many other relatives that my mind became confused with family.

My father's death had occurred two weeks before I was due to sit the Central Welsh Board's School Certificate Examination. Everyone was kind and sympathetic, particularly D. J. Williams and Siân, who made me have lunch with them each day and even suggested that I should stay with them. When the results were known, I found that I had passed in all subjects with credit, with the exception of Latin and History, in which I obtained supplementary certificates the following year.

The Sixth Form differed from the lower classrooms. It had two tables, some chairs and a chest of individual lockers. We were only about a dozen students, and those who studied science spent most of their time in the laboratory. My subjects were English, Welsh and Geography, for each of which there were few enough students to gather around one of the tables with the relevant master. During the English lessons, D.J. would sit at the head of the table, usually holding the edges of his academic gown, except for the occasional removal of his right hand when he would place his forefinger on his upper lip, or form a ring with his middle finger and thumb, as he emphasised some point or other. We would crawl through Chaucer's 'Prologue' and 'Pardoner's Tale', line by line, and when it came to a Shakespearean play, each one of us would have to read a part, or several parts. When we were plodding through *Richard II* in this manner and came to the first speech of Lord Willoughby, D.J., his eyes glistening mischievously behind his thick lens glasses, turned to Willie J. Rees and asked: 'Will you be Willoughby, Willie?'

I was appointed a prefect, and also secretary of the Debating Society and, when the Sixth Form was supplied with bookcases and had its own library, I became the librarian. In my second year at the Sixth I was appointed Head Prefect and School Captain.

During that year, an attractive young woman came, straight from Bedford College, to join the staff as teacher in German and Botany. She had blue eyes and her blonde hair was plaited *fraulein*-fashion round her head. She was Nest, the daughter of Dr Gwili Jenkins, Professor of Hebrew at Bangor and currently the Archdruid of Wales. I quickly decided to take German and Botany as subsidiary subjects and she and I became close friends. She took a cottage on the Parrog at Newport, aptly called *Camelot*, and for us it became a cabin of bliss, with 'magic casements opening on the foam of perilous seas' as we snuggled in front of a spitting log fire reading German love poems. We walked over the cliffs on moonlit nights to Aber Rhigian, which I was so happy to share with her, and up to the tors of Carn Ingli.

We went to Nevern one Sunday afternoon. Hand in hand we walked beneath the dark canopy of age-gnarled yews that lead to the church door, pausing at one that weeps blood-red resinous tears in defiance of all known laws of nature and beyond man's understanding. One legend stated that it bled from the broken heart of a maiden disappointed in love, and another that it was from a branch from which a man had been hanged for the crime of another. We stood before the stone erected to commemorate Vitalianus Emeritus, and the memorial to Maglocunus son of Clutorius, now a church window sill, and read again the words in remembrance of George Owen of Henllys, lord of Cemais, and of Catherine Warren of Trewern and of the many Bowens of Llwyngwair. In the churchyard I showed her the high cross, raised in honour of some notable, perhaps a prince, whose name cannot be read, and the tomb of Ioan Tegid, one time vicar, who had helped Lady Charlotte Guest to translate *The Mabinogion*. We climbed the hill behind the church to the Pilgrims' Cross, embossed upon the naked rock. She knelt before it and, looking up at me, said: 'Shall we say one little one for our future happiness?' After supper that evening, she wrote an article for the *News Chronicle*, which appeared under the heading 'The Wonders of Nevern', and I wrote a sonnet that was later published in *The Dragon*, the college magazine, and then in a book of verse entitled *Awen Aberystwyth* (The Muse of Aberystwyth).

We behaved impeccably as mistress and head boy at school, and no one suspected that we were otherwise until D. J. Williams and Siân came to tea one Saturday. After tea, D.J. rather pointedly referred to the trials of his courtship days and told a story about the time when he unwittingly crossed a mountain ridge that was the boundary between his parish and the next. Suspecting that he might be after a girl from their parish, a gang of lusty fellows, instead of beating him up, gave him some plug tobacco and made him chew it. They watched him fixedly as he chewed away, and he returned their gaze through watery eyes. Instead of spitting out the burning tobacco juice, he swallowed it and, before long, he began to feel giddy, and then the world began to go round, and he was left lying on the ground, desperately hanging on to two tufts of grass in case he should fall off the revolving planet.

Nest's parents came to stay at Camelot and her father, Gwili, as the reigning Archdruid, was glad to hear that I was preparing to sit the examinations of the Gorsedd of Bards and looked forward to admitting me as a member at the Royal National Eisteddfod when it visited Fishguard in the following August, but he died before then. One evening, while talking about his warm friendship with the Anglo-Welsh poet Edward Thomas, who was killed at Arras in 1917, he turned to me and said: 'Now when you and Nest are settled down together . . .' The sudden, matter of fact nature of his words startled, and frightened, us both and, before long, our joyous romance came to an end.

When it appeared in the local newspaper that I had passed the Central Welsh Board School Certificate, a deputation arrived at the house comprising the chairman, vice-chairman and treasurer of the Newport Parish Council and Burial Board. Following the customary pleasantries, the chairman explained that his Council had been faced with a little problem in that certain deficiencies had appeared in the Council's accounts due to the clerk having 'borrowed' some money in order, it was surmised, to 'clear the slate' at one of the local public houses and had forgotten to repay the sum involved. Someone had read of my scholastic success and had assumed that I would be able to keep accounts and write letters until they could find a more qualified person. It would be appreciated if I could help them out of their present impasse. I would, of course, be remunerated at the rate paid to the retired clerk, namely £10 per annum. I knew nothing about the work but, in order to help them and also to meet the challenge involved, I agreed and, at the age of sixteen, I became the youngest clerk of a parish council in the country.

I was soon to learn that the position was a sensitive one, both with regard to personalities and to the peculiar position of Newport as an ancient borough and *caput* of the barony of Cemais. The Steward of the Barony was also designated Town Clerk of the Town and Corporation of Newport, and the Mayor, Aldermen and Burgesses, who comprised the Court Baron and Court Leet, were inclined to look down upon the Parish Council as a newfangled body that had only been in existence less than forty years. My duties were also made more than usually arduous by the implementation of the Rights of Way Act 1932 which demanded a full survey of all footpaths in the parish for the first time ever.

The business of the Council was carried out in Welsh, but the minutes were written in English. When I asked if they would like to have them in Welsh, they said that they had taken it for granted that they must be kept in English, and some were of the opinion that to do otherwise would be 'a contravention of the Act.' They asked me to ascertain that it would be in order and, if so, to produce the minutes in the language in which the discussions and the resolutions were made, and this was done. *The Daily Express* got hold of this story and carried a report under the banner headline: ANCIENT COUNCIL ADOPT WELSH AS THEIR OFFICIAL LANGUAGE. It claimed that Newport Parish Council was the 'first South Wales body to carry out this policy' and stated that I had resigned in order to further my studies at Aberystwyth. It described me as 'an ardent Welsh Nationalist' and, to the displeasure of the members, it added that 'the decision of the council is regarded as a victory for the Welsh Nationalist Party.'

When I left, to go to college, the Council decided to gave me an illuminated address in appreciation of my services, that was solemnly presented to me by the chairman at a special meeting and tea party, to which the Mayor and Mayoress and other dignitaries, as well as the councillors' wives and my mother, were invited. The eulogies and panegyrics delivered, in speeches and in verse, would have made anyone think that I had served the council for half a lifetime and that I was now going into well-earned retirement.

At a meeting of the Court Baron and Court Leet held in November 1934, my name was put forward as 'a fit and proper person' to be a Burgess of the borough of Newport and I received a letter from the Steward of the Barony stating that 'it is not usual to appoint anyone under age, but as you already hold a responsible position, it is possible that the Court may make an exception in your case. When the next Court is held about the time of the June fair, you had better be in attendance!' The Court was held on 12 July 1935 and I became the only person ever to be admitted a burgess under age. I took the oath and kissed the Bible, and took my seat among the burgesses, each one of whom appeared to be old enough to be my grandfather.

Since the early part of the thirteenth century, the mayor has been appointed from a list of names of three burgesses prepared by the Aldermen and Burgesses from which the Lord Marcher of Cemais selects the first name. He is the only mayor left in this country to be so appointed. He is also unique in one other respect. When the Representation of the People's Act of 1949 decreed that mayors would be appointed in May, rather than in November, I managed to persuade the Court Leet that the Act did not apply to the mayoralty of Newport and, as a result, the Mayor of Newport and the Lord Mayor of London are the only two mayors now installed in November.

In those days the Court was held in the smoke room of the Llwyngwair Arms, which had an anteroom in which the mayor donned his robe. Once a year, following the installation, the members of the Court would retire upstairs for the mayor's 'banquet', which was a simple meal of cold beef, potatoes and swedes, and a generous supply of beer. Once the meal was over, the Mayor would propose the loyal toast, which would be followed by toasts to the Barony, the Mayor, the Town and Trade, the Local Authorities, the Services including the Merchant Navy, the Clergy and Ministers, the Press, and the Host and Hostess. The multiple toasts were given individual responses: the Services by a member of each of the armed services, and the Merchant Navy; the clergy and ministers of all the denominations, and County, District and Parish Councillors would respond on behalf of their authorities, so that up to thirty speeches were made and the 'banquet' would go on far into the night.

When John Bowen-Evans became mayor, in November 1935, he asked me to be the Mayor's Secretary. This was the first time for anyone to hold such an office, and it was done in a voluntary capacity but, as an occasional perk, he used to take me in his car to Cardiff. This was something of an experience, for he was a demon driver. 'I used to play a lot of rugby,' he used to say, 'and when I see a gap, I'm through it!'

The coronation of King George VI and Queen Elizabeth took place during John Bowen Evans's mayoralty and I had to make the arrangements for the celebrations. The main event was the Coronation Eve Masked Ball for which I turned up as The White Sheikh, and my friend Rosie came from Llanybyther dressed as a houri. The next day, I led the Carnival similarly attired and mounted on a grey horse, and when we got to Newport Square, the horse reared on to its hind legs, like a circus horse, and I saw old Uncle Tom standing there, by his expression proud to see that I had been able to hold my seat in the saddle.

We produced a guide book to Newport, using the photographic blocks that had been used in the previous guide, published in 1916. The Mayor, in a foreword, thanked Roy Saunders for his cover sketch, and Lloyd and Ivor Richards for the text, but never forgave himself, he kept on saying afterwards, for omitting my name, who had obtained all the advertisements and seen the publication through the press.

When John Harries succeeded as mayor in 1937, I could not refuse helping him in the same manner, especially as he was married to Tavia, my friend John Elliot Davies's aunt. He and Tavia insisted that I should go with them to Pembroke Castle when the Princess Royal came to inspect the Girl Guides. When he was introduced to her, he turned towards me and said: 'And this man is my right hand, Your Royal Highness!'

There was little to entertain young people at Newport, beside the tireless efforts of the church and the chapels to provide talks and debates, but these did not appeal to everyone. Once a week, there would be a cinema show at the Memorial Hall, through the enterprise of Dewi Evans, the district surveyor, who devoted much of his time providing entertainment for the townspeople, and for the young in particular. The films we saw were not the latest releases, but they were classic films, mostly featuring Charlie Chaplin in films like *Shoulder Arms* and *Madamoiselle from Armentiéres*. Not infrequently, the projector would break down, or the film snap, and there would be pandemonium with children running about in all directions, until the cinematograph would flicker again and all eyes would be glued to the silver screen.

Once a year, the amateur dramatic society would put on a play at the Memorial Hall, and it invariably would be one with a Welsh setting, like J. O. Francis's *Poacher*, or a Welsh language play. The Hall was packed on such occasions, not only with playgoers but also with the curious who had come to see their relatives or acquaintances perform on the stage. When I took part in Wil Ifan's *Yr Het Goch* (The Red Hat) as a Napoleonic soldier wearing pipe clay breeches with a flap codpiece, the buttons shot off and the flap fell down, but I was fortunate in having a bicorn hat in my hand ready to provide cover. Once a year, also, we were visited by Will Haggar and his travelling players, most of whom were members of his family. They would perform a different play each night for six nights, many of them appearing year after year, like *East Lynne, Maria Marten or the Murder in the Red Barn, The Sign of the Cross* and, best of all, *The Maid of Cefn Ydfa*, the sad story of the young maiden whose father made her marry the son of the local squire, when she was in love with a poor thatcher, Wil Hopcyn. Haggar, although he was a master of disguise, was always recognisable by the timbre of his voice, and it was he who always had the leading part in the play.

The land upon which the Hall was built had been given by the widow of the old Doctor Havard on condition that intoxicating liquor should never be served or consumed on the premises. The trustees never sought to remove this restriction, which they also interpreted as the donor's wish to forbid dancing in the hall. In order to register our protest, some of us held a dance on the old ninth green on the golf links, where we danced to music provided by a portable gramophone. The next morning there were rumours running through the town of the debauchery that had taken place, the drunkenness and the fornication in the ferns. The truth was that we had a couple of flagons of ale to share among a dozen fellows and, as it had been raining during the day, there would have been little comfort on a bed of wet bracken. The trustees eventually relented, however, and a dance was held at the Memorial Hall, for the first time, on 29 December 1933.

The following year it was decided that there should be a Mayor's Ball held on Boxing Night. This required some persuasion as the Mayor that year was Caleb Morris, who had been a police officer at Aberdare and was a deacon at Ebenezer, and was opposed to dancing. Nevertheless, he came to the dance, wearing his mayoral chain, arriving at the Hall a little before midnight. At the stroke of midnight, he mounted the stage and in a loud voice that silenced the general chatter he roared: 'Ladies and Gentlemen. I crave your indulgence for a few moments . . .' and went on to say how pleased he was to be there. The Mayor's Ball was held on Boxing Night for years afterwards.

Boating could be pursued in the estuary on untroubled waters but occasionally a high sea would drive in waves that were several feet high. This happened one summer evening but it did not prevent Jim Mendus and his brother, Donald, and I from venturing forth. We rowed head-on into the waves broncho-style, so that at times the boat sat on its stern, and then leapt off the crest of a wave and landed with a great flop on its belly in the trough. Soaked to the skin by the spray and laughing madly, we ignored the cries of people standing on the sea walls calling on us to return, until we felt that we had done enough to display our bravado. Some times we would row out to Carreg Edrywy off Morfa Head, perhaps trailing a mackerel line, and at other times, especially on summer evenings, we would row up river, reaching the pool below the rhododendron strewn lawns of Llwyngwair on a high tide. One romantic evening, I took Mavis, who was on holiday at Newport, on such a voyage. It was a good strong tide that took us along, needing hardly a touch of the oars except to steer the boat round the sweeping bend by Pig-y-Benet, and clear of the dark rocks below Sheep-hill, and under the Bridge, and between tall banks of sedge and reeds, where the swans were nesting, and then beneath oak trees with branches hanging so low that we could hold on to them. I tied the boat to a tree and we went ashore and sat on the bank. Time went by, and when we returned to the boat, the tide had ebbed more than I had expected. We had to walk back all the way to the Parrog, through tall sedge and over marshy ground and there was a sizeable gathering waiting to tease us as we arrived there, rather bedraggled and more than a little embarrassed.

On another occasion I took Mary Brake Baldwin up river, but she preferred the hills. She was a niece of Stanley Baldwin, the former Prime Minister, and was an artist who wanted to paint all the time. One day a scene in the Gwaun Valley caught her eye and we sat in a field above Tygwyn Farm all morning, painting the vista down river. She later finished the picture with trees from Hyde Park and had it hanging in the Summer Exhibition at the Royal Academy the following year. I took her to see Lady Lloyd at the castle and while we were having tea, she made a quick sketch of the town, a copy of which she later sent us both. We climbed to the summit of Carn Ingli one evening, to watch the sun as it sank into the sea, halfway to Ireland and gaze at it in silence, as those who had dwelt among the ramparts around us had doubtless done two thousand years before. As we scrambled down the scree, sheep and rabbits scurried from their nibbling in the round hut circles and enclosures, or from breaks in the breast-high bracken, until we came to the cushion gorse and the heather, now rich in tones of gold and purple. Before we left the bracken, I saw the figure of a man rushing away from us and I realised that it was Johnny Witten, the hermit of Carn Ingli. Johnny, registered as John Evans when he was born in 1875, had been brought up by his grandparents and had a habit of sucking a 'witten', or dummy, until he was a grown lad. There was some doubt about his paternity, and one rumour claimed that Dr Joseph Harries of Werndew, the exorcist, was his father. It was said that he wanted to go to sea when he was fourteen years of age but his doting grandmother had prevented him. After his grandparents died, he used the furniture for firewood, and then the rafters and the timbers of the cottage until there was nothing left but the walls. With time, the walls crumbled and all that remained was the open chimney, in which he sheltered. When the weather demanded it, he lit a fire on the old hearth and on cold, bitter nights, he doused the fire with a damp sack and curled up in the warm ashes. He fled at the sight of a stranger and spoke only to the mountain people, and the doctor and, sometimes, he would stay and wait for me, as I used to give him cigarettes. His monkey eyes twinkled all the brighter for the grime on his face as he reached for one, and I had to be careful not to burn his tangled beard or shaggy eyebrows as I offered him a light.

As I walked along a country lane one night, someone flashed a light on me and then turned it on himself so that I could see that he was a policeman and, in confirmation, he said: 'I am the new policeman, PC Ben Williams. I take it that you are on the way home.' We turned into a gateway and had a long chat during which it was apparent that he was endeavouring to get to know the locality. The arrival of a policeman by the name of Ben caused some confusion as the Reverend Ben Morris was generally known in the community by that name and it became necessary to refer to the one as the Reverend Ben and the other as PC Ben. The two had a testing confrontation one evening, when PC Ben called at the Golden Lion allegedly, as usual, 'in connection with his duties'. Mrs Evans, the landlady, served him with a pint of beer in the little room behind the bar and he had hardly taken a sip of ale when he heard the booming voice of the Reverend Ben, who was wont to call after taking the weekday evening service, coming down the passage. There was no hope of escape, so the PC put his pint on the floor by his feet, and placed his helmet over it. The Reverend Ben came into the room and sat opposite him. They exchanged pleasantries, but any further conversation between such disparate people could not be sustained and, before long, they just sat, each waiting for the other to go. The PC could not lift his helmet, and the Reverend could not have his glass of whisky until he went. In the end, the minister had to give way, leaving the PC to enjoy his beer.

He was drinking in the back room of the Llwyngwair Arms, late one night, when I was there after being to the farm sale at Berry Hill, when the telephone rang and someone informed the landlord that the Berry Hill haystacks were on fire and that the policeman was nowhere to be found. We set off immediately and found the haggard one inferno.

Berry Hill, formerly the grange of the lords of Cemais, had been purchased by the Bowens of Llwyngwair in the eighteenth century. Its tenant, Mr Brown, drove himself around in a pony and trap, always wearing a bowler hat. He spoke to no one, unless it was necessary, and then in English, as he came from the south of the county. One day, Sir George Bowen told him that, owing to rising costs, he would have to raise his rent, and he must have been taken aback when Mr Brown replied: 'Oh no, you will not Sir George!' and walked away. He had taken offence at being asked to pay more rent, after being a tenant for a long time, and he gave Sir George notice that he was leaving the farm. Seventeen massive stacks of hay and corn that filled the haggard were sold by public auction. It was the custom at such sales to provide unlimited supplies of home-brewed ale so as to encourage the bidding, and it was no different on this occasion. The sale dragged on into the afternoon, until it was almost dark, it being October, before all the buyers and would-be buyers had departed. There was some concern, however, because Old Man Belton had been seen sleeping under one of the stacks as people were leaving. By the time the fire-fighting appliances came, the haggard had all but burnt out and no remains of a body were found. Arson was suspected, but no one could prove anything.

A new tenant arrived and, by the end of the season, he had good cause to be pleased with the harvest, having a full haggard. One night, however, exactly eleven months after the fire, there was an alarm and there was nothing that could be done to save the great stacks from being consumed by fire once more. Everyone knew that it was the work of a fire-raiser, and names were named, but the proof was absent.

The one hostelry where PC Ben was not welcome was the Sailors Safety at Pwllgwaelod, not only because it was not on his beat, but that the landlord did not like him. This small inn, built for the use of seafarers, and of farmers and hauliers who brought their carts to unload the little ships that came laden with coal and culm and limestone, had been kept by Jack Harries, whose brother, Dewi, owned the Glan Hotel at Dinas and other inns in the vicinity. Dewi would supply Jack with a barrel of beer, but when he came for the money, Jack would say that there had been no custom and that he had asked the lads in the village to come and drink it before it went sour, or some such tale, to avoid payment.

The inn, situated at the bottom of a deep valley, with only one narrow road leading to it, had been bought in the mid-twenties by Arthur B. Duigenan of whom nothing was known save that he was Irish and that he had been a merchantman in India. He had extended the premises by erecting a square building, which became the bar and which he furnished in a manner unknown hitherto in local public houses, that is to say, with settees and comfortable arm chairs, and with a rug on the floor. He had brought a massive sideboard from Calcutta, the upper part of which he placed against the wall to hold glasses and spirit bottles with optics, and some Indian ornaments, while the lower part formed a great ornate bar, from which hung a wooden board bearing Duigenan's own version of a verse from the *Rubaiyat of Omar Khayyam*:

> *Ah, make the most of what we yet may spend,*
> *Before we too into the Dust descend*
> *Dust into Dust, and under Dust to lie,*
> *Sans Wine, sans Song, sans Sailors Safety, and – sans End.*

Duigenan, known to his friends as 'Dag', had been educated at Trinity College, Dublin, where he was a fellow student of Oliver St John Gogarty, whose lodgings were opposite his. One night, he told me, Gogarty, more than a little drunk, staggered to his own front door, as best he could on tiptoe, and rang the bell. He then produced a key and, after some fumbling with the keyhole, opened the door, which he closed quietly after letting himself in. He crept up to his bedroom, which was above the front door, and threw open the lower half of the window and, leaning out, called: 'Who's there?' He then dashed downstairs and out through the door and looked up to his window saying, in a timid voice: 'It's me, Oliver Joseph St John Gogarty, God!' He returned upstairs and, looking down from the window, in a reproving voice said: 'Oliver St Gogarty, you're drunk again!' Then, he rushed down and pleaded: 'Drunk I am, dear God. But never, ever again!' Up the stairs again and from the window, again in the role of God, he granted himself absolution saying: 'In that case, Oliver Joseph St John Gogarty, you may enter.' Then, once more, he came down to the door, fell on his knees and, with hands together, said: 'Thank you, dear God. Never again,' and disappeared into the house for the night.

Sometimes, on winter evenings, Dr Havard and I would go down to the inn and, there being no other customers, Dag would invite us into his 'snug' and on occasions he would reach for *Songs of a Sourdough* or *Rhymes of a Rolling Stone* and, after adjusting his monocle, he would read the poems of Robert W. Service, 'the Canadian Kipling', in his low gravelly Irish voice, his favourites being 'The Shooting of Dan McGrew' or 'The Cremation of Sam McGee'.

When some Royal Navy ships anchored in Fishguard bay, the crews flocked to the Sailors Safety and Roy Saunders made a cartoon sketch of a jolly sailor sitting on a bench outside the inn with a slightly abandoned young lady on his knee, and called it 'The Fleet Sin'.

Dag would often drink a toast to himself and his wife, Jim, which he sang to the tune of 'Father O'Flynn':

> *So here's health to ye Arthur and Jim.*
> *When ye leave this earth at Fate's fickle whim,*
> *Yer maker will meet yer, St Peter will greet yer,*
> *So here's health to ye Arthur and Jim.*

I had been the only boy from Newport to obtain the Higher School Certificate at Fishguard and to proceed to college. The choice of profession for young people in rural Wales in those days, was largely limited to teaching or preaching. My experience of religious instruction in the Sunday school, and a general study of comparative religion, left me with no choice, but before one could embark on a teaching career, it was necessary to spend a year as a student teacher. I was fortunate to be placed at my old school at Newport, teaching Standards IV and V alongside the deputy headmaster, T. J. Francis. I taught at the school at Newport until it became time for me to go to college at Aberystwyth. On my last afternoon there, the whole school assembled and the headmaster, T. R. Davies, presented me with a travelling trunk on behalf of the school and pupils.

I arrived at Aberystwyth at the end of September 1935 and having previously found 'digs' at No. 11 Laura Place, a Georgian house with spacious rooms facing St Michael's Church and separated by a narrow alley from the College Refectory, so that there was constant conflict between the church organ and the honky-tonk of the Refectory piano. I had stayed there for a week when I came to sit the entrance examination the previous April. Then I had met a number of students, and would-be students, and had been put through the beer test. We met at the Black Lion and, after a while, moved on the Plough where we were expected to consume, and hold, a fair quantity of beer under the vigilance of some senior students. At a late stage in the evening, we were joined by R. A. Wing, lecturer in Law, who later fell foul of the law, and his wife, who became Governor of Holloway Gaol.

Eric Allington Hughes, a second year chemistry student and a competent chess player, was already in residence at No. 11 and, soon after my arrival, we were joined by Bernard Garel-Jones, whose father was the chaplain to the Marquess of Anglesey and vicar of Llanidan and Llanfairpwllgwyngyllgogerychwyrndrobwllandysiliogogogoch, and whose mother was French. He had been partly brought up by his maternal grandmother at Le Mans, and had been educated at Canterbury Boys' School and, he hastened to inform us, had not had 'much experience' with girls. We took upon ourselves to advise him on this subject and to warn him against having too close a contact with the fair sex, and when we found that he had been in the company of a young lady of the town, rather than of the gown, Hughes brought home some powder from the Chemistry Laboratory which he sprinkled in the chamber pot under Bernard's bed. When he next used the jerry, froth quickly rose to fill the pot, which drove him into such a panic that we had to confess.

We held a mock election during which the candidates were in constant danger of being kidnapped, but they all arrived to address the eve-of-poll meeting. As the last speaker sat down, six male students solemnly walked into the hall carrying a stiff body on a board on their shoulders. They got on the stage and, as the front pair knelt down, the 'stiff' became upright and revealed that he was an Adolph Hitler look-alike. He shot out his arm and yelled: 'Heil Hitler!' and proceeded to harangue the assembly in a flood of gibberish-German. It turned out to be Bill Mars-Jones, later His Honour Sir William Mars-Jones of the Queen's Bench Division, proving once again that he was the greatest comedian in college.

I was at Aberystwyth when Dr Albert Schweitzer paid a visit to the college, in December 1935. Of him it has been said that 'in terms of intellectual achievement and practical morality he was the noblest figure of the twentieth century.' After studying theology and philosophy at Strasbourg, Paris and Berlin, he had declared that he would live for science and art until he was thirty years of age, and would then devote the rest of his life to serving humanity, and he was now sixty years old. He spoke in German, with his wife acting as interpreter, and told us how he had set up a hospital to fight leprosy and sleeping sickness at Lamberene in French Equatorial Africa, and spoke of his 'Reverence for Life.' With his great lion head bent forward, he then sat at the organ and gave a recital in aid of the hospital.

One of the saddest days of my life was the day Grandma died, on the eighth of March 1938 in the bed in which her William had died sixteen years before, and in which, as a small boy, I had slept with her. She was eighty-four years of age and, apart from being widowed, she had lived a full and happy life, and had suffered no serious illness and experienced no great tribulation. Her death numbed me and, for a long time, I could not believe that she was no more, but she left me with a treasure house of memories so that, for me, she is immortal.

Throughout the time that I was at college I suffered a number of ailments and periods of acute depression which culminated in a nervous breakdown. I was also conscious of the effort that my mother, in her widowed state, was having to make to maintain me there and I felt that it was time I started to work as soon as my health permitted. Professor Daryll Forde said that he would keep a place for me in the Geography Department so that I could rejoin the course, and Professor (later Sir) Thomas Parry Williams expressed the hope that I would return and, eventually, take up an appointment in his department as a lecturer. The Vice-Chancellor, Gwilym Owen, urged me to take up angling as a hobby, which I would find restful.

When I had recovered sufficiently, D. T. Jones, the Director of Education, asked me if I would like to occupy myself by doing some teaching and offered me a job as a relief teacher. My first appointment was at Narberth where, without any experience other than as a student teacher, I was put in charge of the County Primary School as the headmaster, Aaron Edwards, had been taken ill. On arriving in the town, I went to the De Rutzen Hotel only to be told that it no longer offered accommodation. Some gentlemen in the bar, having overheard my request, suggested where I might obtain bed and breakfast and, on hearing the reason for my visit, said they were all friends of Aaron Edwards and introduced themselves as Mr Thresh, the bank manager, Mr Holland, the dentist, and Mr Bentley Mathias, solicitor, and insisted on buying me a drink. The very next evening, I was invited to a dance at the De Rutzen Hotel and there met the Baron de Rutzen himself. His ancestor had come from Courland on the Gulf of Riga to marry Dorothea, daughter of Nathaniel Phillips of Slebech, and he himself, was married to Sheila, daughter of Sir Henry Philipps of Picton Castle. He was killed in the war and his widow married Randolph Plunkett, Lord Dunsany.

I then went to Abercuch in July 1937, to take charge of the school there, and stayed at the Mill House, in the yard of which James Davies, the well-known turner, had his turnery. For some of his work he used a foot-lathe which had changed little in design for two thousand years, but his lathes had been driven by a mill wheel until the recent introduction electric power. One day I saw him working on a piece of wood that was as black as ebony, which he had found, he told me, in the water under the old mill wheel. He had already fashioned a fruit bowl from it, which he had sent as a little present to his great hero, David Lloyd George, and he was now making another which he proposed sending 'to the new Queen'.

At the foot of the hill was the Nag's Head, the landlord of which, while digging his garden one day, saw what he thought was a large rat hiding under the rhubarb leaves and dispatched it with his garden spade. The creature was identified as a coypu, a rodent imported from South America, but no one has yet explained how it had travelled from the fens of East Anglia, where it was bred for nutria fur, to the banks of the river Cuch.

I would sometimes go to Llwyndyrus to see Sir John Lynn Thomas and his collection of relics. Sir John had retired to Llwyndyrus in 1921 and began to take an interest in archaeology and to propound theories that were unacceptable to historians. The gardens were furnished with long tables to display thousands of stones each of which, he maintained, had some particular Stone Age function. He told me that wherever he went he found stones of some significance which he brought back to add to his collection. On the right hand of the drive was a massive chair-like stone in which there was a mark that looked like the fossil of a bird, and a recess which, he assured me, was to hold the blood of young maidens sacrificed by the druids. Along the road, beyond the house, was a disused quarry in which Sir John had discovered an 'altar of Moloch', and below it, where the river Teifi flowed alongside the road, he had found the landing place of early man, which had later become a Roman harbour. From the Phoenicians onward, mariners and traders had not been able to resist exploring the river Teifi and to navigate its waters as far as Cenarth Falls, and some had stayed, leaving a distinctive race, which Sir John called 'Estuarine'. He told me that his discovery of their landing place was the result of a dream that he had experienced. Here was *Allwedd holl Gymru,* 'The Key of all Wales', of which early chroniclers had written, and which he adopted as the title of his book, subtitled 'Surprising Relics of Prehistory on an Old Estuary – River Teifi'. He was unhappy because historians did not take his work seriously.

I was ill again, with pleurisy. The doctor came to see me every day, and then twice a day, which I did not regard as a good omen, but I only got worried when some elderly ladies, who normally came only to pay their last respects, called to comfort my mother. The news reached Aberystwyth and the editor of *The Dragon,* the college magazine, had prepared my obituary. On a pencil sketch of me by the Pontarddulais artist Haydn Thomas, that was being exhibited at the Inter-College Art Exhibition, someone had scribbled *Post mortem.*

When I had recovered I taught at Letterston and at Dinas before being sent, in November 1938, to St David's to take charge of the County Primary School. I stayed at the Grove Hotel which was kept by Mrs Richards, a stern, white-haired lady, and her husband, and their unmarried daughter, Winnie. In the early evenings the leading gentlemen of St David's would call at the little back room of the Grove: there were the three bank managers, Rees of Barclays, Dan Lewis of Midland and Jones of Lloyds, and there was Captain Calder, in his coast guard's peaked cap, and others. The character I loved best was Fred Howell who came each evening accompanied by three or more of his Welsh spaniels. He was a member of the well-connected Howell family of Trewellwell who had nothing left but his dogs, that kept him warm at night in the little cottage he occupied at the bottom of Goat Street.

While I was at St David's, Geraint Dyfnallt Owen, who was by now a BBC producer, asked me to prepare a feature on the well known Welsh ballad, *Y Mochyn Du* (The Black Pig). The ballad had been written by John Owen, a farm servant at Felin Wrdan, near Eglwyswr, who later became a Methodist minister and was deeply ashamed of having written the verses. I was fortunate in being able to borrow his manuscript autobiography from his daughter, and to benefit from her recollections of her father. The broadcast took place in April 1939 and, in response to requests, it was repeated in February 1949, with John Griffiths as producer. Some time after that, I was asked by Sir William Llywelyn Davies, the

National Librarian, to write a potted biography of John Owen for *Y Bywgraffiadur Cymreig* (1953), and for its English version, *The Dictionary of Welsh Biography* (1959).

My contemporaries, by now, had left home and I had made new friends among those who had come into the neighbourhood. One was Victor Davies, who was a native of Llanybydder, with whom I visited his cousins, the Mansels of Maesycrugiau, and became friendly with his sister, Rosie, who later went to live in Trinidad. He was captured by the Japanese during the war and had a bad time before he was rescued and taken to hospital in Australia, and died not long after the end of the war. Another was John Elliot Davies, whose parents had bought Cotham Lodge and who had recently been discharged from Midhurst Hospital where he had been cured of pulmonary tuberculosis. The house had a great walled garden where his parents hoped that John would be able to work in the open air to build up his strength, but he did not relish the idea to the same extent. He had a great ability to write humorously and was told on one occasion that his work could not be accepted for publication because it was too much like a P. G. Wodehouse novel. During the growing season he spent part of the day in the greenhouses, producing quantities of tomatoes, and the rest of his time he spent reading books, or playing billiards in the billiard room his father had installed on the top floor of the house. I was often invited to dinner and afterwards we would play a game of billiards with the old man. At other times, John and I would set off in the car and go to Cardigan or Haverfordwest or make for some remote inn, like the Tufton Arms or the Sailors Safety. At one time, we frequented the Webley Hotel, formerly the Poppit Inn, near St Dogmael's, where we occasionally met the proprietor, Dr W. E. Hurst, who spent most of his time in Egypt where he had been involved in the building of the Aswan Dam, for which he got the CMG. When he came home on leave, some years before the war, he heard in London that the Admiralty proposed to establish an arms depot at a place called Trecwn in West Wales and, when he called at the Black Lion at Cardigan and asked some fellows at the bar where he would find Trecwn, they directed him to a farm of that name above the Teifi estuary. He promptly bought the nearby Poppit Inn which he converted at considerable expense into the splendid Webley Hotel, the walls of which he hung with the antlers of antelopes he had shot in Africa. But when the Admiralty came, it was to another Trecwn, near Fishguard. He had engaged, as manager of the hotel, a man of tremendous charm, one Major Grier, who had spent some time in the Middle East with Lawrence and we listened as he spoke of the desert and 'the lure of the East'. I had always wanted to go to Tibet but my plans to go there were thwarted by the murder of Gareth Jones, the young Welsh journalist from Barry. Major Grier provided me with a new ambition and I applied for a job I saw advertised, as a teacher at Amman, Transjordan, with responsibility for teaching English to the royal children, but the war came to prevent all travel.

I had also acquired some girl friends, among whom was Mollie, whom I first met at a dance in Solva. She was the younger daughter of Canon Evans, the vicar of Whitchurch, the parish in which Solva stood, and she lived at home, at the vicarage, with her parents. Her brother Raymond was to become Dean of Monmouth, and her other brother, Alan, was still at Oxford but was shortly to be sent down, allegedly, for knocking over a double-decker bus with his Austin Seven. The Vicarage was a fine Georgian house, and old-fashioned in that it was overstocked with Victoriana and Edwardian furniture. Mrs Evans greeted me as a new-found son, and I was invited to tea and to supper as often as I pleased, and to stay nights and weekends, only the 'Rev', as the vicar was known to the family, was not to know. This was not difficult as he spent his time in his study and only appeared for the main meals, when he still seemed immersed in the substance of the next Sunday's homilies.

I met Dodie Crowther, from Rugby, when she came for a holiday and, on one occasion, she arrived in a new car that her father had given her. The following day, being Sunday, we went to a service at St David's Cathedral and, in the afternoon we took the car up Newport mountain to Bedd Morus, and went for a walk across the gorse-and-heather-clad heath. Coming down the mountain I warned her that there was a shallow ditch aslant the road ahead, but she ignored it and lost control of the car as we crossed it, and the vehicle did a half somersault and came to rest on its side. I managed to switch off the engine and we crawled out with some difficulty and without suffering any harm.

I first went to Rugby to see Dodie at apple blossom time, driving through vast orchards, pink and sweet smelling. She took me on a sight-seeing tour, to Market Harborough to see John Fothergill at the Three Swans; to the site of the battle of Naseby; to Rugby School, and to Stratford-on-Avon, Kenilworth, Coventry, Warwick and Leamington Spa, where we had tea in the Pump Room to the music of Henry Hall and his orchestra. After church on the Sunday morning, we called at the Dun Cow at Dunchurch, and I found it a strange experience, coming from the Sabbatarian prohibition of Wales. to see the bar, with its great log fire in the middle of the room, full of people who had been to church and were now enjoying each other's company over a drink before going home to lunch.

Siân Evans was a student at Aberystwyth who came to stay with a college friend at Newport when I met her. She would reel off nonsense rhymes as we walked over the cliffs, among them a topical version of Lewis Carroll's 'Jabberwocky':

> 'Twas Danzig and the Swastikoves
> Did heil and Hittle in the Reich;
> All Nazi were the Lindengroves
> And Herr Neurath Justreich.
> And as a Polish oath they swore,
> The Grabberwock, with eyes of flame,
> Came Goering down the corridor
> And Goebbeled as he came.

She fell in love with Cwm Rhigian, which we visited every day and bathed among the irises in the stream. I went to see her at her home near New Quay, and sat over Cwm Byrlip as the sun was setting, as Siân said, in 'the dregs of dying day'.

TO WAR IN JERUSALEM

A Golden Bowl filled with scorpions.
– Arab poem.

THE NEWS WAS NOT UNEXPECTED when we heard that German troops had crossed the frontier into Poland on the morning of the first day of September 1939. I had been helping to distribute gas masks round the town during the previous week and had made preliminary arrangements for receiving evacuees, should the need arise. The Carnival Ball that was to be held in the Memorial Hall that evening had been cancelled in view of the blackout order that had come into force. I had already endeavoured to join the Pembroke Yeomanry, but had been told that, with my medical history, there was no likelihood of my being accepted for active service.

Earlier that year, when the magnolia had burgeoned for the second time, and the blossom had appeared again among the ripening apples, Mother had shaken her head and muttered 'Flowers out of season, sorrows out of reason,' and I remembered her words as she and I listened to the Prime Minister declare on the Sunday morning, that we were, from that moment, at war with Germany.

John Davies came after lunch, and we went for a walk to the Cwm, where we saw my old friend, Captain David George Tudor, commonly known as 'The Aga Khan' because he had served in the Indian Army and had a stateliness and grandeur that would befit an Imam. He had also served in France during the 1914-18 war and we sat in the corner seat above the sea and listened to what advice he could give us on how to survive in the Army.

The following day, John Harries, the mayor, and his wife, Tavia, invited John and I to lunch at their house, Trewarren, that stood on the other side of the river. Harries greeted us on the balcony with mugs of ale and excused himself in order to continue his discussion with John's father, also John Davies, which, we suspected, concerned our fate and future as they saw it. John and I sat each side of a garden pool and watched the goldfish swim lazily beneath the water lilies. On the river's edge below us, a heron stood poised ready to spear its next meal, and I thought how vulnerable the goldfish were. The elders eventually appeared, having obviously come to a decision. They had both served in the Army in the Great War, and had horrifying memories of Ypres and Verdun and Passchendaele. 'We think,' the mayor said, rather nervously, 'that you two should join the Air Force. You wouldn't then come back minus a leg or an arm or something.' 'That's right,' added John's father, in his customary blunt manner, 'You'd either come back in one piece or . . .' and he broke off into a chortle so as to avoid finishing the sentence. Tavia then came at the door and called: 'Come on, you lot. You must be starving.' Her eye caught the heron. 'Look at him,' she said, 'the lone spirit on the waters!' We went inside and Tavia, in an effort to be cheerful, said: 'Let's see what's on the wireless.' The one o'clock news came on and we heard that the *Athenia* had been sunk, with the loss of twelve hundred lives.

John and I set off for Cardiff the next morning, disregarding the advice of the elders, to see if we could enlist in the Army. We saw troops in full kit at road junctions as we travelled and, in the city, others were guarding buildings, or walking armed in the streets. When we arrived at the recruiting office, we joined a queue of young men waiting to enlist, but they came away in rapid succession as each one was told that the Army could not take any more recruits at present but hoped to able to do so in a week's time and suggested we should return then. When we did so, the story was similar, and we decided to try elsewhere. I went to Bristol and at each recruiting office, it was no different. I stayed with Jim Mendus, who was working at the Bristol Aero Works at Filton, and he took me to the newly opened *Mauretania*, visiting the several 'decks', and then to The Grotto where we met a number of his friends. When I rejoined John at Cardiff I found that he had got fed up with waiting for the Army and had been accepted by the Royal Air Force, but for ground duty only. After several more fruitless attempts, I finally succeeded in enlisting in the Royal Army Service Corps at Llanelli, where my attestation papers were signed by Colonel Audley Lloyd of Court Henry, a cousin of Sir Marteine Lloyd.

There was no one to meet me at Aldershot railway station and I had to find my own way to Mandora Barracks, where I saw a frail creature, his baggy trousers about to fall off him, staggering across the barrack square carrying a sack of coal, while two strapping fellows sauntered behind, one of them with a shovel in his hand. After having my particulars recorded, and being given a number, I was taken to an asbestos-clad hut and told to find myself a bed there. I spotted the fragile coal heaver, now turned stoker, feeding a stove around which the occupants of the hut were huddled. They took no notice of my arrival, and carried on exchanging yarns and experiences in a Babel of dialects, among which I identified Cockney and Scouse, Brisstle and Brum, Geordie and Zumerzet, before I was observed and was able to ask if there was a spare bed. 'Let's get down town,' said a wee Geordie later on, 't'see boozers, and maybe a bit o' skirt.' The streets were in fact lined with 'bits o' skirt' for the streetwalkers of London, as always in time of war, had become camp followers. After a couple of days digging trenches and filling sandbags, in my blue pinstriped suit, for there were no uniforms available, we were told to be ready to move. A military band led us in procession, still in our civilian clothes, to the station. When it played *Men of Harlech*, I thought of my fellow countrymen who had set out for Agincourt and Creçy, Sebastopol and Waterloo, but when it struck 'Will ye no' come back again,' we cheered the wry humour of the bandmaster and joined in the chorus.

We arrived at Bulford Camp, near Amesbury, and marched to Kiwi Barracks, a collection of rust-rotten corrugated zinc huts that appeared not to have been occupied since the 1914 war. I was issued with service dress uniform and kit, and was interviewed by the commanding officer who told me that I should apply for a commission. We were taken on long route marches towards Tidworth at daybreak, and were made to suffer under a midget Cockney drill sergeant who had dedicated himself to the breaking of our spirit with endless square-bashing and fatigues.

On the first Sunday afternoon I sneaked out of the barracks and went to Stonehenge, where I found myself alone with the megaliths. I moved among them, and touched the bluestones that were of such significance that men had hauled more than eighty of them over land and sea, four thousand years ago, all the way from the Presely Hills to this sacred place. I was alone with the ghosts of those who, in the dawn of history, had known and held in reverence the places I knew and revered. I hugged each bluestone pillar as though it were a friend of long ago.

We were confined to barracks one evening, and it was rumoured that we were to leave for France in the morning. Reveille was at five and we were ready for inspection by the commanding officer by seven. We left by train at nine and by half-past-six that evening we arrived at Birmingham and were taken in convoy to Harborne Barracks. There we had to sleep on the concrete floor of the drill hall, having been given two blankets each, which did little to protect us from the icy wind that drove in through gaps under the huge doors. I found that I had been posted to the Light Armoured Brigade Company of the Armoured Division, the members of which were local Territorials. We, who had joined them, were newly enlisted volunteers, not known to them or to one another, and naturally curious about our respective backgrounds. From the response to the question 'What were you doing in civvy street?' it became apparent that we were drawn from many walks of life, ranging from lorry-drivers to lawyers, but when the question was addressed to our Company Sergeant Major, Tom Poyner, a veteran of the Great War, he answered: 'Part of me time I worked for the Brumajem Corporation, and part of me time for His Majesty the King.' He did not go on to say that his engagement with the Birmingham Corporation was as a bus conductor, while his part-time occupation in the name of the King was that of assistant to the official hangman, Albert Pierrepoint. I had to share an office with him, and, often in the dead of night, as though he were giving his conscience an airing, he would tell me in detail how an execution is carried out and what happened when he hanged Rouse and other murderers.

We did some drill at Harborne, and training in the use of the rifle and the Lewis Gun. I was again called before the commanding officer, Major Field, and told that I should submit an application for a commission. In the evenings we visited various hostelries and, in particular, the Casino, where the commissionaire's waxed moustaches looked like a pair of pheasant tails. We talked about snipping off one side with a pair of scissors, but thought better of it.

My great joy at Harborne was that I was able, at weekends, to visit my friends, the Woolridges, at their lovely home, The Birches, at West Hagley. Margaret, the daughter, took me riding through the woods and over the surrounding countryside, and sometimes she would come to town so that we could go to the theatre together. I took her to see Constance Cummings in *Saint Joan*, and to *The Importance of being Earnest* with John Gielgud, Edith Evans, Margaret Rutherford and Gwen Ffrancon Davies at the Prince of Wales' Theatre.

We were at Harborne for a little over a month and then, suddenly, one Sunday morning in November, we were told that we were confined to barracks. I managed to get over a wall so as to arrive at The Birches in time for lunch, after which Margaret and I went riding. The fallen leaves were crisp under the horses' hooves as we rode through the woods, and pheasant and the odd covey of partridge took flight as we crossed stubbled fields. We went past Milton's Seat and Hagley Hall, the gardens of which had provided inspiration for the poet's description of the Garden of Eden in *Paradise Lost*, and entered a lane to make our way homeward. Suddenly, my horse bolted and it was as much as I could do to protect my face from overhanging boughs and brambles. Ahead, where the lane met another, was a low hedge which we took with ease, but landed heavily on the steep slope the other side, narrowly missing a cow that lay peacefully chewing its cud. The horse suffered no damage and I succeeded in getting back into the saddle though I had hurt my leg. We returned as the family had gathered round the log fire for tea and, after a hot bath, Margaret drove me to Harborne. I had planned to get into the barracks by scaling the same wall but this was not now possible, and I had to report to the guardroom. I was told that I must appear before the commanding officer in the morning, but as we had Reveille at five and had to join a troop train at the station by seven, I avoided being put on a charge.

We arrived at Newark-on-Trent before noon and, as there was no accommodation at the camp on Sconce Hill, we were billeted in private houses and given a ration allowance of four shillings and sixpence a week. I spent the first night on picquet duty and got to a comfortable bed in Hardwick Avenue at nine o'clock the next morning, and slept the day through. The following day were visited by the divisional commander, Major-General George Clarke, who informed us that we were now in the 1st Cavalry Division, which was mobilising in that area prior to proceeding on active service overseas. The division comprised a number of Yeomanry Regiments, the officers of which were largely drawn from county families and included a selection of the peerage and baronetage from the Duke of Roxburgh down.

A hard frost lay over England that winter, turning every tree into tinsel. The birches on Sconce Hill were hung with icicles that glistened in the noonday sun and, at night, they jingled with the slightest stir in the air. The daily drudgery of army life was relieved, of evenings, by dances in the Corn Exchange and in the Elite Chambers, where we met scores of ATS girls stationed in the vicinity, and the cheerful fires of the Saracen's Head and the Robin Hood provided a welcome refuge from the cold. It was at the Robin Hood that I met Pip Sainsbury who had recently joined us and who drank Pim's No. 1 until, later in the evening, he invited me to join him in a bottle of Veuve Clicquot. I informed him that I was not keen on champagne and that, in any case, I could not afford it on my pay of a shilling a day. He told me, unaffectedly, that he had a private income of £19,000 a year from his grandmother and he felt embarrassed drinking the stuff alone. And so we drank the Robin Hood dry of Veuve Clicquot 1929, half-bottles and all, and got ourselves into high spirits. One night, Sainsbury discovered that by stepping on the rubber pad beside the traffic lights as we came away from the pub, the traffic on the Great North Road would stop, and by continuing to do so, there would be a queue of heavy lorries back to Bawtry. While we were thus engaged, a party of soldiers came down the road singing a Welsh hymn, *Duw mawr y rhyfeddodau maith* (Great God of the boundless wonders), and we all went off together to the Corn Exchange to a dance.

By now I had been appointed clerk at the Commanding Officer's office and found myself privy to much inside information. When our embarkation orders came, we were told to paint 'Port Q' on our kit bags, to indicate our secret destination, which I had discovered from a coded message was Haifa. C.S.M. Poyner speculated that it referred to Alexandria or Port Said and when I eventually told him that it was Haifa, he said: 'There you are. I said Egypt, didn't I!'

An orderly brought me a parcel which contained a copy of Dylan Thomas's new book *The Map of Love*, with warm love from Siân. Siân had come to stay for the weekend when I was at home on embarkation leave, and greatly comforted Mother, and she came to see me off at the station, where we said our last farewells in the cold sombre dawn. She commemorated the occasion in a poem 'To D':

> *Blue, dim-lit station deserted;*
> *Sleeping, humanity-laden train;*
> *Identity-less passengers*
> *A handshake, a kiss.*
> *Your black hair,*
> *And waving a white handkerchief.*

She hoped that *The Map of Love* would bring me some cheer in whatever leisure I had in the Army and enclosed a little Welsh poem she had written:

> *Mae'r sêr perlog yn pylu*
> *Fel blodau gwyw ar ddôl.*
> *A glywi di'r dylluan*
> *Yn ubain ar dy ôl?*

(The stars grow dim, like withered flowers in the meadow. Hear you not the owl's lament?)

I never saw Siân again. She married an RAF officer who had a distinguished war record, and she died in Khartoum comparatively young. Many years after the war, her sister rang me to say that she had experienced Siân's 'presence' in the old homestead, and that she wished to be remembered to me. When the National Eisteddfod came to Haverfordwest, in 1972, the Crown was presented by the Farmers Union of Wales at the instigation of my brother, and it was made of fine filigree silver by Siân's daughter, Jocelyn, who has since become famous and her silver work decorates cathedrals and royal palaces at home and abroad.

On our last night at Newark Sainsbury, as he was too young to come abroad with us, invited the C.S.M. and I to dinner at the Robin Hood. We suspected that it would be the last decent meal we would have for some time and we gorged ourselves on roast duck and champagne. We returned to camp an hour before we were due to march to the railway station to take the train to Southampton and during that period the C.S.M. had got hold of a bottle of Scotch and was in a drunken stupor. We took it in turns to drag him on his heels through the snow all the way to the station.

We arrived at Southampton in a bitterly cold dawn and had to spend the day wandering about the streets until we gathered at the dockside at midnight and embarked on a number of small ships. The *St David*, which I used to see at Fishguard Harbour was there, but now painted white, with a large Red Cross on its side to indicate that it had been converted into a hospital ship. I found myself on the *Tynwald*, that normally crossed to the Isle of Man, sharing a dormitory cabin of 25 berths and after the long day and restless night on the train, we were asleep before the ship sailed. I woke in the night to find the vessel tossing violently, with kit bags being hurled in all directions. I looked around me in the dim light and saw that the other berths were no longer occupied. I immediately thought that the ship was going down and that I had been left alone in the cabin, which had become an air bubble. I leapt out of bed, fully clad and in my greatcoat as commanded in case of enemy attack, and dashed up the gangway, to be greeted on deck by a shower of sea spray. There was no light anywhere but I could make out the bulky figures of my cabin-mates, either leaning over the ship's rail and consigning to the deep that in which they had overindulged, or lying in wet heaps on the deck, caring not what the future held for them. I returned to the solitude of the cabin and slept until the morning. Those who had suffered most, and had vowed never to touch a drop ever again, were among the first to sample the *vin* at Cherbourg, while some of the others sought solace in the arms of *mesdamoiselles*, and the British Military Police and the Gendarmerie had some trouble in gathering them at the railway station platform at the time of departure.

We had not travelled an hour out of Cherbourg before the heating system failed and each compartment became a refrigerator, and its windows sheets of ice. I shared a compartment with the four Henson brothers, whose photographs had been featured in the *News of the World* and other Sunday papers as they had been released from various gaols in order to boost recruitment. They had not been together for years and I was fascinated to hear them talk about prison life, comparing notes on the ways in which they had tricked the 'screws' in various gaols. At daybreak one of them went out of the compartment and returned with the stump of a candle which he had 'borrowed' from someone's kit bag, and with it, he proceeded to thaw a peephole in the thick ice of the carriage window, hoping to be able to look out, but it was of no avail as the outside of the window was also frozen. The dawn had broken as the train arrived at Tours. We were able to open a carriage window and I could see small boys running along the platform offering bottles of champagne at some ridiculously low price. As we pulled out of the station, the C.S.M. appeared at our compartment door and handed me a battered enamel mug full of cheap champagne and said 'To return the compliment!'

We saw not a blade of grass in France, as the countryside lay buried under a shroud of snow, and the rivers flowed under sheets of ice. The edge of the sea was frozen at Marseilles and the east wind went through our thick clothes as we crossed the sidings to board the troopship *Dilwara*. We were taken below deck and each issued with a canvas hammock and shown how to hang it from hooks that were fitted in the low ceiling of a vast room with a steel floor. We returned to the deck and watched our horses being brought aboard, while dockers unloaded a cargo of hides from another ship. Dark, olive-skinned women strolled along the quayside mockingly inviting us ashore.

The *Dilwara* sailed out into the bay leaving Marseilles under a haze which the setting sun turned into a purple pall. We were joined by the troopship *Devonshire* and four others, and set off in a convoy under the protection of the destroyers HMS *Vampire* and HMS *Voyager* of the Royal Australian Navy. We rounded Cap Croisette and saw, silhouetted against the remnant of the day, the outline of Chateau d'If, where Edmond Dantes had been incarcerated, in *The Count of Monte Cristo*. The convoy was soon in utter darkness and we were not allowed to strike a match, or to smoke, on deck, but before long the full moon rose red out of the mist and lit the sky and the silver sea, and our convoy. By the time we had all slung our hammocks, they were as close tight as sardines in a tin, and the only way to travel was to crawl on all fours beneath them. Such movement was to be avoided at night, when the condition of the floor was sometimes none too savoury.

The sea got up in the night and the hammocks swung in harmony with the creaking timbers of the ship as we ploughed through the Gulf of Lyons. A number of horses had to be thrown overboard, and the condition of others was causing concern to our vets. By the next day, the sea was quieter. We saw no land, except Pantalleria, its white cottages looking like scattered sheep on its green slopes. At night we marvelled at the phosphorescence in the wake of the ship. We played 'Crown and Anchor' and had lifeboat drill daily and, on the Sunday morning, the chaplain held a service on deck, using a tea chest draped with the Union Jack on which a cross of olive-wood had been placed, as an altar. We sang 'O God our help in ages past' as though it were Armistice Day, and the Padre reminded us that we were about to set foot in the Holy Land. During the service, one of the chaps standing behind me noticed a rash on the nape of my neck and when I went to show it to the Medical Officer, he sent me to the isolation hospital saying that he was taking every precaution as there had been some cases of meningitis on the previous voyage. I felt pampered to be given Maconochie's M & V ration for supper, but spent a restless night, with a high temperature. Even so, it was a treat to have a bed instead of a swinging hammock.

As the *Dilwara* docked at Haifa, I was carried ashore on a stretcher and taken by ambulance to the isolation hospital. I have little recollection of the journey, or of arriving at the hospital. I only remember being woken the next morning by a cool hand on my brow, and the tender words of a nun standing beside the bed. I saw that the windows were heavily barred and, through one of them I could see oranges hanging like lanterns among glossy green leaves, and bougainvillaea laying purple tresses on a ruined wall. It transpired that I was in a German convent that had been requisitioned and converted into an isolation hospital. The German nuns had been allowed to remain, but they were soon replaced by male orderlies who were regular soldiers and who, they confessed, had joined the army to escape justice in the U.K. They flashed their gold watches and compared 'Nablus time' with 'Tulkarem time', indicating the raids in which they had been pilfered, and they regaled us with horrific tales of what occurred during 'The Troubles' in Palestine, between 1936 and 1939. They had burned villages and raped Arab women, in retaliation, they claimed, for barbarous acts committed against our troops, such as when the Arabs sent the Colonel a parcel containing the severed head of one of his soldiers, with his genitals sewn up in his mouth. This story I was to hear repeated, as though it had happened in every other regiment.

When I was allowed to get out of bed, and given a suit of hospital blues and a thin red tie, I sat in the window and saw that the garden had rows of trees, lemon and orange and olives and palms. In the street outside the garden wall, tottering donkeys strained under unbearable loads, and grossly fat Arabs straddled others while their even fatter wives followed on foot, like stately ships. Behind us rose Mount Carmel, 'the Lord's vineyard' perennially green and famed for its beauty in Old Testament times and, halfway up its slope, shone the golden dome of the modern temple of the Bahai, who believe that all religions should unite in brotherhood, love and charity.

I got up early on the day of my release from hospital, and took a last walk in the garden under a honeysuckle coloured sky, and plucked an orange from a tree for my breakfast. The cicadas already sounded like little sewing machines in the olive trees, and butterflies flew in uncertain flight from flower to flower on the bougainvillaea. Giant geckoes were warming themselves on the stuccoed walls and staring eyelid-less as though they were seeing the world for the first time. After breakfast, I collected my pack and went through the hospital gates with a sense of regained freedom. As I walked up the street I saw an orthodox Jew, in his caftan and curly locks, coming down the pavement towards me, with his dark-eyed daughter walking beside him on the outside of the pavement. As we got nearer, he changed places with her, as though to set a barrier between us.

I spent the night at the Peninsular Barracks at Haifa and caught a train the next morning for Sarafand. The railroad hugged the coast so that nothing more than a strip of sand separated it from the Mediterranean Sea. A caravan of camels soft-footed it along the strand carrying, maybe, spices, maybe contraband. The sand then gave way to the salt pans of the Palestine Salt Company that reached as far as the Pilgrims' Castle at Athlit, between the walls of which Arabs sheltered where proud Crusaders had taken their last stand against the infidel. Little remained of the once whitestone city of Caesarea, that Herod had built to honour Caesar Augustus and from which Pontius Pilate had set forth to celebrate the Passover in Jerusalem, without expecting to have to wash his hands at a memorable trial. The *fellahin* were ploughing in the open fields, some with oxen, and some, incongruously, with a camel and a donkey side by side. The Plain of Sharon was carpeted with the flower that bears its name: not the yellow-cupped Hypericum that we call the Rose of Sharon but *havelet*, as the Hebrews call the narcissus. This was the flower that Solomon had in mind, in his *Song of Songs*: 'I am the rose of Sharon, the lily of the valleys'. Nor were his lilies of the valley the ones that grow in our gardens, but the Hebrew *kalaniot*, 'tears of blood', anemones. Solomon in all his glory wore no more colourful a mantle than the Plain of Sharon on that spring morning.

Zichron Yaacov and Binyamina sounded like villages out of the Old Testament, but they were Zionist settlements founded by Baron Edmund de Rothschild in 1883 and named in honour of his father, Jacob, and his brother, Benjamin. Hadera, meaning 'green' in Arabic, was so-called from the colour of the malarial swamp which the Jews had drained to build the town. It was now lost in orange groves, and the sweet perfume of the blossom drifted in through the carriage window. Past Qaqun, Qalqilya and Jiljilya, we came to Lydda, reputedly the home of St George, the patron saint of England, over whose shrine the Crusaders erected a cathedral, upon the remains of which a Greek Orthodox church and a mosque now stand side by side. An army truck met me off the train at Lydda station and took me through ragged rows of prickly pear, and elegant lines of eucalyptus trees, to Sarafand to rejoin my unit. Sarafand was a permanent Army camp, with additional tented accommodation, standing on sand. In among the marram grass there grew flowers that were strangers to me: dark brown iris and purple convolvulus, and blue pimpernel that was just like the scarlet one that my grandmother called 'the guinea-an-ounce flower', and there was southernwood, that she called *shiligabûd*. Chameleons climbed clumsily over slender branches and leaves and stones, and shamelessly changed their colour to merge with their environment. At night, sleeping under canvas, one heard new sounds, from the chirruping of crickets to the chilling cry of jackals. One was even more aware of these sounds when on guard duty at nights, for which we had to take our turn. After one such night I watched the stars fade and give way to a sky of deep purple that changed to wine red and then scarlet and then gold. A cock crew, and then another, and another. In the distance a bugler of the Gordon Highlanders sounded Reveille and then a train blew its whistle. 'Wish that bugga' were pulling in to Sunderland,' said little Geordie and, to my considerable surprise, a fellow standing beside him rejoined: 'Wish it were pulling into Haverfordwest' I found that he was a native of that town, named Reynolds. In the evenings we would walk along a sandy road, through orange groves and vineyards, to Rishon Le-Zion, 'the first in Zion', a settlement established by Russian Zionists in 1882 and now the centre of the wine industry in Palestine. We would sample the wines and return singing barrack-room ballads and bawdy songs as we shuffled through the sand back to camp.

One day, we were told that we would be allowed to go up to Jerusalem and several Army trucks were laid on for the purpose of conveying us there as part of our cultural recreation. The road ran past eucalyptus and ancient olive trees, to Ramle, founded by Suleiman bin Abd-el-Malik as his capital city. The minaret of his white mosque, was known as the Tower of Richard the Lionheart, and the Crusader Cathedral of St John, had become the Great Mosque, and nearby was the Ramle War Cemetry where 1,600 dead of the Great War lie buried. At last, we entered the Holy City, holy to the three great religions of the west but, in the words of an Arab poet, 'a Golden Bowl filled with scorpions'. No one can approach Jerusalem without a tinge of excitement at the prospect of entering the city that one had been taught to regard as the nearest place to heaven on this earth. I remembered the words of Sarah Harries, who had told us at Sunday School that the streets of Jerusalem were paved with gold, but here they were, coated with tarmacadam and oil and the droppings and urine of horses and mules, donkeys and camels.

Our transport took us to the Jaffa Gate, where the wall built by Suleiman the Magnificent was breached in 1898 to allow the Kaiser to enter the Old City in great style. A clamour of Arab guides squabbled for the privilege of showing us the sights, and we were fortunate in our choice of Faiz Dakkar, who was to remain a helpful friend for as long as I was in Jerusalem. He took us down David Street to the cobbled and covered *Souk*, one moment dark and lined with tall windowless walls, the next bright and gaudy with all the colour and bustle of an oriental bazaar and dense with the smells of spices and leather, fish and food, garlic and candle grease. We wormed our way among veiled women, and squat elders counting their prayer beads, sinewy little men staggering under the weight of a sideboard or a grand piano, pack mules, and soundlessly striding camels. A blind man and a man with no legs, and a Quasimodo cripple, all cry *baksheesh*. A young woman with doe-like, entreating eyes, held out her hand as her baby suckled her breast. Was Mary, 'the maiden that is makles . . . Goddes' mother', such a one as she?

We arrived at the Church of the Holy Sepulchre to find its façade buttressed by a complexus of iron girders that concealed the architecture. In a niche by the door sat a Muslim who had charge of the church, for none of its Christian sects could be entrusted with the keys of the holiest place in Christendom. Constantine the Great, after his mother had discovered the 'true Cross', built a basilica that covered Golgotha and the tomb of Christ. It was burned by the Persians and destroyed by the Fatimids, and restored by the Crusaders. We entered the dark interior and climbed unlit steps to Calvary, where all was silent save for the shuffling of feet and the mumbled prayers of the devout. We descended the stairs and stood by the Stone of Unction, where the body of Christ was anointed, before moving to the high-domed Rotunda beneath which lies the Sepulchre. One by one, we stooped low to enter the marble-lined chamber in which hung forty-three lamps placed there by the various sects. Beside me a peasant woman kissed the satin surface of the marble tomb, and her body shook with emotion. We came out quietly, each with his own thoughts and impressions, and afraid to express them, lest one should be regarded as gullible or heathen. I recalled the words of Sir Ronald Storrs, former Governor of Jerusalem, when he said that 'the faking of the holy sites and the indignity with which, even when authentic, they are now misrepresented . . . is an affront to the intelligence.'

There can be no more historic site in the world than Mount Moriah. Here Abraham prepared to sacrifice his son, Isaac. Here was the threshing floor that David bought from Araunah the Jebusite on which to build an altar. Here Solomon, built the first temple, that was destroyed by Nebuchadnezzar but was rebuilt by the Jews when they returned from their captivity in Babylon. Herod raised his own temple here, which Titus demolished and made room for Hadrian to build his shrine to Jupiter, which Constantine the Great despoiled. Where Mohammed ascended to Heaven, a mosque was built that surpassed even the Mosque of Mecca in magnificence. It all lies within the precinct of the Haram esh-Sharif, 'the noble shrine', that covers the south-eastern quarter of the Old City. At its southern end is the Mosque el Aksa, raised in the eleventh century but restored with Carrara marble columns, a gift from Mussolini, and a ceiling donated by King Farouk of Egypt. Its pulpit of cedarwood and ivory was the gift of Saladin and beside it is shown 'the footprint of Jesus', from the time he drove the merchants out of the Temple. In the middle of the Haram stood the Dome of the Rock, an octagonal edifice of mathematical precision lined with marble and glazed Persian tiles and mosaics. The representation of living things being forbidden by Islamic law, the mosque is lavishly decorated with calligraphic flourishes. A forest of marble columns of different sizes, some marked with crosses showing that they had been taken from a Christian church, holds up the massive gilded cupola. The imprint of 'Mohammed's foot' is also shown, and a reliquary contains snippets from the 'Prophet's beard'.

The Golden Gate, the main entrance to the Temple, through which Jesus rode an ass on the first Palm Sunday, was sealed by the Moslems to deny access to non-believers, and to confound the Jewish and Christian tradition that the Messiah, at his second coming, will enter through that gate. The subterranean Stables of Solomon are, in fact, Herodian, and holes in the supporting pillars were made by Knights Templars to tie their horses and camels. An Englishman, with his dog, strolling past the Damascus Gate, one evening towards the end of the nineteenth century, lost the animal, and eventually heard it bark somewhere beneath the city wall. The dog had discovered Solomon's Quarries from which stone had been taken to build the Temple of Solomon above, so that the chronicler in the *Book of Kings* was able to say that 'no sound of hammer or pick or any iron tool was to be heard in the Temple while it was being built.' The walls of the caves were as though they had been carved in snow, and any building built of its stone would have been a glistening white.

While we were at Sarafand, Frank Pynor and I were selected to go on a training course in Jerusalem which was a doubly attractive proposition in that we would be away from the heat and the sand and, no doubt, would find time to explore the Old City. The officer in charge was Captain Lancefield Staples who, I was comforted to observe, wore the badge of the Welch Regiment. The Carmelite Monastery in the Vale of Bekaa, the psalmist's 'vale of tears', had been vacated for our purposes, and Frank and I each had a monk's cell as a bedroom. As we walked in the monastery garden one evening, a pretty olive-skinned young woman gazed at us from an adjoining verandah and I felt compassion for the brethren when they strode in the garden. The monastery was within easy reach of the Old City and we were, therefore, able to visit the holy places whenever we wanted. I went to the Church of the Holy Sepulchre on Palm Sunday, *Sul y Blodau*, 'Floral Sunday' to us, when flowers are placed on graves so that every graveyard looks like a garden, but here they carried palm leaves in procession after procession. The Latin, or Western, Church held Pontifical High Mass at six o'clock in the morning, and in the afternoon set out in solemn parade from Bethany over the Mount of Olives, following the route of the first Palm Sunday, to Jerusalem. The Greek Orthodox Church, for whom it was the first Sunday in Lent, and the Armenians, for whom it was the second, held their services and processions within the Church of the Holy Sepulchre from seven in the morning onward, each sect carefully avoiding the other, for the Christian religion is nowhere more divided than it is within its holy of holies. The Church of the Holy Sepulchre is shared by six persuasions, each insanely jealous of the others and fiercely protecting the area it claims as its own. The Latins own a half of Calvary, and the Greek Orthodox the other half; the Armenians possess St Helena's chapel; the Copts, a small chapel behind the Sepulchre; the Syrians, a chapel in the Rotunda, and the Abyssinians have to worship on the roof of St Helena's chapel, but claim possession of the tomb of Joseph of Arimathea. The Sepulchre and the Stone of Unction are common property. There is no place for Protestant or Puritan on Calvary.

On Maundy Thursday, towards evening, I followed a pilgrimage to the Garden of Gethsemane. In the fading light, the olive trees in the Garden seemed so ancient that it was easy to believe that they had been there on the night of the betrayal. On Good Friday, I walked up the Vale of Hinnon, the Gehenna of the Bible, the place of eternal torment where sacrifices were offered to Baal and to Moloch, and past Birket es-Sultan, where noisy Arabs were holding a sheep and goat market, and through the bustling *Souk* to join the procession along the Via Dolorosa The route has varied over the centuries and there is little chance of the present one corresponding with the original, as most of the fourteen Stations of the Cross were fixed in recent historical times. It begins at the Fortress of Antonia, named in honour of Herod's friend, Mark Antony, where the *praetorium*, the place of judgement, stood and where Pilate is said to have washed his hands, though he is more likely to have done so at the Citadel, where such trials normally took place. Then, past the Place of Flagellation, to where Pilate handed Christ over to the Jews at the arch named *Ecce Homo*, 'Behold the Man'. Although the arch was not built for another century, the pavement stones bear the scratch marks of games played there by Roman soldiers, and the Sisters of Zion, who were lovingly washing the flag stones, broke off to show me the face of Christ on a veil, a replica of the Turin Shroud. The third station of the Cross is where Christ stumbled, and the fourth, where he met his mother. At the fifth station Simon of Cyrene helped him carry the Cross, and at the sixth St Veronica wiped his brow with her veil. He fell again at the seventh and at the eighth he told the women of Jerusalem not to weep for him but for their children. The ninth is where he fell for the third time. The Via then goes through the Abyssinian Monastery, but processions of other sects are not allowed entry and so they have to retrace their steps and go into the bazaar to get to the Church of the Holy Sepulchre within which are the five remaining stations: the place where they shared his vestments, where they nailed Him to the Cross, where the Cross stood, where the body was embalmed on the Stone of Unction, and the Sepulchre.

There was another 'holy sepulchre', known as the Garden Tomb which General Gordon of Khartoum had invented in 1883. A skull-like rock face outside the Damascus Gate, first noticed by the German Otto Thenius, was declared to be Golgotha, and a rock-cut tomb in a nearby garden, said to be the one that Joseph of Arimathea had prepared for himself and his family, in which the body of Christ had been laid. It had two chambers and a channel along which a stone was rolled to cover the entrance. A hole above, and to one side of, the entrance, would have admitted the shaft of light that revealed the empty sepulchre to the women who came with prepared spices and unction to anoint the body. A tomb set in a peaceful garden surrounded by trees and shrubs and lined with flower borders was more acceptable to many people than the over-ornate, overcrowded Church of the Holy Sepulchre with its divergent sects and quarrelsome priests. Among these were members of the English community in Jerusalem, one of whom, the aptly named Mr Arbour, was the custodian. He had no hesitation in proclaiming that this was the true site, and he showed me a German map of 1582 which had a tomb marked on this spot. He pointed to the remains of a temple of Venus above the tomb, with a phallic representation, that Hadrian had built in order, he maintained, to desecrate the tomb of Christ. When Arbour returned to the UK early in 1944, his place was taken by Mrs Phelps-Richards who persuaded me to buy some mustard seed, fine as dust, as I sat with her one Sunday evening when the almond trees were pink-laden with blossom and the sweet smelling air of peace reigned over the garden.

Frank and I explored the Old City and its environs together. One day we were walking in the garden of the Pêres Blancs Monastery, built on the site of the house of Joachim and Anne, the parents of the Virgin Mary, and where she was born. The garden flowers filled the evening air with their fragrance, and Frank, in his soft tenor voice, broke into 'Dan Cupid hath a garden', but when I started naming the flowers, he said: 'Flowers and I, I'm afraid, are distant friends!' We then went on to the Pool of Bethesda, where Christ cured the man 'who had an infirmity thirty and eight years' by commanding him to rise and take up his bed and walk. The command was written on a tablet beside the pool in many languages, including Welsh: *Cyfod dy wely a rhodia!* We climbed up towards the city, shoulder high in globe artichokes that grew in profusion beneath the walls of Jerusalem, as though they had been enriched by blood spilt in battles there.

We went to Bethlehem and watched the pearl craftsmen at work outside the Church of the Nativity. Some of the people have fair hair and blue eyes: it is said that they are descended from the Crusaders, but more likely from the soldiers of the 1914-1918 War, some say.

During my visits to the Old City I frequently met Faiz Dakkar, our original guide, and he introduced me to his friends in the *Souk*: the shoemaker, the butcher, the spice-merchant, the kolinjan-bead seller, who had a monkey living on his shoulder, and Ali the barber. I went into Ali's shop one day and, as soon as I sat in the chair, he asked me: 'You know Siddi Lorenz? I cut hair for Siddi

Lorenz.' When I told him that I came from the country in which T. E. Lawrence was born he almost threw his scissors and comb into the air, and announced the fact to all who sat around smoking their bubble pipes and proceeded to cut my hair with flourishes. Giving Lawrence a haircut had been the high moment of his tonsorial career, as he regarded him as the saviour of the Arab peoples, but now, 'Siddi Lorenz he dead: all Arab dead.' As I emerged from Ali's, I was summoned by Hassan Effendi, the Turkish spice-merchant, who greeted me as always, in his piercing voice, with: 'My brother, I am so anxious for you.' He introduced me to his friend, Sheikh Abdul Hamid, and handed me a mousetrap, saying: 'There for you! For to catch Mr Hitler!' and then laughed so loud as to frighten the pigeons that were sheltering from the heat of day.

After completing the course at the Carmelite Monastery we were posted to regiments and units in various parts of the Middle East. I was fortunate in being posted to Q branch at HQ Palestine and Transjordan, which shared the two top floors of the King David Hotel with the Palestine Administration. Although we had a separate entrance, on the south side of the hotel, one could at any time descend the main staircase to the ground floor where it was not unusual to see young King Feisal II of Iraq taking tea and behaving very much as a six-year-old boy should do, and sometimes having as a playmate his cousin Hussein, who was to become King of Jordan.

When I arrived at Q, the Assistant Quarter Master General was Brigadier 'Bruno' Brunskill, who had a black patch over his eye, and a small dog that yapped constantly. Under him was Colonel Freddie Forestier-Walker, whose family had connections with the Cardiff area, and he was succeeded by Colonel Henry Somerset Parnell Hopkinson who lived at Llanfihangel Court, Abergavenny. The other officers were Major A. G. Readman, of the Yorkshire Greys, Captain Gerald Best who later owned Rowland Ward, the taxidermists, Captain N. M. Ekserdjian, a bushy-moustached Armenian, and Captain Andrew Man, who came to live in Pembrokeshire after the war.

I was not aware, until I read the book *To War with Whitaker*, of a scene that had taken place in the room across the corridor from my office, when its author, the Countess of Ranfurly, who had been sent home with the other officers' wives, was brought before the Brigadier because she had broken ship and had returned to Palestine. Brunskill told her, in no uncertain terms, that she could not stay. He had brought Andrew Man into his office as a witness and the Countess, in her book, says that he did so in case she would scratch out his other eye!

The King David Hotel commanded a view of the walls of the Old City from its windows. Across the road, on the other side, was the YMCA, with its 150 foot tower, irreverently referred to as the tallest erection in the Middle East, and one of the joys of working at Q, especially on a Sunday evening, was to hear the carillon that rang forth from that tower, sometimes chiming hymn tunes that were familiar to me as a boy.

We were billetted at the Tannous Building, a block of car show rooms and offices requisitioned from the Tannous brothers. It lay below the Jaffa Gate in the Vale of Hinnom, and the standard of accommodation was basic, comprising an iron bed and a small bedside cupboard, standing on the open floor, and a mosquito net that one had to fix to a girder the best one could. There were bedbugs everywhere. We stripped the bedsteads regularly, and trained blow lamps on to every corner and hinge, and stood the legs in tins filled with paraffin, but still they came, sometimes by concealing themselves in the folds of the mosquito net and descending upon us at night. One old soldier maintained that bugs were able to live in the woodwork of an empty house for seven years without a feed. The Tannous bugs gorged themselves on our bodies, and the stench of their squashed corpses was nauseating. Lying in bed at night, I could hear distant Arab music, sounding like a fly caught in a spider's web, and the grinding songs of the cameleers who had brought cargoes of oranges and were spending the night coiled up among the golden pyramids beneath the city walls, and camels belching noisily as they chewed the cud.

Frequently, after supper, we would retire to the roof of the billet and look out on the Tower of David and talk of the future and what it might hold for us. Bob Yunnie, a corporal in the Black Watch, was the most despondent of us all. At thirty years of age, he was older than most, and had worked as an insurance agent before the war. He was convinced that he would never again see his wife and three-year-old son in his native Aberdeen and was impatient for more active service and openly stated that he wanted to join 'a suicide squad and get it all over with.' One evening, he was no longer there. No one knew where he had gone or what had happened to him, and I heard no more about him until, after the war, I read the book *Popski's Private Army*. 'Popski', Lieutenant-Colonel Vladimir Peniakoff, a Russian by birth, had joined the British Army in Egypt at the beginning of the war, and had served with the Long Range Desert Group. He had persuaded the authorities to let him form his own unit of five officers and eighteen other ranks and, for the lack of any other name, Colonel (later General Sir John) Hackett had called the unit 'Popski's Private Army'. The first officer he had recruited was Bob Yunnie who, after he had left us, had been commissioned in the Libyan Arab Force. He served in the PPA with great distinction and was awarded the Military Cross. In April 1945 he received the news that he had always feared: his son, now aged eight, was dead, He asked for a home posting and, to Popski's intense disappointment, chose not to return. He was unable to settle at home, however, and became a mercenary soldier in Central Africa, where he died in the 1950's.

Tannous was below the Tower of David near which a gun was fired to proclaim sundown and sunrise, during which time Moslems are allowed to eat and drink, throughout the month of Ramadan, It was eventually realised that our situation was a vulnerable one and we were moved to the Mercantile Building, facing the Central Post Office in Jaffa Road and backing on to the Russian Compound, within the confines of which stood the Russian Cathedral, the Law Courts, the headquarters of the Palestine Police, and the Prison, where executions took place.

A great advantages in being promoted Sergeant was to leave the Mercantile Building and move to the Sergeants' Mess at Gelat House, which had been the residence of an Arab notable in the select area of Talbiyeh until it had been requisitioned by the Army. It had a well maintained garden, with palms and almond trees, and walls that hung with sweet jasmine. The bar was in the charge of Trumpet-Major Sam Parry from Flint, and we were served by Arab waiters, each wearing a long white caftan and a red fez. Mustafa, the head waiter, disappeared one day and returned a week later saying that he had had to go to Hebron to avenge the killing of his father's brother.

One of the first secret communications with which I had to deal when I got to Q Branch was a letter from the Turkish Consul addressed to the General requesting his help to obtain for the Turkish Navy a supply of 3,500 tons of coal 'of the South Wales quality which is used by the British Navy' and specifying twelve coal mines from any of which the coal should be supplied. Names such as 'Lewis Merthyr' and 'Dowlais' were immediately familiar to me, and even others that had suffered from mis-spelling, like 'Frendale' and 'Gambrian', but some, like 'Nykyesus Nacional' were quite unrecognisable. It was requested that 'the quality of carbon from the Penrikyber Navigation coal mine is not less than 80%.'

As our task was to provide defence against attack by the Germans against the Middle East, it was necessary that we should be prepared for such an eventuality, and to this end we were taken on manoeuvres. Armed with a mess tin, a blanket roll and a rifle each, those of us selected piled into army trucks before daybreak and set off for a destination that was no more than a grid reference in the foothills of Judea. As we approached our rendezvous, trails of dust revealed that other convoys were converging on the same place, and the importance of the exercise was indicated by the presence of the GOC, General Sir George Giffard. When night came, I gathered a few sheaves of corn to protect me from the stubble, but could not sleep as beetles and other insects crawling among the stalks beneath my head sounded like a herd of elephants stampeding through a forest. I lay on my back, under the purple canopy of the universe, watching the stars in their courses and thinking, as never before, how small I was, and failing to believe that out there, in the galaxy of a myriad worlds there was no one who might be thinking similar thoughts. I remembered how Major Grier, at the Webley Hotel at St Dogmael's, had spoken of the lure of the East, and felt that I was already enslaved to it. The moon bobbed up like a huge orange balloon and woke me from my reverie, and the unfamiliar chorus of jackals, crying like babies, and maybe wolves and striped hyenas, made sleep difficult.

We moved on soon after daybreak and stopped near a village that was simply a cluster of mud houses separated by alleys of trodden earth that were also used as drains. Women carried trusses of sheaves on their heads to the threshing floor where men flailed the corn so that chaff and dust rose round them in a cloud of gold. We carried out manoeuvres in the neighbourhood of Abu Ghosh, a village on the road from Jaffa to Jerusalem named after a notorious brigand, Issa Mohammed Abu Ghosh, a man of Circassian origin who had joined Napoleon's army. Napoleon, in camp near Ramle, had sent him to occupy the deserted, but strategic, village of Qiryat el-Enab. When the French retreated, Abu Ghosh was left, or forgotten, and he remained to rule that mountain district and to exact tolls from those who went by, and those who had not the money were put in a baking oven until they were ransomed. That he could also be a gentleman was revealed when Lady Hester Stanhope came by with her cavalcade of eleven laden camels, servants, mamelukes and janissaries, and he gave the eccentric lady her first taste of Arab hospitality. She was invited to pitch her gaily coloured tents in his olive groves, and sheep were killed in her honour and a feast, prepared by his four wives, comprised stuffed vine leaves, pilaffs of lamb and chicken, and small marrows filled with rice. The brigand was captivated by her charm and when he found that she was a kinswoman of Sir Sydney Smith, the hero of Acre, he insisted on mounting guard over her encampment personally.

I went to Nablus, one day, with Major the Honourable Henry Charles Hovell-Thurlow-Cumming-Bruce, later Lord Thurlow, who had been ADC to the High Commissioner until his recent appointment as Military Secretary. A flock of vultures that wheeled above some camels at Shu'fat may have seen that one was weak with age and about to become carrion. Towards Bir Nabala, the wattle towers in the vineyards, and dwellings carved in the rocks were in marked contrast to the Royal Air Force landing ground at Qalundiyah, or the tall wireless masts at Ramallah. When these masts were erected, the learned one among the local Arabs explained their purpose to his people. 'Imagine you have a dog,' he said, 'a long dog, so long that its tail was here in Ramallah, and its head was away yonder in Damascus. Now if you trod on the dog's tail, here in Ramallah, it would bark and bite your brother in the faith in Damascus. That, my friends, is telephone. But if the same dog, with its tail here in Ramallah and its head way yonder in Damascus, had its body taken away, and then you trod on its tail and it would still bark and bite your brother in the faith in Damascus, that, my friends, is wireless!'

Yellow broom and dog roses were in bloom at Sinjil, so named after the Crusader knight Raymond de St Giles, Count of Toulouse. Women worked in the fields at Sychar whence the woman of Samaria had come to draw water and had met Jesus at Jacob's Well. At Nablus people poured out of the mosques, it being Friday. The city of Nablus, from the Greek *neapolis*, had displaced the older Shechem, where Abraham had pitched his tent on entering the land of Canaan and had set up the first altar to Jehovah, and where Joshua led the Israelites after crossing the Jordan. When Hugh Foot was Assistant District Commissioner here, he overcame the age-old custom of inflicting injury on one's enemy by cutting down his olive trees. On receiving such a complaint, Foot would impose a collective fine on the whole village sufficient to recompense the owner, so that it became pointless to cut down an enemy's tree if it were known that he would be compensated. The practice soon ceased, except that sometimes a villager would cut down his own trees and claim the compensation.

Before the end of 1940 we started making preparations for an invasion of Syria and I was put to work on Operation Explorer plans with Major Readman, but his place was taken, shortly afterwards, by Captain the Honourable David Lloyd, whose father, Lord Lloyd of Dolobran, the Colonial Minister, had turned down Dr Weizmann's offer to form a Jewish fighting force to assist the Allies and, even more recently, had refused to allow the 1,700 refugee survivors of the *Patria*, sunk in Haifa harbour, to remain in Palestine. In the circumstances, it did not appear tactful to have posted David to Jerusalem, but I did not detect any hostility towards him, although it must be admitted that his presence may not have been known. We would sometimes talk about his Welsh ancestors, the Lloyds of Dolobran, who claimed descent from Aleth, king of Dyfed, and from Sampson Lort of Stackpole, and who were Quakers and ironmasters and founders of Lloyds Bank. After working all day, one Sunday, and most of the night, everything came to a halt on the Monday morning when David announced that he had lost a top secret file and asked me for a Woodbine to steady his nerves. Woodbine was the finest cigarette we could buy and came, when available, full-size and sealed in round tins of fifty. Early in 1941 came the news that his father had died, and he succeeded as the second baron.

Our immediate concern was the activity of the pro-Axis Rashid Ali, who had seized power in Iraq in April 1941 and had declared a Jihad, or holy war. He had already captured Rutbah, and was getting ready to attack Habbaniyah. General

Wavell, the General Commander-in-Chief, Middle East, was heavily occupied with the campaign against Rommel in the Western Desert and was disinclined to release troops for Iraq, but a force, called 'Habforce', was put together at short notice under Major General William Clarke, while a flying column, commanded by Brigadier Kingstone and known as 'Kingcol', dashed across the desert to Habbaniyah. There was a growing fear, particularly among the Jewish community, that Rashid Ali's move was part of Hitler's plan, following the fall of Crete, to invade Syria, and then Palestine, as one claw of the Mediterranean pincers. Camouflaged German aircraft had landed in Damascus, with the agreement of the Vichy General Dentz, and the appearance of enemy planes over Jerusalem was considered to be imminent.

Saturday, 24 May 1941, had been an unusually warm day in Jerusalem, and one of more than ordinary turmoil and commotion as we had receiving a visit from General Wavell and had to explain to him our proposals for Syria. I had been working since eight o'clock that morning and, when I was leaving at six, I was asked if I would return at eight, and be prepared to do a night shift. When I got back after a hasty supper and a short rest, I was confronted by an administrative instruction that had been approved by Wavell, and required urgent action. In addition, on account of Wavell's presence, dispatch riders arrived throughout the night bearing messages that could not be passed by telephone and that demanded immediate replies which the duty officer, Captain Henry Hunloke, and I had to concoct between us. Henry Hunloke was the Member of Parliament for the Western Division of Derbyshire and had been Parliamentary Under-Secretary at the Home Office at the outbreak of war. He was married to Lady Anne Cavendish, the youngest daughter of the Duke of Devonshire, and he was the man chosen to stand in for the monarch during rehearsals for the coronation of King George VI. Wavell returned to Cairo the next morning, where he met De Gaulle and got his approval to Operation Exporter upon which we were engaged. After a hurried breakfast that morning, I went back to the office again, forgetting that it was my off-duty Sunday, and my twenty-fifth birthday. While I was ruminating, Ben, our orderly, called me to the window to see, below, in front of the King David, a young woman turn towards the hotel and lift her dress to reveal that she wore no undergarment. She then moved on, but only to return at intervals as though she had been engaged by the enemy to distract us from our invasion plans. For much of the time, David Lloyd and Brigadier Brunskill and I, were sprawled on the office floor sticking pins in large scale maps of Syria and the Lebanon. I managed to get away that afternoon but had to get back to the office to face yet another night on duty. I was, by now, so tired of the plan, and of the hours I had worked, that I was tempted, as I sat in the office that Sunday evening, to lift the telephone and give the code word that would set in motion the invasion of Syria, but consoled myself by thinking about the chaos and commotion that such an exploit would cause.

Operation Explorer went into action during the night of 7-8 June, when a mixed force under General 'Jumbo' Wilson, comprising the 7th Australian Division, a brigade of the 4th Indian Division, two regiments of the 1st Cavalry Division, one of which still had the horses that we had brought out with us, a battalion of the Special Services Brigade, and the Free French under General de Gentilhomme, moved on Syria with a three-pronged attack: at Deraa, targetting on Damascus; at Merjayoun and up the valley of the Litani river towards Zahle and Riyaq, and along the coast towards Beirut. On the eve of the invasion, a unit of the *Haganah*, which had explored the border country in preparation for the invasion, together with a small Australian detachment, set out to capture the sentries on a pair of bridges north of Iskanderun before the French would blow them up. The unit was led by Moshe Dayan who was serving a ten year sentence for being a member of the *Haganah* and had been released to assist the British forces. In the engagement, Dayan received a wound that resulted in the loss of an eye, and the damage to the socket was such that he had to wear an eye-patch for the rest of his life. My friend, Mino, from Tiberias, had also undertaken an exploratory sally of his own. He had set out in his truck, with a quantity of British flags, and had penetrated into Syria for a distance of nine miles simply by going up to the guard posts, most of which he knew, and ask the guards to take down the French flag and hoist a Union Jack in its place.

I placed a large map of Syria on the wall of room 412, which I had now been given for my own use, and stuck flags in it to indicate our progress, which was slower than we had anticipated. General Dentz had refused to capitulate, even when we were at the gates of Damascus, and 'Habforce', reinforced with Indian troops, was moving up the Euphrates valley. Damascus fell on the day Germany invaded Russia, and Palmyra after it, but it was not until our troops had surrounded Beirut, on 11 July, that Dentz silenced his guns and sought terms.

Early the next morning we left for Acre, to prepare the terms of surrender. It was already warm when we arrived there, soon after nine o'clock, and we had too much on our minds to do more than take a glance at the domes and the minarets of the faery city, its golden walls washed by a sea the colour of lapis lazuli, or to remember that it was exactly 750 years since Richard Lionheart's Crusaders had captured it from Saladin. The Old Acre, or Akko, of the nineteenth century BC, remained in the hands of the Phoenicians until the Israelites came, six centuries later. The Ptolemies of Egypt took it and called it Ptolemais. Pompey conquered it for the Romans but deprived it of its supremacy by developing Caesarea, further south, as a port. It came to life again following the Arab conquest of 636, and achieved added importance when taken by the Crusader Baldwin I in 1104. It surrendered to Saladin in 1187, who held it until Richard's conquest four years later. The Mamelukes destroyed it and it lay in ruins for close on half a millennium, until Daher el Omar made it 'the port for Syria'. Napoleon failed to seize it, but the Egyptian Ibrahim Pasha took it from the Turks in 1832 and held it for nine years before it was captured by the British.

We assembled at Sydney Smith Barracks, named after the admiral who had saved Acre from Napoleon in 1799. In an ordinary Army hut, 'Jumbo' Wilson, with the Australian General Laverack, and General Catroux, of the Free French, sat facing the Vichy French delegation led by General Andre de Verdilhac, Deputy Commander-in-Chief of the French troops in Syria and the Lebanon, acting in the name of General Henri Dentz and the French High Command, who was in a rage because someone, an Australian soldier we suspected, had stolen his *kepi*.

My task was to type the peace agreement, the twenty-two clauses of which were amended, altered, redrafted and repositioned time and again, until the final document bore little resemblance to the original draft. It was so hot that I took my Oliver typewriter outside and set it on a table in the shade of an acacia tree. As I was banging out one of the many versions of the top secret document, I became aware that I was being watched. I turned round and found a moon-face peering over my shoulder, and before I could complete my expletives, he apologised and said 'I'm a War Correspondent. My name is Richard Dimbleby.'

It was approaching eleven o'clock that night before I was able to produce the final agreed version of the *Agreement governing the cessation of hostilities in Syria and Lebanon between General Sir Henry Maitland Wilson, GBE, KCB, DSO, General Officer Commanding in Chief of the Allied Forces in Palestine and Syria, acting in the name of the Commander in Chief, Middle East, on the one hand, and General de Verdilhac, Commander of the Legion of Honour, Deputy Commander in Chief of the French Forces in Syria, acting in the name of the French High Command, on the other*. As General de Verdilhac was about to sign the convention, the lights went out. We were in complete darkness and General Wilson uttered a thunderous oath, but in no time, a dispatch rider wheeled his motor cycle into the room and trained his headlight on to the table and the convention was signed.

The moon lay its silver sword across the bay as we left Acre, and we travelled back over Samaria, that was white with moonlight. I felt very tired but quietly thrilled because I had brought away with me a copy of the agreement, and one of the pens used in its signing, about which I could tell nobody.

To my surprise, we had to go to Acre again the next day, and yet further amendments had to be made to the agreement, but even then it met with stern criticism on the grounds that we had been too lenient with the Vichy French in granting them honours of war and allowing their troops to retain their personal arms There was less for me to do that day and I spent most of it talking to Richard Dimbleby, during which we discovered that we had mutual friends in Nest Gwili and others connected with the BBC. The French continued to argue over every point that was raised, and the new agreement was not signed until eight o'clock that evening. Captain Hogg, of the Bengal Lancers, and I were invited to the Australian mess, near Safad, for a meal and some drink, on the way back to Jerusalem and we left there about midnight. I saw the bright moon shine on a dome and a minaret in Jenin, and then I went to sleep.

General Wilson issued a Special Order of the Day on 15th July, which stated that 'The Secretary of State for War, on behalf of the Army Council, while sending his congratulations at the conclusion of the campaign in Syria,' wished to thank everybody who took part and hoped that 'never again will Imperial Troops have to fire upon the brave soldiers of a recent Ally, nor the Free French oppose their countrymen in battle,' and mourned the losses suffered in this conflict, 'unnatural but forced upon us.'

Despite the revised agreement, there was still considerable dissatisfaction on both sides. General de Gaulle was so displeased that he threatened to withdraw Free French troops from British command, and the argument continued until General Spears and General de Larminat met in Cairo on 23 July and agreed on an 'arrangement fixing interpretation' to be given to the Armistice Convention. The following day, Spears, with the Earl of Oxford and Asquith, called at the King David Hotel on their way to Beirut. At the end of July, I had to prepare a further covenant for signature by General Wilson and General de Larminat, acting on behalf of General de Gaulle, relating to the repatriation of Vichy prisoners-of-war. It had transpired that General Dentz, in violation of the terms of the armistice, had flown Allied officers who had been taken prisoner-of-war, to Greece, and they had been taken by train across the Balkans and Germany to France. He and thirty-nine Vichy officers were then arrested and detained until our officers were brought back from Marseilles.

The Times, in its account of the armistice, referred to 'the magnificent service rendered by a young Welsh poet who displayed remarkable ability during the crisis following the surrender of the Syrian Forces,' and someone wrote from home to say that one of the London papers had stated that 'the Syrian armistice had been drafted by Wales's youngest bard.' I suspected Dimbleby.

British soldiers could not expect to be received with open arms by either Arab or Jew after the 1936-39 'troubles', when the bad behaviour of the few had branded the many. In time, however, it was realised, by the English-speaking Jews in particular, that we who had recently arrived in Jerusalem were, in effect, civilians in uniform. My first contact with the Jewish community occurred when I called at Aaronson's book shop to buy a copy of H. V. Morton's *In the Steps of the Master*, and it transpired that Aaronson had been employed at Foyle's Bookshop and knew my friend Will Griffiths who was in charge of its Welsh Department. He invited Frank Pynor and I to his house the following *erev Shabat*, Sabbath eve, which is a time when Jewish families are 'at home' to their friends and acquaintances. We talked about many things and especially about Jews the world over, and I was interested to learn that Haile Selassie's minister in London was a Falasha, an Ethiopian Jew, and that there were Jews in China whose Old Testament ended with the story of Lot.

The following week we went with the Aaronsons to a garden party given by Mrs Levy at Mahanaim, her Hebrew-English School. Mahanaim was an old Arab house which had an orange tree growing at the door, and a garden full of roses and cyclamen, mimulus and nicotiana, and oleanders, and a goldfish pool, shaded and cool under a canopy of pines and eucalyptus trees. Mrs Julius Rothschild, whom I met there, invited me to her home, Abcarius House, to meet her husband. Julius Rothschild was born in Eisenach where, he was proud always to add, Johann Sebastian Bach had been born. He and his wife had left Germany when the Great War was looming and had settled at Haifa, and had remained there until their house was bombed, when they moved to Jerusalem. He had met T. E. Lawrence in the Hejaz, and again at a feast given by Sultan Atrash Pasha, the chief of the Druse, among whom he had spent some time. He had never been able to fathom the Druse religion, which was a mixture of Christianity and Islam with mysterious rites that are of older origin. Their original home was the Lebanon but in the middle of the nineteenth century, they had clashed with the Maronites, their historic enemies, following which the French drove the majority of them to the wilderness of Jebel Hauran, since known as Jebel Druse. Jebel Hauran was the granary of Syria, and when a famine threatened Haifa in August 1918, the mayor had asked Rothschild to take advantage of his friendship with the Druse, and with Jemal Pasha, the Turkish commander in Syria, to obtain some wheat. When he got to Jemal's headquarters, he found the Pasha in a black mood and so he wisely went away and returned the next day, when Jemal greeted him like a blood-brother and gave him letters of safe conduct and orders to be supplied with grain. After the Turks had been driven out of Syria the following October, Rothschild befriended Shukri Bey whom Lawrence had appointed governor of Damascus pending the arrival of Feisal. While talking about other creeds, Rothschild told me that he had come across a sect at Haifa that worshipped in a stone circle on top of Mount Carmel on moonlit nights, and he became very excited when I told him that I was a member of the Gorsedd of Bards of the Isle of Britain that holds its ceremonies within a stone circle. He had studied the history of the Celts in central Europe, in Wallacia and the Po Valley and in southern Anatolia, and had delved into the mysteries of druidism. He pointed out that there was a close similarity in written Hebrew between the words 'David' and 'druid', and that *magen David*, 'the shield of David', had been misread as 'the shield of the druid', whatever that may have been.

He himself, though born a Jew, had embraced the Baha'i faith. The Baha'i are the followers of Baha'u'llah, who had proclaimed himself the Twelfth Imam, and of his son, Abbas Effendi Abdul Baha, KBE, who advocated the unity of all religions, and peace among men. Baha'u'llah and Abdul Baha are buried in a golden domed mausoleum set in a Persian garden on the lower slopes of Mount Carmel. Rothschild said that he found the faith soothing and when I asked him if that was the reason he appeared to be such a happy man, he answered with the story of the unhappy king who sent out his armies to find the shirt of a happy man, but the only happy man they could find was a poor shepherd, who had no shirt. We then talked about English words borrowed from Arabic, such as admiral and algebra, and Rothschild said that he had once heard an Arab claim that Shakespeare derived his name from the Arabic *sheikh es kebir*, 'the great teacher,' and that there was a current joke that Hitler's true name, Schikelgruber, was a corruption of *sheikh el garbah*, 'the leader with the whip.'

He was engaged at the time in writing two books: one about castles and fortresses and he told me that he had learned a deal about Welsh castles in the process of his researches. The other was a book on the fortifications of Jerusalem, and when he found that I had a Rolliflex camera, he asked if I would take some photographs for the book. We set off, one sunny afternoon, and walked through the olive groves above the leper hospital, and stopped to speak to an Arab peasant leading a gazelle, that had a neck like that of a swan and large soft eyes, which he said was his pet and lived in his house. We walked round the city wall taking pictures of the Damascus Gate, the Dung Gate, Herod's Gate, Jaffa Gate, the New Gate, Sion Gate and St Stephen's Gate, and the gates of the Haram esh-Sharif. As we passed St Stephen's Gate, towards evening, the massive gates were slowly closing, and a small boy ran towards them, screaming in case he should be locked out.

Rothschild took me to Ein Karem where the Virgin Mary came to visit her cousin Elizabeth, then bearing the child that was to become John the Baptist. The Church of the Visitation commemorates the meeting of the two mothers-to-be, and above the grotto where John is said to have been born stands a fortress-like Franciscan Monastery. Two young monks, one from Spain and the other an

American, took us into the church, decorated with marble reliefs, and an altar of lapis lazuli. Rothschild sat at the organ and played a Bach chorale to which the Spaniard sang melodiously. Elderly Russian nuns emerged from their whitewashed cottages and stood about in their immaculate gardens. The more ancient ones had crossbones on their head cloths as a reminder of their mortality, and one of them approached us and offered us slices of melon or a glass of water drawn from *ein karem*, 'the well in the vineyard.' Among the tall cypresses, the almonds and the pomegranates, stood a marble plinth on which, in shining bronze, lay the Baptist's head.

Rothschild, gave me a scarab that he had found during excavation at Acre. It was made in about 1300 BC, which was the time when the Pharaoh Rameses II swept north through Canaan and marched on the Hittites at Qadesh, and it bore the hieroglyphs *mer en neb ta*, 'the blessing of the gods be upon you.'

A number of Jewish ladies of British origin took upon themselves to provide some comfort for young men from the United Kingdom, and from the Commonwealth, who now found themselves in uniform in a strange, and largely hostile land. They invited some of us to their homes, and they formed a club where one could have a cup of tea and, above all, a chat, and they also persuaded a few English-speaking Jewish young women to come to the Club to entertain us in conversation or with a game of cards or, occasionally, as dancing partners. Chief among these wonderful women was Sophie Adler, who had been born in England of Jewish parents and was married to Professor Saul Adler. Adler was a name in the world of tropical medicine, but he was also known for his absent-mindedness. When I arrived at the house for dinner one evening, a little before the other guests, and asked where Saul was, Sophie replied with a question: 'Yes, where is Saul? I sent him upstairs to change half-an-hour ago.' She ran up the stairs and found that having taken off his clothes, he had, by force of habit, gone to bed, where he was fast asleep.

It was at Mrs Ulitzer's garden party that I first met Shoshanna. It was a large garden, parched on account of the summer heat, but with pretty girls where flowers normally bloomed. Among them Shoshanna, which is Hebrew for a rose, caught my eye immediately and, as I approached her, she asked me in which regiment I served. 'Can't you see from my badge?' I teased her, to which she replied: 'I don't look at people's badges. I look at their eyes.' And in her own eyes I saw only beauty and, could it be, an early message of love. I met her frequently after that day, but only when she was in the company of other girls. Then, one day, she invited Frank and I and two other fellows from HQ, to a tea party at her parents' home in Beit Hakerem. Beit Hakerem was a residential area outside Jerusalem, on the road to Ein Karem. The house, stood in its own grounds surrounded by tall cypress trees and pines and covered with a scatter of acacia, orange, lemon and pepper trees. After tea, we played games in the garden and, as I rounded a corner on the other side of the house, I ran into a lady with a fresh, round face and snow-white hair. I apologised, but she launched into a conversation, as though we had already been speaking, about the various Christian sects. She wanted to know the fine differences between them and, after I had endeavoured to satisfy her, she said: 'I take it, as you know so much, that you are a clergyman!' She seemed surprised when I said that I was not, and went into the house. Shoshanna told me afterwards that this was the first time that Ima, which is the Hebrew for mother, had engaged herself in conversation with anyone outside the family since her little daughter, Rahel, had been killed in an ambush in the previous October, when the Arabs had stopped the school bus and set it on fire with the children inside.

Ima invited me to dinner one evening, during which she continued to show her interest in religion. She listened with attention while I told her that in Wales that evening, being a Sunday, a thousand preachers would be getting into the *hwyl* as they reached the climax of their sermons and that the people sang in parts, as Giraldus Cambrensis had pointed out eight centuries ago. She spoke about her childhood in Latvia, and of her desire to become a doctor, but her parents would not hear of a young lady of her station taking up a profession, even as noble a one as medicine. However, her insistence had prevailed and they had allowed her to go to study in Edinburgh, then the leading medical school in Europe. She and her chaperone, Katerina, arrived in this country and took a sleeper from King's Cross, but they could not sleep. When the train stopped at a station, she asked Katerina to lift the blind to see where they were and was told they were at Bovril. The train stopped again and Katerina, in response to the same request replied: 'Funny. We're still at Bovril!' When the train stopped once more she informed her mistress: 'We're now at another station also called Bovril!' I was interested, years later to hear Peter Ustinov say that his mother, when she arrived in this country, had baffled the immigration authorities by stating on her landing form that she had been born at St Petersburg, educated at Petrograd, and had embarked at Leningrad, and had gained the impression that every station in England was called Bovril.

After qualifying and returning to Libau, she had married a doctor named Borochov whose father appeared in the *Encyclopaedia Hebraica* as 'Abba Yaacov Borochov, rabbi,' and they had come to live in Palestine where, like so many immigrants, he had Hebraised his surname as Brachyahu, 'beloved of God'. I never heard his first name, as he was always known as Abba, the Hebrew word for father. During the 1914-18 war he had been made to serve as a medical officer with the Turks in the Lebanon, and it was there that Shoshanna, or Anna, as she preferred to be called, was born. When the war was over, they had settled in Jerusalem where Ima had helped Henrietta Szold to establish the Hadassah Hospital, on Mount Scopus, in which Abba was the head of the Department of Hygiene. She was a fervent promoter of the rights of women and had represented Palestine at the World Congress of Suffragettes at Copenhagen and elsewhere, and had met Sylvia Pankhurst and other leading Suffragette figures. She also promoted the care and welfare of children and was critical of the 'incubator' methods of the *kibbutzim*, and felt that 'cuckoo-mothers' deprived their children and were themselves deprived.

From the time the Germans had invaded Latvia in June 1941, she had received increasingly disturbing reports from Libau, where her aged father, and her brother, lived. As time went by, there came horrific accounts of the massacre of Jews in Minsk, Kiev and in Lithuania. She had heard that, in Latvia, Jews were having to strip naked and were being shot in rows, standing above ditches which they had been made to dig to be their graves. She naturally feared that her father and brother would be among them, and when I tried to comfort her by saying that even the Germans could not be that inhuman, she insisted that the reports were from a reliable source and that it sounded like just another chapter in the persecution of the Jewish people. She seemed to be reconciled to the suffering of her people, but the brutal killing of her small daughter had caused her hair to go white. She told me that she had a shock of red hair when she was young and when I said 'How nice!' she observed: 'Red hair is always nice – on someone else's head!'

I wondered whether it was some form of warning when Ima told me, that she had an aunt who had married a gentile, who was the governor of one of the provinces, despite the disapproval of her father, who had cut her off from the family and read the service of the dead over her name in accordance with the Hebrew tradition. I also wondered what was in her mind when she asked me to plant a palm tree in the garden. 'It will be there as a remembrance of you,' she said.

October 6 was the first anniversary of the murder of little Rahel, and I knew that the family would not want to be disturbed. I went to Beit Hakerem, however, and stood by the garden gate, which was closed, and looked at the house, dark in mourning. I listened to the soughing of the soft wind in the pines and watched the moon hide her face behind a black cloud, and left.

Anna and I walked over the hills towards Beit Vegan the next day. Across a ravine stood the village of Ein Karem and there were vineyards on the slopes below us, each with its watchtower, fragile as though it had been built of twigs. A pine tree stood alone, which made me recite *Ein fichtenbaum steht einsam* . . . to which Anna responded with a poem by Bialik that spoke of a white dove alone in a karub tree. A vulture wheeled above a place where we found a cluster of bones, that appeared to be those of a sheep. We gathered *kalaniot* (anemone) and *rakevet* (cyclamen) that grew profusely on the hillside and rested on a rock as an Arab shepherd boy came by with his flock, playing his flute the while. He stopped and rebuked us saying that, according to his faith, it was immoral for a young man and a young woman to be alone together in such a remote place, and went his way, leading his sheep and playing his flute.

We went to a concert given by the Palestine Orchestra, at the Edison Theatre at which the conductor was Felix Weingartner, and the programme comprised the *Symphonie Fantastique* from Berlioz's 'Life of the Artist'; Weber's 'Invitation to the Waltz' which Weingartner had orchestrated; Milhaud's *Trois Rag-Caprices,* and Mendelssohn's *Ruy Blas* Overture. I had worn my 'blues' for the occasion, with buttons and badges of rank shining and looking formal alongside Anna's black dress, unrelieved save for a brooch of gold leaves which her grandmother had worn as a young girl in Latvia. As we entered the foyer, she met some friends and I went ahead. As I stood waiting for her by an inner door, with the tickets in my hand, two old ladies came up to me and asked me to conduct them to their seats. I felt somewhat crestfallen when I realised that I had been taken for the commissionaire.

After supper, Anna and I would sit in the garden where we had made our own little bower under the pepper trees. There we would be alone in the world and talk about our past and our future, which we rather feared. One night, as the harvest moon peeped at us through the pine trees, she declared her love with the words *Ana bahubbek*, and later, she wrote me a letter which she signed 'Yours for the duration', although we had hopes that it would be longer.

We walked along the walls of Jerusalem one evening when the moonlight was so bright that we could see gazelle grazing under the pines in Herod's garden, and the expanse of artichokes outside the wall was a sea of silver. Above David's Gate we met some of Anna's friends and one of them, Nahama, broke into song and sang *Yerushalayim shelee*, 'My Jerusalem', so that her voice carried out over the Vale of Kidron. We then supped at the Jaffa Gate, on *kebab* and pigeon, *halkoum* and nuts and Turkish coffee.

Zeev Raban was, perhaps, the best known artist in Jerusalem. Over his door was a carved lion, *raban* in Hebrew, and beside it, a lamb, symbolic of his own gentle nature. He showed me the original drawings he had made for his illustrated *Shira Shirim*, 'The Song of Songs', and his drawings for the book of *Esther* and the book of *Ruth*, and the illustrated Hebrew alphabet that he was preparing for his little granddaughter. He was a well-versed man who spoke easily about his acquaintanceship with Eric Kennington and Lawrence, and with Eric Gill and Epstein. Anna gave me a copy of Raban's *Shira Shirim*, printed and illustrated, in Hebrew and in English, for Christmas.

We were part of an unending line of pilgrims on Christmas eve, on the road to Bethlehem, winding its way in the moonlight across the Plain of Rephaim, where David fought the Philistines; past the convent of Mar Elias, where Elijah rested on his way to Horeb, and the marble seat that commemorates the artist Holman Hunt, and the whitewashed dome of the tomb built by Sir Moshe Montefiore where Jacob had 'set a pillar upon the grave' of his wife Rachel when she had died giving birth to Benjamin. After a journey of less than six miles we reached Bethlehem, 'the house of bread' to the Hebrews, 'the house of meat' to the Arabs. It first appears in history in the fourteenth century BC when the king of Jerusalem wrote to his Egyptian overlord asking for archers to help him recover 'Bit-Lahmi'. Here David was born, his great-grandmother, Ruth, having 'stood breast high amid the alien corn' hard by. Joseph and Mary were natives who had fled to Galilee to avoid the insecurity generated by the Herodian dynasty. Away to our left, the moonlight rained down upon the fields where 'the shepherds watched their flocks by night'. Jerome stated that Bethlehem lay in a grove dedicated to Adonis and surmised that 'in the cave where the infant Messiah once cried, the paramour of Venus was bewailed.' After the Jews had been expelled by Hadrian, pagan cults were freely followed until Helena dedicated a church above the cave in the year 339. Jerome came to live there in 384 and devoted his time to producing the Vulgate version of the Bible. Justinian rebuilt and extended the church, and his building has remained in use until the present day. The south transept was used for worship by Moslems from the time of Omar, which helped to preserve the fabric, and when Hakim ordered its destruction, in 1099, Tancred rode hard through the night from Latrun to prevent it. After the Ottoman Turks had pillaged its marble and used it to build the Haram esh-Sharif in Jerusalem, the west door was made small by the Mamelukes to prevent other looters from driving their horses and carts into the church. The red limestone pillars of the basilica were decorated with saints and monarchs by the Crusaders: one shows Cathal of Ireland, and another King Canute.

The church was built above one, or more, of the plethora of caves that were used to shelter animals from earliest times. To enter the cave of the Nativity, one has to leave the church by a small door in the north transept and descend a flight of steps. We went down dark stairs, step by step in slow communion with a host of fellow-pilgrims, down to where the manger lay. The cave was heavy with incense and the smell of candle grease, and hung with fifty flickering lamps. Tapestries on the walls could hardly be distinguished from the blackened rock. The harmonious voices of monks and nuns came down to us from the floor above so that one could imagine it to be a heavenly choir. A star of beaten gold bore the Latin to indicate that here Jesus Christ was born of the Virgin Mary, and the more devout, among them Polish soldiers, threw themselves to the floor and kissed the star. Some wept and sobbed in ecstasy. Opposite, carved out of the rock, lay the manger, adorned with many coloured lights, and before it was a small cradle in which there was a baby doll to symbolise the Christchild. Two solemn nuns presided over the cradle, unendingly counting their beads. It was all so different from old Sarah Harries's story of the babe in the manger, with the cattle and the donkeys and the Wise Men bringing gold and frankincense and myrrh.

My first Christmas day in Jerusalem was a day of sumptuous feasting in the Mess: breakfast of porridge and bacon and egg and pork sausage with tomato sauce, and marmalade, and then a traditional Christmas dinner with turkey and all the trimmings, served by the General, Sir Philip Neame, VC, and other red-tabbed officers, in the traditional manner.

Anna and I went to Haifa, travelling through acres of jasmine and orange groves, to stay with her friends, and then we went on to Nazareth following the road that snaked across the Plain of Esdraelon, or Emek Israel, or the Vale of Jezreel, where Deborah, the prophetess, inspired the armies of Barak to defeat the Canaanites. The plain was the site of more battles than anywhere else and is the exemplar of war as Armageddon, the hill of Megiddo, which the Apocalypse gives as the site of the last great battle between the forces of good and evil. The Pharaoh Thutmose III gained a victory here, and Solomon fortified the hill and garrisoned it with cavalry and chariots, and kept his horses in stables built by Ahab. Josiah fell defending it against the Egyptians in 610 BC, and it was here, in 1918, that General Allenby broke the back of the Turkish army and was able to advance towards Jerusalem. We passed the concentric *kibbutz* of Nahalal, and Ramat David named after David Lloyd George, and Affulah, established by American Jews, and Jezreel, where Naboth had a vineyard which Ahab coveted. We came to Ein Dor, where the ageing Saul sought advice from the witch on the eve of the battle that cost him his life. Then on to Beisan, or Beit She'an, with its Roman amphitheatre and Byzantine monastery, before turning north to follow the Jordan past Jisr-el-Majamie and the Rutenberg electricity works, to Samakh, on the shore of the lake that is variously known as Gennesereth, Gennosar, Yom Kineret, Lake Tiberias and the Sea of Galilee. We travelled along the eastern side of the lake to Ein Gev, a pioneering *kibbutz* half way up the mountain and within a bowshot of the Syrian border, which had suffered greatly on that account. The snow-clad summit of Mount Hermon rose above us. Returning to Samakh, we visited Degania, the first *kibbutz* to be established in Israel, in 1909, and went on to Tiberias, the town built by Herod Antipas in honour of his patron, Tiberius. We followed the shore northward to Magdala, where a whitewashed dome marked the spot where Christ met Mary, of that town, whose sin is said to have been much exaggerated. At Tabgha we visited three churches: the church of the primacy of Peter, the church of the multiplication of loaves and fishes, and the church of the Sermon on the Mount. On our way homeward we passed by the Horns of Hattin, where Saladin defeated the Crusaders in a decisive battle in 1187, and skirted round Mount Tabor, which some claim to have been the scene of the Transfiguration.

One day I looked up to the sky and saw a great mustering of storks in a wheeling umbrella over Jerusalem, on their migration from East Africa to Europe. I thought how Jeremiah had noted, long ago, that 'the stork in heaven knoweth her appointed time'. Each year, in spring and in autumn, they gathered in great clouds, and wheeled for hours over Jerusalem, as though they were paying homage to the thrice holy city but they were, in fact, taking advantage of the thermals to gain height.

I enjoyed working in the garden ar Beit Hakerem, especially when performing tasks that were new to me. I had never before picked *mishmish*, the baby apricots, off the tree, nor green almonds, nor had I tied paper bags round ripening bunches of grapes as they hung invitingly under a pergola so as to protect them from the birds and the bees. Sometimes I would water the garden and, occasionally, turn the hose on the iguana-like lizards that were sunning themselves on the walls of the house. On warm evenings we would have dinner on the balcony as spiny geckoes clung to the ceiling and stared down at us. Once, one of them lost its grip and dropped into a bowl of borsch that had just been set before Professor Chernikover, the Egyptologist, which stopped him in mid-sentence as he was talking about the excavations of Flinders Petrie. The name of Sir Flinders Petrie was one that I had held in reverence since childhood. I had heard him mentioned, time and again, by the Reverend Ben Morris when he preached fire and brimstone from the high pulpit at Ebenezer, and in particular when he felt that his interpretation of Holy Writ was insufficiently convincing. He would then invoke the name of Sir Flinders: 'As Sir Flinders Petrie has shown . . .', he would say, and proceed to give a description of Petrie's discovery of the city of Hezekiah at Tel el-Hesi, or of the palace of the Jew's daughter at Tahpanhes. Sir Flinders, by his excavations, had unfolded the mysteries of the Old Testament, had made the Word come true.

I happened to mention Sir Flinders, during conversation, to Betty Larke, the Assistant Commissioner of the Red Cross in Palestine, and she asked: 'Would you like to meet him?' I could not believe that I had heard her words. I had never thought of him as a living human being, let alone that he was alive. 'He is here in Jerusalem', she went on, as though she sensed my disbelief. I came to grips with the reality of the situation, however, when I received an invitation from Lady Petrie to take tea with her and Sir Flinders at the American School of Oriental Research, where they lived.

Lady Petrie met me at the door and led me along corridors to a shaded conservatory where Sir Flinders sat crouched among cushions in a cane chair. His finely carved face had that alabaster quality of old age, and it was set in a fine, neatly trimmed white beard. His delicate features and his slender, soft hands would lead one to believe that he had spent his time confined to a Victorian study, rather than digging for sixty years in the sands of the Nile. Lady Petrie provided ample evidence of industry in this field, however. Her face had been burnt by the sun and lashed by blown sand so that it looked like deep-furrowed leather, which gave her pale blue eyes a stunning brightness behind her gold rimmed spectacles. She wore a henna-dyed dress, of the kind worn by the women of Bethlehem, with embroidery around the neck, and on her head was a battered straw hat. Her ability to get a good day's work out of the most slothful Egyptian was the envy of archaeologists. On first meeting she would appear to be curt and rather forbidding. 'Do you drink tea?' she asked as she approached me with two mammoth cups in her hand, 'or would you prefer water with your biscuit, as Flinders does?' Sir Flinders looked frail and spoke little until he found that I was from Wales. 'Oh, I like Wales,' he said. 'If I had my time over again, I would spend more time on the Presely Hills.'

He expressed his frustration because the war was interfering with his excavations, but Lady Petrie interposed to say that, while he was perfectly capable of pursuing his work in the field at eighty seven years of age, it was time that he got on with his writing. He spoke about his work: how he had found Hebrew hymns written on papyri at Oxyrhynchos, how he had identified Beth-pelet as the home of Benaiah who slew the men of Moab and was 'a lion in the midst of a pit in time of snow', and how he had discovered a hitherto unknown script at Serabit el Khadem in the Sinai desert. The discovery that pleased him most was of the fortress of Daphnae, now Tel Defenna, north of Ismailiyah. An Arab had told him that the citadel mound was known as Qasr Bint el Yehude, 'the castle of the Jew's daughter', and this had reminded him that Tahpanhes was the refuge to which Jeremiah had brought the exiled princesses from Jerusalem as they fled from that city after its capture by the Babylonians under Nebuchadnezzar.

Hilda Petrie proudly stated that the discovery she liked to remember was that of the little statue of Khufu, or Cheops. The tiny ivory figure, less than three inches overall, had been found in one of the lower levels of the stratified temples at Abydos, but its head had been broken off while digging and was missing. She made the workers sift the huge heaps of excavated soil, working by day and by night for three weeks until it was found, the size of a thumbnail, to complete the only known figure of the builder of the Great Pyramid. She reckoned that they were extremely fortunate to be living in Jerusalem despite its proliferation of holy days and holidays, and the lackadaisical attitude for which the key word was *bukkrah*, the Arabs' concept of a more leisurely mañana. 'And so,' she would say, 'you have the Moslems flocking to the Haram esh-Sharif every Friday; the Jews trooping to the synagogues every Saturday, and the Christians going to church on Sunday. You might say that a week in Jerusalem consists of three Sabbaths and four *bukkrahs*!'

She telephoned me regularly, after my first visit, usually for some small service, and would frequently upbraid me for not having called to see Flinders. She rang one day to say that he had been admitted to the Government Hospital suffering from malaria, and would I go to see him. When I got there, I saw that he was in an exceedingly weak condition and I had difficulty in following his words, except that he was full of appreciation of the kindness of 'the good people of Jerusalem'. Six weeks later, on Christmas Eve, he said that he was fully recovered and that he would be out of hospital before the New Year, but he was to stay there for the remaining eighteen months of his life. When I took him a little present on his eighty-eighth birthday he told me that *The Seven Pillars of Wisdom* was being read to him, which reminded him of the time when he had Lawrence, learning to dig, at Kfar Ammar, south of Memphis. Lawrence, writing to his brother, Will, had described Petrie as 'a most exciting individual' and, in a letter to D. G. Hogarth he had said that Petrie was 'enormous fun' but wondered why he had not died of ptomaine poisoning as he ate 'out of week-opened tins after scraping off the green crust inside'. Whenever I saw him, he kept on saying: 'The Welsh have always been a great people,' and he said it again when I took him some daffodils on St David's Day in 1942. Although he was becoming more feeble, his mind was as active as ever, and running ahead of his words. He was always glad to see people and he told me, with great delight, that Mortimer Wheeler had come all the way from the Western Desert to pay him a visit. On one of my last visits to him he gave me a copy of a booklet, *A Vision of the Ages*, which contains a series of historical sketches that were read at a matinee at the London Hippodrome in 1930 as part of the 'half-century celebration of Flinders Petrie's researches in Egypt'. He signed it, almost illegibly, and it was about the last time he put pen to paper.

I had planned to go to see him on the afternoon of 28 July 1942 but I was prevented from doing so by an unforeseen occurrence. That evening, he died.

Lady Petrie sounded cheerful and almost relieved when I telephoned her. 'He died splendidly!' she said, and was grateful for my offer of help. Richard Hughes, the 'Welsh ambassador' in Jerusalem, and I, arrived at the American School in time for the funeral at four o'clock the following afternoon, and there were four or five other people there. Lady Petrie was dressed, as usual, in her henna-dyed dress, nailed shoes and without stockings, but she had put a black ribbon round her straw hat, and wore a small black cape over her shoulders. As we followed the coffin, my mind went back to the Reverend Ben Morris and I thought that he would have been glad to have been in my place to pay his last respects. I thought, too, that if any of the children at Newport had heard of Sir Flinders in the way I had, they would have a vision of the Holy City deep in mourning as a massive cortege moved slowly to sad music along the black-draped streets, thronged with people as the body of the great man was borne on a horse-drawn gun-carriage to its last resting place. I thought how disillusioned they would have been if they knew that his widow and Richard Hughes and I, and a few others, alone formed the cortege following the coffin, draped in the Union Jack on a police lorry, through unheeding streets to Mount Zion. There, friends and representatives of the Government and various academic institutions had gathered for the committal.

I called on Lady Petrie a few days later and was taken aback when she asked me: 'Have you come to see Flinders?' As I was beginning to think that she had become deranged after her recent experience, she added: 'He is here you know.' I did not know at the time that he had expressed the wish that his head should be given to the Royal College of Surgeons and that she had it in the house. It was later taken to the Government Hospital where, a friend told me that she had seen it in a jar, with the beard floating in formalin, waiting to be sent to London. It was not possible for this to be done, however, until the war was over, when it was sent in a box as an item of antiquity.

The American School of Oriental Research, situated outside Herod's Gate, was in the charge of Nelson Glueck, an American archaeologist, who was said to be a member of the American Intelligence Service. I also got to know John D. Whiting, who lived there, and he and his wife invited me to tea, where I met Lady Glubb, who invited me to tea with her the next day. She chatted ceaselessly about old times, and as she spoke I noticed, above her head, a photograph of the installation of the Emir Abdullah as ruler of Transjordan, and another of her son, Glubb Pasha.

Canon Bridgeman, whom I had met one day at St George's Cathedral, invited me to tea at his house in the American Colony. He loaned me some books on Jerusalem and the Holy Land and told me that they had been borrowed by H. V. Morton when he came to write *In the Steps of the Master*. He asked me to come to

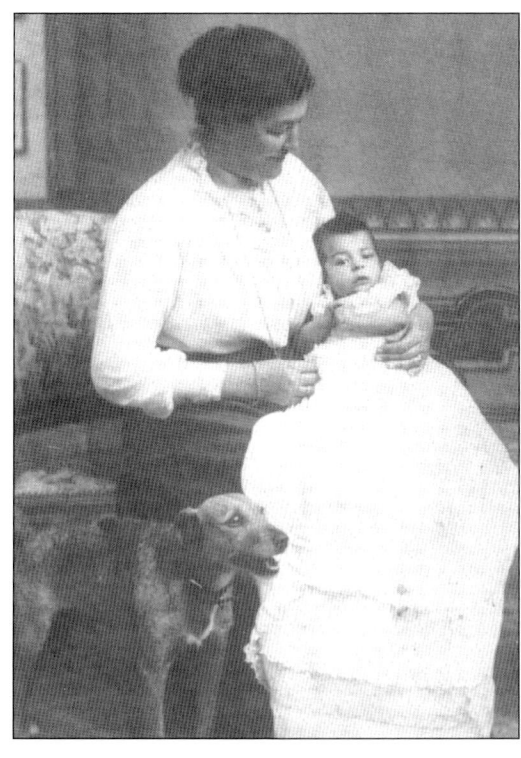

DM with Mother and Dash.

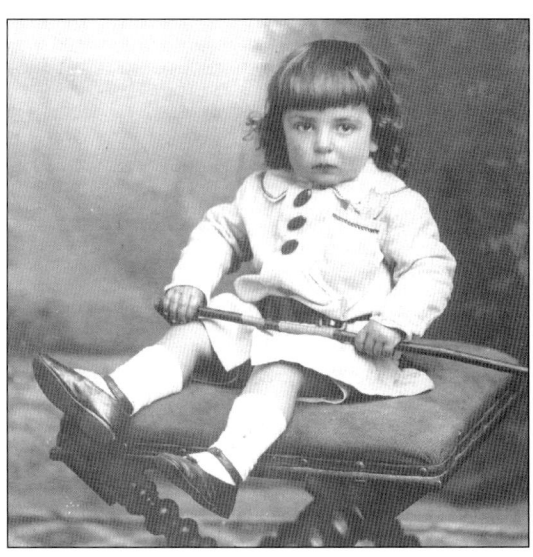

DM aged two.

Mother, Father, Herbert and DM.

Form VI (Upper and Lower), Fishguard County School, 1933.
Front row: Spencer Davies; Miss G. G. Morgan (later Mrs C. B. James), form mistress; Joseph Jones, headmaster; Mary Ford, Glyn Davies. *Behind, left to right*: George Evans, Llewelyn Jones, James David Howell, Alun Johns, Gad Francis, DM, Lambert Sturgess, W. J. Rees, Eurof Martin, Jack Nichols, and Jimmy Stretch.

The first St David's Day Dinner held in Jerusalem, 1942.

Emerging from
The Garden Tomb.

Snow in Jerusalem, 1942.

Planting a tree in the
Land of Israel, 1943.

St George's Cathedral. Jerusalem, 2 February 1944.

Captain Kenneth Gapp; Colonel Hunter; F/Lieut. Arthur Thomas, RAF; DM;
F/Lieut. Arthur Pearl, RAAF; Joyce; Captain Jock Calder; Major Peter Jolliffe;
Lieut. Audrey Mustart, WAAS; Colonel Bindie Carroll; Captain John G. Jones, best man.

At the black tents of Sheikh Abu Daoud of the Suwwahra, January 1944.

Three *mukhtars* leave the wedding feast.

Honeymoon by The Sphinx . . .

. . . and at the Pyramids.

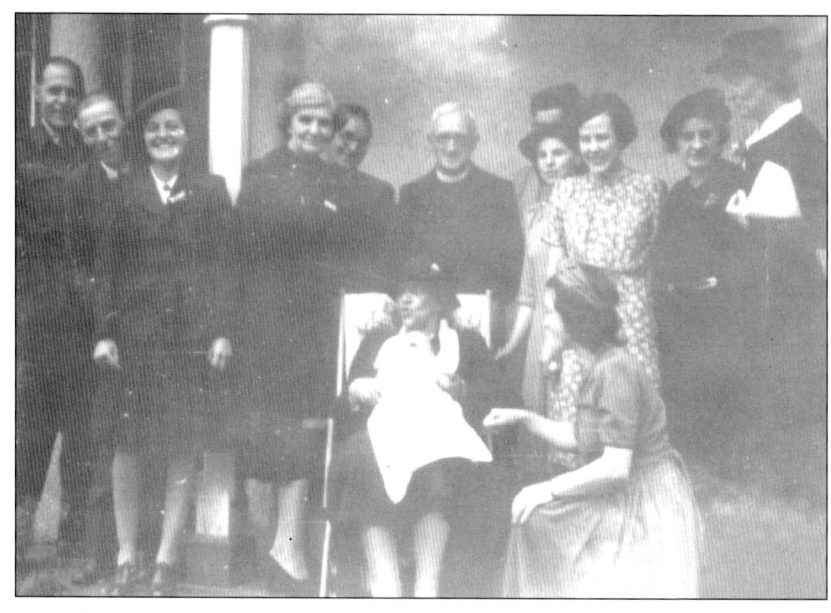

Anthony's christening party, Cotham Lodge, 1945.

Marilyn's christening, St John's Wood Church, 1946.

Newport Castle.

The other side of Newport Castle.

DM, Joyce and Marilyn beside the 'wolves at the door', Newport Castle.

Edna Griffiths and Roger, Betty and Bindie Carroll, Anthony, Joyce, Marilyn, DM, Jon Ord, Eileen Chessum and daughter, Beatrice Ord and daughter.

First *Hen Galan* BBC broadcast from the Gwaun Valley: W. J. Davies; Maria Davies, Penrallddu; DM; Elizabeth Vaughan, Pontfaen House; Rev. H. J. Roberts; Lloyd Richards; and W. R. Owen, producer.

Mayor of Newport, 1950.

Like father . . .

St Curig's Fair revived, 27 June 1951.

First gathering of mayors at Newport: Alderman Wm. John, Tenby; Councillor Eddie Jones, Haverfordwest; DM, Alderman J. R. Williams, Pembroke; Councillor Keri Davies, Cardigan, 27 June 1951. The mayors of Cardigan and Tenby, by chance, were also natives of Newport.

Marilyn dressed ready to present a bouquet to Princess Marina, Duchess of Kent.

Marilyn presenting a bouquet to Princess Marina.

Grant of the Freedom of Haverfordwest to the Lord Mayor of Cardiff (Alderman George Williams) and to the Rev. Baring Gould, 1951. *Front row*: R. Ivor Rees, Town Clerk; Lady Mayoress of Cardiff; Lord Mayor; Mayor of Haverfordwest; Rev. Gould; Mayoress and Mayor of Tenby. *Back row*: Mayors of Cardigan, Neath, Newport (Pembs.), Pembroke, Cowbridge, Port Talbot.

Inspection of his rights of fishery by the Mayor of Haverfordwest (Councillor Eddie Jones) as Admiral of the Port, accompanied by the Mayors of Pembroke, Tenby and Newport, while Councillor John Green secures the boat, 1951.

Anthony, DM, Joyce, Marilyn.

Arriving at the Sheffield Welsh Society's St David's Day Dinner.

a service at the cathedral the following Sunday and introduced me to the Bishop, Graham Brown, after the service. A little later, the Archdeacon, Dr Dawes, telephoned to say that the Bishop wished me to dine with him. There were two QAIMNS nurses also invited, one of whom was to be married at the cathedral some days later. After we had eaten a rather frugal meal, the girls left and the Bishop invited me to his study where, after a while, he switched on the wireless and we heard, on the BBC Overseas Service, that bombs had been dropped in South Wales and that a ship carrying children had been sunk in the Atlantic. He said that he was glad that we had met as he had heard Sir Flinders and Lady Petrie speak of me. I went to the toilet before I left and I was amused to find that the towels and even the toilet paper were of an episcopal purple.

The Bishop invited me to dinner again and eventually persuaded me to be confirmed. I was therefore admitted into the Church of England, with a laying of hands, followed by a tea in the garden. A short time afterwards, he was killed in his car as it was being driven across a level crossing at Ez-Zib, near Acre. I went to his funeral service, at the Cathedral the next day, which was attended by the High Commissioner and Arab and Jewish leaders and members of the Christian, Jewish and Arab communities, among whom I met Mary Booth, daughter of Bramwell Booth, who had recently escaped from Germany and was a bundle of nerves and unable to hold a conversation.

Whenever I picked up the telephone and dialled 'Jerusalem 4709', a cheerful Irish-American voice would answer 'Garden of Gethsemane here!' It was Father Eugene Hoad, a Franciscan monk who hailed from Galway and had spent some time in the United States before coming to Jerusalem. His lively conversation and jolly laughter might not appear, at first hearing, to be in keeping with the solemn occasion commemorated in that garden, but I soon began to value the warmth of his friendship and his genuine pleasure at meeting people. One entered the Garden under an arch upon which was engraved *Hortus Gethsemani*. The name is derived from *gat shemen*, the Hebrew for 'an olive press' which, it is claimed, still lies in a grotto in the garden. The few gnarled olives that remain look as though they could have witnessed the betrayal. The rock upon which Jesus is believed to have prayed that 'the hour might pass away' now lies before the altar of the basilica built, in 1924, on the site of a fourth century Byzantine church, the outline of which is marked with a black line on the floor of the basilica.

Above the Garden is the seven onion-domed Russian church of St Mary Magdalene, that was built by Czar Alexander III in 1888 in memory of his mother, Maria Alexandrova. The body of the grand Duchess Elizabeth Feodorovna lies here, and so, it is said, do the hearts of other murdered members of the Russian royal family.

On a number of occasions while I was at Q, I was informed that I was to be posted, as most of my colleagues were, but each time, at the last moment, I was retained, usually in order to complete the task upon which we were engaged at the time. I thus escaped going to Moascar as a tutor, to H4 on the Haifa-Baghdad pipeline, and to the Western Desert and, by an afterthought, if it were not divine providence, kept from going to Crete, for the colleague who went in my place went on a ship that was lost, with all hands.

From the time that I was enrolled in the Army I was informed that I had been recommended for a commission, but the matter did not progress because my records never seemed to catch up with my movements. After I had been at Q for some time, Colonel Hopkinson became impatient and began to harass the Military Secretary who, eventually, found the papers and, within days, I was summoned to appear before Lieutenant-Colonel Louis Pedretti, the Deputy Assistant Director of Hirings, who was looking for an Area Hirings Officer for Damascus and Aleppo. Within a week, I was interviewed by Brigadier Hayes, the Deputy Director of Hirings, who was on a visit from GHQ, Cairo, and he decided that, rather than go to Damascus or Aleppo, I should be appointed Area Hirings Officer, Jerusalem and Transjordan. I reported to Hirings at eight o'clock the next morning, as a Lieutenant. I had to take over the duties of the Area Hirings Officer for the Jerusalem Area, which extended from Galilee to Beersheba, and covered Transjordan, without any introduction as my predecessor had been posted to Cairo. I was fortunate, however, in having as my clerk and personal assistant, John Asad, who had served under him. Asad was a well-mannered young man, of a respected Christian Arab family in Jerusalem, who anticipated my every wish and whom I found completely loyal, a rare virtue in that part of the world.

Hirings was the department that acquired land and buildings to meet the military requirements of the British Forces in Palestine and Transjordan. Apart from Colonel Pedretti, the staff comprised his deputy, Major Frank Osmond, of the Cheshire Yeomanry, and Captains Whitfield, Lanfear and Stevenson. In addition, there was a civilian staff of about thirty, with Paul Meo, a Greek who looked like Cedric Hardwicke, as chief clerk. Outstanding among the civilians was Dr Leopold Kuenstler, who had escaped from Hitler's Germany in 1938 and was working well below his intellectual ability. The only time I heard him speak of conditions in Germany was when he invited Anna and I to dinner, one *erev Shabat*, from which it was evident that he had had a narrow escape from the fate that befell millions of other Jews. After dinner he showed me an old Hebrew Bible printed in Hamburg in 1587 in which was written, in Gothic script: *Molwch yr Arglydd ac oll Cenetloedd a chydfolwch ef yr oll populoedd. Hibernica*, which he thought was Irish. I told him that it was Welsh, the first verse of Psalm 117.

When I was commissioned I managed to lease part of a flat at Aboulafia House, at the bottom of Ben Yehuda Street, facing Zion Square. The rest of the flat was occupied by Dr David Erlik and his wife Loubah, who were fairly recent immigrants from Kharkov. He was Assistant Surgeon at the Hadassah Hospital, where his salary was £P4 a week, and he was glad of an extra couple of £P's from me for two rooms and a bathroom. Loubah was originally from Pinsk and she would often sit and brood over the fate of her family that remained there and, at other times, would sing sad Russian songs. Her knowledge of English was very limited and I frequently had to use sign language, which she regarded as a hilarious performance on my part. For a time, she had an English teacher, whose English was hardly better than Loubah's and who wanted to teach me German against the day we would be marching into Berlin.

A great advantage in having a place of my own, was the opportunity to have a wireless and to be able to listen to the BBC Overseas Service. *Lilibullero* became a favourite tune, as it was the harbinger of news which, whether good or bad, gave one a feeling of contact with home. There was also the comfort of the opening notes of Beethoven's *Fifth Symphony*, converted by the appropriately named Belgian, Victor de la Vaye, to give the V-for-Victory sign, which the BBC began using on 20 July 1941.

I was able to lease a car for my private use from a cashier at Barclays Bank who could not get a ration of petrol for himself. It was an open tourer Morris Minor, and when I took it to Zachariyah's garage for petrol, he told me that the car had originally belonged to him and that he had chosen the number, M 13 H.

One of my first tasks as Area Hirings Officer, Jerusalem and Transjordan, was to take over the Kaiserin Augusta Victoria Hospital from the Australians. This fortress-like pile dominated the southern end of Mount Scopus, from which Alexander the Great 'spied' on the Holy City before he came to terms with the High Priest, and upon which Titus pitched his camp before he destroyed Jerusalem. Kaiser Wilhelm had erected this massive building for himself, from which he would rule the world, once he had won the Great War, and he named it after his wife, Princess Augusta Victoria of Schleswig-Holstein-Sanderburg-Augustenburg. After the war, however, when the British had been given the mandate over Palestine, it was used as Government House, until it was damaged by an earthquake in 1927. It then became a hospital for refugees and, at the outbreak of the Second War, for Australians, from which I had to transfer it to 16 British General Hospital.

The Kaiser's study was still lined with mahogany, and the walls of the spacious royal chambers were covered with pale green and primrose silk, touched with gold, and decorated with pieces of statuary that included a lion and a lioness representing the Kaiser and the Kaiserin. Asad and I took two full days going from one empty room to another, noting the dilapidation and damages incurred during the Australian occupation. While we were checking the refrigerator, which was the size of a dining room, the door suddenly slammed shut and we soon discovered that there were no means of opening it from the inside. We pushed and banged and kicked the massive door, and shouted. We became colder and colder, and ran out of jokes about becoming frozen stalagmites, and then we began to shiver even though we kept moving and shouting, and kicking the door. I have no idea how long we were in there, but when someone, by a miracle, opened the door, we stepped out, trembling, into what felt like hot air, and I experienced a feeling of cosy warmth and secure comfort. It took some time for us to realise that we had been extremely fortunate, and grateful to an inquisitive orderly who, while walking by, had opened the door of our frigorific prison.

Next to the Kaiserin Augusta in size, the largest building I had to handle was the Fast Hotel, which was the biggest hotel in Jerusalem until the King David was built. When I took it over from the Australian Commonwealth Forces, in whose occupation it had been, it had suffered damages that cost several thousands of pounds to make good, all of which had to be repaired before I could transfer it to the Church of Scotland for use as a hostel and club premises.

I had in my charge 122 properties, ranging from shop or office premises and dwelling houses to hotels and hospitals, airfields and many hundreds of acres of land, some of it barren and some under cultivation as orange groves and olive groves and vineyards and hundreds of acres of corn and other crops that were damaged by the troops in various ways. I felt a little uneasy when I found myself assessing the damages done to a monastery on the Mount of the Beatitudes.

The first person to notice that I had been promoted to the rank of Captain was my grocer, Dolinski. When I entered his shop, that smelt of soused herring and salami, he shouted *Mazel-tov*, and rushed forward to place 'a Cohen's blessing' on my pips. At dinner, at Beit Hakerem, that evening, Abba produced a bottle of his best wine 'to wet the stars'. It was a Saturday evening, and when Dr Kabak came in after dinner, he refused a cigar that I was offering him because three stars had not yet appeared in the sky, the sign that indicated that *Shabat* was over, but when I pointed to my shoulder and said *Yesh shne cochavim* (Here are three stars), he laughed and felt justified in submitting to my bending of the law of Moses.

In April 1942, Major Frank Osmond and I were invited to attend the ceremony of the Passover held by the Samaritans on Mount Gerizim, and we took Anna with us, and Jennifer Foot, who was with her brother Hugh at Amman. When the Assyrians conquered Samaria, and exiled its people, they introduced a mixture of foreign colonists 'and placed them in the cities of Samaria instead of the children of Israel.' These mingled with the remnant that had been left behind, and the resultant interfusion became known as Samaritans. When the Jews returned from Egypt, they would have 'no dealings with the Samaritans,' whom they despised, and it was only Christ's tale of the Good Samaritan that made a term of abuse a byword for Christian charity. The Samaritans regard themselves as the survivors of the remnant that avoided the exile, and they divided themselves into four clans, the progeny of Aaron, Ephraim, Manasseh, and Levi. The descendants of Aaron were the priests, until they became extinct in the seventeenth century and their place was taken by the Levites. They recognised only the Pentateuch, the first five books of the Old Testament. Their population had dwindled to 252 souls, two-thirds of whom lived at Nablus, and the others at Jaffa and Tulkarem. Since 1927 three of the men had been allowed to marry Jewish Yemenite women, so as to introduce much-needed new blood. They lived freely among the Arabs and spoke Arabic as well as Aramaic. When the Jews refused the offer of the Samaritans to help them to rebuild the Temple, they raised a rival sanctuary on Mount Gerizim. This was destroyed by the Jewish High Priest, John Hyrcanus, in 109 BC, but they celebrate their Passover on its site each year, precisely in the manner laid down by Moses.

As we sat having tea in the house of my friend, Captain Constant at Nablus, we could see people make the ascent up the steep slope of the mountain, and I was glad that Constant would take us up the rough track in his jeep. He knew Yaacov Ben Uzzi Hacohen, the community's public relations officer, who spoke English surprisingly well, and took us to seats of honour and presented us to the High Priest, or *Hacohen Hagadol*, Mazliach Ben Pinhas Ben Yitzchak Ben Shlomo. He, the *Hagadol*, provided spiritual guidance for the community and had charge of the holy books, including an ancient Scroll of the Law reputed to have been written by Abisha Ben Pinhas, the great grandson of Aaron, that was kept in a four-foot long silver container. He wore a light grey robe for the festival, with green silk wound round his turban. The turbans of the other priests were wrapped in a white cloth, and the rest wore tarbooshes.

Ben Uzzi, tall and bearded as a patriarch, squatted before us and launched into his obsessive desire to take a party of his people to Hollywood 'so that the whole world, and other forgotten peoples, may join with us in celebrating the Feast of the Passover in the way it was celebrated by our father Jacob, peace be unto him.' He went on: 'On the tenth day of Nissan which, as you know, is the first month in our calendar, we come to this holy mountain, as our forefathers have done over the centuries, and as prescribed in the book of *Exodus*, and pitch our tents here. On the fourteenth day, that is today, as the sun begins to go down, a fire is kindled in the trench we have dug before the altar, and water is boiled in those cauldrons over there, and we wait for the venerable the *Hagadol Hacohen* to start the ceremony. Cue perfect, the *Hagadol* mounted a stone platform and began to read the *Exodus* story of the deliverance of the Children of Israel from Egypt, and the celebration of the first Passover. The people waited with bated breath for him to come to the words relating to the sacrifice. Seven lambs, 'male of the first year and without blemish,' were brought before the altar, each held by three young men dressed in white shirts and *shintiyans* and their sandals tied with string, until, at the given word, a priest cut the throat of each with his sacrificial knife. The blood of each was caught in a bowl, and a bunch of hyssop was dipped in the blood and used to daub the tents as a sign of the Angel of Death. The lambs were then skinned and scalded and cut open and drawn, and the carcasses speared on oak spits and placed in the *tannour*, which was sealed with clay while the lambs 'roasted with fire' for three hours. At midnight, under the full moon, the High Priest led the heads of families, each carrying a straw tray, to the *tannour*, where the clay was broken. The meat was taken out and eaten, with unleavened bread and bitter herbs, hurriedly in accordance with the Lord's injunction: 'with your loins girded, your shoes on your feet and your staff in your hands: and ye shall eat it in haste.' They remained on the mountain another seven days and, on the last day, they climbed to the very summit where the *shechinah*, the visible glory of God, resides and sits on the Seat of Mercy.

When the *Hacohen Hagadol* died the following January, his death created a problem. He had held office since 1932, when he had succeeded his cousin, Yitzchak Ben Amram. The succession normally passes to the eldest son or, failing him, to the next of kin, but the present inheritor, Naji As-Samri, had an affliction and the Lord, in speaking to Moses, as recorded in the twenty-first chapter of *Leviticus*, had ordained that whosoever 'that hath a blemish . . . a blind man, or a lame, or he that hath a flat nose, or anything superfluous, or a man that is broken footed, or crookbackt, or a dwarf, or that hath a blemish in his eye, or be scurvy, or scabbed, or hath his stones broken . . . shall not come nigh to offer the offerings of the Lord made by fire . . . shall not come nigh to offer the bread of his God.' Whether poor Naji had a flat nose or was crook backed or scabbed was not stated: it was simply said that he had a blemish, and this led to a dispute as to the succession. Following the intervention of Abdullah Effendi Kheir, the District Officer, it was eventually agreed that the office should be vested in three priests; Naji Avisha Effendi Hacohen was chosen Reader of the Law on the Sabbath; Aviesha Effendi Hacohen, the conductor of services, with the additional task of maintaining contact with the authorities, and Amram Hacohen was appointed to deal with the community's political affairs. In addition, a committee of nine was set up to manage secular affairs and the settlement of disputes.

I went to Beit Jala, one day, with Toukan Bey, the Arab District Officer, to make peace with the *mukhtar*, Hanna Effendi Makhlouf, and to pay him compensation for damage done to the villagers' vines by our troops, and I then went on to a Russian monastery upon the land of which the Army wanted to erect a secret radio station. I found the superior, the Archimandrite Antony, sitting in his study, that was furnished in Russian style, and when he stood up I could see that his dark brown beard was down to his navel, and his hair to the small of his back. He received me most courteously and agreed to my request.

There were several radio stations sited, usually on hilltops, in my area, and they caused little complaint except, occasionally, for damage to crops. One day, however, I received a letter from Brother Nicholas of the Franciscan Hospice near Ramle, complaining that he had been 'receiving cipher calls through the ether or air' which he thought was 'most unusual as we have never had a Radio in our Monastery.' He believed that the voices were from Jerusalem, and they came to him wherever he was, in his room, in the monastery garden, in church, while out for a walk or in a bus, talking to him all the time and interfering with his 'private parts with their devilish power . . . drawing off the seed . . . until I learned how to prevent it, but even this does not work any longer.' He signed his letter 'by typewriter as they ever touch my hand,' and he invited me to call at the Hospice to discuss the matter.

News of the Jewish persecution in Europe, and later of the massacres, percolated through, but even those who managed to escape from the holocaust were not allowed to enter the Promised Land. Ships that reached the coast of Palestine bearing refugees were turned away, and any who landed were interned. In November 1940, the *Patria*, loaded with nineteen hundred refugees awaiting redirection to Mauritius, was sunk in Haifa harbour by its own passengers, rather than face deportation. Eighteen months later, the *Struma*, a broken vessel carrying 769 Jews who had fled from the pogroms of Romania was cruising aimlessly in the Black Sea while seeking permission to land in Palestine, when it struck a mine and sank, with all hands, save one. The local newspapers were not permitted to publish the story and so they appeared with empty spaces, framed in black lines, in which there were pertinent verses from the Old Testament.

With the advance of Rommel to El Alamein, almost within firing distance of Cairo, at the end of June 1942, there were fears that Hitler's declared ambition to squeeze the Middle East like a ripe orange was in danger of being realised, and the cruel joke given currency was that he was preparing to make a pilgrimage to the Wailing Wall. We had orders to be ready to burn our secret files and plans were in hand to evacuate British women and children. My department was inundated with requests for accommodation of all sorts and it was fortunate that

I had made a rough survey of properties that could be made available at short notice in the event of an emergency. I had given priority to earmarking properties that could be used for additional hospital accommodation and I set off to investigate further some monasteries and convents that I had in mind.

When I got to the Carmelite Convent, a small woman stood in the cool courtyard, with her brown habit pinned up above her knees. Her pale face was swathed in a white cloth, and she was wearing a black shawl, so that she looked like one of the hooded crows that were strutting around the convent. While she hurried away to find the Mother Superior, I wandered through an open cloister where there were tablets bearing the *pater noster* in some forty languages on enamelled tile tablets on the walls. I read the Breton version and tried the Gaelic, and was disappointed not to find it there in Welsh. The little pied sister returned and led me into a small chamber which had three rush chairs, as though they had been taken out of a Van Gogh painting, on one of which I sat and waited. In the wall facing me was a large Gothic arch covered with a black iron grill, from which spikes protruded at each intersection. Behind the grill hung a deep red damask curtain. All was still and silent until there suddenly came a heavenly voice, soft and gentle and more soothing than balm, saying: 'Good morning, Captain. What can I do for you?' Where was she? Behind the curtain? How did she know my rank? Could she see me? All these, and other, thoughts went through my head. I reached for words, and they came stubbornly, and I told her that I was seeking accommodation for those who had been wounded in war and before I could finish my message, the voice answered: 'How I grieve that I cannot be of aid to you, Captain. You see, we are a closed order, cloistered. We are cut away from the world. But I will see what the Mother Superior says: I am only the Sub-Prioress.' I apologised for not having realised that it was so and implored her not to pursue the matter any further. 'Pray do not apologise,' she went on. 'When one is so isolated, it is difficult. However, it's been nice meeting you, and I wish you well. We shall pray for you. We shall pray for you all. Good bye!' I came out into the sunlight half-dazed and with no thought but of that voice. I knew that I would never forget its soothing quality, and that I would never cease to wonder what the face behind the damask was like.

Some months later, I went back to that small chamber, taking Richard Hughes with me, to seek permission for the Lord's Prayer to be placed in Welsh among the other languages. The voice behind the curtain this time was that of the Mother Superior and she spoke in French, but when she realised our limitation in that language, she did her best to communicate with her limited command of English. She immediately warmed to our request and said that she felt that a language with such a close Biblical connection, which we had emphasised, deserved to be represented at the place where the *Pater Noster* was first uttered. There was simply the matter of purchasing a space for the tablet, which we agreed to do there and then.

As the German advance in the Western Desert threatened Egypt, and then Palestine, it became necessary for us to collaborate with the Jewish Agency in order to organise guerrilla activities in the event of invasion. The *Haganah*, though still a proscribed body with its members open to arrest and imprisonment, was given training at a special camp set up by the Special Operations Executive (SOE) at Mishmar Ha-Emek under the expert guidance of Major Henry Grant-Taylor. The *Haganah* was running a risk by revealing its personnel, and particularly those of its secret striking force, *Palmach*, while on the other hand they were receiving training of the kind they had not received since the departure of Wingate. This training was to be of value to them when the mandate came to an end, and during the events that led up to the Declaration of Independence in May 1948.

Jerusalem provided a refuge for Haile Selassie, Emperor of Ethiopia, before he was restored to his throne after the liberation of Abyssinia, and for King Peter of Yugoslavia. They were both provided with residences in Rehavia. King George of the Hellenes came on visits, and so did King Idris of the Senussi, although he spent most of his time at the Continental-Savoy in Cairo.

Harry Beilin was a frequent visitor at HQ and appeared to have access to offices and officers in a way in which no other civilian had, as he was the Liaison Officer between the Jewish Agency and the Army. He was a native of Liverpool and had started life as a sports journalist. His wife, Judy, who worked at the Palestine Broadcasting Studios, came from Norfolk, of an Anglican family, and they had got married in England before coming to settle in Jerusalem. She admitted to me that her conversion to Judaism had not been easy, and she bore her new religion lightly. They invited me to their home where I met their little daughter, Sheila, who called me 'Dill-Dill', and gave me a standing invitation to their *erev Shabat*, the Jewish 'at home', on a Friday evening.

One never knew whom one would meet at an *erev Shabat* anywhere, but this was particularly so at the Beilins as they had such a wide circle of friends and acquaintances. Apart from leading members of the Jewish community, there would be Army or RAF officers or members of the Palestine Police Force, or occasionally of the Palestine Government, and people connected with broadcasting and the theatre. It was there, one evening in January 1943, that I met Teddy Kollek who had come from South Africa, and was to be Mayor of Jerusalem for some fifty years. He was with Gerar, of 'World Window Productions', and we had a supper of bacon and eggs in a Jewish household.

The Beilins invited me to accompany them to the *bar mitzvah* of Harry's nephew, David, at Haifa and we arrived at the house on a Friday evening, in time for the traditional *erev Shabat*. We rose early the next morning and hurriedly prepared to get ready to go to the synagogue. Judy looked at me before we left the house and, as though she could read my thoughts, she said: 'Does it not remind you of the rush to get ready to go to church back home?' When we reached the synagogue, she joined the women, who all sat behind a screen, and I was taken to sit with the men.

One day, Harry took me on a tour of synagogues in the Old City. We first called on Moshe Weingarten, the *mukhtar* of the Jewish Quarter and met his three beautiful daughters, Yehudith, Rifkah and Masha, for whom prayers had been said at the Wailing Wall following their narrow escape from death by electrocution the previous evening. The Hurva Synagogue is regarded as the most elegant in Jerusalem and was the centre of worship for Ashkenazic Jewry. Further on, along the Street of the Jews, was the Sephardic synagogue of Yohanan, which was below the level of the street and was divided into four prayer halls. It was named after a rabbi who prayed here during the destruction of Jerusalem by the Romans, in 70 AD, and among its treasures was the horn which the Messiah will blow when he comes to proclaim the redemption of Israel. Not far from the Dung Gate stood Tipereth Israel, 'the glory of Israel', and across the road was the synagogue of the Karaites, a sect established in the eighth century, of which only three men and ten women survived.

The Beilins were close friends of the Chiziks and the Westons. Yitzchaq Chizik was a District Officer, and his wife, Assia, was French. Laurie Weston was a lawyer and a spellbinding storyteller, born in England, and his wife, Leah, was a *sabra*, as Palestine Jews were known after the indigenous prickly-pear, and a perfect foil to him. They met in each other's houses and went to plays and concerts together, and delighted in each other's company. Harry referred to them as 'The Kurdis': the Kurdis were regarded as a joke people about whom one was told, for instance, that a Kurdi wife had a right to beat her husband with a slipper if he did not give her satisfaction. I was adopted by them as a sort of seventh man, and exhorted to treat their homes as my own and, in the case of the Beilins, given a key to their in house in Ramban Road, to enter whenever I liked. I had met Chizik when he took over from Yussef Marroum as District Officer for Jerusalem: I found it helpful to consult the District Officer whenever I wanted to take over civilian property for the Forces. He, too, was a *sabra*, and as District Officer he spent the greater part of each day dealing with complaints. Each morning the corridor outside his office was tenanted by a line of petitioners: blue-shirted *kibbutzniks*, black-hatted and bearded *yishivebochers*, and Arabs, with their women carrying great baskets of edible leaves or squawking hens, waiting to see the D.O. Yitz gave advice and dispensed justice speedily and fairly, and few ever doubted his word. He had graduated Bachelor of Philosophy and Master of Arts at Chicago University, and a fellow student, Captain Goldberg of the U.S. Army, who came to see him, spoke of him in the highest terms. Another contemporary of his in Chicago was Heismann, who made me sit and have coffee with him, whenever I called at his shop to pay for my hired wireless set, so that he could tell me about Yitz's philandering in that city. Yitz retaliated by disclosing that Heismann had been a crony of Al Capone.

I got to know about Chizik's family when I went with Yitz to a ceremony held near the settlement of Huldah to commemorate the death of his brother Ephraim, who had been killed in an Arab ambush there in 1929. To my amazement, I found myself facing a monument on which were three carved figures which, Yitz explained, were his brother Ephraim, his sister Sarah, who had been killed in another ambush, and the third figure was the 'Unknown Soldier', representing those who had lost their lives in similar circumstances. This was the first 'graven image' in the Land of Israel. Yitz introduced me to his surviving sisters, Hannah and Zipporah, and brothers Aaron and Baruch. Baruch, I knew, had written the standard handbook on botany in Hebrew. A detachment of soldiers arrived, dressed in uniform that I did not at first recognise. They eyed me suspiciously, for they were members of the *Haganah*. They saluted the monument, and the banner of David that hovered over it. Baruch read the *kiddush* and Hannah read some words in Hebrew, and we went away, leaving the monument standing peacefully between a palm and an olive tree.

Yitz was dark and olive-skinned, and lacked polish. His petite, blonde French wife, Assia, was the antithesis in almost every respect: always lively and ready to cook a meal. I was regularly invited to sample her meals, and often the Beilins and the Westons would be there as well, especially on *erev Shabat* when Assia would light the candles in the traditional manner. Sometimes there would be a more formal dinner party, such as when Moshe Shertok and his wife came and Yitz would mix a pretty potent cocktail to set us off.

I was invited to Shertok's for *erev Shabat*. Shertok was to change his name to Sharett and become Prime Minister of Israel in succession to Ben Gurion. Moshe had always just returned from somewhere and was full of exciting stories. On one occasion he had been on a visit to Britain and the USA and on another, he was just back from Cairo where he had been to meet Lord Moyne, Minister of State in the Middle East and he was in a depressed mood as Moyne had told him that he was advocating a proposal to the British Government for the solution of the Palestine problem based on partition, when the Zionists were calling for the establishment of a 'Jewish Commonwealth' in Palestine. Moyne was assassinated a year later by two members of the Stern Gang, who were hanged for his murder.

In the way that some people see their world through rose-tinted spectacles, Laurie Weston saw his through tortoiseshell framed pebbles as 'a damned funny place'. Each new day brought him face to face with situations which he tackled, according to their gravity, either with hilarity or with apparent disregard. He had been brought up in Jerusalem, of parents with an Anglo-Jewish background, and it was in a synagogue there that he had married Leah, who was as necessary to his life as an arm or a leg, and went to lived in a penthouse flat in Rehavia, the fashionable part of Jerusalem. Laurie was a qualified solicitor and he was working with the Custodian of Enemy Property when I first met him. He then joined the Army and was given the rank of Major in the Judge Advocate's Department but, to his great disappointment, he was posted to Cairo, from which he endeavoured to escape and return home at every opportunity.

The quickest way of getting from Cairo to Jerusalem was to make for the outskirts of the city early in the morning and hitch a lift across the Sinai desert in a military vehicle. Laurie was thus engaged one Saturday morning when a large staff car pulled up and as he opened the rear door, he could discern that its occupant, from his red collar tabs, was a high ranking officer. He sprang a salute and apologised, saying that he would not have dreamt of stopping the car had he not been standing there for three hours and that his wife was desperately waiting for him in Jerusalem. The high ranking officer told him to jump in and sit beside him and not to apologise any further. Laurie was incapable of holding a conversation with anyone for long without relating one of his funny stories, and so it was with the high ranking officer. He regaled him with hilarious accounts of what happened at the Judge Advocate General's office, and of strange happenings in Jerusalem, and spoke about his wife, Leah, all interspersed with risqué stories and barrack room tales which seemed to delight the high ranking officer and made him laugh uncontrollably. Before they were half way across the Sinai, he appealed to Laurie to desist, otherwise the ache in his sides would become unbearable. He shared his sandwiches with Laurie who, when they stopped the car at Beersheba, took him and his driver to an Arab coffee shop that he knew and then, they continued their journey, through Asluj and Hebron, until they got to Jerusalem. The car pulled up outside the King David Hotel and the high ranking officer thanked Laurie for making the journey pass so quickly, and invited him, with his wife, to dinner at the hotel the following evening. Laurie accepted the invitation with gratitude and got out of the car, holding the door as he gave a stiff salute. He shut the door, and quickly opened it again, saying: 'By the way, sir. Who do I ask for?' The high ranking officer replied: 'Just ask for George.' Laurie burst out: 'There you are. Ask a silly bloody question . . . George who, for God's sake?' The officer smiled and said: 'George of the Hellenes!'

I discovered that the Dead Sea was no longer dead when I went to visit the Daniel Sieff Institute at Rehovot, where Dr Volcani produced a glass vessel which, he stated, continued an amoeba found in the salt ridden waters. The Institute had been built to commemorate Daniel Sieff, who had committed suicide in 1933 at the age of seventeen. The distraught parents, Israel Sieff, of Marks and Spencer, and his wife, bearing in mind the boy's enthusiasm for science, asked Dr Chaim Weizmann to suggest a means of perpetuating his name in a beneficial manner and he had put forward the idea of an institute of scientific research. As we approached the Institute we were greeted by an attractive young woman, who was Weizmann's niece, and was working on some aspect of synthetic rubber, and by Weizmann's sister, Anna, who entertained us to lunch at the Institute Club.

Dr Chaim Weizmann and his wife, Vera, arrived after lunch, looking rather travel weary and, after a brief conversation, they retired to their house, the surround of which was landscaped so that it looked like an English garden.

Anna Weizmann then took us to Givath Brenner where we met Enzo Sereni, who had left Rome, where his father was a surgeon to King Emmanuel III, and was one of the founders of the settlement, with its floral gardens and lawns edged with box. He had volunteered to be parachuted behind enemy lines to gather intelligence and to find escape routes for Jewish survivors and for Allied pilots who had bailed out over enemy territory, and was waiting a call. He was later captured by the Nazis and taken from camp to camp as the Germans retreated, before being put to death at Dachau in November 1944. Further tragedy befell his family when, during a memorial ceremony held for him, a plane, bearing a message from President Weizmann, crashed into the crowd and killed, among others, one of Sereni's children.

I first met Mino at the Savoy, a restaurant in Jerusalem to which Anna and I had gone to join the 'Kurdis' for dinner. He was a thick set man, with a squint, and hands that crunched one's fingers. Harry had introduced him as 'the King of Tiberias' and explained that he had the fishing rights in the Sea of Galilee. As in any conversation in Jerusalem, the talk got round to 'the Troubles' of 1936-39, when he alone among the Jews of Galilee was able to move among the Arabs, as he was a blood-brother of Abu Arab, who ran a café in Tiberias. The British Police had dealt harshly with him as they could not fathom his position and had given him the treatment they gave to both Arabs and Jews so that he had suffered doubly at their hands. From recalling those cruel times, he would suddenly turn to speak of the nights he spent fishing on the Sea of Galilee, watching the fish swim, pink in the light of the moon. As we parted, he promised to kill a sheep if I came to Tiberias, and I was able to take up his invitation just over a month later.

Tiberias stands, seven hundred feet below sea level, on the edge of the Sea of Galilee, or Kinnereth, as the Hebrews called it, from its shape, like a *kinnor*, or lute. It was built as a health resort by Herod Antipas and named by him in honour of his patron, the Emperor Tiberias on his sixtieth birthday. Solomon knew of the curative properties of its hot springs which, because of the foul smell of their sulphurous waters, were deemed to spring from the nether regions. After the destruction of Jerusalem in 70 AD it became the seat of the Sanhedrin and it continued to be a spiritual home for the Jews and a seat of learning for Hebrew scholars.

Mino lived in a large house above the town, overlooking Kinnereth. As he held the fishing rights, he was known to the Arabs as *Malik samek*, the king of the fish. When I arrived, he called to his *walad* to kill a sheep and prepare it in my honour. His wife, Marianne was away at the time, for which Mino apologised and explained that we would have to look after ourselves but that the *walad* was able to cook and would see to our needs. We had our evening meal, Arab fashion, and Mino ate most of the sheep that the *walad* had cooked on a spit in a courtyard behind the house. We then went to see Abu Arab in his café by the lake where we were royally entertained with arak and coffee and company.

Whenever Mino came to Jerusalem he would telephone me with a curt message: 'Mino here. See you at Mohammed Cohen's,' and I would go to a tiny café set among the traders' stalls in the *Souk*, that was run by the most tolerant of Arabs. No one knew why he, a good Moslem, suffered being known as a 'Cohen' by Mino, as it would have caused most Arabs to lead a mini-Jihad, but Mohammed merely smiled and was pleased and privileged to cook the fish that Mino had brought from the Sea of Galilee, and the meat that Mino had carefully selected at a nearby butcher's stall. There would also be a *walad* standing by, ready to fetch more arak or whatever we required. The fish would usually be Sultan Ibrahim, that looked like red mullet, or carp, or *musht*, a member of the wrasse family.

The Chief Censor telephoned me one day and asked if I would censor letters written in Welsh. I agreed and, from time to time, I had to call at the Chief Censor's Office where I sat in a room with a civilian and two Army officers. A notice hanging on the wall, signed by Owen Tweedy, head of the Government's Public Information Office, claimed that:

> A CENSOR NEEDS THE EYE OF A HAWK, THE MEMORY OF AN ELEPHANT, THE NOSE OF A BLOODHOUND, THE HEART OF A LION, THE VIGILANCE OF AN OWL, THE VOICE OF A DOVE, THE SAGACITY OF SOLOMON, AND THE IMPERTURBABILITY OF THE SPHINX.

The Chief Censor's secretary was Arminta MacMichael, the High Commissioner's daughter, and she gave me a close and, sometimes disrespectful, insight into the life and attitudes of the upper class British community in Jerusalem. One day she brought me a letter which, she said, was 'Welsh in French', as on the envelope was written *Cette lettre est ecrite en Wallisien*. I opened it and started reading: *Koena foki kua au tae fai tohi atu kota ku*, and came to the conclusion that it was written in a Polynesian language. I then noticed that it had been addressed to a sergeant in the Free French Forces by one Benjamin from Nouman, New California, and realised that it was in Wallisien, the language of the Wallis and Futura Islands, French protectorates near Western Samoa, in the South Pacific. Another time she handed me a Christmas card addressed to a nun in Bethlehem, with greetings in Irish from Eamon de Valera.

Arminta married Lieutenant Bowman at St George's Cathedral and, after the war, she became the wife of Toby Lowe, the Conservative MP for Blackpool North until he was ennobled as Lord Aldington in 1962. He sued Count Tolstoi for defamation in connection with his wartime activities and was awarded damages of £1 million or more, which he is not likely to receive as the Count says that he has no money.

Lady Petrie had asked me, one day, if I had met 'the other Welshman in Jerusalem', and suggested that I should call to see Richard Hughes at his flat, above the British and Foreign Bible Society's shop in Tancred Lane, near Allenby Square. When I arrived, I was given the warmest of Welsh welcomes, and that in my native tongue, which I had not heard spoken since I had left home. Richard Hughes came to Jerusalem in 1892. As a young man in his native Betws-y-Coed he had suffered from pulmonary tuberculosis, the scourge of Wales in those days, and he was advised by his doctor to seek a warmer and drier clime. His father, having paid for his fare and given him some money to support himself, handed him a £10 note so that he could have a decent burial. Whenever he repeated the story, he always added with a twinkle in his eye and putting his hand in his waistcoat pocket: 'I still have the £10 note.' He spoke Arabic fluently, and he knew the Arabs. 'With all their faults,' he used to say, 'I love them still'. Whenever there were family squabbles in Metullah or tribal strife in Beersheba that no one could settle, the Government would send its Director of Lands, Richard Hughes, and all would be peace again. He regarded those who were not Christian as infidels, however, and would comment that when the Moslem prayed in the Harem esh-Sharif his face was towards Mecca, but his back was towards Calvary. Despite his involvement with the Arabs, he commanded the respect of the Jewish community and, when he was ill in hospital, the *mukhtar* of the Jewish Quarter in the Old City told me that they had been praying at the synagogue for the restoration of his health. When his wife died, he moved into the flat and had, as his housekeeper, a wiry, one-eyed little Arab woman, called Haroub, who moved about the house as silently as a shadow, and was always within earshot whenever he wanted anything.

He invited me to 'Sunday dinner' and, in the afternoon, we went for a drive in a hired car that was always available, with the same driver, whenever he ordered it. As we drove past Shu'fat, he said: 'That's the place that is shown on old maps of Palestine as "Nob?", with a question mark after it.' The vines were heavy with grapes in the vineyards at Ain Farah, 'the place of still waters', and the figs were green. Tell el-Ful, 'the hill of the beans', was Gibeah, where Saul reigned as king in the first royal castle in Israel. Jib was Gibeon, a great city when the Israelites entered Palestine in about 1200 BC but was now a picturesque Arab village on a rock that stood rising from the plain where many gory battles were fought, and where Joshua bade the sun stand still. We stood over the Vale of Ajalon and sang *Nant y mynydd*, for no reason except that it was a valley in the hills, albeit without a running brook, and that thoughts of the hills of home were ever with us. Tel el-Nasbeh, thought to be the site of Mizpah, 'the mount of joy', reminded me that my mother had a brooch with Mizpah written on it in gold. We came to Imwas, one of three places that claim to be Emmaus, and saw gangs of Italian prisoners of war at work in the fields. We stopped at Beth Horon to speak to an aged Arab who swore that the ancient beside him was his father and that he was 120 years old. We joined the road from Jaffa at Abu Ghosh, facing the hillside upon which David took up his sling and slew the Philistine giant, Goliath.

I wanted to gather together the Welsh people, service and civilian, in Jerusalem and wrote a letter to *The Palestine Post*, in January 1941, inviting those who would like to attend a St David's Night's dinner to get in touch with me. I wrote the letter in Welsh, and the response was poor, but it made history, according to the managing editor of the paper, Gershon Agronsky, who maintained that it was the first time ever for the Welsh language to appear in a Palestine newspaper. As there was no prospect of a dinner, I thought that we might have a broadcast programme to mark St David's Day, and so I went to see Ralph Poston, the Controller of the Palestine Broadcasting Studios (PBS), who let me have half-an-hour at prime listening time on the first of March for that purpose. I prepared a script and got Richard Hughes and Iorwerth Jones, a British police officer, to read it with me. The only suitable music at the PBS was a record of *All Through the Night* sung by the Barclays Bank choir, and one of Edward German's *Welsh Rhapsody*, both of which I used. The broadcast engendered considerable interest and I began to receive letters and telephone calls, which gave me enough reason to make another attempt to bring the Welsh together. On the morning of St

David's Day, Richard Hughes had telephoned that he had found a daffodil for me to wear. I wore it in my hat which caused people to turn their heads and stare at me as though I had straw in my hair. He invited me to his house the next evening and we dined alone, talking about old times in Betws-y-Coed and in Newport, Pembrokeshire. As the Children of Israel had wailed by the waters of Babylon, we sat in the place for which they had grieved, yearning for our 'Jerusalem' in Wales.

Hughes was remarkably fit for his age, considering that he had been sent here to die half a century earlier, but he frequently suffered from minor complaints, and he would only have to sneeze twice for Haroub to ring the Government Hospital and say: 'Struws not well!' Within moments there would be an ambulance at the door. One day, he had suffered a haemorrhage, following an expedition to Jericho shooting *chukar*, but when I went to see him he demonstrated his fitness by singing the opening bars of *Mentra Gwen*.

In response to my request for the names of Welsh people, Sergeant Gallanders, of the Palestine Police and a native of Neath, brought me a list of the Welshmen serving in the Police Force in Jerusalem, and of nurses in the QAIMNS. I received a message to call on Major Kenneth Nicholl, ADC to the High Commissioner, at Government House, whose family home was the The Ham, near Cowbridge, and I met D. T. Lewis, master of St George's Cathedral School, Mrs Bamford from Llanrwst, Mrs Rachel Chinn who was a cousin of James Eaton-Evans, Haverfordwest, and a number of other civilians. Richard Graves invited me to take tea with him and his sister, Clarissa, at their home, called *By a Fig Tree*, as it stood by a fig tree. Their father, Alfred Perceval Graves, had published *Welsh Poetry Old and New*, and their step-brother, the poet Robert Graves, had written affectionately in his autobiography, *Goodbye to All That*, of the house where the family had spent its holidays at Harlech. but Richard did not consider himself 'sufficiently Welsh' to become involved in any Welsh activity. He was a Government officer and was to become the last mayor of Jerusalem under the British mandate. I met him, years later, at the corner of Oxford Street and Park Lane, still wearing the broad-brimmed black hat that he wore in Jerusalem and discovered that he was a fellow member of the Savile Club where he was affectionately known as 'Graves Superieur'.

When I felt that I had sufficient names, I called a meeting at which the Jerusalem Welsh Society was formed. Richard Hughes was appointed chairman and I was asked to be the honorary secretary. We held fortnightly meetings when someone gave a talk – Richard Hughes spoke of his half century in Palestine – or there would be a reading of Welsh poems or similar entertainment, and there would always be singing. By virtue of my appointment I was able to obtain the use of the Menorah Club and of St Andrew's House for our meetings and activities free of charge. In addition to the regular meetings, I arranged an occasional *noson lawen* at which our members or visiting Welshmen performed.

Ralph Poston let me have another half-hour for a St David's eve broadcast in 1942, and offered the services of Joseph Gruenthal with his harp for accompaniment. I got Afif Boulos, a Syrian Arab, to sing 'Watching the Wheat' and other Welsh songs, which he did with a sweet tenor voice. Lieutenant Colonel Bill Buckley, the Deputy Assistant Provost Marshal for Palestine, rang me that morning and asked me to meet him at Hesse's Restaurant at noon. We talked about his house, Castell Gorfod, near St Clears, and otter hunting on the Teifi and the Nevern, and about our mutual acquaintances. He then took me to lunch at Darouti's and apologised for being unable to attend the dinner, but said that he would detail a posse of military police to keep an eye on the Tel Aviv Hotel, on Zion Circus, where we were holding the dinner. There were ninety people present, and we 'called the counties': I was the only one from Pembrokeshire.

We raised a rugby football team, and arranged a Wales v. The Rest match on the Police Rugby Ground. This took place one Sunday afternoon, when the slopes of Mount Scopus echoed with *Sospan Fach* over and over again and, although one of our men was injured early in the game, and had to be taken to hospital, we won by eight points to five. For the uninitiated the sight of goal-posts decorated with giant leeks and hung with saucepans must have proved a little puzzling.

Preparation for the 1943 St David's Day dinner, again fell on me, and this time there were 125 persons present, as the Welsh choir of 1st Army Tank Brigade was on leave in Jerusalem. Early in the evening, the PBS Children's Choir, under Esther Solomon, sang a selection of Welsh songs in a programme that I had written, called *Gwlad y Gân* (Land of Song). The children were mainly Arab and Jewish, with some English, Scots, Irish, Armenian and other nationalities, but they sang as though they were Welsh. For the main broadcast, I took the microphone in imagination to such places as the Rhondda Valley, Strumble Head and Caernarfon, ending with the chairing of the bard ceremony.

Flying Officer T. Elwyn Griffiths, of Llandybïe, came from Cairo to see me to discuss his journal for Welsh men and women serving in the Middle East, *Seren y Dwyrain* (The Star of the East). He wanted me to be the Jerusalem correspondent. The first issue had already appeared and it continued, under his guidance, up to the end of the war and after the war, he founded *Undeb y Cymry ar Wasgar* (Society of the Welsh Overseas).

I contributed an article to *The Palestine Post* under the title 'St David of Wales: From the Hills of Jerusalem Holy', and *The Palestine Illustrated News* carried a report of our activities with a picture of the Archdruid Elfed admitting the King and Queen, as Duke and Duchess of York, into the Gorsedd of Bards at the Swansea Eisteddfod in 1926. Karminski, the editor of the glossy magazine, *Life in Palestine*, asked me to write a feature comparing Wales with Israel. My article, 'Two Lands – Wales and Israel', was well received and was favourably reviewed in the Hebrew paper *Ha'aretz*, but it was to cause trouble later.

The *Palestine Post* was the English daily covering Palestine and the Levant. It was founded in 1932 under the editorship of Gershon Agronsky, who was a leading and influential personality in the community in Jerusalem in particular, and in Palestine in general. I got to know him and his deputy editor, Ted Lourie, and members of the staff, including Julian Meltzer and Fay Andronovitch, through contributing articles relating to Wales and Welsh life in Jerusalem. One day, Agronsky asked me to write an article for a series that he was commencing under the title *I Remember . . .* and I wrote a nostalgic piece which was later picked up by the local newspapers in this country.

I was kept in touch with Wales, not only by letters from family and friends, but also by communication with people like Sir William Ll. Davies, the National Librarian, and D. R. Hughes who sent me copies of *Cofion Cymru*, a small journal published by him on behalf of *Undeb Cymru Fydd* and issued to Welsh men and women in the services, until the last issue, the sixty-second, appeared in June 1946. *The Liverpool Daily Post* referred to my message in that number and stated that 'Captain Dillwyn Miles says that there had been much criticism of what Wales did for her scattered children, and that much of that criticism was justified. "We saw," he writes, "clear signs of the Scots' care for their regiments all over the world. We saw things done for French and Poles, Indians and Yugoslavs, Czechs and Chinese. But never anything for the sons of Gwalia. We had to build our own tabernacles in the wilderness." Is not this true of Welsh everywhere and at all times? They have always had to build their own tabernacles. Captain Miles pays tribute to the care and kindness shown by Welsh churches and, in particular, to those who were responsible for *Cofion Cymru*.'

At the Officers' Club I met Captain John Gwilym Jones from Corwen, who remembered me at college. John was in Public Relations and had recently arrived from the U.K., and brought some blank records which had been given to him by Aneirin Talfan Davies of the BBC at Cardiff and which we were able to use to send messages home. He had a colleague, Lieutenant Nicholas Andronovitch, of the Public Information Office of the U.S. Armed Forces, who came from Georgia and spoke with a fascinating Southern drawl. In appearance he looked as though he were the original Jimminy Cricket, and he drove around in the only clean Jeep I had yet seen. He became friendly with Saalah Russota, an artist, but she fell out of his Jeep one evening and broke her arm. After the war she came to stay with us at Newport Castle and painted Anthony and Marilyn, as tiny tots, playing snail races on the flat-topped stone that stood in the centre of the circular lawn.

Whenever I walked into the Officers' Mess at 16 General Hospital, which now occupied the Kaiserin Augusta, I was greeted by Captain David Llewelyn (Pinkie) Davies whom I had last seen at Haverfordwest where he was busy eradicating the pulmonary tuberculosis which had carried away so many of our young people, my friends among them. He was a large, jovial man, and when I arrived at the Mess accompanied by an ATS officer, as he got up, the cane chair that he so amply filled would cling to his body, as though it were a snail's shell.

An article by John Waller in *The Citadel* entitled 'To a Party of Afif Boulos' reminded me that it was there that I met Myfyr Bryn Davies, Professor of English at Fouad I University, Cairo, and his wife, Bill. Bryn, tall, dark and handsome with a grey streaked beard, and walking with a limp, was glad to meet someone with whom he could converse in Welsh. More than forty years later, when I was browsing in Lears' Bookshop in Cardiff, I heard someone walk out of the shop and immediately recognised the limping footsteps as his. I ran out and caught up with him on the pavement, to his immense surprise. We went across the road to the Royal Hotel where we had a long talk about old times in the Middle East.

As I was leaving the King David Hotel one day, in June 1942, I met my old friend, James Gibson, the Cardiff ship owner. He was delighted to see me and told me that he had recently been to Newport, where he normally went for his holidays. He had been sent to the Middle East by the United Kingdom Commercial Corporation and was on his way to Tehran, after he had inspected the ports of Jaffa and Haifa. But first he wanted to go to the military cemetery on Mount Scopus to visit the graves of his colleagues in the London Scottish Regiment who had fallen in Palestine in the Great War. We found them among the graves of 2,542 men and one young woman, set between low hedges of rosemary and tended with roses and lily of the valley, red poppies and wallflowers.

I took him to dinner at the Officers' Club and then to Beit Hakerem. He was captivated by the parents, Abba and Ima, and completely entranced by Anna whom, he kept on telling me afterwards, I should marry without delay. He spoke about his wife, Toff, the former Russian Countess Anitoff, and of their daughter, Jennie, from whom he had never been parted for more than a week before. He asked me to accompany him on his tour of the Palestine ports and we set off in a chauffeur-driven car the next day. When we got to Jaffa and started to walk round the harbour, we were approached by the naval officer in charge, Lieutenant Commander Barton, who told us we were in a restricted area and to consider ourselves under arrest, but Gibson soon convinced him that this was part of his work for the UKCC and invited him to join us for dinner at the Gat Rimon Hotel where we were staying. We were up early next morning and, after visiting Petah Tiqvah and Binyamina, we were at Haifa before noon, calling upon McCullum, the head of the Haifa Shipping Agency, who took us to lunch at Pross's before making an inspection tour of the harbour.

He called for me the following afternoon, having already collected Anna, and Ima, whom he had persuaded to come with us to the Dead Sea. We went to Jericho, where he had been stationed during the Great War, and visited Elijah's Well and the Winter Palace. We had tea at the Kallia Hotel, on the edge of the Dead Sea, where Ima had not been for ten years, and we returned for dinner at Beit Hakerem. The next day, which was his last before leaving for Tehran, I took him to the Church of the Holy Sepulchre, so that he could say a prayer for Toff, and then to the *Souk* to visit my friends at the Spicers' Market. Anna and I had dinner with him at the King David that evening and, after taking her home, we returned to my flat when we 'tired the night with talking'.

Squadron Leader W. R. (Dick) Davies rang to say that he had been given my name in Cairo and asked if we could meet. I invited him to lunch at the Club and from that first meeting we became close friends. He was a chaplain in the RAF and had left a wife and young son at Briton Ferry, where he was a Baptist minister. He had served in the Western Desert where, he said, he had held services for all denominations, and also for Jewish soldiers in Libya, and had been much involved in burying the dead after El Alamein. I took him to the Beilins' *erev Shabat* and he was soon adopted as a friend and was always known as 'The Padre'.

One day, he brought his 'boss', Group Captain T. Madoc Jones, senior RAF chaplain in the Middle East, who was a native of Llannerch-y-medd, to see me. Madoc was highly conscious of his senior position and made it clear that he was the superior officer. The Padre, on his part, obviously despised him and when Madoc was appointed to adjudicate the poetry at the Cairo Eisteddfod, Dick asked me to submit a poem that would test Madoc's ability to undertake the task. I obliged by writing a sonnet in which archaic and obsolete words were strung together in a way to indicate that they conveyed the profound thoughts of someone lost in the desert, and submitted it under the pseudonym *Ibn Kharif*. A few days later, Madoc telephoned The Padre from Cairo seeking my assistance in adjudicating the poems submitted, saying that he had found 'one sonnet written in classical style difficult to interpret' I told The Padre to tell him that I was not available.

I was not able to attend the Eisteddfod, which took place on 25 September 1943, and I had forgotten all about it until I arrived, rather late, at a party at Agronsky's house the following evening. The party was in full swing and, as I entered, John Gwilym Jones, called out in a loud voice 'Here comes the bard!' He had read in the *Egyptian Mail* that I had been awarded the prize for the sonnet. They all cheered, although no one knew what it was about, and a dark-skinned woman leapt from her chair and gave me a big kiss. I was then introduced to her and found that she was Josephine Baker, whom Ernest Hemingway had described as 'the most sensational woman anybody ever saw.' She had abandoned her *chocolate arabesques* for the duration of the war and had donned the uniform of a lieutenant in the Women's Auxiliary of the Free French Forces as a cover for her intelligence work, for which she was decorated with the *Croix de Guerre* and the *Legion d'Honneur*.

I arranged with the Reverend Donald McGillivray, to borrow St Andrew's Church for us to hold a service in Welsh. The service comprised a reading of the 137th Psalm by Richard Hughes, and 1 Corinthians I, 3 by me. When I had invited The Padre to preach a sermon, he asked me whether I had a text in mind, and I suggested 'How shall we sing the Lord's song in a strange land?' It was a strange feeling to be singing 'There is a green hill far away' and other hymns that one had learnt at home in the place that had inspired them, and at the first Welsh service ever held in Jerusalem.

Anna took me to the Edison Theatre to see a Hebrew play performed by the Habimah Theatre Company. It was called *Ha-Dybbuk* and the renowned Hanna Rovina was playing Leah, the merchant's daughter whose father would not allow her to marry her truelove, the poor Hanan, as he wanted a rich husband for her. Hanan dies of a broken heart but his *dybbuk*, an indefinable spirit, like a straying soul, takes possession of Leah. The wedding feast proceeds, by tradition including the paupers' dance. In their black velvety caftans, and ringlets dangling below their soup-plate hats, the men dance a dance that was weird and spectacular and unforgettable. It was not necessary to understand the dialogue as one was captured by the ritual and mysticism and occultism and kabbalism, and there was such passion in the spoken word. To the sound of music from the *Song of Songs*, the soul of Leah unites with the soul of Hanan as her body falls dead.

I hardly missed a performance by the Habimah after that. I saw their *Michal bat Shaul* (Michal, daughter of Saul), and their *Yerushalaimm ve Roma*, and a dozen others. One of these, *Cochav ha-Shachar*, was a Hebrew translation of Emlyn Williams's *Morning Star*, and I was immediately struck by the characterisation of Brymbo Watkyn by the actor Reuben Klatzkin, a portrayal that I recognised as a type of Welshman I had known in childhood: grey-haired, whiskered but with a clean upper lip; wearing a black jacket, oatmeal breeches and buttoned leggings. I wrote to Emlyn Williams the next day and he replied to say how pleased he was, and how highly he regarded the Habimah players. I sent a copy of his reply to the

Habimah and, shortly afterwards, when I went to see their *Eternal Jew* with the Beilins and Abba Eban, and we took some of the cast afterwards to Hesse's for dinner, Klatzkin and Hanna Rovina told me that they were greatly pleased with Emlyn's appreciation.

Wolf Hildesheimer and Larry Lawler came to see me one day to discuss the formation of a Literary and Arts Society and wanted me to be a founder member. The society was eventually formed as 'The Jerusalem Forum' and I was appointed to the committee, the main function of which was the preparation of a programme of speakers. Dr Nelson Glueck, the American archaeologist gave a talk on 'The Archaeology of Transjordan', and we had a poetry reading by Christopher Scaife, former Professor of English at Cairo University, and an address by Taha Bey Husseini, the blind Egyptian writer and scholar. Dr H. C. L. Bertram described his time in Antarctica. Professor Ifor Evans of London University, spoke on 'The Traditions of British Journalism', when he and I had an opportunity to exchange a few words in Welsh.

The St David's Day broadcasts had brought me into close touch with the staff of the Palestine Broadcasting Studios responsible for the production of English language programmes, provided in addition to programmes in Arabic and Hebrew. The controller, Ralph Poston, returned to England in 1941 to enter holy orders, leaving Ruth Belkine and Judy Beilin, as producers, and Richard Humphrey, as news reader. Poston was replaced by R. D. (Reggie) Smith, portrayed as Guy Pringle by his wife, Olivia Manning in her *Levant Trilogy*, which was made popular by its television presentation as the serial *Fortunes of War*. Reggie had a permanent urge to produce plays, his most memorable production being *The Importance of Being Earnest* with Richard Humphrey as Algie and Judy Beilin as Lady Bracknell. They, too, did the reading in a lecture Reggie gave as a prelude to a season of broadcast Shakespearean plays. He gave me the part of Fluellen in *Henry V*, and other plays in which I took part were *The Coming of Arthur*, *The Muse of Fire*, *A Christmas Play*, *The Apple Cart* and James Joyce's *Ulysses*.

I frequently met Stephen Haggard at the Broadcasting Studios, especially when we were rehearsing *Henry V*, in which he was Henry. He was a Captain in the Intelligence Corps, working in the Department of Political Warfare, and had not long arrived from England. James Agate, in his autobiographical *Ego*, wrote that, while having supper at Rules, Gwladys Wheeler had introduced him to 'a young man who looked the oddest compound of scarecrow and eaglet. Leaping to the conclusion that the young man wanted my advice about going on the stage, I promptly jumped down his throat with the warning that six months of the hardest profession in the world . . . would kill a whippersnapper so completely devoid of physique . . . when he stammered something about being already in it and having served three years with Reinhardt.' This nonplussed me and gave him a chance to talk, which he did very intelligently. He told me his name was Stephen Haggard.' Later, Agate was to write, after seeing him perform in a mediocre play, that Haggard had made an enormous impression on him and expressed the view that he was 'a born actor, with a queer pathetic face, half boy-Christ and half-faun.'

We frequently had meals together at the Officers' Club and after breakfast one Sunday morning he sat, with his chin cupped in his hand, and listened without moving a muscle, and with his eyes fixed on mine, as I described to him, at his request, the intricacies of *cynghanedd*. I quoted William Barnes's 'Do lean down low in Linden Lea' to give him an idea of the echoing of consonants and then gave Welsh examples. He kept on repeating lines from Wilfred Owen to see whether there were traces of *cynghanedd* in them. The next morning, at breakfast we discussed his own poem, 'Harmonica' which had appeared in *Modern Reading*, No. 1.

He considered that he should not have been sent abroad as he could have done the job he was doing equally well in England, but cheered himself by saying that he had been told that he would be leaving for Cairo before long. One morning he called at the PBS and told Judy Beilin and Ruth Belkine that he was leaving that day for Cairo. He then kissed them both, which he had never done before, and left without another word. When I called at the Studios some days later, I found Judy and Ruth in tears. They had just been told that Stephen had been killed in a car accident. One of his colleagues confirmed that he had been in love with the Egyptian wife of a Government officer and that she had promised to elope with him that day, but had failed to appear at the station, and it was thought that he had committed suicide on the train.

In his letter to his sons, which he had written before he was posted overseas, and was published posthumously under the title *I'll Go To Bed at Noon*, Stephen wrote: 'Nowadays one cannot help feeling that each action, each word, each pleasure may be one's last, and it intrigues me to think that the Fool in *King Lear* may be the last part I shall ever have played, and that the last line I spoke upon a stage should be the uncannily appropriate one with which the Fool is so arbitrarily dismissed to his death by Shakespeare: "And I'll go to bed at noon."' He had played the Fool in the Old Vic production of *King Lear* with John Gielgud. In view of the manner of his death, the subsequent words seemed prophetic: 'Although I haven't yet actually severed my ties with civilian life, I feel like a man in a railway carriage, who doesn't really belong anywhere. He isn't at his place of departure, and he hasn't yet reached his destination.'

One day, Anna told me that she had decided to join the ATS. She had, for a long time, felt it her duty to make her contribution towards the war effort, beyond being employed as a secretary at HQ, and so she enlisted and was posted to Sarafand where, on the first morning she was served breakfast by Colonel Pedretti's wife, who had joined a little before her, but in no time she was posted to Moascar where her commanding officer was Junior Commander Cripps, a daughter of Sir Stafford Cripps. Shortly after her departure, Senior Commander Kathleen Morrison-Bell, whom I met after the war as County Councillor for Northumberland, came to seek accommodation for an ATS Company that was to be stationed in Jerusalem, and I took her to see the Mercantile Building, which she considered suitable. I never ceased to marvel at the speed with which confidential matters became public knowledge, but I was a little surprised to be told by a Czechoslovak monk, while visiting his monastery on the Mount of Olives the next day, that he understood that 'women soldiers' would soon be coming to the Holy City and asked that I should give him an assurance that they would not come anywhere near his monastery.

When 512 Company ATS eventually arrived, I called to see that they were properly installed and found the commanding officer, Junior Commander Diana Little, a stunningly beautiful girl. I took her to dinner at Hesse's that evening, where she had a hypnotising effect, for almost every officer present came to our table to speak to me on some pretext in the hope that I would introduce them to her.

Hebron is one of the oldest settlements in the world. About four thousand years ago, Abraham 'moved his tent and came and dwelt by the oaks of Mamre which are in Hebron.' He bought a cave, in the field of Machpelah, from Ephron the Hittite in which to bury his wife Sarah when she died, and there he lies, and his sons Isaac and Jacob, and their wives, Rebecca and Leah, and Joseph too. When I arrived in Hebron, for the first time, I went, as arranged, to the Mayor's house and, to my surprise, found the Town Council there assembled. The hawk faced Mayor, I already knew, was a friend of the pro-Axis Haj Amin Husseini, the Grand Mufti of Jerusalem, and was not to be trusted. After a round of salaams and coffee, but before I could tell them that I wanted to take over eight houses in the poorer quarter, the *mukhtars* of the neighbouring villages of Halhul and Idna arrived and there was a noisy exchange of greetings all round once more. They had heard of my visit and had hoped that I might lease some land or property in their villages. We had hardly settled down again when the Grand Mufti of Hebron, Sheikh Tewfiq Tahboub, came, with his retinue, and there was a general commotion until it was made clear that he now occupied the seat of honour and was in charge of the proceedings. He was a man of tremendous charm, and dignified as a prince. The whole atmosphere changed with his arrival and I stated my requirement while they were all in a good humour. It was treated as though it were the least I could ask as a contribution to the war effort.

The Grand Mufti charged me to call on him whenever I came to Hebron, or if there were anything that I felt he could do to be of help. He took me to the Haram el-Khalil, the mosque beneath which is the cave of Machpelah, and introduced me to his kinsmen, Ali Fawzi Effendi Tahboub, the sheikh of the mosque, and Atef Abdul Hafiz el Hamoun, its custodian, and told them to see that I was received properly whenever I went there. The Haram el-Khalil still has the remains of walls erected by Herod the Great surrounding the mosque, the minarets of which were built by Saladin. The cenotaphs of Abraham and of the members of his family, each covered with richly embroidered palls, render Hebron sacred to Jew and Christian and Moslem alike. The destroyed houses in the Jewish quarter were a reminder of the massacre of 1929, when the Arabs killed all the Jewish inhabitants. A hole in the wall permitted barren women to throw petitions, written on bits of paper and addressed to Sarah, into the cave. A footprint on a stone in the floor of the mosque was said to be Adam's, following a Jewish legend that Adam and Eve, after they had been thrown out of Eden, had settled in Hebron, and were buried there.

When I went to see Abraham's Oak, I was warmly welcomed by Brother Jakob, a Russian monk. He picked up some fallen acorns, which he gave me, and took me to his monastery to meet the abbot, who gave me wine of the grapes of the vines of the Vale of Eshcol.

Sheikh Ali Abu Hassan told me, when I was in Hebron once, that all Arabs fear the *debbeh*, the striped hyena, because of its hypnotic powers. They believed that it would lead them to its lair, entering which they would strike their heads against the overhanging rock and fall victim to the creature. 'But,' he added, 'as the Arabs live from day to day, by the will of Allah, they do not allow such matters to worry them.'

A sign in the village of Deir Suneid which read: 'Fair dinkum dealing Greek tailor', was the first indication that I was approaching 'Aussie' territory when I was going to Gaza to meet Major Dow, of the Australian Imperial Forces, whose office, he proudly proclaimed, was Napoleon's HQ in 1799.

I then went on to meet Sheikh Frei abu Maidan, sheikh of the Hanajreh, one of the seven Bedouin tribes of the Beersheba desert. I met him in the *souk* at Gaza, in a small Arab cafe outside which men were polishing pans with their feet in the sand. We were joined by Aref el Aref, the District Officer for Gaza, and I explained to them our requirements, which we had in mind in the event of invasion. The muezzin summoned the faithful from the minaret above our heads as we went our separate ways.

I stayed the night at the Australian Officers' Mess from the roof of which one could see where the battles of 1917 had been fought, and also look into the 'glasshouse' where convicted Aussies spent most of their time sunbathing.

The road from Gaza to Beersheba was a rough track, and a lonely one. At first there were acres of corn, with widely scattered encampments of Bedouin waiting for it to ripen. Then, there was only sand and broken ground. From the highest point along the track, at Tel abu Hureira, my driver and I could see the inverted black cone of a whirlwind moving across the desert, which we were fortunate to avoid. For a while we followed the old 1917 railway and, when we reached Beersheba, there was a camel mart in progress. Beersheba, 'the well of the seven', over which there was a dispute between Abraham and Abimelech, has been a cause of complaint among nomadic peoples ever since. We then travelled north, through Edh Dhahiriyah, an evil looking oasis, and, in the middle of nowhere, the car broke down. My driver, who was a Jew, soon repaired it saying that he was glad to get away as the ruined site, nearby, was all that remained of the *kibbutz* destroyed by the Arabs in 1936, in which some of his best friends had lost their lives.

The Bedouin Arabs of El Ghor, the area to the south of the Dead Sea, have negroid features and are said to be descended from Sudanese slaves purchased in Mecca and brought back by pilgrims who had made the Haj, and then sold to the merchants of Ma'an. One of their number, Sheikh Abdul, was a considerable landowner, and one day, he called to see me concerning a land dispute. His face was coal-black under his white *keffiyah*, which was kept in place by an *ega'al* of gold, and he wore a pale lilac kaftan and a brown goats' hair *abbayiah* over it. He attracted considerable attention as he walked down the street in Jerusalem looking like someone who had walked off a production of *The Desert Song*.

Winston Churchill, when he was Colonial Secretary, boasted that the Hashemite Kingdom of Transjordan was 'created one afternoon in Cairo.' In fact, it was in Jerusalem. At the end of the 1914-18 war, Husseini ibn Ali, King of the Hejaz, who, on the advice of Lawrence, had changed sides and had led the revolt against the Turks, expected to be granted hegemony over the Arab countries. His eldest son, Ali, would succeed him in the Hejaz; Abdullah, the second son, was to be King of Iraq, and the third, Feisal, King of Syria. Feisal assumed the throne of Syria, but was soon ejected by the French, and he then proclaimed himself King of Iraq. The infuriated Abdullah gathered a force of two thousand tribesmen and marched on Ma'an, and moved on to Amman, proclaiming himself Emir of Transjordan.

When the mandate over Palestine was given to Britain, it was assumed that Transjordan was included and, in March 1921, Churchill and Sir Herbert Samuel, the High Commissioner in Palestine, met Abdullah and Lawrence at Government

House in Jerusalem. In less than half an hour it was agreed that Abdullah should be recognised as Emir. Churchill appointed Lawrence as Chief British Resident in Transjordan, but he could not get on with Abdullah and, in the following October, he was succeeded by St John Philby. Philby, on the other hand, got on too well with the Emir and allowed him to get into debt to such an extent that the country had to be virtually taken over by the Palestine Government, and the more stern Colonel (later Sir) Henry Cox was appointed Resident in 1924. He remained in office until 1939 when he was succeeded by his Assistant British Resident, Alec Kirkbride. Kirkbride had fought in Feisal's army with Lawrence, who found him so taciturn that he referred to him in his *Seven Pillars of Wisdom* as 'Kirkbride the summary'. I found him vague and inclined to avoid decision on the score that he left such matters to his underlings. His Assistant, Hugh Foot, later Lord Caradon, on the other hand, complained that he was tired of 'doing nothing important' due to lack of delegation by Kirkbride who, he said, had 'an alarming capacity for being silent.' Despite what Foot said, however, it was not easy to get him to commit himself and, invariably, I had to turn to Ledger, the lively factotum, who knew all the answers.

Emir Abdullah was an intelligent man, and a good Arabic poet. He retained his friendship with Ibn Saud, who had driven his family out of the Hejaz, and with Moshe Sharett, the Prime Minister of Israel. He was married three times, firstly to a cousin, and secondly to a Turkish lady. He was said to have married his third wife to pacify turbulent tribes in the southern parts of the emirate. She was black and the story goes that when his sons, Talal and Taif, returned from hawking and found her in the palace, they held a gun to their father's head and told him to get rid of her. He built her a house across the ravine and he was to be seen, of evenings, a pathetic, but devoted, little figure, walking up the hill to see her.

As a protection from the ever present threat of attack by the Wahhabi warriors of Ibn Saud, the Arab Legion was formed, under the command of Captain Frederick Peake, better known as Peake Pasha. It was recruited, at Abdullah's request, not exclusively from Transjordan, but from all the Arab countries. A special section of the Legion, known as the Desert Patrol, was recruited from the Bedouin tribes, and was placed under the command of John Bagot Glubb, who had been born in Preston in 1897 and educated at Cheltenham College and the Royal Academy at Woolwich. After the Great War he was sent to organise a native police force in the new state of Iraq and, in 1930 he was transferred to Transjordan, then under a British mandate. In 1938 Glubb succeeded Peake in the command of the Arab Legion, which was part police and part soldiery. The police wore helmets, while the soldiers had their long hair covered by a red and white check *keffiyeh*, or head cloth and wore caftans and cloaks with long sleeves, from which they were known as 'Glubb's Girls'. He made them into an efficient and well-disciplined force, and he himself was one of the most influential figures in the Arab world, respected by high and low. He was a minute figure, strutting with an air of importance that one felt was justified considering his prestige and influence among the Arabs, who knew him affectionately as *Abu Huneik*, 'the father with the small chin,' not that he was chinless but because a face wound had left him with only half a chin. Hugh Foot reckoned that Glubb had a knowledge of Arabic and the Arabs that was far superior to that of Lawrence, but got none of the glorification. In the end he was curtly dismissed by King Hussein.

The Transjordan Frontier Force was formed in April 1926, partly from the disbanded Palestine Gendarmerie, which had been created in 1921, and partly from the Arab Legion Reserve. It later comprised Arabs, Circassians, Druse and a few Jews.

Although the prospect of war had kept me from going to Amman as a teacher, I now found myself there in my capacity as the Hirings Officer for Transjordan, and I felt excited to be driven down the winding road through the hills of Judaea on my first visit there. The road goes past the village of Bethany, or El Azariyeh as it is known to the Arabs in remembrance of Christ's restoration of Lazarus to life, and it then plunges into the wilderness of Judah, mile after mile of barren hills with no sign of life until one comes to the Inn of the Good Samaritan, now but the ruined walls of a khan, or caravanserai. The hill above is a fortified site called Qalat ed-Damm, 'the castle of blood', from the red sandstone of the surrounding countryside. A track to the left was the old road down the Wadi Qilt to Jericho, along which is a Roman aqueduct and, hanging from the side of a cliff, the monastery of St George. It comes as something of a surprise to see a sign at the side of the road marked 'Sea Level', and it was from there on, that I found the road quite terrifying. The car swerved and skidded round the numberless bends, one moment swinging into the face of the cliff, the next narrowly missing the edge of a precipice that plunged into the dried-up stone bedded wadi deep below. I shouted at my Arab driver but he simply threw both hands into the air, exclaiming that it was the will of Allah that we should either get to Jericho, or not, and there was nothing he could do about it, except get there as quickly as possible. I was glad when we reached the foot of the hills, over eight hundred feet below sea level, to follow a straight road to Jericho, which appeared as a mirage in the shimmering heat across the parched lands of the Jordan Valley.

After the arid flats of the plain of Jericho, with its withered thorns and bones, clean picked by jackal and vulture, and bleached by the sun, the road came to Allenby Bridge, built during the 1914-18 war and named in honour of the Allied

Commander-in-Chief, before it entered Wadi Nimrin and began to climb the mountains of Moab. A brook bounced down beside the road and, every now and again, lost itself among oleanders and papyrus and scarlet flowered pomegranate bushes. In the bed of the stream stood 'Jericho Jane', the gun that shelled the British in their camps at Jericho, and was blown up by the Turks when they had to retreat.

The village of Shunat Nimrin appeared to be untenanted, except for some savage looking men, armed with daggers and rifles sitting in front of a roadside cafe sipping their coffee. Away to the south was Nebo, where Moses got his glimpse of the Holy Land, and I sang to myself the old Welsh hymn, *Dwy aden colomen pe cawn* . . . 'had I the wings of a dove . . . I would fly to the top of Mount Nebo to see the fair land beyond.' Es Salt seemed to be a straggly village, or should one say a town, for it had a municipal council and secondary schools for boys and for girls. Even so, the *mukhtar* was holding court on the open square. Its people were reputed to be the enemies of the Emir and of everybody. Suweileh, at 3,400 feet, was windswept and clean, and had the biggest threshing floor I ever saw. It is a village of Chechens from Daghestan, and Circassians, from the west of the Caucasus, planted there by Sultan Abdul Hamid II to protect the fringe of his Ottoman empire. The road descended gently for the next dozen miles to Amman, the Rabbath-Ammon of the Old Testament, where Og, King of Bashan, had his 'bedstead of iron . . . nine cubits was the length thereof and four cubits the breadth of it,' that is, about sixteen feet by seven, which correspond to the measurements of the burial chamber discovered by Gustav Dalman there in 1918. Here Tobiah ruled over the Ammonites, until the Tobiads became the vassals of the Ptolemies. Ptolemy II Philadelphus named it Philadelphia, 'brotherly love', even though he had slain his own brothers.

Amman began its present existence as a Circassian settlement, but since it became the capital of Transjordan, its population was predominantly Arab. When I got there, it had the appearance of a large village built along fissures in the three thousand foot plateau of Moab, with houses often clinging to the sides of the ravine. There was only one hotel, the Hotel Philadelphia, hard by a Roman amphitheatre that teemed with ghosts in the moonlight.

I called on Kirkbride, at the British Residency, on my first visit to Amman, and informed him that we wanted to requisition further properties in the town. Most of these belonged to the Bisharat family, a family that I got to know well, and was always most hospitably received in their homes, particularly by Najella and her sisters, who made me feel that I was their only contact with the great wide world. When I approached Wasif Bisharat, and told him that I would have to take one of his finest houses, which had the most beautiful bathroom I had ever seen, for the use of the commanding officer of 96 Area, he saved my embarrassment by offering it to me, fully furnished, as it stood, free of rent.

I met Hugh Foot soon after he had been appointed Assistant British Resident and with him was his sister, Jennifer. We met again when I took Diana with me, and had lunch at the British Residency. I also took her to Zerka, the Biblical Jabbok in the land of Gilead. Ruins scattered over the desert were the remains of the palaces built by the Umayyads in places where game was plentiful so that they could hunt with their falcons, salukis and trained cheetahs.

My private life changed considerably with the advent of 1943. Anna, having joined the Palestine ATS, had been posted to Moascar on the Suez Canal, and I missed her greatly. I also had to leave 58 Aboulafia as Mrs Erlik had given birth to a baby boy, and I was so occupied with finding accommodation for other people that I had no time to find any for myself.

Then, one day, I was invited by Maxim Piha to share his house. Piha was the son of the head of the Bank of Romania and was of an aristocratic Franco-Jewish family, the scion of which was the Baron de Menashe. He had been a brigadier in the Free French Artillery but had been invalided during the early part of the war and now had nothing to do save living on his money, and establishing small factories, which he did to provide work for the unemployed poor. The house, Anis Jamal House, in Talbieth, was one of the finest residences in Jerusalem, and no house was more richly furnished. Every piece of furniture was French period, or otherwise exquisite, and had been brought by him from his home in Paris, from which he had fled at the beginning of the war. Among the treasures that he showed me were the stole worn by Marie Antoinette's priest when he stood with her at the guillotine, a handkerchief of Napoleon's, the gold threaded tabard of a Venetian herald, and a collection of gold purses. I accepted his invitation with alacrity.

The sight of a British officer driving a private car along the streets of Jerusalem, especially one that was an open two-seater, was so unusual that I was occasionally stopped by British policemen in the Palestine Police Force, and asked to show my licence or insurance or to account for my journey. One April evening I was driving past the Garden of Gethsemane with an attractive young lady beside me, when I was stopped by a British Inspector of Police and charged with misuse of petrol, although I had told him that I was on duty and on my way to visit the nuns at Bethany, at their request. It transpired that the inspector had had his eye on the young lady and had made unsuccessful advances to her.

I was often invited to a feast by one of the *mukhtars* of the villages surrounding Jerusalem. The *mukhtar* of Malkha, Sheikh Fatma Abu Darwish would invite me to bring some friends 'to tea', but the tea, which was served in the shade of a spreading pepper tree, consisted of a spring chicken, one for each person, followed by a selection of sweetmeats. For a meal other than 'tea', the fare consisted of a sheep, killed and cooked for our benefit and served on a large dish on a bed of rice. We all sat round the dish and helped ourselves by tearing off bits of meat and rolling the rice, using only the left hand, in the traditional manner. Unlike their brethren in the desert, they normally paid regard to our susceptibilities by refraining from offering us the eye of the sheep.

Snow seldom fell in Jerusalem and, when it did, old men would say that they knew it was on the way from the manner in which the starlings roosted. In January 1942 there was a heavy fall and, as it thawed during the day and froze again at night, the streets became winding ice rinks. The driver of the No. 37 bus had a stove, with burning coals, beside him as he guided his skidding vehicle towards Beit Hakerem, and sang merrily as he did so. In Anna's garden the palm trees held the snow in their palms, and the cypress branches splayed out under its weight. The setting sun made the snow-capped hills of Judaea blush.

One day I took Diana to the Mount of Temptation. On our way we called at the Winter Palace at Jericho, built in great splendour by the Omayyad caliphs for their hibernation in the seventh century. We then went on to Tel es-Sultan, buried beneath which lie the walls of the Jericho that 'came tumbling down' when Joshua's men blew their trumpets. Ten thousand years ago, people had settled at this oasis, the powerful spring of which produces a thousand gallons of water each minute, and established the oldest city on earth. By now, seventeen cities lie, one on top of the other, each shrouded by the dust that a kind wind blew to hide its ostentation, or its shame. One of them was given by Antony to Cleopatra, as an expression of his love, or was it to keep her eyes off Jerusalem. Ahead of us stood Jebel Quruntal, up which, St Matthew tells us, Jesus was 'led up of the Spirit into the wilderness to be tempted of the devil' and, having fasted for forty days, the Prince of Darkness tempted him to turn the stones into bread. We climbed a winding goat-path along which solemn faced monks drove their mules laden with worldly goods. We stopped now and again to look back over the valley of the Jordan and the Dead Sea and the purple backdrop of the mountains of El Kura and El Kerak, of Ja'far and Qara Shihan. We rounded a bend to find the crenellated walls of a monastery, clinging to the face of a cliff. An ancient monk sat at the entrance and fixed his one eye on Diana, following her every movement, as he answered each of my questions. He had been there fifty-one years, or thereabouts, he said, banished after he had broken loose for a fortnight in New York. A less crabbed monk then greeted us and said his name was Yoachim and more or less hinted that we should ignore the ancient one, whose name was Gabriel. He presented us to his brethren and insisted that we should take coffee with them. I looked at their faces and found every eye upon Diana, and I wondered whether they would be able to restrain any ribaldry in the cloisters after we had gone. Brother Yoachim took us round the monastery, built over a medieval cave-church. He reverently touched the stone upon which Christ is said to have sat while arguing with the devil. The path to the summit of the Mount of Temptation passed through the monastery and when we got to the top, Diana sat on a broken wall, the remains of a pre-Christian fortress against a scallop-lined arch, behind which one could see, in the distance, an outline of the Mount of Olives.

On Tuvah Sh'vat, the festival of the trees, Gregg, the Assistant District Commissioner, and I were invited to a ceremony to be held at the settlement of Ma'aleh ha-Khamishah, and we took Diana with us and her new second-in-command, Subaltern Joyce Hasluck who, I later discovered, lived at Monkton Old Hall in Pembroke. When we arrived, we found the District Commissioner, Keith-Roach, who was known as 'The Pasha', already there, together with Hadassah Samuel and other Jewish notables. We were invited to plant a tree each. Diana planted hers next to mine, and the Sephardic Chief Rabbi, Ben Uzziel, came and stood over us and blessed us and the trees. I felt that I would have to return one day, to see whether my tree was providing shade from the sun, or beautifying a trysting place for lovers. We walked along a bosky path, which The Pasha wished to be christened there and then 'The Soldiers' Way'. He insisted that Diana and I should sit with him and the Chief Rabbi at the top table.

That evening, Yitz Chizik, who had also been at the ceremony, gave me a copy of his *Political Parties in Palestine,* an address he gave, to the Royal Central Asian Society in London in 1933, reprinted from the journal of that society. In it he wrote: 'To Dill, in memory of a glorious day on which a tree was planted by him at Ma'aleh ha-Khamisha in Palestine, where there are more political parties than trees!' When my children were born, some years later, instead of the traditional pusher-spoons or christening mugs, they received from our Jewish friends, in this country and in Israel, certificates to say that so many trees had been planted in their names in the Land of Israel.

SYRIA AND THE LEBANON

IN MAY 1943 COLONEL PEDRETTI told me that he wanted me to take over the office at Tripoli and to become Area Hirings Officer over an area that covered western Syria to the Turkish border, and the Lebanon. As I had not had any leave for three-and-a-half years, I was given seven days, and I decided to go to Egypt. The train left Jerusalem station at a quarter past two and wound its way, for two hours, down to Lydda, where passengers for Cairo changed trains and, if fortunate enough, got a sleeper. I shared one with Major Howard, whose father was a Major General and who was on his way home. We stopped at Gaza, where we were given a free meal of sorts and were able to buy a bottle of beer. Thereafter, we crossed the apparently untenanted wastes of the Sinai Desert as the cloudless sky turned orange and then red and then into ever deeper shades of purple, until darkness came and a myriad stars brightly studded the heavens.

Unable to sleep, I got up when we reached Qantara, at three in the morning, and took my time eating breakfast before I got off the train at Ismailia at five. I bathed and shaved at the Palace Hotel, and rested a while before setting off for Moascar to meet Anna, who was waiting for me. We walked back into town, along the Ismailia Canal, to the *Hotel des Voyageurs*, where I had booked accommodation and where the menu indicated that there were no shortages in Egypt. In the afternoon we lazed in the French Gardens, beneath casuarina trees above which black kites mewed noisily. King Farouk's yacht waited its turn, with other ships and feluccas, to proceed along the Suez Canal, and boys, their shining brown bodies unclothed, bathed in the waters of Lake Timsah.

I left the next morning by RAF transport for Heliopolis. The road running along the Canal was lined with tall palm trees past which *feluccas* quietly sailed. Water buffaloes under yoke drew water from deep wells and, where the water table was shallower, men turned large Archmidean screws to bring it to the surface. We passed huge army camps on sandy wastes at Qassassin and Tahag, and we called at Tel el Kebir.

On reaching Cairo I went, with a letter of introduction from Laurie Weston to his aunt, Mme Spring-Gay, one time mistress of King Fuad. She said that there was no accommodation to be had anywhere in the city, and then took me to meet the manager of the Continental-Savoy Hotel who said he could manage to let me have a room. While we were having coffee on the verandah of the hotel, she introduced me to the Egyptian Minister of Defence and other notables.

I went to the Gezira Club to meet Jimmy Williams who had been a schoolmaster in Cairo for many years. He and Lloyd Richards were at school together in Cardigan and I remembered Lloyd telling me how Jimmy had crossed the Sahara Desert in an Austin Seven when he had been attacked by Arabs whom he had beaten off with a spade. We talked about his early days at home in the parish of Llantood which he so memorably recorded later in his book *Give Me Yesterday*.

I walked alone among the Pyramids and stood before the Great Pyramid, built in about 2500 BC of 2½ million massive limestone blocks, to the memory of Cheops, or Khufu, whose only known likeness was the seven centimetre statuette that Flinders Petrie had found at Abydos. The guide said it would take only twenty minutes to get to the top, but it was nearer half an hour before I, breathlessly, and he, laughing at my inability to keep pace with him, reached the platform on the summit. On our descent we entered the Great Hall, the King's Chamber and the Queen's. Khufu's son, Khefren, built a slightly smaller pyramid nearby but he embellished it by having the Sphinx hewn out of limestone rock. I was aware that I was in the presence of one of the Seven Wonders of the World, and went quietly to the Mena House Hotel for some tea.

Returning after only a few days' absence from Jerusalem, I felt as though I were returning to the bosom of the family. I was more loath to leave than ever. I recalled that Sir Ronald Storrs had said: 'For me Jerusalem stood and stands alone among the cities of the world . . . There is no promotion after Jerusalem.' I went to the Old City and spoke to my friends, the Spicer, the Quilt-maker, the Copperbeater, the Cobbler, the Tailor, but did not dare tell them that I was going away.

I found that efforts had been made, in two quarters, to keep me in Jerusalem. Edwin Samuel made every endeavour to have me transferred to the Government as an Assistant District Commissioner, and Major 'Chick' Nathan wanted me in GSI 12, of which he was the officer in charge. His Brigadier agreed to the transfer, and got my Brigadier to agree, but only when a suitable replacement had been found.

There were farewell parties arranged at the Services Club, the Officers' Club and at the office and elsewhere. As none of their houses was large enough, the 'Kurdis' had arranged with Piha to have a huge party at Anis Jamal House to which they had invited my fellow officers and friends. The final farewell was at a dinner party at Hesse's which the Padre gave and to which he had invited the Beilins, the Chiziks, the Westons. We had a specially prepared meal and the consumption of wine may be judged from the messages scrawled on the menu cards which mischievously overestimated my capabilities as 'the despair of all Jerusalem mammas' who could 'beat Don Juan at a canter', and as 'the man who was prepared to try anything twice'. There was laughter, there were kisses, there were tears before we went our separate ways.

The Padre had conveniently arranged to visit his flocks in the Lebanon so that he could drive me to Tripoli in his staff car, complete with trunk, valise, kit bag and bookcase. As we left I was overwhelmed with a feeling that I was being torn away from the great happiness of my life. 'If I forget thee, Jerusalem . . .'

We set off through Nablus and Jenin, and crossed the Plain of Esdraelon to Haifa and Acre, and climbed the slopes of the Mushaqqa Hills, which Josephus called the Ladder of Tyre, until we reached Ras en Naqura, on the frontier between Palestine and the Lebanon. We passed the khan at Iskanderoun, and the white cliffs of Ras al-Abyad, and came to Tyre, the city founded by the Phoenicians five thousand years ago, that had withstood the might of Sargon and Sennacherib, but had failed to restrain the sea and the sand, so that only the ruin of a Crusader cathedral remain, and pyramids of *Murex purpurea*, the molluscs that yielded their colour to provide Tyrian purple for the robes of Roman emperors.

A fleet of fishing boats lay at Sarafand, another Sarafand, the old Zarephat to which Elijah escaped from the drought of Israel and performed the miracle of the widow's cruse. On an island off Sidon were the ruins of Qal'at el-Bahr, 'the fort by the sea', a Crusader castle, and another, the castle of St Louis, stands near the town, After crossing the river Awali, a road to the right leads to Djoun where Lady Hester Stanhope came to live, in a half-ruined monastery, when the convent she occupied at Mar Elyas, near Sidon, was no longer large enough to accommodate the poor and the persecuted to whom she gave refuge. Here she found the solitude she desired, surrounded by perilous rocks above which eagles and vultures hovered, and with jackals, wolves and hyenas howling at her gates. Here she died twenty years later, in 1889, and her remains lie in a corner of the garden, where the air is perfumed with jasmine and roses. We passed through Khan Nebi Yunis, named after Jonah as it is believed that it was here that the whale 'vomited out Jonah upon the dry land', and then through Shuweifat, the home of the Lebanese Druse emirs of the Arslan family, where a statue of a former emir stands. The reigning emir was said to be in Germany consorting with the enemy.

We stayed the night at Beirut and dined at *Le Cercle des Officiers*, where the Padre told me that he would be happy to marry Anna and me. We then went to The Dugout, an aptly named dive in which an elderly woman sang bawdy French songs, and sat in the corner marked *Coign des Roués*. When I called at the Hirings office in Beirut the following morning, I was greeted by an attractive ATS officer named Sheila van Damm, whose father owned the Windmill Theatre.

The mountains come down to the sea north of Beirut, and Nahr el Kelb, the

Dog River, breaks through a gorge which, according to legend, was guarded by a fierce dog that barked so loudly at the approach of an enemy that it could be heard even in Cyprus. The river, on the other hand, may be named from the story of Anubis, the dog diety, that aided Isis in her hunt for the body of Osiris, that had been washed up on the shore at Byblos. Those who came that way commemorated their passing in hieroglyph and Greek, Latin and Arabic script. Seventeen graven tablets bear the cartouche of Rameses II, the stele of Nebuchadnezzar, the effigy of Asarhaddon of Assyria, the arms of the Mameluke Sultan Barkuk, and the name of Caracalla. Napoleon III obliterated the name of Rameses to substitute his own. A tablet recalls the entry into Damascus, and another the occupation of Beirut and Tripoli in 1918. Our invasion of Syria in 1941 is also recorded. The water of Nahr Ibrahim, further on, runs red at certain times of the year for it is, they say, the blood of Adonis, the beautiful youth who, when hunting in this valley, was killed by a wild boar. The tears shed by Venus, who was in love with him, cover the hillsides with anemones.

Byblos is the Gebal of the Book of Kings, from which the modern Arabic name, Djebeil, derives, and it was famous for its masonry and shipbuilding, The Crusaders called it Giblet and built a castle on its Acropolis, and a cathedral dedicated to St John, that is now a mosque. The mountains of Lebanon reached the coast again at the handsome cape of Ras Cheqqa that was once known as Theouprosopon, 'the face of God'. Men were working on the new railway, to connect Haifa to Tripoli, and there had been a landslide which kept us from passing for an hour and more.

We arrived at Tripoli in the evening and I unloaded my belongings at the spacious villa that I was to occupy. Its windows, I noticed, were close covered with heavy iron bars, relieved with interwoven decorative wrought iron work, and I could see that the surrounding villas were similarly fortified.

Taraboulos esh-Sham, or Tripoli, stands on the delta of the Qadisha river, which has its source near the Cedars of Lebanon. It is surrounded by groves of olives and oranges, apricots and figs, all of which are so freely watered that, in summer, the weather is unbearably hot and humid. One lived in a permanent state of perspiration, even without any clothes, and nights were made insufferable by having to sleep under a mosquito net that inhibited the movement of air. The town was founded in about 800 BC by the joint action of the three cities of Tyre, Sidon and Aradus, hence its name. There are no traces of the temples and palaces built by the Seleucids and the Romans, or of the Moslem library that held a hundred thousand volumes. The Crusaders besieged it and cut it off by building the hill Mont Pelerin, now the citadel, Qal'at Sinjil, the castle of Raymond St Giles.

There were only three other British officers stationed in Tripoli, the Town Major, Major Sergeant, who kept on saying that 'the bloody place was full of dogs and wogs'; his assistant, Captain Careless, a quiet man, and the chaplain, Captain R. D. Grange-Bennett, (G-B), who had been vicar of St Augustine's at Bristol before joining up. About half a dozen other officers ate at the Mess but they were stationed either at the port, El Mineh, or on surrounding sites.

I took over as Area Hirings Officer, Syria and Lebanon from Captain Grose, who was as unhappy to leave as I was to arrive. It was typical of the Army to remove two people who were happy and competent in their work, and place them where they did not want to be. The work at Tripoli was interesting enough, but my one ambition was to return to Jerusalem.

Lieutenant de Sozier, the French Liaison Officer in Jerusalem, had given me a letter of introduction to the Vicomte de Mentque, the Conseilleur at Tripoli, and I called on the Naval Officer in charge of El Mineh, the port of Tripoli, at the estuary of the Qadisha, Commander Oxley, who was a cheerful old salt, with no ambition but to maintain the place as a rundown version of a French port. The harbour was occupied, almost entirely by fishermen and boat builders who were busy building ships to a design that would have been familiar to the Phoenicians.

Entertainment in Tripoli was limited to the Roxy Cinema, where reels were sometimes shown out of sequence, and two night clubs of a poor sort, the *Moulin Bleu*, with a two-girl cabaret, and the Lido, where olive-skinned young ladies endeavoured to persuade one to buy them green drinks at ten Syrian pounds a time. There were occasional dances at the *Unione Sportive* and I went there, one evening, to a charity dance with the Vicomte de Mentque and George Arida, and danced with several women, none of whom spoke English. Apart from the Mess and the Officers' Club, there was the Kookaburrah Bar that was kept by a Mr Cohen.

G-B brought his Deputy Chaplain General to see me, as he was a Welshman. Colonel D Ainsleigh Jones, hailed from Llandysul and was a cousin to Dorothy, the wife of my cousin Howard. A week later, he brought another of his superior officers, who was also a Welshman and a Deputy Assistant Chaplain General, Lieutenant Colonel D. D. Lloyd Evans, a native of Trefin and a cousin to 'Trefin', the Grand Sword-bearer of the Gorsedd of Bards and, later, Archdruid.

While we were having coffee, one day, G-B spoke of an incident that had taken place on the train in which he was travelling to Cairo some months earlier. An officer in the Intelligence Corps sat opposite him, he said, who looked pale and not at ease with himself and did not wish to make conversation. Eventually, he got up and walked out into the corridor and shot himself. His name, he said, was Stephen Haggard.

Rumours of thievery in Tripoli soon proved to be true. On account of the heat, windows were left open at night and a favourite ploy was to try to steal anything that could be reached through the grill. One night I woke to find a long bamboo pole reaching for my tunic which I had placed on the back of a chair in the middle of the room, and surprised its holder by grabbing the pole out of his hand. Another night, after I had gone to bed, Haj, the ghaffir, who kept an eye on my villa, came to the bedroom window to warn me that there was a thief on the prowl that night. Next morning, at breakfast, the Chaplain and the Town Major and his assistant all complained that they had been visited. Haj protested that he had seen nothing but, under pressure, confessed that he had seen a boy later identified as a lad from El Mineh, called Yusef Mitri Dibo. He was put under surveillance and was trapped in a lavatory on the third floor of a building, but by the time the gendarmes arrived, he had escaped. The expertise of Syrian thieves was illustrated by the way they were able to remove an EPIP tent, in which twenty soldiers were asleep, without rousing one of them, and the men would wake up under the open sky.

A narrow plot of land separated my villa from the next and, several times when I looked out of my bedroom window, I could see a pair of beautiful, dark eyes, behind the grill of the window opposite, looking fixedly in my direction, which I found somewhat embarrassing as, in that hot and humid atmosphere, I wore no clothes. The lady's eyes were not averted even when they met mine and, on one occasion, she blew a puff of cigarette smoke in my direction, but when I smiled, there was no response. I wondered whether she was blind. I then discovered that she was the wife of Judge Yanni, and came to the conclusion that her behaviour was innocent, arising out of a boring existence. One day, I received an invitation to dine with them and found myself one of a party of six, the other male being Captain Lawson, our Political Officer, who spoke Turkish. The difficulty in communication became a source of hilarity as the evening wore on, with gestures growing more grand and more intimate by the hour.

As I walked along the *Place de Serail*, one evening, I saw a British officer speaking to a gendarme, obviously seeking information and gesticulating in a manner that reminded me of my old friend Major Llwyd Williams, solicitor, of Fishguard. His back was towards me, so I walked round the *Place* in order to gain sight of his face, but by the time I had reached the other side of the square, he had turned, still flailing his arms as he tried to make the gendarme understand. In the end, I approached them and, before he saw me, I asked in Welsh if I could be of help. Llwyd swung round, dropped his arms and said: 'Well, good God!' I took him to the Officers' Club and it took a few pink gins before we could convince ourselves that it was not a dream. We spent the night at my villa, talking about home, the people we knew and the things we did before the war. Halfway through the following morning, he arrived at my office with a puzzled look on his face. His mission, which he had not bothered, or found time, to mention, was to find accommodation for his unit, still in Egypt, and he had come to see the Area Hirings Officer whom he now found, to his surprise, was me. I took him to Kalmoun, and along a lane lined with figs and vines, pomegranates and bramble, to Majlaya, where we found a suitable site.

Two roads lead from Tripoli to the Cedars of Lebanon, one on either side of the Qadisha river. I followed the southern bank one morning, soon after dawn, so as to avoid the heat of day as much as possible. The corn grew tall, to reach the branches of the olive trees, at Dahr el Ein. In the village of Amioune a church stood on a pinnacle of rock, and at Kusbah a monastery clung to the cliff face, much like the one on the Mount of Temptation. The road wormed its way along a narrow valley, beneath towering crags and steep mountain slopes covered with pines and cypresses, or terraced and planted with mulberries and vines.

On the brink of a precipice, like a cluster of jewels in the morning sun, there was a village. I asked my driver what it was called and he said 'Tirzah', and I thought of the words of Solomon in *The Song of Songs*: 'Thou art beautiful, O my love, as Tirzah'. Although there is a Tirzah nearer Jerusalem, I chose to think that Solomon could only compare the beauty of his love to this one, and I also thought that no one who had not seen its beauty as I had seen it that morning could have understood what Solomon had in his mind

Besharreh stands amid gardens and vineyards and mulberry trees and is one of a number of villages along the western foothills of the Lebanon Mountains to which the wealthy escape from the humid heat of Tripoli. It was the birthplace of the Lebanese poet and artist Jibran Khalil Jibran who had lived the life of a hermit here before going to Paris, where he studied under Rodin. In his verse, he is considered to have come under the influence of William Blake. His grave is decorated with stalactites brought from the nearby Qadisha Cave, where the flood-lit spray of running water gave stalactites and stalagmites a wonderland image.

The road beyond Besharreh, that leads to Baalbek, passes by the Cedars. At one time, cedars grew over large areas of the Lebanon but only five groves remained, the largest of which, comprising some four hundred trees, stood here, in an amphitheatre below the steep slopes of Djebel Arassia. They measure up to forty feet in girth and are said to be up to fifteen hundred years old. When Solomon built the Temple in Jerusalem, King Hiram of Tyre sent him timber from the cedars of Lebanon.

While I was having lunch at the Long Range Desert Group Mess, by the cedars, Colonel Prendergast, one of the founders of the Group, was intrigued to find that his family may have originated at Prendergast, Haverfordwest, before they went to Ireland as part of the invasion of 1169. I returned to Tripoli along the northern bank of the Qadisha, through Ehden, another mountain resort which, an old Maronite priest confided in me, was the nearest place to paradise. Through pine and cypress forests, the road wound down to the plain, where it ran between olive groves and vineyards, and through Zegharta, which General Allenby considered was the worst place in the Middle East for malaria.

I found the people kind and interesting. A monk from Achache came and asked me to come and taste the wine in his monastery. Another monk, from Deir el-Ambar, who was dirty, smiled when I gave him a bar of soap. Sister Esther, from the convent at Besharreh, called and invited me to take tea at the convent. The furniture in my villa was hired from Tewfiq Baddaoui Jabbour Effendi, who had made his money in cotton in Nigeria and he frequently called to see that all was well and, one day, he brought me a *mishmish* tart that his wife had made.

As one approaches Amrit, on the road to Lattakia, to seaward stands a massive black cube of stone, known to the Arabs as the Tower of the Snails, that commemorates an unknown Phoenician, while to landward two large tombs of the fifth century BC, known as The Spindles, bear traces of Phoenician art. On one side of the river Amrit are the remains of a rock-cut temple where Phoenician statues were found, and on the other side, stood a vast stadium. After crossing the river, the island of Ruad came into view, as though it floated on the water. This was Arvad, whose people are mentioned in Genesis and praised by Ezekiel as redoubtable soldiers and sailors. The island fortress was encompassed by a wall which is the finest surviving piece of Phoenician masonry, and it was the final foothold of the Crusaders in Syria. Tartous, the ancient mainland city of Antaradus, was the last stronghold of the Templars. Their castle occupied a corner of the town and its massive keep, standing on the shore, had a postern at sea level. The cathedral of Notre Dame de Tortose stands roofless in the middle of the town. It is claimed that its altar was the first to be dedicated to the Virgin Mary, and that St Peter celebrated Mass upon it. Here Raymond of Antioch was assassinated by the Assassins, an Ismaili sect who doped themselves with hashish, and were thus known as the *hashishin*, 'the hashish eaters'. They developed their own brand of murder, that became known as assassination, under their chieftain who went by the name of Sheikh el-Jebel, or the Old Man of the Mountains. It was to this church that Alice of Champagne, widow of the king of Cyprus, came to marry another prince of Antioch, at the bidding of the King of Jerusalem. She had given herself to an emir, an infidel, and was made to change her mind, but change her heart she could not and, at her marriage she wept more tears 'for her lost love than there were pearls in the embroidery of her wedding gown.'

The sea road leading northward into the territory of the Assassins is guarded by the great Crusader castle of Marqab, its black basalt towers standing out against the chalk ridges. Originally an Arab castle, it was taken by the Hospitallers who made it into an impregnable refuge for pilgrims and for the sick and wounded. In its prime it had a garrison of a thousand soldiers and a population of two thousand families. When, eventually, it fell to the Mameluke Mansour Qalaoun, the Arabs claimed that it had done so with the aid of the archangels Gabriel and Michael.

Lattakia is one of the several Laodiceas of the Romans, the one in which Dolabella was besieged after Caesar's murder, and known as Laodicea-by-the-Sea to distinguish it from the others. To the Phoenicians it was Ramitha, but it was named Laodicea in honour of his mother by Seleucus I Nicator, he who realised the importance of elephants in battle and manoeuvred four hundred of them, mounted with archers, to victory at Ipsus in 301 BC.

Pipe smokers are familiar with the name Lattakia for some tobacco mixtures contain black strands of its tobacco, recognisable by a most distinctive aroma. That aroma was fixed in my nostrils for ever when I was taken into the bonded store by its owner, Edouard Sa'adi. There, layer upon layer, piled to the roof, was all the uncut Lattakia tobacco in the world, waiting to be exported, subject to the exigencies of war. The tobacco, once harvested, is dried in the sun and 'smoked' for up to five months with Syrian oak wood, until it is black and exuding its peculiar fragrance. It is then mixed, in the minutest quantities, with other tobacco to produce certain brands. No man could enter a crowded room, or pass me on the road, smoking such a mixture without it being immediately detected by my nose.

I had gone to see Sa'adi at his office, which stood on the dockside, near where Lawrence stated that he had been shot by a Turk. It looked like a Victorian solicitor's office, and it was there that he and his brother, both nicely porcine-faced, arranged the world distribution of their unique tobacco. I took him to Slenfe to hand back a house which had been occupied by the GOC, 10 Armoured Brigade. We had lunch at the Slenfe Hotel which he had built at a cost of £40,000 and leased, as it stood, to Guidon's, a branch of Lucullus, for £100 a year. When I gave him back the keys of his palatial house, he refused to take any rent for the period of its occupation by the Army, or any compensation for damages.

Slenfe is a mountain resort for the prosperous merchants and government officials of northern Syria. It is set among pine forests and deciduous woods with bracken and brambles in which blackbirds sang. We followed a track through the village of Juriye, and on to Nebi Yunis, in the Alaouite Mountains, from which there was a panoramic view of the Anti-Lebanon and the valley of the Orontes below.

On our return journey we visited Qal'at Sahyoun, originally a Byzantine fortress which the Crusaders converted into a castle occupying a narrow ridge with a precipitous ravine on each side, and named it after Saone, in France. The Crusaders cut a deep fosse across the only approach, leaving a tall pillar, rising over a hundred feet from its floor, to support a wooden bridge. Even so, it fell to Saladin in 1188 and was never recaptured, so that it remains a unique example of earlier Crusader work. So vast an area does it cover that Saladin was able to build a town within its walls, which was occupied up to the nineteenth century.

As we travelled back, Sa'adi showed me fields where Suleiman el Mirchet, the chief of the Alaouites, grew his hashish. The Alaouites, or Ansariyah, inhabit the Alaouite, or Ansari Mountains and the coastal region of northern Syria, with their capital at Lattakia. Their religion is pantheistic and those who betray its secrets are found dead with their tongues torn out. They have no place of worship but they hold ritualistic dances at night, which may derive from the worship of Astarte, the Syrian Aphrodite.

The Alaouites are not to be confused with the Druse, who regard Jethro, priest of Midian, in Egypt and father-in-law of Moses, as their progenitor. They number around 200,000, living mostly in the Jebel Druse and the Lebanon, with a sizeable contingent resident in Galilee. They speak Arabic but remain apart and do not intermarry with Arabs. They derive their name from Darazi, a renegade Turko-Persian Christian who adopted the Shiah heterodoxy of the Fatimid Caliphs who were descended from Fatimah, the daughter of Mohammed, and her husband, Ali. The distinctive dogma of the Druse religion is the deification of the mad Caliph Hakim who utterly destroyed the Church of the Holy Sepulchre in September 1010 and who said to Darazi: 'Go into Syria and spread the cause in the mountains.' His death, or more probably his murder, while taking his usual evening walk in the Mokattam Hills, served to strengthen the belief of the Druse in his return to lead his people to 'a new and happy age'. Their religion remains a mystery, except that it is a variation of Ismaili, an offshoot of the Shiah division of Islam. Their *kalwah*, or meeting places, are concealed, high in the mountains, and they believe that the dead go to China. 'Happy are the people of China at your arrival', says the hymn sung at Druse funerals, and they have a firm belief in reincarnation. They do not pray as they regard prayer as an interference with the will of God. Under their leader, Sultan al Atrash, they launched a revolt against the French in 1925 and swept across to Damascus, and were only subdued after their capital at Suwaida had been captured.

Another mysterious sect had its centre at Qubbet el-Beddaoui, a village north of Tripoli, where a house of worship, looking like a mosque without a minaret, is a monastery of the dervishes, whether of the dancing or howling variety is not known. Near it is a large basin teeming with fish which are held to be sacred and, therefore, may indicate a connection with the Syrian goddess, Derceto, who neglected her daughter, Semiramis, and was changed into a fish. Corn is specially grown to feed the fish and, as I threw a handful into the basin, there was a great troubling of the waters as the fish rushed to the surface to devour the floating grain.

Krak des Chevaliers may be the best known of the Crusader castles, but few would recognise it by its name on the map, Qal'at el Hosn, or its Arabic name, Hosn el Akra, 'the fortress of the Kurds'. Lawrence regarded it as 'perhaps the best preserved and most wholly admirable castle in the world.' A fortress was built here by the emirs of Homs early in the eleventh century, to defend the Gap of Homs, and they garrisoned it with Kurdish soldiers. It was occupied by the Crusaders before the end of that century and ceded by Raymond of Tripoli to the Knights Hospitallers. The Saracens consistently failed to capture it, but it fell to the Sultan Beibars in 1271. The castle rises out of a marshy plain against a curtain of bare moorland and stands on a spur of the foothills, looking much as it must have done when the Hospitallers left it and, as one approaches its turreted walls, one could expect the guard to turn out and make its challenge. There was nothing but silence, broken only by the screaming of a kestrel disturbed from its eyrie, and the echoing of my footsteps as I moved from hall to hall, through colonnade and courtyard, and into the chapel of the castle that later became a mosque. On a flat roof stood a round table of stone, and those who might have dined there would have had a panoramic view of the sea to the west, of the Lake of Homs to the east and the desert beyond, of the Lebanon and Anti-Lebanon southward, and of the Alaouite Mountains to the north. By an outer curtain wall I picked up a piece of human skull in which a notch had been cut by a battle axe or heavy sword.

Diana rang to say that she was being posted as Staff Captain to GHQ, Cairo, and would like to come to see me before she left Jerusalem, and I agreed to meet her at Beirut. I was held up by road works at Chekka, and then by a lorry that had been hit by a train on a level crossing and its Arab driver killed. It was early evening by the time we got back to Tripoli and, before dinner, we went for a walk along the Tell where every head turned to behold this beautiful woman and the sight, uncommon to them, of a couple walking arm in arm. I took her to the Club, where every officer ogled and aimed for an introduction. We had dinner at the *Moulin Bleu* and then sat above the babbling river Abu Ali before retiring for an early night.

The next morning, I took her with me to Lattakia where the Town Major invited us to lunch and then came with us to inspect a site I wanted near the Turkish border. He showed us some of the espionage routes, and said that spies were shot in public in Lattakia as a lesson to others. On our return journey we walked up the sandy aisle of the roofless, half-buried church at Tartous, and stopped at Qubbet el-Beddawi to feed the sacred fishes. George, my Lebanese driver, kept us supplied with water melons along the journey as it was a scorching day and, as we were travelling in an open car, we caught the sun and, with the sunburn and the hot night, we had little sleep. The next day we set off for Baalbek. I took her to see Tirzah, beauty to behold beauty, and we lingered there. We met Monsignor Keirouz at Besharreh who invited us to lunch but I told him that we had already been invited to the Palace Hotel by the Khouris. M. Khouri brought in a branch clinging with apples, and a red rose for Diana. We climbed the mountain but could get no further than Col Ainata at 8,600 ft. where there were snowdrifts across the road and we had to be content with a distant view of Baalbek. We went to see the Qadisha Cave where the stalactites and stalagmites are like alabaster, and the river flows a torrent below one's feet.

On a day when I was going to Aley, my clerk, Adeeb, expressed a wish to visit his grandmother at the nearby village of Suq-el-Gharb. We drove through vineyards and mulberry groves until we came to the picturesque village and received a warm welcome from the old lady. She sat, wizened and bent, as we sipped our coffee, and babbled toothless to her grandson. As we left, she came up to me and, with a crooked finger, she placed the mark of her tribe in the Hauran, on my cheek, where my old grandmother would have planted a kiss. It made me write a little poem.

The road followed a mountain ridge, through Didde and Fih and Qalat to reach Deir Belamend, the Belmont of the Crusaders, where I called at the twelfth century Cistercian abbey and had to have coffee with the abbot and two Greek Orthodox monks. The monastery buildings, including a refectory with dormitory above, were grouped round a cloistered court and the church had a thirteenth century belfry and a finely carved rood screen that was disfigured by being hung with tinsel and toys of the kind that one could buy on Gamages' Christmas sale. The whole place had a squalid air, however, and the monks were unwashed and dirty, but they had a view that was among the finest across the eastern Mediterranean.

One of the most delightful villages in the Lebanon was Sur, a holiday resort built by Jezzar Bey and one day, when clouds played round the summit of Qurnat es-Sauda and the village was full of greenery and the sound of running water, he told me his life story. He was an illegitimate child, left out of his father's will and cruelly treated by his half-brothers. He left home as soon as he could and went to South Africa where he had made his fortune. He then returned home and bought out his half-brothers and hired them as his servants to work the land. He had married 'an English lady' in Johannesburg, by whom he had had eighteen children, and he had three other wives who, between them, presented him with a son each year, not counting any daughters. He was amazed to find that I had no woman in the house and when I declined his offer to provide me with a beautiful concubine, he came to the conclusion that I was lacking in virility, and sent me a jar of his favourite, and unfailing, aphrodisiac, which consisted largely of marrow extracted from the bones of young lambs and looked revolting.

Aref Khaled Pasha, who had been a general in the Turkish Army during the 1914 war, called and poured a thousand blessings of Allah upon me as he asked for consent to plough his lands, but when I told him that he could not do so yet, he left mumbling, probably, as many curses. He called again a few days later, with another thousand blessings and, when I told him that he could now yoke his oxen, he called down yet another thousand.

At Deir el-Ahmar, on the road to Ba'albek, I was greeted with open arms by Mohammed Sa'id and his brother, the *mukhtar*, when I went to inspect the damage done by the Light Anti-Aircraft Brigade to their vines and fig trees and prickly pears. Mohammed expressed the view that a gentleman like me should have a walking stick and undertook to make one, and asked whether I would prefer to have one made from Syrian oak or an orange tree or an olive tree. Within a week, with two evil-looking henchmen, he was waiting outside my villa as I got up, with a handsome stick made, he vouched, from an orange branch. A few days later, Abdul Ruhman el Dheibi, from the village of El Miniyeh, who had heard of Mohammed's visit, arrived with a pair of walking sticks made from *zaroor*, the medlar tree. One was for me, he said, and the other, thinner and lighter, for my wife, when I should have one.

There was a great parade through the streets of Tripoli on Bastille Day. The French troops, many of them Senegalese, in their red tepis, looked like a field of Flanders poppies moving down the road below us. As soon as they had gone by, an invasion of natives descended on my office, led by Abdul Ruhman el Dheibi. He said that they were workmen from El Miniyeh and that they had not received the pay that was due to them. He felt that, as a British officer, I could do something to help them, and that was why he had brought them round to my office. I told him that it was nothing to do with me, which he knew perfectly well, whereupon he harangued them until they dispersed quietly.

After a while, the medical officer ordered me to take three days' rest, which I could not take, and gave me some medicine. I was told that the humid heat of

Tripoli did not help my condition, and a week later, I had to go to see Colonel Seegar, officer commanding 170 Light Field Ambulance, who wanted to admit me to Sidon Hospital. The following day I informed Colonel Pedretti, when I met him at Beirut, and he offered to transfer me to Damascus as there was no vacancy in Jerusalem, except in a lower rank, which I said I would prefer.

We had farewell drinks at the Mess the night before I left Tripoli and, the following morning, the staff gave me little mementoes and appeared to be sad to see me go. Victor, whom I had scolded more than any of the others, was on the verge of tears. I left without a shred of regret, however, and was mightily pleased to be returning to Jerusalem, which I did on the last day of July 1943.

I found Anna at home, on leave. Her father had said that the grapes were ripening but that 'he who is a head above the rest' was not there to pick the high clusters. She and I picked the grapes together.

I was extremely happy to return to Jerusalem after my sojourn in Syria and the Lebanon, and to sacrifice any seniority or promotion. I resumed by duties as Area Hirings Officer, Jerusalem and Transjordan, but soon found that there were moves to have me transferred to the Intelligence Corps. Edwin Samuel assured me that he was pressing my Colonel, and GHQ, Cairo, to find a replacement, as they had promised to do, so that I could be released, or even seconded, to his department as an Assistant District Commissioner. Major Nathan had also applied for my secondment to Military Intelligence. 'The Kurdis' quickly organised a 'welcome home' party, and, I reinstalled myself in Piha's house, and leased again the Morris Minor, all within a day of my return.

One of the first people to call to see me was Father Eugene, from the Garden of Gethsemane. He said that he was calling to object to the provision of accommodation for pregnant Polish women in Jerusalem. He had the usual twinkle in his eye and I thought that he was joking, but on enquiry, I found that such provision was being sought when Richard Hughes rang to say that he had heard that the Poles wanted to take over Miss Carey's teahouse as a home for this purpose and, within days, I received a request for that to be done. I felt that the English community would never forgive me if I had acceded to the request, and so I managed to persuade them to accept alternative premises.

The RAF wanted a considerable amount of additional accommodation in Jerusalem in the autumn of 1943, and when I went to hand over the Diakoness Hospital to their relevant officer I found that he was Flight Lieutenant Arthur Thomas, nephew of Thomas Thomas of Felin Bryn, Brynberian, the former headmaster of the St David's Grammar School, whom I had known at Newport as he and his mother and brothers and sister came each year there on holiday.

I went to Kfar Tsiyon to meet the Gurkhas and sat with them drinking lemonade when the Staff Captain of the 4th Indian Division arrived and turned out to be Devonald James, the son of the Queen's Hotel at Aberystwyth and a fellow student at college there.

I arranged to meet Hugh Foot at a point, somewhere between Beisan and Irbid, that could only be identified by an eight figure grid reference. After crossing the Jordan at Jisr el Hussein, I called on Said Bey Amoune, who was in charge of the Iraq Petroleum Company's pumping station, near Zor el Basha, and had coffee with him and his wife in their lonely homestead on the banks of the river. He told me that two German spies had been caught in Tiberias the previous day, and complained that Jews were entering Palestine in convoys of Polish refugees. As he spoke, a bulbul did a harsh mimicry above our heads, and a hoopoe poo-pooed along the river bank, while in a nearby bush, a golden oriole, on early migration, and a kingfisher, rivalled each other in brilliance. Hugh Foot was already at the grid reference point and he had with him Abdel Qadr el Hassan to whom I handed back 1,200 dunums of land and properties that we no longer required. We did our business and left, for there was no reason to stay longer than was necessary in such hostile territory.

We came to Aidoun, where the road divided and, if we turned left, I thought, we would pass nowhere until we got either to Baghdad or Bahrein, and then drove through young oak growing on the hillsides, and into Wadi Yabis which, was Jabesh Gilead, that Saul rescued from the Ammonites. I called at Ajlun, where the Arab Legion Mechanised Brigade had a camp, and found Captain John Paul, whom I had known in Jerusalem puzzled, as Emir Abdullah had just been there and had presented him with the Freedom of Transjordan, and we both wondered what that meant. Above Ajlun stood the great Saracen fortress of Qala'at el Rabad, guarding the road from Beisan to Jerash and forming a link in the chain of beacons that enabled the Caliph in Baghdad to send a message to the Sultan in Cairo in a matter of hours. The winding track from Ajlun towards Jerash led through pine trees for a while, and then we passed through the villages of Anjara and Sakhib and Reimon, a dirty hamlet that was once Ramoth in Gilead, one of the six cities which the Lord had commanded Joshua to get the Israelites to designate as 'cities of refuge . . . that whosoever killeth any person unawares might flee thither, and not die by the hand of the avenger of blood, until he stand before the congregation.'

Jerash, the Gerasa of the Bible, was founded by Alexander the Great in about 330 BC. After it had been conquered by the Romans in 63 BC, it became one of the cities of the Decapolis, a league of ten cities designed as a source of Graeco-Roman influence in the Middle East. It established trade with the Nabataeans of Petra, but with the rise of Palmyra and the change in trade routes, it began to decline. It was captured by the Crusaders in 1121 following which it was abandoned and it lay buried under the sand until it was rediscovered in 1806. Its ruins are said to be the most complete of all provincial Roman cities. I stood alone by the oval forum and walked among the fallen pillars of the Temple of Zeus and the Temple of Artemis and the Nymphaeum, and down the Street of the Columns. I left the ruins in the silence of the desert with only the whisper of the wind among them.

Hugh Foot rang one day to say that he had had his wish, to leave Amman, and had been posted to the Military Administration at Cyrenaica with the rank of Lieutenant-Colonel. I rang Ledger, who had taken over his work, but he said that he could not speak to me. He rang back an hour later to apologise and explain that he had Nuri Pasha es-Said, the Iraqi Premier, with him at the time.

Junior Commander Olive Brown, who shared a flat with Diana in Cairo, came to see me looking for accommodation for SSAFA in Jerusalem. She was a native of Portaferry, on Strangford Lough, and a Protestant. I took her to see premises that appeared to be suitable, and showed her the Old City and she came with me to Hebron, where we were entertained to lunch by the Palestine Police in their officers' mess, and were shown the stables that were full of beautiful Arab horses. After dinner at the Club one evening, she complained that I had not taken her to see the Mount of Olives, and there we sat long under the whispering pines talking about her childhood in Ireland. I handed over the premises for her to set up a SSAFA office and, shortly after, she said that she was unwell and was admitted to hospital. I went to see her and found Mrs McConnel, the GOC's wife, already there, and regularly I took her some books or whatever she needed, and we became very friendly.

'WHEN A MAN SHOULD MARRY...'

I ARRIVED BACK AT THE OFFICE one afternoon, in September 1943, to be told by Asad that a most attractive ATS officer had called to ask if I could help her to find accommodation for herself. He said that he had seen her go across the road to a tea room, and that I might find her there, which I did. She told me that her name was Joyce Ord and that she had been posted from Broumana, in Syria, to Q (Movements and Transportation) at HQ Palestine as Staff Movements Officer (Rail). She was looking for a flat and I took her to see several before she settled on a semi-basement in Alfazi Road which she immediately called 'The Kennel'.

Her parents, she told me, were Canadian, of families that had emigrated to that dominion two generations ago. Her father, Lewis Craven Ord, had served in France as an officer with the Canadian Army during the 1914-18 war and her mother had come to London so as to be nearer to him when he had leave from the trenches. Joyce had been born in Kensington, and had returned to Canada when the war was over, where the family had lived at Montreal and at Toronto. They owned some of the islands on Lake Muskoka, where she had spent summer holidays among the Indians. She had two brothers, Arthur, who was a Lieutenant Colonel in Burma, and Kenneth, who was suffering from an unidentified disease similar to muscular atrophy, on account of which he and his mother had been evacuated to Exmouth, where they used to spend their holidays after they had returned to this country and settled at Nottingham. Her father, now divorced from her mother, was an industrial consultant and was at that time advising Lord Beaverbrook in the Ministry of Aircraft Production. She had been entered for Cheltenham Ladies College but her mother had not approved of its atmosphere and so she had been sent to Malvern College.

She had been stationed at Broumana, and was now Staff Officer (Rail) in Q (Movements and Transportation) where, among her fellow officers was Robin Cayzer, later Lord Rotherwick, and, for a while, the Prince Aly Khan, who lived very quietly as though he did not want anyone to know that he was there.

At that time, my private life had become rather complicated Diana wrote from Cairo to say she was miserable there, and enquired tartly whether I had engaged to marry Olive. Anna was in Moascar, and there were others. This was the situation when I met Joyce and, unlike the medieval Welsh poet Dafydd ap

Gwilym who made an assignment with several of his lady loves in a leafy glade while he hid among the branches of a tree, I sought escape.

I was rather involved with Olive when I first met Joyce and it did not take long for the one to become aware of the other. I would meet one for tea and the other for supper and, one day, when Olive was at the office, Joyce called: I gave them tea and talked about the weather. Some days later Olive said that they had had a long talk, in a civilised fashion, which I found rather frightening and I had to tell her that our futures lay in different directions, which saddened us both, and she arranged to be posted back to Cairo.

I saw a good deal of Joyce after that. I took her to the Beilins, and to a party held on the roof of the Westons' house where Laurie was roasting a sheep, Bedouin fashion. I took her to Miss Carey's where we had a good old-fashioned English tea and no one there but English people, as though we were back in England, and I took her to dinner at the Club and elsewhere, but we did not get close together. I learned, afterwards, that she did not want to get too involved with me because she had thought that my name was Myers, and assumed that I was Jewish and lived in Palestine. Joyce was the only ATS officer in Q (Mov & Tn) until she was joined by Audrey Mustart, a South African WAAS officer with whom John Gwilym Jones, became friendly, and the four of us went around together a good deal during our leisure hours.

I took Joyce to Galilee, and when we got to Jenin we found that the road had been blown up, but we got by and went through Beisan to Jisr el Majamie and on to Ma'ad where I had arranged to meet the Mutassarif of Irbid, Abbas Pasha, who was an unreliable Cherkess gentleman whose fingers were festooned with gold rings studded with precious stones. He always wanted to give me one, which I politely refused, stating that soldiers were not allowed to wear rings. We went with him to Samah to inspect damage to crops for which he asked an exorbitant sum in compensation. We then went back to Ma'ad where the villagers were holding out their hands and crying for money. Fortunately, Glubb Pasha arrived and I explained the situation to him and he supported my assurance to them that they would get their money soon, but I did not tell them how much I had in mind. We went to Magdala and Capernaum before returning to Tiberias to stay with Mino.

Fishermen were fishing in the Sea of Galilee as we left the next morning and after passing through Irbid, for the next two hours we crossed the untenanted plains of Moab. I recalled that the Crown had been awarded, at the wartime National Eisteddfod held at Bangor that year, to Dafydd Owen, a theological student, for a poem on *Rhosydd Moab*, 'the plains of Moab', and here was I crossing the real Plains of Moab. From Mafraq to Zerka we saw nothing but empty tar containers, left after building the road, until we suddenly came upon the green vale of Wadi Zerka. At Amman, after calling at the British Residency, we had lunch at the Philadelphia Hotel, and then called at the Arab Legion HQ where a young officer showed Joyce his compact of uniforms. The Royal Cherkess Guard was changing guard at the Emir's Palace.

When Joyce and I called on the Zaharovs in the Bokharian Quarter in Jerusalem to wish them a happy new year, 5704, we found them, in their brightly coloured robes, sitting round the table ready to eat and however much we protested that we had already had dinner, they insisted that we should join them, and places were set for us while we still argued, and glasses of green arak were put in our hands. They already had two guests: Asher Levitsky, a prominent Jerusalem lawyer, and Leopold Schen, the director of the Jewish National Fund in London. This chance meeting with Schen was to stand us in good stead when we were later looking for somewhere to live in London.

Bertram Thomas, the explorer who had crossed Rub' al Khali, 'the Empty Quarter', the Great Southern Desert of Saudi Arabia, by camel in 1931 called at my office to say that he had been appointed Director of the Middle East Centre of Arabic Studies for which the Austrian Hospice, near Damascus Gate, had been requisitioned. The purpose of the Centre was to train British officers in Arab affairs.

The Special Operations Executive (SOE) were given Dr Jamal's house in Talbiyeh, one of the finest residences in Jerusalem, for their use. Its occupants included Captain Anthony Webb, who was later to become Chief Justice of Kenya, Captain Aubrey Eban who, as Abba Eban, was to become Foreign Secretary of Israel, and Major Henry Grant-Taylor. They had previously occupied a house on the Bethlehem road but as they had largely to do with representatives of the Jewish Agency and of the *Haganah*, an Arab neighbourhood was not considered suitable and the house that I got for them in Talbiyeh was more suitable. Grant-Taylor was an expert sharpshooter. I once attended a lecture that he gave, entitled 'Tough Tactics', throughout which he walked up and down the stage of the YMCA Auditorium, twirling and spinning his guns in the best cowboy fashion, and firing at dummies with live ammunition to illustrate his points. He would even draw both guns and fire them together, so that only one shot was heard, and only one hole was made in a patch placed over the heart of the dummy.

One of the tasks of SOE was secretly to prepare the *Haganah*, and in particular its striking force, *Palmach*, in the event of Rommel being able to push through into Palestine and as that threat receded, it became redundant. Before its officers scattered, however, they gave a party at Dr Jamal's house to which they invited the Chief Secretary to the Palestine Government and the Deputy Provost

Marshal. At the party, someone had challenged Grant-Taylor to hit with his revolver a mil coin, the size of a silver three penny bit, placed on the bull of a dart board. He succeeded in doing so, several times, but others who attempted it were not so clever, with the result that the a portion of the wall of the dining room had been gouged out, and the whole place looked as though the eye of a tornado had passed through it. Eban, who was my contact with the unit, hoped that I would be able to settle the matter without taking it further, and when I told him that I would have to put him on a charge, as the responsible officer, for damage to property he pulled a long face, thinking that I meant it. A few days later, Eban, now stationed in Cairo, called to bring me greetings from Diana, and to thank me for the way in which I had handled the Jamal affair, and gave me £P4 as a personal contribution towards the cost of repairs. On the night before I handed the house back to Dr Jamal, I happened to pass by and saw a light inside. I crept in and found the night watchman, Yacoub Yusef Raghab from Abu Ghosh, asleep on a bed, with his dagger beside his pillow. I took the dagger and crept out again. As I reached the office the following morning, Yusef was waiting for me to say that someone had broken into the house while he slept there. His eyes opened wide when I said: 'And even stole your dagger!' He was relieved when I let him off with a stern warning and gave him his dagger back.

Early in November 1943 I was told that it might be necessary for me to take over the YMCA building, opposite the King David Hotel, for a summit meeting between the world leaders, and a rumour was deliberately spread that it was needed for a visit by the Pope. In the meantime, I had to prepare a schedule of the hotel accommodation that was available in Jerusalem. As it turned out, Churchill and Roosevelt met at Mena House Hotel in Cairo when Churchill tried to persuade Roosevelt to agree to invade the underbelly of Germany from the Mediterranean, but Roosevelt insisted on adhering to 'Operation Overlord', the invasion through northern France.

We had taken over most of the King David Hotel and a large marquee had been erected over its front entrance so that no one could see who was arriving there, or leaving. Everyone expected the arrival of Churchill and Roosevelt but had to be content with fleeting glimpses of the service leaders, such as Alanbrooke, Marshall, Dill, Cunningham. Joyce was amused that they should have saluted her as they arrived. When I called at the King David for the bill, Hamburger, the manager, told me all about the visit of the generals. A signal came from the War Office expressing the Director of Hirings' pleasure at the manner in which the arrangements had been made.

As the Christmas of 1943 approached, Yitz Chizik kept on saying that he was thinking of arranging a proper Christmas dinner, with turkey and Christmas pudding. When he discovered that Joyce's birthday fell on Christmas Eve, he decided to have the dinner then, and informed the Beilins and the Westons accordingly. The ladies dressed for the occasion and, for a brief while, one forgot that one was far from home or that there was a war on. That evening, the blackout was lifted and the lights of Jerusalem shone again after the long gloom lasting four years. There had never been darkness, however, for most nights were starlit and, when the moon was full, one could read a book in the street.

I had found a comfortable penthouse flat for Joyce in Gaza Road, which she christened 'The Crow's Nest'. On New Year's Eve we called to see Richard Hughes to convey the season's greetings and then, with John G. Jones and Audrey Mustart, by now his girl friend, we went to the King David Hotel for a goose dinner to which John and I had invited the Beilins, the Westons and the Chiziks. Colonel Pedretti, who had a party at a table the other end of the dining room, came up and, in his customary uncouth manner, took Joyce's hand and kissed it and said: 'This is the nicest little thing I've seen with you yet, Miles!' After the meal she and I went into the garden where, among the cypresses, fountains sprayed silver under the moon. It was the perfect setting in which to ask her to be my wife.

I woke in the morning of New Year's Day regretting that I had not popped the question the night before, but reflected that it would not have been fair to do so when the dance and the wine and the glamour of the moonlit garden conspired to create an unreal situation. Better, I thought, to have left it to the morning, cold and grey, but clear. I spoke of an uncertain future, with prospects that seemed none too bright, and made no mention of the bliss I envisaged, and hoped for, and then asked her if she would come with me, hand in hand, into the unknown. Her response came in tears of joy: above all things in the world, that would be her desire.

We immediately began to plan our tomorrow. The wedding would be soon, for fear of a posting, and in a church in Jerusalem, for the sake of the children to come. She would send for her mother's wedding dress. I regretted being unable to wear my father's brocade waistcoat, and being married at Nevern, as I had always planned. Joyce sent a telegram to her mother saying 'Have indigestion: taking Dill', her mother having said that the only Dill she had known was the herb used as a carminative. I wrote to mine at greater length, and to my brother. Joyce also wrote to her brother Arthur, in the Lushai Brigade in the Far East, and to my mother. Yitz Chizik wrote to Joyce's mother to say what sort of fellow she was going to have as a son-in-law, and Assia offered their house for our wedding reception, but Major Tate of EFI had already stated that we could have it at Allenby Barracks.

John and Audrey came to lunch and gladly agreed to be best man and bridesmaid.

Mino rang to ask us to a party at Tiberias that evening, but we found good reason to decline, and when John grabbed the phone and gave him the news, he said 'Mino uttered a Christian oath and expressed his delight.' We then had to do the rounds to inform our friends. Richard Hughes gave his blessing and would not stop kissing Joyce. Yitz kissed everybody and danced like a dervish, leaving Assia to pour the drinks. Harry and Judy immediately planned a party. At the Club John could not resist disclosing our secret and champagne corks popped instantly. As we left the Club a black cat walked, as though deliberately, across our path, which Audrey swore was a good omen. The next day, Sunday though it was, we had to go to work as we were both duty officers. Even complete strangers who rang offered me their congratulations, which I found baffling until I discovered that the telephone operator had been telling my callers: 'He's got engaged!' That evening we went to a party arranged by Joyce's colleagues at Q (Mov & Tn). Her commanding officer, Colonel Hunter gave her his consent to marry, and Robin Cayzer light-heartedly offered to give her away. I had to ask Colonel Pedretti for his permission and he replied: 'Gladly, were it only to reduce you to my state!' He apologised for his behaviour on New Year's Eve, being a little drunk, he admitted, and gave me a firm handshake and his best wishes.

We went to see the Assistant Chaplain General, Colonel Yelverton, and he made arrangements with the Archdeacon for us to be married at St George's Cathedral on the second of February, Candlemas, at three o'clock in the afternoon. I wrote to Colonel Ainsleigh Jones, the Deputy Chaplain General, 9th Army, at Beirut, asking him to perform the ceremony.

By post that day I received a copy of Lawrence's *Seven Pillars of Wisdom* as a belated Christmas present from Olive. I felt embarrassed and sore, and wrote to her to say that I had got engaged and offered to return the book, which she would not let me do as long as I gave her a copy of one of my sonnets. I also wrote to Anna, with great pain.

When Sheikh Abu Daoud of the Suwwahra tribe heard of our engagement, he sent a messenger to invite us to a feast, for which he would bring his tents as near Jerusalem as the laws of the Bedouin would allow. This was in the wilderness of Judea and as we and our friends approached the black tents, Sheikh Abu Ali, the 'father' of the tribe, rose to meet us with traditional greetings and took us into his tent where he had prepared tea for us. Two lambs had been roasted in our honour, and heaps of fruit laid before us. Sheikh Abu Daoud pounded the coffee beans to a tribal rhythm, which expressed the welcome of the tribe by the measure of its beat. Abu Ali spoke with pride about the antiquity of the Suwwahra and gave us the blessing of the tribe.

Ainsleigh Jones came from Beirut to make the arrangements for the wedding ceremony. As he had not been to the Dead Sea we took him to tea at the Kallia Hotel, and then to Jericho and to Allenby Bridge where we stood by the Jordan and sang the Welsh hymn *Ar lan Iorddonen ddofn* with great *hwyl*. We then took him home for dinner, to which we also had invited Richard Hughes who was always delighted to meet a fellow countryman.

The announcement of our engagement in *The Palestine Post* brought further messages of congratulations and good wishes. It also contained the announcement of the engagement of the General's daughter, Diana McConnel, who had been working at our office, to the Marquess of Douro, the future Duke of Wellington. They were married a few days before us.

At a meeting of the Welsh Society, I heard that my cousin, Major Tudor Miles, was a medical officer at 4 General Hospital at Qassassin. I wrote to Tudor, whom I had never met, and he replied suggesting that we should meet in Cairo. He enclosed a photograph of himself from which I could see that he bore a remarkable likeness to my brother.

Father Eugene Hoad called to say that he regretted that he would not be able to come to the wedding but invited us to the Garden of Gethsemane after the honeymoon for a blessing.

Q (Mov & Tn) held a presentation party for Joyce and gave her a cheque. Colonel Hunter said that he would provide the transport to and from the Cathedral and Allenby Barracks, and two seats on a flight off the Dead Sea in a Sunderland, landing on the Nile, for our honeymoon.

The guest list comprised so many Jews and Arabs that made Joyce suggest that we should invite a few Christians to sing the hymns, and by the time we added the military and members of the British community, the number of invitations amounted to three hundred and fifty. Most of them accepted, and at the wedding, there were also those who had not been invited, so that St George's Cathedral was full of well-wishers.

On the eve of the wedding, my best man, John Gwilym Jones, took a firm hold of me and said that he would not allow me out of his sight until we reached the Cathedral the next day. About thirty of my friends appeared at the Officers' Club for dinner, which was followed by a rousing and riotous stag-party, from which John dragged me away not long after midnight, to stay with him at his quarters. He kept me on a very short leash the next morning but when we arrived at the Club for lunch, there was an urgent telephone message for him: a refugee ship, the *Nyassa*, had landed in Haifa that morning with eight hundred illegal Jewish immigrants and he, being in GSI, had to prepare a report for the Press. While he was engaged in this telephone call, my friends who had gathered at the Club took advantage of his absence to supply me with a few drinks. By two-thirty, he and I were on our way to the Cathedral, to be greeted by the groomsmen, who were Major Peter Jolliffe of the Northumberland Fusiliers; Captain Jock Calder of the Highland Light Infantry; Captain Kenneth Gapp, Intelligence Corps; Flight Lieutenant Arthur Thomas, RAF; Flight Lieutenant Arthur Pearl, Royal Australian Air Force, and Lieutenant. Nicholas Andronovitch of the United States Army Air Force. There, too, to meet us in the cloisters were Archdeacon Hawes and Colonel Ainsleigh Jones.

Old Richard Hughes and Lady Flinders Petrie sat in the front row, where my father and mother would have sat, I felt, had they been there. The rest of the congregation was made up of officers and other ranks, ATS officers and civilian staff, Government officers, and friends from various walks of life, including the *mukhtars* of the surrounding villages and Sheikh Abu Daoud and three others of the Suwwahra who had left their black tents and entered a roofed building for the first time in their lives. Abdul Fatah, came with his bodyguard, each bristling with daggers and guns, who waited outside the Cathedral porch while the service was in progress.

Joyce arrived soon after three on the arm of Colonel Bindie Carroll, a family friend, who had arrived from Egypt to give her away. She was dressed in her mother's wedding dress, which she had managed to have sent out, and her bridesmaid, Lieutenant Audrey Mustart, WAAS, from Johannesburg, wore a pale blue dress. The service began with 'Guide me, O thou great Jehovah' to the tune of *Cwm Rhondda*, and ended with 'O Perfect Love'. We had to sign a variety of forms as we were contracting a 'marriage out of Great Britain and Northern Ireland registered at a military station' and the certificate had to be countersigned by the General Officer Commanding.

As we drove away from the Cathedral to the reception at Allenby Barracks, we passed the sheiks and the *mukhtars* walking on the grassy verge and carrying their shoes in their hands. They were wearing them again by the time they arrived at the Barracks, to be received, by Colonel Hunter, Joyce and myself. Two of the Bedouin sneaked by for the second time so as to give the bride another kiss.

After we had cut the cake with my sword, Colonel Hunter proposed a toast during which he sang Joyce's praise in superlative terms and said that it had taken a Welshman to 'catch' her, and that under the noses of others. As I rose to respond, the orchestra struck 'Land of My Fathers'. John proposed a toast to the bridesmaid and read telegrams from our parents and a host of others, including Major Nicholl, ADC to the High Commissioner; Sheikh Mustafa Bey Husseini, of Jericho, and Sheikh Wasef Bisharat, of Amman, and one, said John jocularly, from Rhosllanerchrhugog with good wishes from Wales. We eventually got back to the penthouse flat in Gaza Road where Joyce removed her name from the door as I carried her over the threshold.

Abu Issa, the *mukhtar* of Lifta, had arranged a feast for us and for our more immediate friends that evening, and there we sat eating Arab food and singing, for the most part, Welsh songs led by the Deputy Chaplain General.

Early the next morning, we were driven down to the Dead Sea where we took off on a Sunderland which was on its way to Pembroke Dock. The plane rose between the walls of the wildernesses of Moab and Judaea, over Sodom and Gomorrah, and down the Wadi Araba, and then swung westward to cross the Sinai desert which, though seemingly barren as the face of the moon, was surprisingly well spattered with the black tents of Bedouin Arabs. We had a severe buffeting as we flew over the mountainous regions of Gebel Hellal and Gebel Maghara, during which the flying boat seemed to drop out of the sky, but afterwards we sailed peacefully over the Great Bitter Lake and Heliopolis and landed on the Nile at Cairo. Among the security officers there to receive us was a Field Censor who insisted on retaining my diary for inspection, although it was written in Welsh, and I refrained from telling him that I was the censor of Welsh letters written throughout the Middle East. He also confiscated the copies of *The Palestine Post* which we had been given that morning by the editor, but allowed us to cut out the report of the wedding.

When we arrived at the Continent-Savoy Hotel, the manager rushed forward and presented Joyce with a massive sheaf of red roses, a gesture engineered, we later learned, by Hamburger, the manager of the King David Hotel in Jerusalem.

The next day we rode on horseback round the Pyramids and the Sphinx, where an old *fellah* told us our fortune in the sand of the Nile. I remembered Sir Flinders Petrie telling me how, when he was digging at Abydos, he had found the only known statue of its builder, King Khufu, or Cheops. We then had tea at Mena House Hotel where Churchill and Roosevelt had had their meeting with Chiang Kai-shek the previous November. The Egyptian journal *The Sphinx* carried a report and picture of our wedding, and of that of the Marquess and Marchioness of Douro.

My cousin Tudor came to see us at the Continental-Savoy. His father was my father's youngest brother, but we had never met. He was a Major in the RAMC, stationed at Qassassin where, a few days earlier, he had mended King Farouk after that monarch had been involved in a car accident. We had tea at the YWCA at Darbhanga House, formerly a residence of the Maharajah of Darbhanga, and dined at the Ambassador's, considered to be the smartest restaurant in Cairo.

Bryn Davies and his wife, Bill, entertained us to lunch at their home the next day, and Bryn took us to the Fuad I University where he was Professor of English.

That evening, we had dinner at Shepheard's with Bindie Carroll and his friend Princess Delafrus Idybulat Khan, who had seen twenty-two members of her family butchered by the Bolsheviks before she was able to escape, first to Holland, and then to Cairo.

We went to Memphis and saw the alabaster sphinx discovered by Petrie, and the giant statues of Rameses II, the Pharaoh of the oppression of the Children of Israel, and went on to Saqqara, to the Tomb of Ti, its walls covered with bold hieroglyphs, and to the Step Pyramid, the first pyramid of all, built by King Zozer to his own glory some six thousand years ago. When we returned to Cairo we found the streets bedecked with flags and bunting in preparation for the celebration of King Farouk's twenty-fourth birthday the next day. It had been our plan to go to Luxor but Joyce became unwell and was found to be suffering from yellow jaundice. We therefore had to return to Jerusalem and were able to travel in the car of a fellow officer, David Elston.

We left Cairo early in the morning. Feluccas sailed noiselessly along the canal and water buffaloes swished their tails among the tall rushes. Children played under the palm trees, egrets hunted the water's edge in fitful darts, and a man turned an Archimedean screw to draw water from the canal. We stopped for breakfast at the United Officers' Club on the shore of Lake Timsah, and crossed Suez on the ferry. The road ran like a steel tape across Sinai and one could not help thinking about the problems Moses faced in leading the Children of Israel over the barren wastes that lay on each side.

After a couple of restful days, Joyce improved sufficiently for us to travel in my little car to Tiberias to stay with our friends Mino and Marianne. Mino looked like a heavyweight all-in wrestler, with a squint that made one eye disappear when he looked the other way. Although he was a Jew, by the name of Goldzweig, he was accepted as a blood brother by the Arabs and, during the troubles before the war, he was able to mingle freely among them as no other Jew could do. Marianne, on the other hand, was petite and fragile as a china doll. She was the daughter of a professor who, she hoped, had escaped from Germany but whose present whereabouts were unknown. When Mino went to seek her father's consent, he arrived dressed as a Bedouin Arab.

The sun had set over the Horns of Hattin and it was getting dark by the time we arrived in Tiberias. Marianne welcomed us and said that Mino had gone to Lake Huleh but would be back shortly. When he arrived he poured us large brandies, as the wine of welcome, and drank half a bottle himself, saying that he was thirsty. Two spring chickens placed on each plate for dinner turned out to be the first course, for then a lamb was brought in on a silver tray and Mino tore off a hind quarter for himself, leaving us the rest of the carcase to pick off tasty morsels. After dinner we went to Abu Arab's for bitter coffee and then on to the Panorama where, upon our entry, the orchestra stopped whatever it was playing and struck up a wild Ukrainian song that it always played to greet Mino. It then played only music requested by Mino or by us, for the rest of the evening and, at one stage, Mino gave a performance of Circassian and Ukrainian dances, that made one marvel to see such a giant dance so that his feet hardly touched the floor. After we got home, Mino gave me a silver Cherkess camel whip of a unique design that had been made by an old silversmith in Quneitra. Inside its handle, was concealed a dagger.

The next morning we sat on the quay wall and watched fishermen setting out in their boats, and as the warm sun bore down upon our bodies, we could see Mount Hermon capped in snow. A duck with her brood of newly hatched ducklings swam in front of us until some boys threw stones at them. Mino came and joined us, saying that he had been up all night as the fishermen had brought in catch after catch, amounting to fifteen tons of sprats, and he went off for a sleep in a nearby house where his friend 'Mary Magdalene' lived, with whom he normally played *t'awla* on the street pavement. Abu Arab, Mino's blood-brother, came to invite us to lunch at his café . He was dressed, that day, in a suit of bright green, but still wore his white *kaffiyeh*. He had a handsome face and when he smiled there were flashes of gold in his teeth. Lunch consisted of fresh sprats, of which I ate a dozen or more, with *tahineh* and cabbage, washed down with arak

We had to make a journey to the *Souk* the next morning, before leaving, to say goodbye to some of Mino's friends. The weather was threatening and a strong wind blew the leaves off the trees as we drove back through Cana and Nazareth, Jenin and Nablus. When we arrived in Jerusalem we found that the Chiziks had arranged a party to welcome us home from our honeymoon and among those present were the war correspondents Alan Moorehead and Edgar Mowrer. There were lots of letters, and a parcel from Colonel Yelverton, our chaplain, who sent us a copy of Aref el Aref's new book, *Bedouin Love, Law and Legend* as a wedding present.

Seren y Dwyrain contained good wishes for us on our marriage, and my monthly article on the proceedings of the Jerusalem Welsh Society, and also a poem I had written at the request of the editor.

There were about eighty people present at the St David's Day dinner in 1944. Richard Hughes, was a patient at the Government Hospital, but he had persuaded the doctors to allow him to attend the dinner, at which he presided and commanded Joyce to sit beside him. Major Davies, RWF, who brought a large red dragon flag that his Prisoners of War had made at their camp at Latrun, proposed the loyal toast. Richard Hughes proposed the toast to *Dewi Sant a Chymru*

(St David and Wales) and devoted most of his address to thanking me for all I had done since I had founded the Society. Major Nicholl arrived late from a party at Government House, and Colonel Buckley came at midnight with a police escort to see that all was well. When we left the hotel, however, we found that someone had stolen my car, but it was found early the next morning, undamaged.

The next day a BBC programme was broadcast from my office under the title *Y Cymry yn Israel 1940-44* (the Welsh in Israel 1940-44), and I also did a five-minute piece on Jerusalem from the Mount of Olives. That same evening, at the fortnightly meeting of the Society, we had a discussion: 'Hills of Judaea or Hills of Home?'

'The Wayfarer in Uniform', in his column in *The Palestine Post*, stated that he had been given to understand that 'the Welsh Rugby side is all set for football glory' that season, and added:

> And talking about Welshmen, Jerusalem has the oldest Welsh Society in the Middle East. Its moving spirit is Captain Dillwyn Miles, or Dilwyn ap Cemais (his Welsh title). He is a Bard (a high-up Druid) and a great enthusiast for all things Welsh, especially poetry and literature. Any fellow countryman in the Services, especially those who speak Welsh, will get a big welcome from him. His ambition is to get enough members to hold an Eisteddfod in Jerusalem. A Welsh paper is published in the Middle East, *Seren y Dwyrain* (Star of the East). But the printers (in Cairo) can only make up one page at a time because Welsh needs so many *y*'s.

Joyce and I went to a performance given by the Rina Nikova Ballet, with Professor Isaac and the Beilins, and afterwards to Moshe Shertok's house for drinks. Nikova and two of the ballerinas also came and one of them, Rahel, sang the funny song *Kukiyeh* for me. Nikova said that she had first heard the song being sung by an Arab in Paris.

I went to Amman, without knowing that it would be for the last time, and ran into Operation Crocodile returning from manoeuvres: a column of Greek trucks extended all the way to Talat ed Dam. The Ghor looked like a battle-field with guns, tanks and lorries everywhere, but I still got to Amman in about three hours. I wanted to see Alec Kirkbride, the British Resident, but found that he was on leave and that Glubb Pasha was 'holding the fort', as he aptly put it. I got Ledger to take over some vacated properties, and told him that the Ghor looked as it had not looked since Joshua had fought the battle of Jericho, but his only reply was that he hoped that they would not damage any of the fossils there. I called on Emily Bisharat and went to the *Souk* to buy sandals for Joyce. As I got down to the Jordan Valley I noticed that Emir Abdullah's summer tents were still pitched at Shuneh.

The daughter of Ben Yehuda, who had revived the Hebrew language, called to ask if I could find her a house, as she was homeless. It was my last act.

A signal came to say that I had been posted to the Royal Artillery Base Depot at Almaza. That which we had greatly feared had come upon us, and we felt that the bottom had dropped out of our little world, and it could mean that I would be sent home immediately, on account of the length of my service abroad, and that Joyce would have to stay as she had only been abroad three years. We had feared that this would happen and had implemented Paragraph 11 of ATS Regulations, which stated that a member of the service, on becoming pregnant could demand immediate release.

The day before I left, a bomb blew up the district police headquarters, killing Assistant Superintendent Scott. A civilian curfew had been imposed, so that only our military friends were able to get to a farewell party that we had organised for that evening. The following evening we had to have special permission to attend a dinner party that had been arranged for me at the Club. Because of the curfew, Harry Beilin organised a tea party at the King David Hotel the next day for all my friends that he could gather. He was of the opinion that the CID had a hand in my posting because of my close contact and friendship with the Jewish community, as it was a known fact that I was on their 'black list' on that account. We had supper alone at home.

Sudkhi, the havildar, looked after my things at the railway station while I handed back the car, M 13 H, before I set off on the train to Cairo. I shared a compartment with Major Carmichael of 16 British General Hospital, who was on his way home so that his wife could have a child before she was too old, and at Lydda we were joined by an Indian medical officer and a Polish diplomat from Ankara. Until then, the weather was dreary, with a *khamsin* blowing and an occasional shower with thunder, but when we got to Lydda it was heavy rain. The Rail Transport Officer, nevertheless, warned us that there might be sandstorms in the Sinai Desert, and we found that he was correct in his forecast soon after we left Gaza. By the time we got to the vicinity of Mazar, the train came to a halt and could go no further on account of sand-drifts. At dawn we moved forward towards Bir el Abd and got some idea of the effect of the storm. The sand blocked our passage at both ends and found its way in through the edges of the carriage windows. There was no food on the train, nor a drop to drink. The Polish diplomat produced a small bar of chocolate which he insisted on sharing with us: it gave a taste in the mouth but did nothing, nor was there anything, to assuage one's thirst.

As I left the flat in Jerusalem I had picked up a copy of the journal *Wales*, No. 3, which had arrived that morning and which I thought would be enough for me to read in the train before going to sleep. After the second night on the train, I had read it from cover to cover several times and I wrote a note to the editor, Keidrych Rhys, claiming that I had derived the most pleasure and benefit from that issue.

Looking out through the window, I could see no sign of life except for dung beetles moving excitedly over the sand, and I wondered why such unattractive creatures should be regarded by the ancient Egyptians as the repositories of the secret of eternal life and be sanctified as scarabs.

The next day the wind was still blowing sand in great sheets across the surface of the desert. Hunger, thirst and a throbbing head made for low spirits. We knew that our location was known, as planes flew over us from time to time, but we were not aware that camel caravans were endeavouring to reach us. A train sent by Joyce, as Q (Movements) Rail Officer, with the aim of towing us back to Gaza, broke down in the effort, and the wind got up again. I wrote a poem: *Dyma hi'n wawr y trydydd dydd* (The third day has dawned). Towards evening, a train came and succeeded in towing us back to El Arish.

We reached Gaza around midnight and were given some kind of skilly that looked revolting and tasted of rabbit, which I could never abide, but hunger takes little account of such niceties. We were advised to eat slowly, as our stomachs would have shrunk, and not to eat too much. I bought a bottle of beer, which I sipped and which was the finest drop of beer I have ever tasted, and felt the effect of its alcoholic content instantly. I screwed the top on to the bottle after a few more sips, and took it on the train where we spent the rest of the night with the same discomfort.

We crawled past Khan Yunis and Rafah, and, after Bir el Burg, it was a relief to see the blue of the Mediterranean coming into view. We stopped at El Arish and at Bir el Abd we met the train from Cairo and gave it a great cheer. At Rumani, on the Bay of Pelusium, we were greeted by a detachment of Bechuanan troops who had been clearing the track from that end and trying to bring us food, which was still unpacked while they, they said, were hungry. The sight of palm trees made me think that we had come upon an oasis, or was it a mirage? We had, in fact, reached the salt marshes of Tell el-Luli.

We had taken most of the day crossing the Sinai and it was early evening by the time we reached Qantara and saw great ships sail by on the Suez Canal, which we eventually crossed. At Ismailia they were selling the *Egyptian Mail*, the front page of which featured our experience under the heading 'The Lost Train'. It was eleven o'clock that night by the time we arrived in Cairo and there, on the platform, was the Cairo City Band waiting to greet us with strident music that one was able to recognise, after a while, as 'God Save the King'. A crowd of people had gathered and speeches of welcome were delivered by various dignitaries, while all we wanted was to get away and make for our destinations. I had to wait two hours on Cairo station for transport to take me to the RA Base Depot at Almaza, which I discovered to be a tented town in which everyone was asleep. I went into the kitchens in search of food but found that everything had been packed away beyond the reach of the congeries of cockroaches that appeared to have taken possession of the place. I found a blanket and curled up in a hole in the sand, and slept.

I went in to Cairo the next day and, on Opera Square, I met Emlyn Williams who was there to put on his play, *Night Must Fall*. He thanked me for my letter telling him that I had seen his *Morning Star* performed in Hebrew and I went with him to Shepheards, where he was staying, and up to his bathroom where we spoke as he shaved. As I had nothing to do, I spent most of the time at the Continental-Savoy Hotel, where I knew the manager, Freddie Hoffman, since we stayed there during our honeymoon.

I could not stop thinking how stupid it was that I should have been given an 'urgent posting' and taken away, once again, from a job that I had been doing for over two years to the apparent satisfaction of my superiors, and sent to a tented camp on the sands of the Nile to do nothing. After another three weeks, I requested, and obtained, some leave which enabled me to go back to Jerusalem, but I had only been there a few days before I received an urgent call to return to Almaza to be told that I had been appointed Liaison Officer with the 1st United States Army Air Force, stationed at Huckstep Camp. On arrival there I was conducted to the Officers' Club and handed my first Bourbon. The unit was to move to an unknown destination, the route to be disclosed to us on our way. I was introduced to Lieutenant-Colonel Ralph P Dunn, the commander, and to Major John N. Dunn, the second-in-command. I immediately christened them 'Overdone' and 'Underdone'.

Colonel Dunn asked me to go ahead 'to blaze the trail', and I opened my instructions to find that my first destination was Haifa, and I decided that I would go via Jerusalem. I set off early the next morning with an escort of one sergeant, one corporal, three Enlisted Men (EMs), and a driver, in a large utility-wagon. We reached Jerusalem at eight o'clock that evening, and I found accommodation for the men at St Andrew's House, leaving the utility in the care of the military police.

From Haifa the unit travelled, in a large convoy of American Army vehicles, across the Syrian Desert to Mafraq. The vehicles were driven by Indian soldiers under the command of Lieutenant Rattan, whose father was the governor of Gujurat, but the American officers, even though they had black EMs, made it clear to me that they did not want to consort with a coloured officer. I found Rattan a good deal more cultured than any of them, however, and I quickly accepted his offer to share his tent, especially when I saw that it was a silk-lined pavilion, spacious enough to provide us with separate bedrooms and supplied with electricity from a small generator and an all-wave radio set, and orderlies to attend to our every need.

My orders were to take the unit as far as Mafraq, where I was to hand over to two South African officers. The American officers had arranged a farewell party for me that evening at their mess and we had hardly charged our glasses when the field telephone rang. It was Joyce reporting that the South African officers had been lost and that I was to take the 1st USAAF to its destination.

We left Mafraq at dawn the next morning, and saw the sun bounce up like a ball of fire. In no time it made the sheets of lava over which we travelled like hot steel-plate. There was no sign of life in any form and one could well imagine that the surface of the moon, or even of the planet Mars, was like that. Our convoy of some two hundred vehicles moved across the desert like a slow sidewinder snake. We took the left fork at Tel el-Asfar, as the other track would have taken us to Saudi Arabia and Bahrein. We were following the Iraq Petroleum Oil Company's pipeline from Haifa to Baghdad and came to the oil pumping station known as H5. After crossing the wastes of Harrat er-Rujeilah we arrived at H4, near Wadi Abu Halrah, where we asked for water, but were told that we could not have any as the water lorry had gone off to water some sheep.

It grew hotter and hotter as we drove languidly across Rijn el-Mulhar to H3 and by the time we reached Rutbah, where we looked forward to a good night's rest, we found that no provision had been made for us, neither food nor drink, nor anywhere to sleep except on the hot sand. Although my duty to make advance arrangements had ceased at Mafraq, I felt embarrassed at someone's failure to do so here, and this was made more acute by the brusque manner in which we were received by the officer commanding the Rutbah station. We left Rutbah as early as possible so as to avoid the heat of day and got to Wadi Mohammedi by noon, with the temperature at 126°F.

I had left Jerusalem with the minimum of kit, as I had expected to return there from Mafraq. I wore only a shirt and a pair of shorts, apart from my underclothes, and had brought my greatcoat in the pockets of which were a razor and some articles of toilet. I took the opportunity, at Wadi Mohammedi, to wash my vest and pants, but the supply of water was meagre and they dried out with grey stripes so that when I wore them, I looked like a zebra.

Rattan shot a gazelle that afternoon and invited the Dunns to join us for dinner. Each day, as we pitched camp, the Indian drivers would get out of their uniforms and wear loincloths, while Rattan changed into his native finery and donned the robes of an Indian aristocrat. The Americans were greatly impressed with the occasion.

We reached Habbaniyah the next morning and found that although it lay beside a vast lake, there was no growth of any kind, and no trace of any bird life, or of any other. It was not until we got to the banks of the Euphrates that we saw the first greenery since we had left the Jordan. We were warmly greeted at Baghdad by Major West, officer commanding Lancer Camp, where we were billeted, and he gave us lunch at the mess, where I met Major Gwynne from Neath. The bar in the mess was built of beer bottles set in cement, with their bottoms facing outward and lit from behind.

Baghdad began as a round city built on the west bank of the Tigris by the Caliph Mansour who had moved his capital there from Damascus. His pride was the Palace of the Golden Gate, in the centre of the city, which was struck by a thunderbolt and rebuilt with even greater splendour by his grandson, Haroun el-Rashid, whose memory has been given a false halo by *The Tales of the Arabian Nights*. A new city, built on the east bank of the river, was ravaged by Hulagu, the brother of Khublai Khan, and his Mongols, and was later occupied by Tamerlane, and sacked again by the Sultan Murad in 1638. Its mosques were built anew soon after, but its bazaars had to wait until the beginning of the nineteenth century.

Major West informed us that all troops were confined to barracks as there had been some ugly bloodletting in the city that day. Major Wiseheart, the M.O., however, had already done a recce. and he invited the Dunns and me to dinner at the Tigris Front Hotel, to get to which we managed to get past the guard at the gate of Lancer Camp. We sat on a sort of pier that jutted into the river so that we had water on three sides, and there were boats going up and down, and gay lights everywhere, a scene that made one think of Venice. We dined and wined well, and rather noisily, and when we had reached the liqueur stage, I saw the figure of a British officer making towards us. He was wearing a red armband and I realised that he must be of the military police, and I warned the others to be prepared to be placed under arrest for having broken curfew. The officer came up to our table, however, and saluted smartly saying: 'Lieutenant-Colonel Evans, Deputy Assistant Provost Marshal. I had hoped to have been able to call on you gentlemen earlier, but we've had a bit of a to-do here in Baghdad today.' I detected a trace of a Welsh accent and was inebriated enough to ask: 'What Evans, look you?' 'Evan Evans,' he replied which led me to be bolder and enquire where he came from. 'Oh,' he said, 'a place you will never have heard of, called Woodstock in Pembrokeshire.' When I told him that I came from the same county, he sat down and joined us for a drink. He gave us a potted portrait of Baghdad, for which he had no great liking, any more than he had for some of his fellow officers, for when I asked him what Major Wynne did, he said: 'He makes tin arseholes for wooden birds!'

He then offered to take us on a night tour of Baghdad and we drove away with an escort of three trucks and a dozen military police fully, armed, until we got to the gate of the old city and, under heavy escort, we walked down a narrow covered way along both sides of which were benches, and upon each bench sat two, or mostly three, prostitutes of all ages and types. There were young women and older women, most of them having dyed their hair, some red, some blue, some violet, some even green, all clad in gaudy raiment and all endeavouring to arouse male desires by lifting their dresses. Men walked up and down inspecting the wares and haggled until they had struck a bargain, when a couple would descend a few steps into a room below street level and perform on a mattress on the floor regardless of any onlookers. Having had enough of this unsavoury spectacle, Evans said that he would take us to more salubrious places. We went to Angela's where Angela, the madame, called upon Fawzia, a lithesome young lady to display her snake-like body to us, and others, no less comely. We were then taken to another house of easy virtue, which was formerly the harem of a wealthy merchant of Baghdad. It was built round a courtyard and a garden, with orange trees and a pool with an illuminated fountain against which gazelle-eyed houris stood and strode so that one could see through the diaphanous pantaloons that alone covered their nether limbs.

The next day was a day of rest for the drivers and Rattan and I set off in his jeep to Babylon, driving most of the way through a sandstorm. As we approached the city one could see that Sennacherib had exaggerated only slightly when he threatened to destroy Babylon so that 'the location of the city and of the temples of the gods would be seen no more'. We stood on the banks of the Euphrates and I could hear, in my mind, the words of the psalmist, and repeated them to Rattan to whom they were new: 'By the waters of Babylon, there we sat down, yea, we wept when we remembered Zion. We hanged our harps upon the willows . . .' And here was I, by the waters of Babylon, knowing how they had felt. We entered the disembowelled city through the gap where stood the Ishtar Gate, once covered in blue-green glazed tiles, with bulls and horses and dragons in relief, that had been stripped by German excavators, and which I was to see, years later, reassembled in a museum in Berlin.

I remembered how old Sarah Harries had told us, in Sunday School, about a bright young boy among the captives, called Daniel, who had interpreted the dream of Nebuchadnezzar, and had made sense of the writing, *Mene, mene, tekel u-pharsin*, that had appeared upon the wall of the palace at Belshazzar's feast, for which Belshazzar commanded that he be clothed in scarlet with a gold chain about his neck, just like our mayor, my child mind thought. The satraps became jealous, and Daniel was thrown in the lion's den, with a stone placed over the mouth of the pit, somewhere near where I was now standing. Ahead lay the great processional way built by Nebuchadnezzar, along which he returned in triumph so many times during his reign of forty successful years and along here in 587 BC, after the sacking of Jerusalem, he led the captive Jews. Away to the right were the Hanging Gardens of Babylon, one of the seven wonders of the world, which he had built to make his country bred wife feel more at home. I looked at the desolation around me and thought of the time when the valleys of the Tigris and Euphrates were so closely settled that it was said that a cock that crew in Mosul would be heard, seven hundred miles away, in Basra.

Babylon only came into full flower during the reign of Hammurabi, who died in about 1750 BC. Literature and science, algebra and astrology flourished then, and Hammurabi coded the laws, as Hywel Dda was to do in Wales a couple of millennia later. On a six foot phallus of black diorite, thirty-four columns of cuneiform writing proclaimed two hundred and fifty laws dealing with most aspects of life, including the law on retaliation: 'If a seignior has destroyed the eye of a member of the aristocracy, they shall destroy his eye', a sentiment that finds an echo in the law of Moses. The phallus was no longer there, but I was able to see it, years later, in the Louvre in Paris. Hammurabi built a great stepped tower, or ziggurat, which was destroyed and rebuilt more than once and which appears in the book of *Genesis* as the Tower of Babel to illustrate the confusion of languages. It was now no more than a stump in a hole in the ground.

The unit drove out of Baghdad across a pontoon bridge before six o'clock in the morning, as people were crossing the Tigris in *qufas* that looked like giant coracles. We travelled along a rough road through Baqubah and Kharnabat and Shahnaban, and came to Qizil Ribat, an unexpectedly pretty village with a tree-lined street. The Jebel Hamrin looked just like the hills of Judea, but the going was stiffer and, to add to our troubles, we were greeted by a sandstorm as we entered Khaniqin, with its rail terminus sign posted Khaniqin City. Here I received orders to carry on beyond Tehran and I was already beginning to get worried as to how I would return, as I had no money or any form of identification, having left everything in Jerusalem. Major Sharpe, the DAQMG (Ops) at Khaniqin offered to lend me money, or to arrange for me to travel back to Haifa on a Nairn Transport bus that ran weekly along the Haifa-Baghdad route, but I could accept neither as I had to go on. Captain Jeffries, the NAAFI officer, let me have a case of whisky, which immediately elevated me to the status of a deity in the eyes of the American officers. Wiseheart found a place for it in the heat-stroke waggon, and guarded it as though it were a Wells Fargo consignment of gold bars.

We crossed the frontier into Iran early one morning and instantly felt that we were in a different country. The men were no longer clad in colourful, sweeping clothes but wore dark grey suits and dark grey, or black, flat caps, and they all looked as woebegone and wretched as their raiment. Police and soldiery wore sinister German-style uniforms, so slovenly as to give a bedraggled appearance. The Shah's attempt to Westernise his people had not been a success.

Iran, or Persia as it was until 1935, was ruled by shahs, or kings, of the Qajar dynasty from the end of the eighteenth century until Sultan Ahmed Shah was deposed in 1921 when there was a military coup led by Colonel Reza Khan, commander of the Cossack Brigade, who made himself prime minister in 1923 and, in 1926, was crowned Reza Shah Pahlevi. He was pro-German and in 1941 he had to abdicate and his son, Mohammed Reza Pahlevi, ascended the Peacock Throne as his successor. The young Shah introduced extensive social reforms but the religious fundamentalists protested against the 'Western-style decadence' and he was forced to leave the country in 1979 when Ayatollah Khomeini proclaimed an Islamic Republic.

Beyond Kachal Kachal there was no sun any more, and dark mountains looked down upon us from either side, and glowered like Snowdonia on a thunder-laden day. It shone momentarily as we came to Qasr Shirin as though it wanted to remind us that this was the palace of Shirin, 'the loved one' of Khosru Parvis II, king of Persia in the sixth century. But she had fallen in love with Farhad, the architect of Taq-i-Bustan, whom Khosru, in a jealous fury, had hurled to his death from a high rock. Beneath the mountains of Sunbula Kuh, at Sar-i-Pul, there were green fields in which hollyhocks grew and, as we approached the Paytak Pass, there were shepherds in sheepskin coats with false sleeves that fell to the ground. At Shahabad, with its Persian gardens and forests of poplars, we met a mile-long convoy of empty lorries marked 'Aid to Russia: UKCC'.

We halted at noon at Chehar Zabad, a name signifying 'four walls' as it lay in a hollow, with mountain peaks on four sides. We set up camp there for the night but Major Dunn and I, with an escort, went ahead to get some provisions at Kermanshah, beneath the snow-capped peak of Kuh-i-Parau. This was evil country, the ideal location for brigands, which led Dunn to talk about 'stickups' and 'hijackings' as we travelled along. As he did so, I saw two armed men hurtling down the craggy slope towards us. Dunn swiftly grabbed his gun and fired in their direction, which stopped the bandits in their tracks and made them disappear among the rocks.

It was cold when we left Chehar Zabad in the early light. Sheep appeared on the road, and their fat tails jitterbugged as they ran ahead of us. At Taq-i-Bustan we halted and went to see some carvings in a huge cave: one of the enthronement of Khosru II in 590 AD, and another of the investiture of Ahuva Mazda Shapur in 310 AD and of his successor, Ardashir II in 380. An inscription in Pahlevi recorded that Shapur was the 'king of Iran and Aniran'.

At Bisitun, beneath images of Darius and of the nine kings whom he had vanquished, was written in cuneiform: *I am Darius, the Great King, King of Kings, King of the Nations, son of Hystaspas the Archaemenid.* After crossing the Zagros Mountains we came to the plain of Sehneh, where a river disappeared into the floor of a mountain valley. On every side there were acres of white poppies in bloom, shortly to provide a rich harvest for the opium pickers, but for mile after mile we saw no sign of human habitation. By the time we crossed the Bidisuk Pass we were in need of water but failed to get any at Hamza'abad and had to wait until we reached Kangavar, a city of the Medes with its sixth century temple to Anahita, goddess of fertility. We then came to Hamadan, the Hagmatana of the Persians and Ecbatana of the Greeks, the chief city of Darius and of his son Xerxes, whose names are perpetuated in *gange-nane*, or treasure-writing, high on the rock faces.

Seven of us packed into an American Jeep to see the sights of Hamadan under the direction of Colonel Tilley, the commandant of 'Camp Park'. He took us to the fort of Darius, which was merely a mound which the driver of the jeep mounted without realising how steep were its walls, so that we were nearly thrown out of the vehicle. It was here that Darius III made his last stand against Alexander the Great. Mount Elevend rose 12,000 feet above us and although it was the month of May, snow clung to its upper slopes. We were taken to a carpet-making factory where women and children sat on suspended planks weaving huge carpets in the traditional patterns. The factory manager pointed to one and said it was the biggest carpet they had ever made: it had taken six years to weave it for a hotel in Turkey at a cost of £400! We made a pilgrimage to the grave of Esther, who had been chosen by Ahasuerus in place of the disobedient Vashti, and the tomb of her uncle Mordechai, who was taken captive in Jerusalem and had brought her to the king's notice. Esther had saved her people from the wrath of the king, and had caused their persecutor, Haman, to be taken to the gallows, in celebration of which the Jews eat 'Haman's Ears', little triangular cakes, at the feast of Purim. The tombs were in a small synagogue and were similar to those of Abraham and his family in Hebron. An ancient rabbi reverently showed me a torah inscribed on parchment the colour of his sun-tanned face.

I left the Americans at Hamadan and had a farewell drink with the Dunns and Wiseheart. Colonel Dunn thanked me for all I had done for them and paid me the highest tribute possible by saying that he would have liked to have me as one of his officers. I went on to Tehran, with two British officers, but we had not got far before we found our passage impeded by droves of tortoises crossing the road, as toads do in this country. Although there appeared to be reasonable rainfall, judging by the verdure of the grass and the trees, the bed of the Qara Chai was dry as a wadi, and one could only assume that it awaited the melting of the snow, which was thick as we crossed the Aveh Pass and, in my summer kit, I felt the cold.

The roads parted at Takestan, one leading to Tabriz and Tbilisi and the other to Tehran. We came to a frontier post flanked by high pillars painted in bands of blue and white, and each surmounted by a red flag, and there were Russian soldiers on guard. It was a sight that filled one with dread. Captain McRae, one of my companions, was able to speak Russian and had travelled the route before, and he explained to the officer in charge of the guard that I had brought the 1st USAAF as far as Hamadan for the purpose of helping the Russians on the eastern front and was now proceeding to Tehran on urgent business. I still feared in case he should ask to see my papers and, as I did not have any, I had visions of being detained as a spy, possibly never to be heard of again. He eyed me suspiciously, I felt, and even when he allowed us through with a twist of his thumb, his eyes never left mine as we moved away. We all three breathed a great sigh of relief. From there on, all road signs had been removed, and we were in unknown territory. We knew, however, that the next town was Qasvin, a town teeming with green copper domes, and along its streets were carts drawn by horses wearing yokes. Russian soldiers spending their off-duty hours walked aimlessly among the native population. We then travelled along the foothills of the Elburz Mountains until we came to Tehran, lying in the shadow of Mount Demavend, that rose to 18,600 feet into the snows.

I went in search of the Q (Movement and Transportation) office to enquire about a return journey and to ask the officer there to get in touch with Joyce in Jerusalem, as I had no other way of establishing my identity. When I got there I saw that the officer in charge was a man named Pritchard whom I had known at college and he was able to obtain a lift for me in an American aircraft to Cairo the following day. After dinner at the Q (Mov & Tn) Mess, I was taken to see the sights of Tehran by some of the officers. Russian troops ambled along the cobbled streets, unable to afford the high price of even the meanest comestibles, let alone drink. I was taken to the Miami Club and other night spots, and everywhere we went we drank vodka, as all other drinks were of a prohibitive price. Those who could not afford even vodka had to resort to a concoction that was described merely as 'wood-alcohol', which drove its imbibers out of their minds. The town was heavily patrolled by British and Russian military police, and we all had to be off the streets before eleven o'clock as a curfew had been imposed on account of an attempt on the life of the Shah.

Tehran had an unfinished appearance. Buildings were half-finished, a spade pushed into a heap of mortar was fixed there for all time, and a wheelbarrow rested tipped on its side for ever in another heap. Everyone had downed tools at some precise moment, when the old Shah had abdicated, I was told. Water ran down open ditches, or *jubes*, each side of the street. Women were washing clothes in one of these ditches, apparently unaware that a dead horse lay in it further up the street, with its legs in the air.

I left Tehran in a DC3. There were nineteen of us aboard the plane which had been stripped of everything, and a wooden bench had been fixed along each side of the fuselage. We rose rapidly above the Elburz and looked out on the snow-clad summit of Mount Demavend. The absence of any form of insulation lowered the temperature to freezing point, and I was glad that I had brought by greatcoat.

Among those on the plane were Frances Cassard and Martha N. Adison who had been entertaining the American troops. The cold was so intense that they asked to be cuddled, and Frances said that I was the first British officer she had ever met and asked me to write my name on a ten rial note. The temperature improved as we flew over Kermanshah and Baghdad. We landed for an hour at Habbaniyah but were given no sustenance, and when we got in the air again we struck considerable turbulence. We flew over Amman, and over the Dead Sea as the pilot was seeking permission to land me at Lydda. I pointed out Jericho and Jerusalem to the others, and the pilot offered me a parachute to float down on the Holy City as he was not allowed to land at Lydda. We had a buffeting again as we crossed the Sinai Desert, and we landed at Cairo at four o'clock in the afternoon. Within half an hour I had found a flight to Lydda where I landed two hours later. I explained to the authorities there the reason I had no papers or permit to land, but they were not prepared to accept my explanation and started to make out an order for my detention as a suspect character. I then asked them to telephone the Movements Officer responsible for my travel, giving them Joyce's office number and her maiden name, so as not to arouse suspicion of collusion, hoping that she would be on duty. She quickly sensed that I was in trouble and issued an order for my immediate release and, for once in her life, told a lie by adding that the Colonel was waiting to see me on an urgent matter. They let me go but warned me that there was no military transport to Jerusalem that evening and pointed out that it would be unsafe to walk. I had no option, however, and had walked about four kilometres, almost as far as Ramle before a vehicle came along. It was a lorry carrying a load of oranges, but the cab was full and the driver said that I could have a lift to Jerusalem if I did not mind sitting on top of the load. This I gladly did, and as I had not eaten anything since dawn, I helped myself to some of the fruit. I then made myself a bed by rearranging the oranges and slept most of the way to Jerusalem.

Having managed to get back from Tehran earlier than expected I thought that I would be justified in taking a few days' French leave. We called on the Beilins and found Moshe Shertok there full of tales about his recent visit to Naples, where he had seen Anna. I had been home only a day, however, when a message came from GHQ, Cairo, to report urgently to AG 3, and I went off on the afternoon train. I travelled with two South African officers who were gold-diggers. One spoke of the danger from lions where he lived, but of the greater danger he expected from the black people after the war.

On arrival in Cairo I found that I had been posted to GSI 12 and started work the next morning at GHQ, under Colonel Russell, who, unlike the run of superior officers, told me that it was his policy to make life as easy and informal as possible for us all. I had feared to mention that Joyce was in Jerusalem in case, true to Army tradition, I would be posted to Algiers or Aleppo, but Russell comforted me by saying that he had already sent a signal to Chick Nathan to say that I would be at GHQ. He furthermore said that he would endeavour to get me to Palestine as soon as an opportunity arose.

I had dinner that evening with Evan John who was writing a book that appeared after the war under the title *Time in the East*. The dust jacket claimed that 'Evan John is worth meeting because of himself' and that he had written 'one of the most diverting and satisfying books that the war has incidentally made possible.'

Part of my work was to scrutinise letters that could contain coded messages, or could be regarded as suspicious in any way and, in so doing, I came across some amusing, and some strange, communications. One young officer wrote to his mother: 'I don't know where I've been. I don't know where I am. I don't know where I'm going. Because I've been reading Security Regulations.' An Army cook wrote to his wife to say that he was in trouble because he had prepared a meal for 27 dancers instead of the 27th Lancers. A soldier wrote to Professor Fleming to ask if the newly invented penicillin would cure his wife's cystitis, which had prevented him enjoying his conjugal rights. A South African officer complained that he had had his 'marbles caught in a Claxon horn', which had caused him considerable pain. Many of the letters were simply crude and basic, arising out of sexual frustration, and some contained tufts of pubic hair or semen, but most envisaged the first night of their reunion. There was invariably a touch of sadness in them, because they were written by people whose one ambition was to return home to their loved ones. An officer writing from Italy to his wife who had upbraided him for wanting a son, confessed that his 'dream of having a Little Michael was born in a slit trench at the bottom of Monastery Hill under enemy fire.' Another, also from Italy, wrote to his wife:

> I was leaning against what remained of a wall of a house when a dirty and ragged little girl found courage to approach me and give me a gardenia. I gave her a tin of food. So out of place amid such scenes of devastation. With the flower in my hand, I read your letter . . . I then placed the gardenia in the little girl's hair. Silly, wasn't it? For no one knew what was in my mind.

We also had to censor sensitive cables, even to members of the royal family. One, from my friend, Frank Pynor, to his girl friend, Bathsheva, was scrutinised presumably because he, as a British officer in India, as he now was, was sending a cable to a Jewish girl in Jerusalem. I have no idea why a cable addressed to Montgomery and signed 'Abdullah of Transjordan' should have come to us. Every soldier swore constancy to his wife, although there was the story of the fellow who confessed that he had met a beautiful Arab maiden and wanted a divorce so that he could marry her, and when the indignant wife sent a cable asking: 'What has she got that I haven't?' he replied: 'Nothing, but she's got it here.'

African troops wrote letters that were so similar in content that one was driven to think that they had been written for them by the regimental scribe. The prime ambition of each man was to go to bed with a white woman, and they all claimed that they had succeeded in doing so, usually with a British nurse. The letter was to be read out by the chief at a tribal gathering and the writer would expect to be greeted, at his homecoming, with a hero's welcome.

Evening entertainment, in the main, was limited to cinemas and café crawling. The nearest thing to a pub was Tommy's Bar, and there was also Mannering's Bar in which a plaque hanging on the wall stated that:

> Mannering's is dedicated to those merry souls of other days who again will making drinking a pleasure, who achieve contentment long before capacity and who, whatever they may drink, prove able to carry it, enjoy it, and remain gentlemen.
>
> – *Mannering's Bar, Cairo.*

The most exciting form of entertainment was to be found at Doll's Cabaret, or at Madame Badia's, both of which featured belly-dancing in the main. The excitement reached a peak at Madame Badia's one evening, when a *suffragi* shot an Egyptian officer over the favours of one of the belly-dancers. The pit, immediately below the stage where the performances took place, was occupied each night by *fellahin*, who masturbated freely at the sight and proximity of the girls.

Loaded Cairo trams were as closely packed as a tin of pilchards, and passengers clung to, and hung out of, the sides so that each tram looked like a branched tree moving noisily along the *sharias*. Every Friday the streets were cleared for the entourage taking King Farouk to the mosque, with an escort of red cars and red motor bicycles closely guarding the royal Rolls Royce.

The quality of his Government was indicated in a report that appeared in the *Egyptian Gazette* stating that Deputy Haroun had been expelled from the Senate because he could not read or write. Three weeks later, a law was enacted decreeing that illiterate Egyptian men under the age of forty-five would have to attend a course of instruction.

There were ingenious Egyptians, however, as the old *fellah* who came in to Cairo from the country seeking somewhere safe to invest his life savings discovered. Sitting outside a café in the Muski, he got into conversation with a townsman in whom he confided. 'It was undoubtedly the will of Allah,' said the man, 'that you should have come to this very café where you would find me, for I am the best person in Cairo to advise you on such matters. Now, come with me.' He took the peasant for a ride on the tram that ran from the city to Heliopolis and, after a while, he said: 'Now, you see that man collecting money from the passengers? He is the conductor. If you were to buy this tram, the conductor would be collecting the money for you and would bring it to you at the end of the day.' The *fellah* was convinced and handed over his savings to the trickster believing that he would buy the tram for him, and was only disillusioned when, at the end of the day, the conductor would not give him the money he had collected. The next morning there was a sign outside Ezbekiah Gardens, in the centre of the city, inviting members of the public, for a modest fee, to come to see the man who had been tricked into investing his life-savings in a municipal tram. The following day the *Egyptian Mail* reported that the man on view at Ezbekiah Gardens, whom thousands of people had paid their piastres to see, was not the stupid *fellah* at all but an impostor.

When I was in Tehran, my friend Graham Johns of Manorowen called at my office in Jerusalem and Asad put him in touch with Joyce whom he took to dinner at Hesse's. A few weeks later I met him in the doorway of the Continental-Savoy Hotel at Cairo and we had an evening full of reminiscences together. The following morning, he set off for Italy where, within a few days, he was badly wounded.

The last of the letters I was to receive from D. J. Williams while I was still in the Middle East was written 'on a July morning when the clouds were full of rain and the trees and the grass heavy with dew, and the croak of a raven forecast more wet weather, and behold,' he wrote, 'I am sitting at a low table in Form II keeping half an eye on the little boys and girls sitting their examinations.' He had first written soon after I had arrived in Jerusalem saying 'Of all the good and faithful students I ever had under me in Form VI, you were the quickest, cleverest and truest of them all, without mention of the missionary expeditions we undertook together, in which I appreciated your company so much. Your present experience in the Army will be of great help to you one day, as Wales is expecting a great deal from you, and those like you, when you return from this present insane business.' In another letter he wrote: 'It is my heartfelt wish that I could be free of my chains and escape back to the old neighbourhood that my heart has never left for even one moment, and there be left alone to draw, like the spider, upon the web of my imagination and, I hope, weave tales. I have three more years before I have the right to a bit of a pension.' He felt that I had shown 'originality and imagination' in arranging to convey greetings in Welsh from Bethlehem on Christmas Day on behalf of the Welsh forces serving in Palestine. 'That is doing something new in history,' he wrote and added: 'I have heard the bells of Bethlehem at Christmas before, but to hear Dillwyn's voice from there would cause a far greater stir within me, speaking in the old tongue from the most sacred spot in the world!'

He had been to Newport to see my mother and wrote: 'She looked like a princess,' he said, 'but like every other mother, praying for the day when this mad undertaking comes to an end.' On another occasion he admitted that he should have written long ago, and meant to do so, 'for you are one of those people that crosses my mind frequently, frequently. And if I had written to you each time I thought about you during the last few weeks, you would have a tidy package of letters.' He and Siân were most grateful for the Hebrew-English calendar I had sent them and which miraculously had arrived on Christmas morning. In his next letter he apologised for a delay in replying to mine, but went on to assure me that 'there is hardly a day that goes by without my thinking about you in some way or another and I comfort myself . . . by believing that these mental messages serve their purpose just as effectively as if they had been sent visually in ink on paper . . . Tonight, then, having read about old Moses in the book of Exodus, after coming home from the chapel service, and before commencing a new chapter in one of Berdyaev's books, here is a letter to you.' He went on to say that he, too, was 'a Bolshi, or something of the kind, at the end of the First War, and for some years afterwards,' but, like Berdyaev, he had turned his back on Communism. It was the time of the School Certificate examinations and he remembered my ordeal having to sit them so soon after my father's sudden death. 'But you came through, more than a conqueror. You are a rare exception, Dillwyn, but few are those pupils who, after they leave school, remain steadfast in the faith for any length of time. They find it easier to find enthusiasm for anything rather than Wales.'

He wrote with great delight to say that they had heard my broadcast, on Christmas Day and he and Siân were most pleasantly surprised to hear me send greetings to them. 'I cannot really tell you how we felt – perhaps as though the King had sent us a prepaid wire to come to breakfast the following morning,' and he thanked me profusely for remembering them both 'in so elevating a manner.' His letter went on to say that they had seen photographs of the wedding and that Joyce looked 'as lovely and natural as though she had been brought up within sight of Carn Ingli' and added that I had 'always had the eye of an artist.'

Rumours of an allied invasion of France began to reach us in Cairo on D-day itself and an account of a landing near Caen was confirmed by Reuters, and by the German radio where the announcer said: 'This is D-day. We will now play some music for the invasion forces!' From the Russian front came news of a shuttle bombing that was being carried out from one end by the 1st United States Army Air Force.

I was delighted to be told that I had been posted to GSI 12, Haifa, and caught a train there that day. My office there was near the port, above a coffee shop, so that the aroma of freshly ground coffee floated in through the window all day long. Once Joyce heard that I was to go to Haifa, she applied for a posting there. We, therefore, spent most of our leave packing and preparing to vacate the flat in Gaza Road. In Haifa, we found accommodation at the Pension Zirker-Tuch-Hammerslag that was situated in a little glen on Mount Carmel and in the heart of the country. The valley was full of bird song in the daytime and, at night, the paths through the pine woods were bright with glow-worms, but it was also the home of a family of jackals that kept us awake with their chilling chorus. After a while, we moved to the Grand Hotel Nassar, which backed on to the harbour and, after dinner each evening we would retire to the roof and watch the movement of ships. Large vessels came and went, and destroyers streaked across the bay at fantastic speeds. Ack-ack guns regularly shook the neighbourhood and tracer shells fired from Acre formed arcs of light across the sky and appeared to bounce on the water, while Verrey lights shot across them and searchlights sent blue pencils of light to sweep the purple sky. Whenever an air-raid siren sounded, the destroyers would leap into action and make out to sea; barrage blimps shot upwards and stood silver in the sky: one broke loose, and went up until it burst and fell flopping down, like a shot bird. Guns raised their probing fingers and searched the heavens for an enemy plane. One evening the sky was red, not from the setting sun, but because another oil tanker had been hit by the enemy and was burning furiously beyond the horizon.

One of my colleagues at Haifa was Captain John Gladstone, KOSB, son of Sir Hugh Steuart Gladstone of Capenoch, Penpont, whose boyhood visits to Hawarden had furnished him with a surprising repertoire of Welsh hymns and melodies. Another colleague was Captain Alfred Downey, a native of Chester-le-Street who had spent most of his life in darkest Africa where, as a young man, he had been shooting lions with the great big-game hunter Frederick Courtenay Selous, whom Rider Haggard is said to have taken as his model for Allan Quatermain. He believed in theosophy, a belief derived from Buddhism and Brahminical mysticism, and belonged to the Theosophical Society, founded by Madame Blavatsky, and he would bring me copies of her writings to study. I suspected that he thought that I knew something about the creed because he heard me mumble to myself the incantation of the Buddhists, *Om mani pad mehoum.*

I went to a meeting of the Haifa Welsh Society and was asked to address the following meeting when I spoke on *Undeb Cymru Fydd*, with Dr Colenso Jones in the chair.

Padre J. R. Lloyd Thomas, who was later to become Principal of St David's College, Lampeter, brought me a package from Cairo which contained the poems that had been submitted for the 'Eisteddfod of Egypt' which I had agreed to adjudicate. I was unable to attend the Eisteddfod and saw an account in the *Egyptian Mail* and discovered that the prizes for the sonnet, the lyric and the humorous poem had all been won by W. J. Jones, Caernarfon, and there was a picture of Lieut-Colonel D. D. Lloyd Evans, ACG, being chaired for his ode, *Y Pyramidiau.*

Through the Beilins and the Chiziks, we already had some Jewish friends in Haifa, who were all extremely kind to us. When Mino heard that I had been posted to Haifa, he telephoned all over the place until he found me. He arrived on a Sunday morning and we gave him lunch at the Nassar. He had brought a bottle of John Haigh with him and called for three glasses, which no one at the hotel ventured to refuse, or charge corkage. He then took us to call on his friend, Shabatai Levy, the Mayor of Haifa, and to see his sister, and her husband who was a solicitor, LLB (London). We had dinner at the home of Mino's old friend, Josef Ermann. Josef regaled us with tales of his adventures with Mino, and especially about the trip they made to Romania. Mino had called on him when he was preparing to leave for that country and he had, jokingly, asked Mino if he would like to accompany him. Mino made no reply but lifted the telephone and told Marianne that he was going to Romania. When they got to Bucharest, they called on Queen Marie, whom Mino had conducted round Galilee on her visit to the Holy Land, and were warmly received and royally entertained. On their return journey, Josef called at the war museum at Istanbul, but Mino stayed outside saying that he preferred to watch the swans on the Bosphorus. On a side table was a photograph of Ermann with the former Prime Minister, A. J. Balfour.

We were invited to the Ermanns every Friday evening, for *erev Shabat*, after that, and we always marvelled at Josef's fantastic tales: how the Emir of Beisan had come to release him from the vengeance of the family of an Arab notable of whose murder his brother had been accused; of how he had ridden from Izmir to Haifa, following roads built by the Romans; how Basrowi, the Agah of the Khetkhan Kurds, who claimed descent from Saladin, had wanted him to become a blood-brother to his son and had made the two of them drink the same mother's milk out of a bowl. He had tried to see the Emira Djunblatt who, after her husband had been assassinated, had ruled the Druse from her Palace at Mouktarr. He had sent her a message saying that he had found gold on her land, but all he wanted was to set eyes on the Emira who was renowned for her beauty. When he was ushered into her presence, however, he found that she was veiled.

As we were walking to the Ermanns' house, on Hadar Ha-Carmel, one evening, a sickle moon the colour of blood sank into the ocean, and Castor and Pollux, above it, left a faint silver path across the water. We left about midnight in a shower of fireflies, which Josef described as 'mosquitoes with lanterns'.

The Army had done its utmost since our marriage to keep us apart and it now proposed to send me home, leaving Joyce behind. We succeeded in defeating the proposal, however, and we were more than happy when Joyce was told by her aptly named doctor, Dr Better, on 11 September 1944, that she was on the way to motherhood.

In September I discovered that we were due to leave the Middle East on the next convoy, which was due to sail early in October. For our last weekend, we went to Jerusalem, but did not disclose to our friends the imminence of our departure. We had lunch with Richard Hughes, and took him to tea at the Café Vienna where we met Bryn and Bill Davies on their way back to Cairo from Syria. Bryn gave me a copy of his paper on Elis Gruffydd, the Soldier of Calais, and his account of the Duke of Suffolk's expedition to Montdidier in 1523.

The Beilins gave us a party one night, and the Chiziks invited us to dinner the next, as though we were on a weekend visit. We left under that pretence the following morning.

That morning, I took one long last look at Jerusalem, as though I had not looked at it enough over the past five years. For most of that time I had yearned for my home in Wales, and now here I was sad to part with a place where I had as many friends and where, despite *hiraeth* and, often, despair, I had known more happiness than ever before. I took the train to Cairo.

Joyce followed two days later, which gave us time to do some shopping and to visit friends who, on our last night, gave us a farewell dinner at Shepheards. After dinner we went out on the balcony to watch a riot that was taking place on Opera Square following the dismissal of the prime minister, Nahas Pasha, by King Farouk that day.

We boarded the train for Port Said the next morning. At Ismailia a gali-gali boy, with a chameleon on his shoulder, came on the train and demonstrated his disappearing chickens trick, which helped to pass the seven hours it took to reach our destination. The Movements Officer at Port Said, whom Joyce knew, was there to receive us. He took us aboard the troopship *Maloja*, and gave us a cabin for ourselves, saying that we were the only couple on board to be so privileged. That night, great ships came up the Canal and passed by like giant shadows. One of them was lit up overall and the troops, on their way home from India, lined the decks, singing *I'm Dreaming of a White Christmas*.

We sailed before noon the next day and passed the statue of Ferdinand de Lesseps. By the time we were out at sea we had grown into a sizeable convoy comprising, among others, the *Monarch of Bermuda*, the *Strathhaven*, *Stratheden*, *Strathmore*, *Johann von Waldheim*, the *Durban Castle* and the *Cape Town Castle*, with an escort of four destroyers. There were some familiar faces on board, including the Marquess and Marchioness of Douro, who had been married a few days before us at St George's Cathedral.

The voyage gave me a chance to catch up with my reading. On our third day at sea, when we were somewhere off Benghazi, the escort vessels fired their guns and dropped depths charges, and the convoy took a zigzag course. Swallows that had summered, perhaps in Wales, flew across our bows on their southward journey, and some birds landed for a brief while on our topgallant and bob stays. Once we passed Sicily the weather grew colder, and the sea more grey and rolling so that the destroyers regularly disappeared into the trough of a wave. Joyce, who loved the sea, was in her element as the *Maloja* pitched and rolled, and her timbers creaked.

Major Bill Wheatley, who had worked with Joyce at Jerusalem, gave her his copy of Francis Brett Young's *Pilgrim's Rest* and turned to me and said that I was 'the luckiest beggar in the world to have won the heart of the loveliest and most popular girl' he had met throughout the war.

The sea was calm again by Sunday morning, when a service was held on the deck. We sat with the Douros, whom we had avoided lest they should, in conversation, discover that we were sharing a cabin, while they had been separated like every other couple on board. We could see the Atlas Mountains for most of that day. Two ships left the convoy for Algiers, and three others joined us. A *chukar* landed on the deck so exhausted that I was able to pick it up and protect it from the ship's cat, a black monster the size of an Easter lamb. The OC Troops joined us as we watched the sunset, and told us to look out for 'the green flash', but we failed to see it. Each night we looked at the glowing phosphorescence that followed the ship, and I wondered whether an enemy aircraft would not be able to spot us in the dark. Having passed through the Straits of Gibraltar in the night, we woke to face an angry Atlantic, and a mist that made sea and air one dreary grey. In the evening we saw the flickering light of the lighthouse on Cape St Vincent. The weather deteriorated and, by the time we came to the Bay of Biscay the ship swayed like a cow's udder and shook to its timbers. For some reason unknown to us, our ship swung to starboard and left the convoy, but only to rejoin it at the rear. Someone said that we would dock at Glasgow and many people suffered from seasickness and cared not where we landed, as long as it was soon. Nerves were not soothed when we were told not to undress as we retired for the night.

BACK TO BLIGHTY

THE *MALOJA* EVENTUALLY DROPPED ANCHOR in the mouth of the Mersey. It was a Saturday and we were told that we would have to remain there until the following Tuesday, when the ship would move up to the 'pool' of Liverpool. No land was in sight, owing to a permanent mist, and all we saw were vessels of all description passing up and down on both sides. It seemed cruel, after five years abroad and having been made to come home, that we were now being kept from setting foot on our homeland. On the afternoon of the Monday, however, we weighed anchor and followed the tortuous course of the channel until we came to the Liver Building, and there we stopped for another day. The ferry boat, *Royal Daffodil II*, passed beneath our bows regularly and, each time, its passengers gave us a cheer. The ship eventually drew close to the quay, where a military band was formed to entertain us, and VAD nurses came aboard to take off the sick, the wounded and the handicapped. We tossed oranges and piastres at the band, and someone threw them a pith helmet. We watched our luggage being hoisted ashore and being laid out in an open shed, under an armed military guard.

We disembarked at seven o'clock the next morning and, when we got to Customs, I found myself alongside Downey, who had travelled on the *Stratheden*. There was no time to feel the thrill of setting foot on 'dear old blighty' as we had to dash to the station to catch the train to take us to Exmouth, to see Joyce's mother, before going on to Pembrokeshire. We shared a compartment with a Colonel Wilson who had served in Egypt until 1935 and who was glad to be brought up to date on Egyptian affairs. I offered him a cigarette, which he was loath to accept as they were on ration, but I assured him that we had plenty, and opened the case that contained them, only to find that the packet of 500 I had bought duty free had been stolen, presumably by, or under the eye of, the soldiers standing guard over our luggage the previous evening.

A thick mist prevented us from having a grand view of the countryside, but it was exciting to be passing through the stations of Crewe and Shrewsbury, Hereford and Pontypool, the first place on Welsh soil, Bristol and Taunton. We took a taxi from Exeter to Exmouth, and arrived there at seven in the evening, and met Joyce's mother, Julia, and invalid brother, Kenneth. Kenneth, who had a promising career as an artist and designer, had been struck by a rare disease which had an effect similar to progressive muscular atrophy. He had been seen by leading world specialists, including one in Romania which had been arranged through his father's contact with King Carol, but to no avail, though it was said that a remedy could be found were money not more urgently required to find a cure for cancer. His passion for the sea had been met, in part, by the purchase of *Tornado*, a vessel beached among the fishermen's cottages on The Point at Exmouth, and converted into a comfortable residence. Swans and their cygnets came to the garden wall and great rafts of wildfowl sailed past the house.

Julia was the daughter of Colonel Robert Lacey Johnson, officer commanding the Canadian Mounted Heavy Artillery Brigade. *The Standard*, of Montreal, on 1 May 1915, gave an account of his funeral which was carried out with full military honours, with representatives of all Canadian regiments taking part. A saluting party of three hundred men with arms reversed escorted the coffin, draped in the Union Jack, on a gun carriage, which was preceded by a waggon bearing the floral tributes, and followed by his charger. The band of the Heavy Brigade led the procession and the pall-bearers were the former commanding officers of the Grenadier Guards, the Highland Regiment, and the 65th Regiment. He was buried at Mount Royal cemetery, where a volley was fired over his grave and the Last Post sounded. The paper carried a photograph of the Colonel, in full dress uniform, and several photographs of the cortège and committal, with captions in English and in French.

After a few days at Exmouth we set off for Pembrokeshire by car. We stopped briefly at Carmarthen to buy flowers for mother. Meeting her after an absence of five years, and bringing her a daughter-in-law whom she had never seen, was a moment of intense emotion, which found relief in warm caresses and a flow of tears. Old Uncle Tom hovered around, not knowing how to meet the situation.

For the next few days I took Joyce to meet old friends and relatives, and to visit the places of my boyhood. We called at Hendre, to see Aunt Bess and her husband, J. O. Vaughan, who thoroughly approved of Joyce, saying that she looked like Princess Elizabeth. We frequently called to see Aunt Bess and invariably had to stay for tea, or supper, while she and I talked tirelessly of our family history. We had tea at Cotham Lodge where John's father took me to the billiard room and told me about John's unfortunate marriage to Daphne.

With Dr Dai Havard and his wife, Iris, we went to The Sailors Safety at Pwllgwaelod where we received a loud and hearty welcome from the landlord, Arthur B. Duigenan. He showed me a letter I had sent him from Jerusalem, which he had pinned to the door leading in to the bar. He told me that his wife, Jim, had died and that he had married 'Little Loisie', one of the maids, who was anything but little. Paddy, the Irish wolfhound, was still there, however, in complete occupation of one of the settees. The drinks were on the house to celebrate my return, and to welcome Joyce, 'the Little Lady'. As there were no other customers he joined us in a meal, of duck and green peas, and brought out one of his finest Burgundies. We also went with Dai and Iris to have dinner at the Webley Hotel at Poppit and found the dining room still hung with the antlers of sable and other antelopes which Dr Hurst, whom I had met in Cairo, had shot in Africa. Dai was full of tales of wartime Newport, some to do with the Home Guard and others relating to a lady, known as Dirty Sal, who had entertained the American GI troops stationed at Maenclochog to such an extent that Newport had been put out of bounds to all GI's.

We went to St David's Cathedral for the enthronement of the Bishop, David Prosser, as Archbishop of Wales in the presence of all the other Welsh bishops, and after the service we called at the Grove Hotel where Winnie was still behind the bar, though more than a little ravaged by the years.

We had dinner with D. J. Williams and Siân at their house, the former *Bristol Trader* at Fishguard, when D.J. spoke entertainingly about his Jewish fellow prisoners, Tannenbaum and Pinkus, at Wormwood Scrubs. He said that he would consider retiring next year so that he could go back to his native 'square mile' at Rhydcymerau, but Siân reminded him that they did not have a car and that he had not even visited the area for a long time. As we had some spare petrol coupons we took them on a round trip, and I was more than rewarded to see D.J.'s delight in returning to his old haunts. On another occasion, when we were there for tea, Waldo Williams arrived at the house. He was on holiday from Pwllheli, where he was teaching at the time. He knew of my movements and said that he had seen my letter pinned in the bar at the Sailors Safety. Siân said that she did not know that he frequented public houses but he was quick to reply that he had enjoyed the mince pies he had had there with the tea.

We called to see Grandma's house and found it much as it was when I last saw it, for Uncle Tom had virtually closed it down, and sensibly, had gone to live with Mother. The Welsh oak dresser, still shining, was laden with the same jugs, lustre and otherwise, and the clock ticked and struck the hour, for Tom had wound it regularly every week. But there was no fire and it was cold, as I had never known it.

I took Joyce for a walk over the cliffs to Aber Rhigian and saw a sad sight. The pebbles had been removed, to provide a foundation for Brawdy airfield, even though there was an inexhaustible supply of such pebbles at nearby Newgale. I felt angry that the valley had been exploited by a speculating Cardiff solicitor, who had purchased Feidrgaregog Farm and had endeavoured to close Cwm Rhigian to the public. The place was littered with the rusting skeletons of the machinery employed in removing the stones, and the remains of a hideous summerhouse stood neglected on the river bank. The valley itself was unspoilt. We walked breast-high in bracken to the hazel tree copse.

I invited Joe Williams, the clerk of the Newport Parish Council, to go with me to the valley, to see where the course of the river had been diverted over the footpath and strands of barbed wire placed across it. The map that I had prepared under the provisions of the Rights of Way Act 1932, when I was clerk, was produced as evidence of the existence of the footpath down the length of the valley. and the Chairman of the Cemaes Rural District Council came and cut the barbed wire.

I attended the Court Leet for the installation of the rector, the Rev. Jeffrey Jones as Mayor in succession to Alderman E. R. Gronow, both of whom spoke kind words about my service overseas and Alderman Gronow referred to the correspondence that I had maintained with him during that period.

The alderman and burgesses gathered outside the Llwyngwair Arms on the following Sunday morning in order to parade to church for the civic service. As it was a bitterly cold morning, some of us were admitted to the bar for a little medicinal whisky, despite the Sunday closing law. The mayor became rector again and conducted the service. At the stroke of eleven o'clock, we observed the two minutes' silence. After the service we paraded to the Memorial Hall, the ex-servicemen wearing their medals, and there another service was held and another two minutes' silence observed and wreaths laid at the 1914-18 war memorial in the hall. Old Stone, the postman, an Englishman who came to Newport after the Great War, his red hair now grey and wearing a chest-full of medals, stepped forward and, as a member of the British Legion, mumbled a brief oration. A uniformed bugler sounded the Last Post and the Reveille. The congregations of the three chapels had also made their way to the hall and, after the united service, I met the Rev. Frank Lee, of Bethlehem Baptist Chapel who said: 'So you are that Dillwyn Miles I've heard so much about.

A letter came from the Palestine Government saying that they understood that I was no longer in that country and that they would send my papers to the Colonial Office if I wished to return as an Assistant District Commissioner. The War Office sent Form AFO 1669, stating that I had served 1,457 days in the Army, whereas more than 1,900 days had gone by since I signed my attestation papers. I received a letter from the War Office asking me to appear before a Selection Board in London at noon that day. I rang the Adjutant who told me to wait until I had another call, which came within two days. I caught a night train and arrived at Paddington at half past six in the morning and, after having a shave and breakfast at the Great Western Hotel, I walked to Marble Arch. In

Oxford Street I saw the damage caused by a V2 bomb the previous night: many people had been killed and a taxi had been blown into the middle of Selfridges. I went to No. 39 Frognal, a house in which Pavlova had lived, by noon to meet the Board, which comprised a Lieutenant Colonel in the VIIIth Hussars and two Majors, one of whom I was told was a psychiatrist. They immediately took me to the Mess where we had some gin and tonic and a good lunch before I formally appeared before them. After a friendly chat, they told me that they had no job for me, unless I wanted to join an Air Photography Intelligence Unit, or take charge of a Prisoner-of-War camp, but thought that it might be better if I waited for something more suitable.

A letter from Judy Beilin found me although it was simply addressed to me at my mother's house, as 'Manora, Pembrokeshire, UK'. It said that Reggie Smith would shortly be retiring as Director of the Palestine Broadcasting Service and she wanted me to apply for the post. I had to reply that with Joyce expecting a baby, Mother and Uncle Tom being so unwell, apart from the fact that I had not been released from the Army, I regretfully could not do so. By the same post, there was a letter from Yitz Chizik to say that there was a vacancy for an Assistant District Commissioner in Jerusalem for which he wanted me to apply.

Joyce was enraptured by the beauty of the countryside, and the warmth of the people. She would have liked to settle down at Newport and so, of course, would I if I could only find some acceptable means of subsistence. She suggested that we should live at Grandma's house, and we talked about building a cottage among the trees in the depth of Cwm Dewi; we looked at the remaining storehouse on the Parrog with a view to its conversion into a dwelling, and we were tempted by a mountain cottage which had a glorious panoramic prospect over the northern slopes of the Presely Hills and the home of my forefathers. Members of the Golf Club committee asked me to consider buying the club, which I was offered for £4,000.

Herbert and Janet and Joyce and Anthony and I spent Christmas day quietly with Mother and Uncle Tom, fearing that it would be the last Christmas together. We listened to the bells of Bethlehem, and heard messages broadcast by those who were still in the Middle East.

The people of the Gwaun Valley still celebrate the New Year on the thirteenth day of January, and we were invited to the *Hen Galan* supper at Trefach Farm. The evening was spent most convivially in story telling and song and one was never allowed to empty one's mug of ale before it was filled again, so that one had no idea of the consumption. The BBC got to hear of *Hen Galan* and asked me to do a broadcast feature, which I did from Pontfaen Farm one year, and from Ffynnondici the next. Although I had no reason to think so at the time, these broadcast programmes gave publicity to the celebration, and I regretted having done them. However, some good came out of a programme I did from Pencnwc, the cottage home of Andrew Thomas and his sister Eliza. Andrew sang an old song, *Bwmba*, from his repertory of folk songs which led to him being 'discovered' as a folk singer in his late seventies. My friend Seamus Ennis came and recorded many of his songs for the BBC library. Eliza, too, made her mark by singing *Tiwn y Sol-ffa*, a mixture of tonic sol-fa notes and words which was later placed on record and became popular as a song. One *Hen Galan* night at Andrew's cottage when the place was already full of neighbours and well-wishers, some men from Fishguard arrived and, seeing that there were no more mugs available, one of them grabbed a lustre jug from the Welsh dresser and went to fill it with beer. He was very drunk and could not see that the froth rising to the surface was not the head of beer but the accumulated fluff which had gathered in the bottom of the jug. This was the jug in which Eliza had kept odd buttons and pins and when the fellow drank the beer, his mouth was full of them and he spat them out all over the floor.

I received an invitation, or more precisely a command, to call on Mallt Williams at Plas Pantsaeson. Born Alice Matilda Langland Williams, the fourth child of Dr John James Williams of Llanfeugan in the county of Brecknock in 1867, she had come under the influence of Lady Llanover and was more than a little eccentric. She espoused a number of patriotic causes and, each year, she topped the Welsh Nationalist Party's St David's Day Fund with a donation of £100. I had received letters from her in 1938 because she believed that the Ministry of Defence was about to establish a bombing school on Carn Ingli and she wanted me to rouse the people of Dyfed in defence of 'the holy mountain'. She wrote seemingly, with a stick from the hedge, with few words to a page, in a sort of pidgin Welsh. When I arrived at Pantsaeson I found that she had taken to her bed since the death of her brother, Jim, who used to go around dressed as a Welsh aristocrat of the thirteenth century, or rather his impression of one. Beside her bed was an old Irish harp which, she maintained, had been made by an Irish harp-maker in 1000 AD.

The BBC in Wales produced a series of programmes devoted to the works of war-poets called *Cerddi'r Hogiau*, and I was asked to provide a selection of my poems so that one or two might be included in one of the programmes. The producer was T. Rowland Hughes, the chaired bard, and he wrote back to say that he would like to use all the poems that I had sent him and asked if I could send him some more as he wanted to make an exception in my case and devote a whole programme to my work. I was at Exmouth when the programme was broadcast, on 12 February 1945, and although Joyce and her mother listened with me, there was no one to tell me how good or bad they sounded. Wil Ifan,

T. J. Morgan and Prysor Williams read twelve poems: *Ain Karem, Mair Wyryf* (Mary the Virgin), *Y Glaw Cyntaf* (The First Rain), *Y Glaw Olaf* (The Last Rain), *Pysgod Y Duwiau* (Fishes of the Gods), *Mamgu* (Grandmother), *Bedd y Cerddor* (The Musician's Grave), *Gŵyl Dewi 1944* (St David's Day 1944), *Ar Goll yn Sinai* (Lost in Sinai), *Cwm Rhigian* and *Breuddwyd Milwr* (A Soldier's Dream). D. J. Williams wrote in glowing terms after the broadcast, saying that he was proud of his old pupil and that the poems had *'blas y Dwyrain a thinc o hiraeth'* (the savour of the East and a touch of longing).

I was called to London again, to appear before the War Office Selection Board at the War Office, and was told by Colonel Pope, the presiding officer, that there were no suitable vacancies. I had been invited to stay the night with Leopold Schen, and his wife, and I went to meet him at his office, next to the British Museum in Great Russell Street. I had hardly entered the room when a V2 bomb landed not far away and shook the whole building, and we found that another had landed near his home, in Finchley Road, when we got there. Schen spent the evening furnishing me with news and gossip from Jerusalem, whence he had just returned. Henrietta Szold had died, and so had Annie Landau, whom I remembered as the headmistress of the Evelina de Rothschild School. Abba Eban had married an Egyptian Jewess called Suzy Ambache, in Cairo. Moyne's murderers, hanged that morning, had gone to the gallows chanting the Jew's last prayer.

The next day I had lunch with my cousin, Tudor, at Chelsea Hospital, where he was medical officer. The hospital had been founded in 1682 by Charles II, after the Duke of Monmouth, his illegitimate son by a Pembrokeshire woman, Lucy Walter, had told him that Louis XIV had built the Hotel des Invalides for maimed and elderly soldiers. In the afternoon, he took me to his home in Wimbledon to meet his wife, Lilian, his son, Peter, and his daughter, Gillian, and our mutual cousin, Muriel, daughter of father's brother James, who was married to Pascal Pardoe and lived at Hendredenny Hall, Caerffili. We returned to the hospital to spend the night and, as we arrived at the gate-house, some pensioners were celebrating the birthday of one of them with a firkin of beer and they insisted we should take a drink with them. One of them had been chauffeur to the Duke of Windsor when he was Prince of Wales and had some amusing, and revealing tales to tell about his royal master's night visits. V2 bombs made sleep well-nigh impossible, particularly after one had landed so near that the ceiling plaster fell down upon my bed.

In May 1945 I was invited to become the Labour candidate for Pembrokeshire at the General Election. The sitting member, Major Gwilym Lloyd George, had for some time held ministerial rank and had neglected his constituency. I knew little about the policies of the Labour Party and was still, nominally, a member of Plaid Cymru. I was nominated by nine of the local Labour parties, and eight other nominees had one nomination each. I was led to believe that I was the popular choice, being local and Welsh-speaking and recently out of the Army, although I was told that I must not appear in uniform at the selection conference. Only four of the nominees appeared at the conference and we had all made our speeches and answered questions and were waiting for the chosen one to be called, when a fifth arrived, breathless and dressed in the uniform of the Rifle Brigade, with cross strapped Sam Browne shining. He was Major Wilfred Fienburgh and he apologised for being late, saying that he had flown from Field Marshal Montgomery's headquarters in Hamburg. He was selected, beating me, I was told, by one vote.

I supported Fienburgh throughout the election campaign in the following July. Lord St David's and I took it in turns to preside at meetings addressed by visiting politicians, like Malcolm Stewart and D. R. Grenfell, 'father' of the House of Commons, who urged me to find another seat and told people that I was 'the most promising candidate in Wales'. Wilfred paid little regard to the local stalwarts and quickly made enemies within his own ranks, including his agent. Gwilym retained the seat but with a majority of only 168 votes and it was said that if I had been selected, my local connection would have given me the required majority and more.

D. J. Williams was furious when he heard that I had allowed my name to go forward as prospective Labour candidate, but at the same time, I received a letter from J. E. Jones, the *Plaid Cymru* secretary, inviting me to stand as the Blaid candidate for Cardiganshire. I was also asked to attend the *Blaid* summer school at Llangollen, there to meet Saunders Lewis, the president, and other *Blaid* leaders, who wanted to hear about the Jewish settlement in Palestine. I told them about the *kibbutzim* and *moshavim* and suggested that the *Blaid* should conduct an experiment by acquiring a farm and convert it into a settlement for young people so that they would not have to cross Offa's Dyke in search of work. I also explained how the Jews had set about reviving the Hebrew language, which had been dead for many centuries, save in the synagogues, and had formed specialist groups in order to coin new words for things that did not exist those centuries ago. They all said that these were marvellous ideas which they would consider carefully and would invite me to meet them again to discuss matters in greater detail. I heard nothing, and nothing was done.

The National Eisteddfod was held that year at Rhosllannerchrugog and, at the Gorsedd ceremony, the Herald Bard, Captain Geoffrey Crawshay (Sieffre o Gyfarthfa), handed me a staff and asked me to be a Marshal of the Blue Order. I was also elected a member of the Gorsedd Board, of which I was to remain a member for the next fifty years. During a concert held in the Eisteddfod pavilion on the Thursday evening, when the band of the Welsh Guards took part, with David Lloyd as soloist, a ceremony took place at which the Archdruid Crwys and the Bishop of St Asaph, on behalf of the Welsh people, extended a welcome home to those who had served in the Forces. Captain Evan Jones, Commodore of the Atlantic Fleet, and I were deputed to respond, and we were received with tumultuous applause. I found, for the first time, that it was far less of an ordeal to stand before ten thousand people than ten.

The following day, just before noon, a choral-speaking competition was interrupted by an announcement from the Eisteddfod platform that the Japanese had surrendered and that the war was over. A great silence fell upon the vast audience as Elfed, the blind poet and former archdruid, was led to a microphone on the platform. He raised his right hand and said '*Gweddïwn*', and prayed, and after praying, he gave out the hymn *Cyfamod hedd, cyfamod cadarn Duw* (Covenant of peace, the firm covenant of God) which was sung as it had never been sung before, with fervour and thanksgiving and with tears of joy. The people then dispersed and went their ways, some seeking a quiet corner where they could give vent to their feelings. The agony of six long years was over.

Nurse Price, the district nurse, strongly believed that children should be born at home. She was a stout lady, with a porcine face that concealed a devilish sense of humour. 'You can always tell a child's paternity during the first hour of its life,' she used to say, 'And I have seen the spit image of some of the leading gentlemen of this town at such times – some of them more than once!' Joyce was admitted to Cardigan Hospital, however, as the baby was overdue and I waited anxiously until he was born, at ten past four on the morning of the eleventh of May, weighing eight pounds and twelve ounces. We had decided that he should be named Anthony, because we liked the name, and Ord, after his mother's family. I sat down and started to write 'A Letter to My Son', which I never finished:

Newport, 11 May 1945, 4.45 a.m.

My dear Anthony,

Half an hour ago you raised your first cry in the hospital at Cardigan. It was ten past four in the morning, and here am I, at home, writing to you your first letter.

I write with that same sense of urgency that was upon the Children of Israel as they were leaving Egypt. For, although the war has now been over three days, I have not been allowed to discard my uniform, as an Army officer, nor am I likely to do so for some time yet. I am expecting a call every day, and in case it should come suddenly, I am writing to you now, at this moment and without delay, as I would have had to do had you been born when I was first called to war, five and a half years ago.

You have come into this world at the end of a most cruel and destructive war. There is no one who has not suffered on its account, unless they are pygmies in the Amazon or Innuit of the Arctic snows. This, if it had any, was one of its redeeming features, as there will not be an end to wars until all have suffered the pain of a young soldier's widow left with her fatherless children.

Your mother and I agonised as to whether we should give you life, in such troubled world. We have lived through years of hate and holocaust, and we have given those years of our lives in the belief that we were doing so in order that those who came after us should have a better life.

We met in Jerusalem, in the Land of Israel, the home of three of the world's great religions, and yet the scene of more bloodshed than any land. No place could give us less heart, yet there still remains, within our breasts, some of that faith in the future that we all but lost with the fall of the leaves in the autumn of 1939.

You were conceived in Jerusalem, the Holy City, in which our love for each other, your mother and I, was born, and where we got to know the true meaning of happiness. And it was on the heights of Mount Carmel, on a sunlit Sunday morning, that you gave the first sign of your existence, and there never was a more joyous day.

Anthony was christened, in water we had brought from the Jordan, at St Mary's Church at Newport on 23 July 1945, by my cousin, Binnie Vaughan, then a curate at Carmarthen and later to become Bishop of Swansea and Brecon. John Elliot Davies's mother gave a christening party for us at Cotham Lodge, and this was the last time my mother appeared in public. His godparents were John, and John Gwilym Jones of Wrexham, my best man, cousin Margaret Vaughan and Zabette Hermite, Joyce's friend in Paris. Among the telegrams we received was one from Leopold Schen stating that twenty trees had been planted in Anthony's name in the Land of Israel.

PALESTINE HOUSE

THE DAY AFTER ANTHONY WAS BORN, while I was busily engaged in attending meetings in connection with my nomination as a Parliamentary candidate, I received a letter from Sir Wyndham Deedes asking if I would care to apply for the post of National Organiser at Palestine House in London. Sir Wyndham had been awarded the Distinguished Service Order in the 1914-18 war and appointed a Commander of the Order of St Michael and St George; he had reached the rank of Brigadier-General and had been one of Allenby's brightest intelligence officers, before he became the first Chief Secretary of Palestine under the British Mandate. Palestine House had been established in order to create a better understanding of Palestine under the mandate with its commitment under the Balfour Declaration of 1917 to set up 'a National Home for the Jewish People' in that country. Its affairs were governed by a committee, under the chairmanship of Sir Wyndham, that included Viscount Cecil of Chelwood, Lord Horder, Dame Sibyl Thorndike, Sir Hubert Young, Sir Andrew McFadyean and Victor Gollancz. I appeared before them, as one of five candidates, one of whom was my old friend from Tripoli, the Reverend R. D. Grange-Bennett, now vicar of Ruislip. I was offered the post and accepted it subject to being released from the Army. Sir Wyndham wrote to the Adjutant General, and went to see an old pal at the War Office, but to no effect. Although the Army had been unable to offer me a suitable job for so many months, and despite the fact that the date of my release could not be far away, they would not let me go. In the end, I decided to move to London so as to be ready to take up the appointment on release, and also to be able to spend some time at Palestine House and to undertake some preparatory work. Two days before our move, I received a letter from the War Office stating that I had been posted to the Infantry Records Office at Warwick.

The Records Office was based at St John's House, in Warwick, a historic timbered building, which I found myself sharing with about twenty other officers drawn from various regiments. I was put up at the Officers' Club but the next day Captain Cyril Montrose, of the Royal Warwickshire Regiment, asked me if I would like to share his apartment at the Courtenay Hotel at Leamington. Cyril, or Monty as everybody called him, was a Jew who had been brought up in Birmingham, where his family had anglicised its name of Rosenberg to Montrose.

He had a cavalry moustache and occasionally wore a monocle, and we were both amused when he was approached in a London pub by a couple of American GI's who asked if they could take his photograph because they wanted to 'take a picture of a typical English gentleman!' He had been married but the marriage had not been successful. One day he invited me to lunch at Simpson's-in-the-Strand and to accompany him, afterwards, to the Law Courts where we heard his wife's uncontested application for a divorce being granted. That evening he took us, and his friend Ria, who was understudying Mary Morris at the Lyric Theatre, to dinner at the Albany, where he had a set of chambers.

Monty had previously shared the apartment with the son of a well known Midland brewer who had taken a young lady out to dinner one summer's evening and had been invited back to her home. While they were making love on the couch in the front room, the young lady sprang up and said: 'Quick! Father's coming down stairs!' He, seeing the bay window wide open, leapt through it, unaware that there was a basement area below, into which he fell and broke a leg. It turned out to be a compound fracture and he had been granted indeterminate leave, and I was invited to take his place. The other permanent residents at the Courtenay were civilian and included a brother of the Scottish painter, Sir Muirhead Bone, whose *View of St Paul's* was one of the most striking records of war devastation in London.

The work at Warwick was soul destroying in that it consisted of checking the war records of infantry officers and men, a task that could have been performed by corporals rather than by captains. My only comfort was that I was due to be demobbed in three months' time, but when I was told that my release would be deferred for three months I had no compunction in going to the MO who said that, on account of my fibrositis I was in no fit state to work and gave me fourteen days' sick leave 'to start with.' After a few days in bed I was able to move more freely and, at Sir Wyndham's suggestion, I began to set up my office at Palestine House.

Palestine House was a fine Georgian house at Number 18 Manchester Square, formerly Bentinck Square so named after the Bentincks, Dukes of Portland. It was tucked into a corner of the square, across the road from Hertford House that had been built in 1786 by the Marquess of Hertford to house the art treasures he had collected and had been enlarged by his successors in title until it passed, in 1860, into the hands of Sir Richard Wallace, since when it has been known as the Wallace Collection. The house had spacious rooms with fine Adam fireplaces. The artist Peter Ray had been engaged to do the decoration and to prepare a display of models and photographs to illustrate the activities and current developments in Palestine, and there were some busts by Oscar Nemon, who complained to me that no one bought his work.

Nemon was born in Croatia and had studied at the *Acadamie des Beaux Arts* at Brussels. He had emigrated to this country in 1939 and had been given English lessons by Sir Max Beerbohm. He came to the notice of Sir John Rothenstein, director of the Tate Gallery, and Sir Karl Parker, of the Ashmolean Museum. After the war he made statues or busts of most of the famous, including Montgomery and Eisenhower and Mountbatten, and Churchill, together with the Queen and the Queen Mother, When I visited him at his Kinnerton Studios he was working on a bust of Paul-Henri Spaak, the Premier of Belgium and first President of the United Nations Assembly. He often spoke about his life in Brussels and Vienna and told me that when he was modelling the busts of Sigmund Freud and Theodore Herzl, he had begun to appreciate the Jewish contribution to civilisation and he wanted to raise a temple of Humanities on Mount Sinai as a tribute to it by a Gentile.

When we moved to London we stayed for a few days with Joyce's father and his second wife, Ruby, in Purley. His book *Secrets of Industry* had almost been sold out in this country and had been published in the United States and in Canada, which pleased him immensely. In the first chapter, explaining why he had written the book he stated that, apart from his desire to improve the efficiency of British industry, 'other influences were at work. My son had joined the Commandos. My daughter was in an antiaircraft battery.' He congratulated me on my appointment and offered to help by introducing me to influential people and, in particular, to the leaders of industry.

Through the good offices of Leopold Schen we obtained a studio flat on the corner of Finchley Road and Lymington Road, opposite the Hampstead Library. It belonged to Mrs van Praagh whose daughter, Peggy, at that time was assistant director to Ninette de Valois at Sadler's Wells, and became celebrated as Dame Peggy van Praagh, founder of the Australian ballet.

After staying a few nights at Purley, during which time I went to see AG 7 at the War Office, asking to be given a job or else released so that I could start work at Palestine House, we took a train to Exmouth. Although we got to Waterloo in good time, the train was full and we had to travel, with Anthony in his pram, in the guard's van. Julia met us at Exeter, and told us that Japan had accepted the terms of surrender and that tomorrow would be VJ Day. We celebrated with a dinner at the Maer Bay Hotel and then went to The Strand where the people of Exmouth were singing and dancing in the street and, at the appointed hour, a huge bonfire was lit. I quietly recalled my memory of the burning of the Kaiser when the Great War ended in 1918.

Arthur arrived home from Burma, where he had been with the Lushai Brigade, to find that his wife, Esme, had gone off with another man, taking their son,

Michael, with her, and leaving their little daughter, Shirley to be brought up by her father. One day, he invited me to lunch at his Club, the Devonshire, in St James's. It was a buffet lunch and, as I went to help myself at a side table, an elderly gentleman who had just filled his plate, fixed his eye on my tie and asked: 'When were you in The Horse, sir?' I had no idea what he meant, which obviously irritated him, for he repeated sharply 'When were you in The Horse, dammit?' I mumbled, half-laughing, 'Oh, that's my school tie,' for it was the red and green tie of the Fishguard County School, and I was not aware that it resembled the tie of The Poonah Horse. He looked me up and down in a way that indicated that he regarded me as a rank impostor, and stumped away, dragging a leg and all but spilling the food on his plate. An amusing sequel to that story occurred when my friend Major Francis Jones, later Wales Herald of Arms Extraordinary, was a member of the Surrey Yeomanry. The other members were most of them titled and, from time to time, they foregathered at the Berkeley. They were there, one evening, enjoying their drinks, when Albert Bowen, from Fishguard, arrived on his way home from Kenya. Francis introduced him all round and, as he shook hands with one of the titled officers, a marquess no less, who was wearing the Poonah Horse tie, he blurted: 'Good Christ! When were you at the Fishguard County School?'

On a day in October my brother rang to say that he was home from Italy, having been granted compassionate leave on account of Mother's failing health. I did not recognise his voice, as I had not heard it for six years, and it sounded mature and gentle. He came to London the next day, bringing with him a small kitten for Anthony, which we were not sure that we wanted to have in our first floor flat. We took him to dinner at Martinez's Restaurant, in Swallow Street, that evening, and he and I sat up late as we had much to say after so long a separation.

The following morning, we went for a walk on Hampstead Heath while Joyce was preparing Sunday lunch. He told me that he had found himself dancing with a Palestine ATS in Naples one evening. She had told him that she came from Jerusalem and that her name was Anna, and he had responded by saying that he had a brother in Jerusalem who had written home about a girl of that name, whereupon she said: 'That's me!' He had fallen in love with her and planned, when he returned to Naples, to ask her to marry him, but he did not return to Naples and, a few months later, he married Janet Rees, of Whitland, who used to spend her holidays at Newport when she was a young girl.

When I arrived at Palestine House I was given £50 to purchase books, than which nothing could be more pleasant. I went to Edwards's shop in Marylebone High Street, and to Foyle's where I met Will Griffiths, who was in charge of the Welsh Department, and who was later to open his own book shop, specialising in books about Wales, assisted by his three brothers, in Cecil Court off St Martin's Lane. Foyle's was a great meeting place for Welshmen as long as Will was there and I had to call there regularly. Geraint Dyfnallt Owen was there one day, on his way home from Bucharest, and Alun Llewelyn Williams happened to call as well so that, with Will, we had a real Welsh session.

The author Maurice Pearlman, came to see me and brought with him Maurice (Moshe) Rosette, of the Jewish Agency, a native of Swansea. I later met Rosette in the Lobby of the House of Commons, when Harold Macmillan came by and greeted him. 'By the way Harold,' he said, 'meet my fellow-countryman, Dillwyn Miles!' Macmillan looked me up and down, obviously unable to decide whether I was Jewish or Welsh. Rosette later became the first Clerk to the Israeli Parliament.

I had dinner at the Savoy with Senator Gillette and Judge Bennett and other members of a deputation from the United States League for a Free Palestine, at which the other guests were James de Rothschild, Dr J. J. Mallon, CH, Warden of Toynbee Hall and Judge Greenridge from British Honduras, and David Bernhard of the 'The Londoner's Diary'. I met Edouard Atiyah, a leading protagonist of the Arab cause, at a debate between him and David Horowitz at the PEP Club, at which Moshe Shertok and one of the Nashashibis I had known in Jerusalem, were present.

At a party at the Schen's flat, on an evening before Leopold, as president of the Jewish National Fund, was leaving for Jerusalem, Sigmund Freud's daughter asked Joyce whether our baby had dark hair, as we both had, and when she was told that he was fair with light blue eyes, she said: 'Oh yes, I hear that in Palestine lots of little Jewish children are born with fair hair and blue eyes!'

I went to hear the appeal of William Joyce, 'Lord Haw-Haw', against sentence of death, at the Central Criminal Court, at the Old Bailey, before Lord Chief Justice Caldecote and Judges Humphreys and Lynskey, and heard Sir Harvey Shawcross, the Attorney General speak for the Crown. He was hanged two months later.

As well as meetings and lectures, most of them illustrated by film, we held receptions at Palestine House, and sometimes arranged recitals. Myra Hess came, and Harriet Cohen gave a piano recital and, during the interval, Susan Verney sang some Ladino folk songs. Louis Golding came and read from his book *The Glory of Elsie Silver*, when one of his most attentive listeners was Gwen Ffrancon-Davies.

Towards the end of November, 1945, we had a 'house warming' at Palestine House which was attended by about 150 people, among whom were Lords Walkden, Glenconner, Swaythlng, Sir Andrew McFadyean, Sir Geoffrey Leon Mander, Dr James Parkes, Sir George Gater, a number of Members of Parliament and many of my friends, such as Reggie Smith, who was now back in this country and working at the BBC, and his wife, Olivia Manning. Sir Wyndham had asked Joyce to receive the guests with him and, towards the end, when people were already leaving, a man arrived and said that he was 'a great friend of Dillwyn Miles' and did she know him? When she explained that she was my wife, he stated that he and I had not actually met but that we had been in correspondence when I was in the Middle East. He said that his name was Keidrych Rhys. I was very glad to meet him, although I would have preferred to have done so at some other time, for I was busy talking to the remaining guests, and generally looking after their enjoyment. Fortnum and Mason, who had brought along the food, were already packing the hampers, but I got them to open them again so as to provide for Keidrych, who appeared to be very hungry. He reminded me, which was not necessary, that I had written to him from the marooned train in the desert, and kept on asking 'What do you think of Wales?' but I did not know whether he referred to the country or to the excellent magazine called *Wales*, which he edited. He then came home with us, and we talked far into the night about both Wales and *Wales*.

Keidrych took me to the Wig-and-Pen Club, founded by Dick Brennan soon after the war, opposite the Law Courts where Fleet Street begins, to cater for the two professions whose emblems it bore in its name and badge. A timbered Tudor building, that alone had survived the Great Fire of 1666, it was in itself an attraction. Its members included eminent legal eagles and journalists such as Hannen Swaffer, and 'characters' like Gilbert Harding. One day, the new Club ties were displayed behind the bar: one blue and one maroon, bearing the emblem of the Club, a wig and a quill. Keidrych told the barman that he would like one of each and, when he received them, he handed me the maroon one. I refused to take it, protesting that I would not wear the tie of a club to which I did not belong, but he was insistent and finally pushed the tie into my coat pocket. The barman, in no time, produced a form which he asked me to sign and so I became a life-member of the Wig-and-Pen Club for five guineas.

In 1957, when Alan Villiers took *Mayflower II* across the Atlantic, Dick signed on as cook and the walls of the Club had several photographs taken on the voyage, in addition to the first edition front pages of Fleet Street newspapers announcing momentous events, such as the outbreak of war or the death of the king, and a frieze of portrait sketches of the more prominent members ran round the bar. On one occasion I took Bill Thomas, the Haverfordwest butcher, whom I had met in London to the Club for dinner. I took Dick to one side and warned him that Bill was a good trencherman and that when he ordered steak he expected a generous one. Dick took the tip and produced a thick slice of meat that covered the plate to the extent that there was hardly room for three peas besides. Bill looked at it and, in his gruff manner, said: 'What the hell's this? Back in Ha'rfordwest, where I come from, they put a thing like that between two pieces of bread and call it a sandwich. Get me another!' Dick was incredulous. 'You don't really mean it, sir!' 'Of course I do,' growled Bill, 'and while you're about it, bring half a chicken with it!'

I was now working for most of the time at Palestine House, while still on sick leave from the Army, and had to make the journey to Warwick every fortnight to see the Medical Officer and he, as a mere formality, gave me 'another fourteen days'. On 3 December I was taken to the hospital at Warwick where I was given yet another check-up and was told that I would not be called for any more medical examinations as a recommendation would be issued for my release on medical grounds.

When I arrived home from Warwick the following evening I found my brother there, sporting a release telegram that he had received that morning and had caught the next train. I noticed, however, that the telegram bore my regimental number and that it referred to my release, and not his. I envisaged the disappointment this would be for my mother, who was dying and did not want him to leave her and return to Italy. I would readily have allowed him to take my place had that been possible. The next morning, I reported at the London District Recruiting Depot, as ordered, by ten o'clock. I was sent to Chelsea Barracks for a medical examination and from there to Olympia to collect an issue of civilian clothes. I chose a dark blue pinstriped suit like the one I had before the war, and a green porkpie hat because it was the only hat that would fit my head.

In view of my mother's condition, I then took my brother to the House of Commons to see his Member of Parliament, Major Gwilym Lloyd George, as I knew that a note from him would lead to an extension of leave, and this kept him from returning to Italy.

We travelled overnight to be with Mother for a couple of days. Then, soon after we had returned to London there came the news that Uncle Tom had suffered a heart attack and that there was little hope that he would recover. I got the first available train and arrived to find that he was already dead. He was 68 years of age and, following a service at St Mary's Church, he was buried beside his father and his mother in the churchyard there.

Once again there was the aching business of leaving Mother, who was now more convinced than before that we should not meet again. I travelled back home on Christmas Eve with a heavy heart, and yet joyful at the prospect of spending his first Christmas with our little son. We placed a stocking at the foot of his cot and pretended that he understood that it was Christmas as he happily opened present after present. We sat round the table, the three of us, and ate our dinner of goose and stuffing and plum pudding. We then went to Wimbledon to join Tudor and his family and, after tea, sat and listened to my broadcast talk 'In Bethlehem' being read rather badly by an actor in Cardiff.

We travelled to Newport again on New Year's Eve and spent most of the night with Mother, sitting around her bed. I returned to London the following morning, leaving Joyce and Anthony with Mother. Two days later Joyce telephoned me to say that Mother was sinking and, again, I caught the first available train and arrived home to find that she was already in a coma. She died shortly afterwards and was buried beside my father, following a funeral at which tributes were paid to her by the rector and the ministers of the three chapels in the town.

After Mother and Uncle Tom had died, and we were to settle in London, there was no purpose in keeping Grandma's house. We emptied the loft of everything, but the smell of small apples, and I went over the house for the last time. Each room was now silent, yet I could hear voices that were familiar to me but that would never be heard again except by me.

I took up my duties as National Organiser at Palestine House, wearing my 'demob' suit and, for the first time for over six years, a shirt that was not khaki in colour. My first appointment was at Bristol University to meet Professor McInnes, the blind professor of Imperial History and, in the evening, to address a meeting of the Royal Empire Society. The next day, after having tea at the Roman Baths, I spoke at a meeting of the Society at Bath where, at the end of the meeting, one of the members said that I should deliver my speech 'to the House of Commons!'

My father-in-law, Lewis Craven Ord came to dinner and, on his arrival Leopold Schen and his wife called to see the baby. Joyce asked them to stay for supper and I shuddered when they accepted, for I knew that she was in the process of roasting a joint of pork. Fortunately, there was also some veal available, which they had, and Schen congratulated her on being prepared for such an eventuality. He and the old man got on famously and the evening ended with Schen inviting Lewis to deliver a lecture in Jerusalem, which he had to decline on account of his other commitments. I was invited to lunch at the Royal Empire Society, the next day, to hear him address the Industrial Co-Partnership Association. On the Sunday afternoon we went to Purley to meet his cousin Lewis Redman Ord, known as LR, who was on a visit from Canada.

Julia discovered that *Tornado* was no place to spend a cold winter and so she bought Foxholes House, a large house built by one of the cider kings. While I was pottering about in the garden there one afternoon, I heard a car zoom up the drive and saw that it was a Rolls Royce bearing the number A 1. It belonged to Julia's friends, George Pettyt and his wife and, over tea, I heard how they had resisted vast sums of money offered for the number from *A1 Atora Beef* Suet and *A1 Shag Tobacco* and the like. When George died in 1952, he left the number to his friend Trevor Laker, of the John Bull Tyre Company, later acquired by Dunlop.

My work at Palestine House took me all over England and Wales meeting the leaders of the local communities and addressing meetings in an effort to interpret the situation in Palestine. I went to Liverpool to meet Archbishop Downey and Bishop Martin, Lord Leverhulme and the Lord Mayor, Alderman Luke Hogan. In Durham I met John Twemlow, Sam Watson, the Trade Unions leader, and addressed a meeting at the University, with the Vice-Chancellor in the chair. I was taken to meet a number of people over lunch at the Liberal Club at Newcastle-on-Tyne by Sam Phillips, who showed me the John Ord School that had been established by Joyce's ancestor in the sixteenth century. At Cardiff, Sir Frederick Rees, Principal of the University, and a native of Milford, was very pleased to see me and he presided at a meeting which I addressed at the Angel Hotel at which George Thomas, then a recently elected Member of Parliament, was the other speaker. At Swansea Rotary Club, Judge Rowe Harding, the former Welsh international rugby player, said that they were grateful for a balanced view of the problem. I spoke at the University's International Affairs Society that evening.

George Thomas invited me to lunch at the House of Commons and introduced me to Goronwy Roberts, later Lord Goronwy-Roberts, and Barnett (later Lord) Janner, and we all had tea with John Strachey and Tom Driberg, later Lord Bradwell. They urged me to have another stab at the Pembrokeshire nomination in time for the next General Election, and Goronwy Roberts invited me to lunch at the House with a view, he said, to persuading me to seek a more suitable seat to contest at the next election. George Shepherd, later Lord Shepherd, who was the secretary of the Labour Party, said that he hoped that Fienburgh would stand for Mile End, so that Pembrokeshire would be free for me. Another day, I had tea at the House with Alice Bacon, who introduced me to Hugh Gaitskell, Raymond Blackburn, Ben Levy and J. B. Hynd, Chancellor of the Duchy of Lancaster. We were later joined by James Hoy (Leith) and Ian Mikardo (Reading) and Morris Orbach (Willesden).

When I addressed the British India Commonwealth League at Brighton, with Sir George Morgan-Webb in the chair, I was surprised to find among those present Sir Alfred T. Davies, who was secretary to Lloyd George and he gave his recollections of the time of the Balfour Declaration. The Rev. Pitt Bonarjee also spoke.

I was invited to address the 17th Battalion, Parachute Regiment at Bulford prior to their departure to the Middle East. When I left Bulford in 1939 I had hoped that I would never see it again but I found the whole place transformed. Gone were the dilapidated and rusty huts that we inhabited and permanent brick buildings stood everywhere. I spoke to the battalion, about four hundred strong, in a palatial hall-cum-gymnasium, and could not resist telling them of the incredible change that had taken place.

Lorna Wingate came to seek help in writing a biography of her famous husband and I took her to lunch at Martinez. Her mother, Mrs Moncrieff-Patterson, later called seeking help to find a fund-raising secretary to raise £100,000 in order to establish a memorial to Wingate.

Aubrey (later Abba) Eban, whom I had known in Jerusalem, came to see me at Palestine House and said that he had been asked to take over the Information Department of the Jewish Agency at 77 Great Russell Street upon his release from the Army. He invited us to his parents' home in Harrow, where there was a party for Moshe Shertok. We were invited again, for dinner, when Shertok was there and, this time, he entertained us with stories about his dealings with Arab leaders, and especially the Emir Abdullah with whom he had a special rapport. Aubrey and I met for lunch when he returned finally from Palestine and he liked my idea of having a reception at Palestine House for British service men and women who had served in Palestine during the war so as to present them with an opportunity to maintain contact. When Aubrey came to lunch at the flat, and stayed for the rest of the afternoon discussing Palestinian affairs, I little thought that, one day, he would be Foreign Secretary and Deputy Prime Minister of Israel.

H. St John Philby came to speak at Palestine House on Saudi Arabia. I knew that he had been particularly interested in the Palestine problem and that he had proposed to Dr Weizmann, who was President of the World Zionist Organisation at the time, and Moshe Shertok, then Political Secretary of the Jewish Agency, that in return for a subsidy of £20 million paid to Ibn Saud the Jews would be able to take over most of Palestine and that the old city of Jerusalem should have the status of a 'Vatican City'. After the lecture I had dinner with him and Sheikh Hafiz Wahba, the Saudi Minister in London and during the meal Philby said that he would like to propose my name to the Royal Geographical Society as a Fellow.

The mayor took the chair at a meeting I addressed at Southport, and there were about a hundred people present. After the meeting, an Irishman who had asked several intelligent questions at the end of my address, invited me to his home at No. 20, The Promenade. He said that he was Dr Clement, a general practitioner in the town, born in Limerick. His conversation consisted largely of raising questions to which there were no apparent answers, on realising which he would say: 'Och, the asininity of it all!' and launch on another intractable subject. He poured generous measures of Irish whiskey, and his attractive wife, Victoria, brought coffee for me and for herself, and tea for him. From her conversation she revealed that she had a much clearer understanding of world affairs than her husband, and I corresponded with her for a while.

Several months later, I saw a photograph of Dr Clement and his wife, Victoria, on the front page of the *Evening Standard*. He had poisoned her and had similarly disposed of two previous wives. He had felt the finger of suspicion point at him, and had committed suicide, and a young doctor who feared that he might be charged with being too hasty in carrying out the post mortem had also taken his own life.

Arnold Lunn came to Palestine House to give a talk on 'Christian Minorities in the Middle East', and Sir Ronald Storrs gave an address on Egypt. The Hon. Edwin Samuel, newly arrived from Jerusalem, called to see me at Palestine House, but would not give a talk on the present situation in Palestine on the grounds that what he had to say would please nobody. At the request of Sir Wyndham I wrote to Field Marshal Smuts to invite him to address a meeting at Palestine House during his visit to this country but he replied regretting that he could not fit it into his programme.

At a meeting of the London Pembrokeshire Society I was shown a copy of the programme of the old London Pembrokeshire Club, as it was then known, which listed all the peers who had any connection with Pembrokeshire as patrons, and I was asked if I could obtain the patronage of present day peers. With this in view, I approached Viscount St David's who invited me to lunch at the House of Lords. The only relevant peer there that day was Viscount Simon who said that he was proud of his Tenby connection and would give the Society his support. At another meeting of the Society, the Secretary, Arletta Black, embarrassed me by producing a copy of the *Western Mail* in which I was described in an article headed 'A Second Lawrence of Arabia'.

We had, for some time, been trying to find more suitable accommodation and, at long last, I was offered a flat in a block edging on Regents Park. We went to see it and, although the rooms were rather small, it seemed comfortable and convenient enough for us to decide to take it. We got home just ahead of a storm of unbelievable ferocity. Blinding flashes of lightning were accompanied by almost instant deafening claps of thunder, and torrential rain converted Finchley Road into a rushing river. At the same time, as though set in motion by the storm, Joyce's labours began. I telephoned Dr Zeitlin, as arranged, and he set off immediately and although he only had a short distance to travel, he took an interminable time arriving. I was getting frantic, but Joyce remained calm and attempted to distract me by giving me various jobs to do. The doctor and the nurse eventually arrived together and Marilyn was born within five minutes of their arrival. Five minutes later, I saw her, and was speaking to her mother as though nothing much had happened. A short time later, I was holding the little bundle in my arms. Marilyn had been born, on 26 July 1946, at half past six in the afternoon, in a storm that had brought London to a standstill.

At a Gorsedd ceremony held in a leafy glade in Dyffryn Park during the Royal National Eisteddfod at Mountain Ash in August 1946, the Princess Elizabeth placed her hands between those of the Archdruid Crwys and became a member of the Gorsedd of Bards of the Isle of Britain. She was admitted into the Ovate Order, as her parents had been twenty years earlier at Swansea, wearing a green robe, the material for which she herself had produced, as cloth was still on ration, under the bardic name *Elisabeth o Windsor*.

At the National Eisteddfod held at Colwyn Bay in 1947, in the absence of the Herald Bard, Captain Geoffrey Crawshay, I was asked to take his place and to lead the procession of bards through the town and to the Gorsedd Circle in Eirias Park. That evening, Cynan took me to a *noson lawen* at Eirianws, a remote farmhouse in the hills above the Conway valley, that had once been the home of John Williams, Dean of Westminster, Lord Keeper of the Great Seal, and Archbishop of York. Cynan was given the seat of honour in the *simne fawr* in the large farmhouse kitchen as Telynores Dwyryd and her sister, Gwenllian, played their harps and their father, Ioan Dwyryd, sang *penillion* till the oak rafters quivered.

Joyce's uncle, John Ord, the Harley Street specialist, invited us to dinner at his house, called Pin River, in Willesden Lane, as his sister, May Ord, was there on a visit from Canada. She gave Joyce a brooch containing a curl of hair, which her kinswoman, Anne, daughter of William Dummer Powell, Chief Justice of Upper Canada, had worn when she was drowned when the SS *Albion* sank.

In September 1946 we moved to a flat on the corner of a newly built block on the edge of Regents Park. On the Sunday following our move, Marilyn was christened at St John's Wood Church by the Archdeacon of London, the Venerable D. H. Gibbs-Smith. She, like Anthony, was christened in water we had brought from the Jordan, which had been boiled again and again but still gave off a sulphurous odour.

Douglas Butterworth wrote from Birmingham to say that some of the survivors of 550 Coy RASC had formed a 550 Club. Major Duncan Riddell had given him my address and Frank Pynor had remembered that I had kept a copy of the nominal roll on which I had entered the private address of each member of the unit. I sent him the copy which enabled him to communicate with those who had served in the unit and the Club was formed.

London was swathed in mist, thick as cotton, as I left early one morning, and so it was as I drove through Dunstable, Northampton and Chesterfield to speak at the Rotary Club at Huddersfield and, in the evening, the International Affairs Group at the Huddersfield Technical College, which largely consisted of foreign students, including several Palestinians. The next two days I spoke at the Rotary Clubs at Barnsley and at Pontefract, where I stayed at the Red Lion Hotel.

As I came down the stairs that evening I could not believe my eyes when I saw that the person standing at the reception desk, with an elderly gentleman beside her, was Marianne, Mino's wife, from Tiberias. She, equally unbelieving, stared at me, and neither of us spoke until I asked: 'Marianne?' 'Dillwyn!' she replied, and we embraced. The old man was her father, Professor Falck, who had escaped from Hitler's Europe during the war. He was internationally recognised as an expert on tree diseases and he had come to England to advise some timber curing firm on the treatment of dry rot. He was pale and frail and I tried to conjure his expression when Mino arrived on his doorstep to seek the hand of his daughter, dressed as an Arab sheikh.

I was invited to address the Arts Society at the University College of Wales, Aberystwyth, and felt rather nervous to appear before my former lecturers, now professors, and other luminaries who sat in the audience. I had been invited to stay the night with Professor Gwyn Jones, professor of English, author, and editor of *The Welsh Review*, who presided at the meeting. I dreamt that the house was flooded and, at breakfast, found that it had been, on account of a burst pipe.

I had lunch with the college staff when I went to address the International Society at Nottingham University, among whom was W. D. Evans, professor of geology, and author of a book on the geology of north Pembrokeshire, later ennobled as Lord Energlyn. He jokingly asked me if the volcanoes beneath Fishguard Bay had been active lately. That evening I addressed a meeting at Lady Fletcher's house in Nottingham. Mrs Woodward, a friend of Julia's, was there and she had been asked to propose a vote of thanks to me, which she did glowingly and then left immediately. I had noticed that her chauffeur had come in through a French window and had given her a message as I was speaking, but I did not know until afterwards that he was telling her that her house had caught fire. I stayed at the Black Boy and, the next morning I went to see Cavendish House in The Park, where Joyce had lived and which was now the Judges' Lodgings. I then went on to address the Derby International Society.

I addressed meetings arranged by the United Nations Association at Southall, Slough, Woking, Derby, and elsewhere throughout the country, with audiences of up to 450 people, as at Newcastle-on-Tyne, and public meetings at Loughton, Hastings, West Hartlepool, Berwick-on-Tweed, Darlington, South Shields, Whitley Bay, Sunderland, Rawtenstall, Nelson, Heywood, Burnley, Preston, and the High Schools at Manchester, Burnley and Stockport.

I spoke at a number of Rotary Clubs in the London area, and to a hundred and fifty others in various parts of the country. The Rotarians at Merthyr distinguished themselves by continuing to ask questions for half and hour beyond the usual closing time and they were sufficiently impressed to write to Sir Wyndham. At Cardiff, I had lunch with Huw Wheldon, then director of the Arts Council for Wales, who offered to speak at our meetings. I had tea at the BBC with Dafydd Gruffydd and Elwyn Evans, both of whom had served in Palestine and held diametrically opposite views, Dafydd being pro-Jewish and Elwyn pro-Arab. I suggested that they take part in a broadcast debate, which I would chair, but they did not seem anxious to do so.

I kept on addressing meetings of Rotary Clubs, international groups and political parties, from Brighton to Berwick-on-Tweed, from Harpenden to Harlech, covering some two hundred meetings a year. Most times one came away feeling that something worthwhile had been done, but occasionally one wondered whether it was worth the effort. Rotary Clubs frequently left one empty: they are all different and yet all the same. The time allocated to the speaker is whittled down by greetings to visiting brethren or discussion on some domestic matters, so that having been told that one had twenty minutes, the time available was often reduced to fifteen or even ten minutes. Then having rushed or curtailed one's address so as to allow time for questions, no one dares speak as it is now approaching two o'clock and the members must get back to work. Worse still, in the vote of thanks, and on the members' faces, was a complacency and a feeling that they had dealt with that particular problem and could now wash their hands of it.

During a tour of Rotary clubs in North Wales I stayed with John and Bethan Jones, and met Bethan's father, Louis Jones, who was the Registrar for North Wales. He told me that he remembered old Siân Owen, the woman wearing the Paisley shawl in Curnow Vosper's famous painting *Salem*, and the other people who appear in the picture.

At the Prestatyn Rotary Club, Sir Wynn Wheldon, former secretary to the Welsh Board of Education, endeavoured to persuade me to return to Wales. I had already given the matter some thought, and there was also the discomfort suffered by Joyce in having to bring up two small children in an all-electric flat that was unheated, except for two short periods each day, on account of the rationing of electricity. Were I back in Wales, I thought, I could always chop down a tree to make a fire that would keep us warm. The idea of returning to one's native heath grew stronger as time went by.

NEWPORT CASTLE

THE DECISION TO RETURN HOME came on the slopes of Cader Idris one Sunday evening. I had left the family at Newport while I went on a tour in North Wales, and had taken John Davies, Senior, of Cotham Lodge, with me as far as Dolgellau. We stayed the night at the Royal Ship Hotel and, as it was a bright April evening, we went for a walk and started climbing the path up Cader Idris. I expect that I must have mentioned my difficulties in London to him during conversation, and he said: 'Why don't you come back to Newport? Why don't you come back to live at the castle? Lady Chelmsford has left, and it is vacant.'

When I returned to Newport I took Joyce to see the castle. It was much as I had seen it last, before the war, only now it was empty, without the furniture and the pictures and the deep carpets that I remembered, and the moat that was flooded to provide water to drive the miller's wheel, and had a boat on it, was now dry and overgrown with brambles and water-parsnip and young willows. We instantly decided that we would take it and went off to Cardigan to sign a lease with the agent, after having informed the miller that there was a dead cow beneath the drawbridge.

The arrangements were all but completed when I got word that the Pembrokeshire County Council had set its eye on the castle and had appointed a panel to inspect it with a view to converting it into a children's home, and I was advised by the barony's solicitors to move in as soon as possible. I received this advice on a Saturday and was told that the inspection was to take place on the Monday. We therefore gathered what camping kit we had, and bought some more at John Barnes, and set off for Newport, and entered into occupation of the castle until the furniture arrived. We set up our camp bed in the principal bedroom, and the cots for the children, now aged two and one, in the round tower.

From the time of their birth they had slept from the moment they were put to bed until the next morning but on this night they both woke and cried uncontrollably, and it was some time before Joyce was able to soothe them to sleep again. The same thing happened on the second night, and again on the third. The morning after, I met my brother who remarked on my worn appearance, and when I explained to him the cause, he asked where the children were sleeping.

On being told, he immediately said: 'That's the haunted room,' and insisted that we should remove the cots to another bedroom, which we did, and the children slept uninterruptedly from then on.

Neither Joyce nor I found any evidence of a ghostly presence, although we slept many nights in the tower bedroom afterwards, nor anything unusual beyond regular visitations by horseshoe bats, which I endeavoured to catch by throwing my wife's underwear at them, thinking that the nylon would defeat their radar. Of course, there were the tales that I had heard in childhood of the Lavender Lady, so named because she was preceded by the scent of that herb, a small hedge of which grew below the bedroom windows, incidentally, but it was always the friend of a friend who had seen her. Some said that she was a young maiden who had been thwarted in love and had taken her own life, while others believed that she was the widow of a knight who had failed to return from the Crusades.

The castle was part of the estate of the lords of the barony of Cemais. When I was a small boy it was occupied, from time to time, by the then lord and his lady, Sir Marteine and Lady Lloyd. After Sir Marteine died, in 1933, I spent many hours with Lady Lloyd, listening to her tales of her life and family. Above all, she would tell me about her son, Martin Kemes Arundel Lloyd who, she would say, was born on a Friday, got whooping cough on a Friday, had pneumonia on a Friday, broke his collarbone three times on a Friday, and was killed on a Friday. He was killed as a Captain in the Grenadier Guards leading his men into action on the Somme in 1916. He had always sent her a red rose on her birthday, echoing a custom among the tenants of the barony to pay their rent with a red rose on the Feast of St John. When he was in the trenches in France and unable to find a red rose, he sent her a little flower that grew beside the trenches which later became famous as the Flanders Poppy.

In the stables, down by the moat, I found some discarded items including a pair of broken figures which I rebuilt. They were wolves, representing the arms of the Lloyds of Bronwydd, *azure* a wolf salient *argent*. Each had its forepaws resting on top of a shield and I placed them one each side of the front door, and I was thus able to say that, while some would complain about having 'the wolf at the door', I had two at mine.

As the castle stands on a knoll above the town, it exposes a steep slope of green grass that is visible above the houses. Cows looked enormous when seen on this slope and sheep appeared out of place, apart from requiring a lot of fencing to keep them in. It struck me that geese would look better there, and so I purchased fifty and allowed them to roam without hindrance. The townspeople were delighted with their appearance, and all went well until one Sunday when a deputation from Bethlehem Baptist Chapel arrived at the door after the morning service, asking if I would mind keeping the geese at home on Sundays as that morning, when the minister was getting into *hwyl* in his sermon, the geese had walked up the aisles calling their 'gawk-gawk-gawk' instead of 'Amens' and, what was more, leaving their messages on the chapel floor. After this, the geese took to wandering and, when Christmas came, they had to go the way of all Christmas geese, and the grassy slopes, and the whole place, seemed empty without them.

I had mentioned to Joyce that a nook by the Great Keep would be an ideal site for a few beehives and I returned home one day to find that she had been to a sale and had bought three hives for me. The next task, which she could not have fully appreciated, was to bring them home, and this was more than ordinarily difficult because they stood in a garden behind a row of houses. They could not be taken out through the house, and there was no other way of approaching the garden except by climbing some hedges and crossing neighbours' gardens. All went well until we were getting the last hive out over a hedge into Berriman Lane, which was a steep cul-de-sac with a couple of cottages, that had their water closets at the end of the lane. One of my helpers stumbled and the bees came out in clouds and made for the gap above the door of the water-closet where, unbeknown to us, George Jenkins the postman was sitting on the seat and quietly reading the local paper. The door was flung open and out shot George grasping his postman's trousers about his ample waist, but he lost his grip and the red-striped blue garment fell about his ankles, and he went head over heels revealing an expanse of flesh at which the bees instantly made aim. We bought an extractor and other equipment and had quantities of honey, and Joyce made mead which was unexpectedly potent, as some of our visiting friends discovered.

In order to save on our meagre petrol ration I bought a governess car, with harness, and then set about the more difficult task of finding a suitable pony. I went to Maenclochog fair and to several farm sales before succeeding in getting hold of a gentle creature called Fancy. With Fancy in the shafts, Joyce could take the children shopping, and go to the beach and for pleasant rural rides.

A friendly farmer brought a collie pup that was almost tortoiseshell in colour. 'Something for the children,' he said. The little dog became a family favourite and was named Ianto, and survived even falling out of Anthony's bedroom window beneath which, fortunately, was a grassy scarp down which the dog rolled until it found its feet.

Another farmer friend told me that he could let me have a pig, and that he would come along to kill it and dress it up. Joyce brewed for the occasion, in the traditional manner and, unbeknown to us, the farmer gave Anthony some beer. Joyce noticed that he appeared sleepy and took him off and put him in his bed, and some hours later, he woke up with a headache and all the symptoms of a hangover.

She brewed again when it was time to gather the hay. After the demise of the geese, I had allowed the grassy slopes to grow hay and, as it was old pasture that had never been ploughed, there was a fine, sweet smelling mixture of clover, buttercups and yellow rattle, sorrel and eyebright and oxeyes. Friends and neighbours came to help us gather the hay, in the way it was done before the war, and children tumbled among the hay cocks. When day was done, we all sat down, some thirty of us, round the long table in the kitchen for the harvest supper, which Joyce had prepared, and as much of her home-brewed ale as anyone could drink.

I felt privileged to be invited to become a member of The Pint Club, which comprised a select few who met in the small back room of the Golden Lion each evening at nine-thirty and were allowed to remain there by the law-abiding landlady, Mrs Evans, until half-past-ten, half-an-hour after closing time. Dr Dai Havard sat in the armchair and was considered 'chairman', maybe because he was chairman of the bench. Captain John James Seaborne and Captain John Morris, Ivy House, both long retired master mariners, sat each side of the fire, the latter with a spittoon strategically placed beside his chair into which he spat unerringly before launching on one of his stories. 'Did I tell you about the time we got drunk before we got to Australia?' he would ask, and on being assured that he had not, he would spit again and pull at his pipe until clouds of smoke billowed up to the ceiling, and then after a measured pause, he would add: 'As a matter of fact, we were drunk by the time we got to Crymych!' Crymych was the nearest railway station in those days and a horse-drawn coach ran regularly from Newport to meet the trains.

Despite his travels and knowledge of the world, John did not believe in such 'newfangled devices' as the wireless, which he dismissed as that 'bloody man in the box', and when Dr Dai arrived at the Pint Club one evening and said that an atom-bomb had been dropped on Nagasaki and had flattened the city, John simply spat in the cuspidor and sucked his pipe and said: 'Bloody nonsense. I know Nagasaki – great big buildings like Liverpool, or London. Impossible to flatten buildings like that. I know Nagasaki well. Matter of fact, I knew a girl there. Natasha was her name. No, they wouldn't flatten Nagasaki. Bloody nonsense!'

Once a year he brought a large pudding basin full of the finest looking strawberries as a present for Betty, the daughter of the Golden Lion. 'How do you manage to grow such fine strawberries?' I asked him. He looked at me as though I was deficient in common sense. 'I don't weed 'em. Don't you see? When I don't weed 'em, the bloomin' birds up in the trees won't see them, and the bloomin' slugs and snails get 'tangled in the weeds, and I get the strawberries!'

Captain Seaborne, rubicund of face, soft of voice and quick of smile, sat in the other corner of the fire. He had retired from the sea at the end of the Great War and his life subsequently had been taken up with a daily game of golf, weather permitting, and early each evening, the euchre school that met in the billiard room, huddled round the fireplace and demanding silence, which virtually prevented us from using the billiard table. Seaborne was less of a story teller than John Morris, but more of a practical joker and full of innocent tricks that he played on people, as he did once on James Thomas, Bohemian Stores, immediately across the road from his house. After James Thomas had retired from selling paint and other household requisites, he had little to do save stand in the bay window of his front room, where the shop was, and watch the world pass by. Whenever a horse would leave its droppings on the road, he would rush out with a bucket and shovel and scoop it up and place it on his rhubarb bed. On one occasion, a horse stopped immediately outside the house and left a perfect mare's nest on the road. While James went for his bucket, Seaborne dashed out and planted a small Union Jack on the steaming heap, and retreated to his own front window to watch the old man bend down to scoop the manure, and as he saw the flag, he froze, then looked round him, before gathering the heap and rushing indoors with his mysterious prize.

As a general practitioner in a rural area, Dr Dai had a fund of stories arising from his experiences over a period of forty years. There was the winter's night when he was woken by a young man beating at his door saying that his father was dying. The snow was thick on the ground and the young man had brought his truck, with chains round the wheels, to fetch the doctor and take him to is father's cottage in the heart of the Presely Hills. Where they could go no further in the truck, the young fellow had tied two ponies to a post to take them on through the deep drifts. As they approached the cottage, almost buried out of sight in the snow, Dai could hear the old man groan and, when he got inside, he found him lying on his bed, holding his belly and complaining that he had a pain, 'something terrible'. Dai, suspecting colic, asked what he had eaten for supper. 'Oh, only some warmed-up *cawl* and some bread and cheese and pickles. Nothing much, Doctor bach.' Asked if he had taken anything for the pain, he said; 'Well, yes. Mari, the wife, suggested that I try some of that Sloan's Liniment.' 'Did you rub it on your tummy, or what?' inquired Dai. 'Oh no, Doctor,' replied the old man. 'I took two spoonfuls. It was after that the pain got unbearable!'

In the autumn of 1947, I was asked to return to Palestine House for a short period and to do a speaking tour in the north-east of England. I had agreed to meet Richard Llewellyn, who had bought a cottage above Newport Castle, in London, for him to take me to the Savile Theatre by to see Reginald Tate's production of Richard's play, *Noose*. After a day or two, I set off to address meetings in the north-east of England. I stayed the weekend at the County Hotel at Newcastle where, at breakfast on the Sunday morning, everyone was reading the Sunday newspapers, which had such banner headlines as 'Priestley tells America', referring to an open letter that J. B. Priestley had written to the Americans on their attitude to the situation in Europe. No one appeared to have noticed that sitting at a corner table, also engrossed in a Sunday newspaper, and enjoying his breakfast, was J. B. Priestley.

When I got back to London, Teddy Kollek took me to lunch at the Athenaeum and told me that Weizmann was on the point of resigning from the presidency of the World Zionist Congress because an American delegate, at the Congress meeting at Basle, had called him a demagogue. I took Sir Wyndham to see him at the Dorchester Hotel some days late. He was still very depressed and feeling that he had been abandoned by the people for whom he had devoted his life, but he seemed brighter when he came to tea at Palestine House the following week. Lord Samuel also came to see Sir Wyndham and I felt that it was an historic occasion to be in the presence of the two men who had worked so hard in the early days of the mandate.

I was invited to speak at the Haverfordwest Rotary Club, and I spoke again to the Club a number of times over the years and, in particular, in September 1997, exactly fifty years after I had first spoken. After that first meeting, David Hughes Lewis, the resident tutor, suggested that I should become an extra-mural lecturer for the University College of Wales, Aberystwyth, to speak on Middle Eastern affairs. I told him that I would do so provided I could also do courses on local history, which would lead me to make a closer study of the history of Pembrokeshire. I took sessions, of ten or twenty lectures, on each subject for the next thirty years.

In an endeavour to create a more subjective interest in the environment, I invited R. M. Lockley, then living at Dinas Island Farm, to give a talk on the natural history of north Pembrokeshire at Newport. After the meeting, he came to look at the bats in the crypt and the adjoining ruined tower and, over supper he told me that he had named the character featured in his books as 'The Baron' because he reminded him of Baron Munchausen and his extraordinary tales. He said that his name was Harries, and that he was connected to the Harrieses of Tregwynt.

A letter from Major Francis Jones, who was writing the official history of the war at the Cabinet Office, appeared in the *County Echo*, regretting that there was no historical society in Pembrokeshire and calling for the formation of one, and he went on to state that 'a young man of great drive and ability has returned to roost in his native Newport. Perhaps Captain Dillwyn Miles, now that he is among "his ane again," will do some recruiting among the homagers of the Lord Marcher and persuade them and others to form a society.' My old master Stanley Richards, home on leave from Cyprus, then wrote to say that he, too, hoped that I would do something about it, adding that 'Dillwyn has been to Arabia and I would like to see him emulating Lawrence in digging into the past, even if he cannot emulate Lawrence's camel-riding exploits!' I indicated that I would be prepared to call a meeting with a view to forming a 'Pembrokeshire Historical Society' provided sufficient interest was shown, but I was told that there was a local branch of the South-West Wales Historical Association already in existence.

An embarrassingly flattering article appeared in *Y Cymro* under the heading *Bardd, Milwr, Cymodwr* (Bard, Soldier, Conciliator) referring to my work in the Middle East, and another in *Y Tywysydd*, as one of its series on 'famous Welshmen of today', *Cymry Enwog Heddiw: Captain Dillwyn Miles, FRGS.*

Our predecessor at the castle was Lady Chelmsford, widow of Viscount Chelmsford, GCSI, GCMG, GCIE, GBE, Viceroy of India. Lady Chelmsford was a granddaughter of Lady Charlotte Guest, who had translated *The Mabinogion*. One of her daughters was married to Lord Inchiquin, a bas-relief of whom I discovered when I was clearing out the stables. Another, Margaret, aware of my interest in her great grandmother's work, gave me a copy of *The Diaries of Lady Charlotte Guest*, edited by her kinsman, the Earl of Bessborough.

Members of the London Appreciation Society came to visit the castle, and one of them asked me if I could lend him a pen and some Indian ink, and a stool upon which he sat and produced a splendid drawing of the castle. He was Hanslip Fletcher, whose drawings appeared in the *Sunday Times* every Sunday and he asked if I would agree to his drawing of the castle appearing the following Sunday, adding that if I wrote to Lord Kemsley he might let me have the original drawing. It arrived in a handsome frame in which it has hung in my study ever since.

The writer H. J. Massingham called as I was leaving to attend a Court Leet at The College at Felindre Farchog and he gladly accepted the invitation to accompany me. This was the Court to which the commoners of the locality, together with those of the parish of Dinas, brought their grievances, and Geoffrey George, Steward of the Barony, explained to Massingham that there were courts also still meeting at Eglwyswrw and Llanfyrnach, beside the Court Baron and Court Leet at Newport. Present at the Court was Ianto'r Hafod, otherwise Evan Phillips, who was Beili'r Bryn, the bailiff of the Presely Hills, and had in his possession a book in which were registered the sheep earmarks of all those who were entitled to graze their sheep on the hills. Drawings of pairs of ears appeared in rows down the recto pages, and on the verso the description of the mark, such as *Hollt ar y dde a thwll yn yr aswy*, meaning a slit in the right ear and a hole in the left. By this mark, an owner was able to identify his sheep and claim any strays during the *stra*. The *stra* took place twice a year, towards the end of June and in October. Farmers and shepherds would set off early in the morning, on horseback and on foot, to sweep the hills and round up the sheep. The animals were driven from Moel Trygarn to Parc-y-boty, and the ones that were not claimed there were taken to Mirianog, where they were joined by flocks from Carn Alw and Carn Breseb. The unmarked wethers were then driven to Hafod Tydfil where sheep from Carn Goedog, Carn Twm Ffranc and Banc yr Hafod would have been gathered. At Hafod Tydfil the men would partake of cakes and ale towards which they would have already contributed their scot. Unclaimed sheep were herded to Tafarn-y-bwlch where they were met by flocks brought from Pen Foel Fedw, Carn Lladron, and Pen Bwlch Gwynt. Unclaimed and unmarked sheep were then driven to Newfoundland and placed in the fold there and kept for up to seven days, when any sheep still unclaimed were sold by the Bailiff. After his costs had been deducted, together with those incurred by the Steward, the proceeds were handed to the lord of the barony.

Anthony was now four years old and, on my birthday, he took himself down to Mansel Evans the Draper's shop and bought me two handkerchiefs with his pocket money. He was by now full of expressions such as 'Good gracious!' and ready to chide his sister with remarks such as 'You little rascal!' Marilyn revealed her power to charm men at an early age when, as we were at tea at Hendre one Sunday, old J. O. Vaughan, who never paid any regard to children, took her on his lap. Whenever I saw him afterwards his first words were 'How's little Marilyn?' The children found the castle an ideal place to play the game of 'hide and seek'. There were the ruined towers, the steps down to the drawbridge, the rhododendrons bushes, and the woods and the stables, beyond the moat, so that it could take a long time for the one to find the other. More often than not, however, they did not have the patience for a prolonged search, not even indoors. I heard Anthony, hiding in the tower room say, as he could hear Marilyn approaching 'You needn't look for me here Marilyn, 'cos I'm not here!' One Sunday, after we had been to church and were walking up the footpath to the drawbridge, Anthony kept on repeating 'Thy Kingdom come,' and then turned to his mother and asked 'Mummy. When Jesus comes, will he be coming along the road or up this path?' Another time he asked 'Why doesn't Jesus give the weather forecast?' While I took them over the mountain, one day, near Bedd Morus, Marilyn picked some wild cotton and was saying to herself 'Likkle fevvers the baa-sheeps have lost!' I was pleased when old Mr Thomas of Scolton Lodge came up to me and said: 'Your two are the most mannered little children in Newport.'

I responded once more to Sir Wyndham when he asked me to speak at the annual conference of the Council for Education in World Citizenship at Buxton on 'Britain and Palestine' with the Reverend Gordon Lang, MP for Stalybridge and Hyde, nephew of Cosmo Lang, Archbishop of Canterbury.

In June 1947 I received a letter from Herbert M. Vaughan, a member of the Ancient Monuments Board for Wales, stating that my name had been 'recommended as a good Local Correspondent in the Newport-Fishguard district' for the Board which, he added, was 'attached to HM's Office of Works, London.' Having indicated that I would be prepared to be of help, a letter came from A. J. Taylor, Secretary of the Board and Inspector of Ancient Monuments for Wales enclosing particulars of the duties of a Local Correspondent which were, in my case, to keep the Board informed of all matters affecting the listed monuments between Fishguard Fort and St Dogmael's Abbey, and inland to Moel Trygarn, Pentre Ifan and Cilgerran Castle.

My first test came by accident, one Saturday morning, when Willie Owen, clerk of works of the Cemais Rural District Council, brought me some plans for inspection. As he was leaving the castle, he casually remarked that they were 'flattening those old heaps on Pencrugiau', and went on to say that there was a bulldozer working on the site that morning. The 'heaps' formed the largest collection of Bronze Age barrows in north Pembrokeshire, known as Crugiau Cemais. The land upon which they stood had recently been bought by Morton Smith, the landlord of the Black Lion Hotel at Cardigan and I telephoned him to explain that these were scheduled monuments and part of our priceless heritage. He told me that he knew better than the archaeologists: these were mounds of sand, and of no great antiquity, and he had therefore decided to get rid of them. In any case, barrows or not, he could not make contact with the man on the bulldozer as he was busy in the bar of his hotel. I set off immediately in the hope that I would be able to persuade the bulldozer driver, or else frighten him with dire consequences. When I arrived on the scene, I found that the man had fallen off the bulldozer and damaged his leg, after taking off only one slice of the seven barrows, and had been taken to hospital. Crugiau Cemais was thus saved and word soon got round for, some weeks later, another bulldozer driver informed me confidentially that he had been commissioned by a farmer to demolish the Iron Age site at Penrallt, Llantood, which gave me enough time to have a preservation order issued.

The Memorial Hall at Newport had been built to commemorate those who had lost their lives in the 1914-18 war, and the question arose as to whether it should now be regarded as a memorial for the men who had died in 1939-45 as well, and a committee, of which I was a member, was appointed to consider the matter. Once we had decided that the hall should be the memorial for the two wars, the placement of the tablets caused heated discussion. The brass tablet bearing the names of the fallen of the first war was placed in a place of honour at the back of the stage, but it was hardly ever in view as it was either concealed by the cinema screen or by scenery set for a drama performance. Even so, there were some who wanted the two tablets, side by side, on this wall and I had to do some pleading to have them placed on facing walls below the stage so that they would be visible at all times, before this was agreed. Then there was argument when we came to discuss the order of the names and which to include. The 1914-18 tablet was headed by the name of Captain Martin Kemes Arundel Lloyd, Newport Castle, and then according to rank, but it was felt that the new tablet should have the names in alphabetic order. While the names of the young men born and bred at Newport were not in any doubt, there were others whose entitlement was questioned. There were those who had married local girls, and there were those whose families had come to live at Newport during the war. There was the young RAF officer who had married the daughter of an incomer family, and who had been killed on the day after the war ended. And there were other problems, like the one presented by the mother who would not allow the name of her son to be included as she expected him home daily, although everyone knew that he had been lost at sea. These matters led to endless deliberations before the two memorials, now placed on facing walls below the stage, were unveiled on Remembrance Day 1949.

Monday, the opening day of the Bridgend Eisteddfod will long be remembered for its torrential rain. My old Army friend Monty Montrose, who was staying with us at the castle, expressed a desire to come to the festival and we set off in his car on a rather dismal morning. By the time we got to Stormy Down the rain obliterated our vision and all cars had to pull in to the side of the road and watch a brown torrent rushing by. We stayed at the Wyndham Hotel where there was a goodly company of Eisteddfod figures, among whom was Trefin, the Grand Sword-bearer. I introduced Monty to him as 'my friend Montrose' and Trefin immediately turned to me and asked: 'Not the Duke, is it?' 'But of course,' I jokingly replied and Trefin livened and said: 'I am so pleased to meet you, your Grace. I once had the privilege of being taken fishing on your river at Drymen, and I should very much like to go there again.' 'With pleasure,' said Monty, adjusting his monocle as we were leaving, 'Any time.' I only realised the consequence of my wicked joke when I heard that Trefin was telling everybody what a nice fellow the Duke of Montrose was and how he was looking forward to fishing his rivers again.

When the Archdruid called on the winner of the Chair poem to stand, a hush fell over the vast congregation until a lone figure got to his feet at the back of the

Pavilion. Excited voices in the audience could be heard saying 'It's Dewi Emrys.' The cognoscenti raised their eyebrows, for it was the unwritten law that a poet would not compete again after winning the Crown or the Chair three times. Dewi had already won the chair at Liverpool in 1929, at Llanelli in 1930 and at Bangor in 1943, but he had a justifiable feeling that he had been unfairly treated by the critics and by the bardic establishment, and this was his revenge. As he sat in the chair, he looked around him with a defiant air as much as to say 'To hell with the lot of you!' After we had returned to the robing rooms I went to shake him by the hand. There was a tear in his eye as he said: 'As long as Pembrokeshire remembers me, all is well!' The party to celebrate his victory that night was a jolly one and it was well gone midnight when Humphrey ap Evans, now Humphrey Drummond of Megginch, Keidrych Rhys and T. H. Evans and I, left Bridgend: in Humphrey's car, and came home with me.

Gwenallt, who was my lecturer in the Welsh Department when I was at Aberystwyth, called at the castle to ask me to conduct a party of Welsh intellectuals on a tour of Palestine, which I had to decline. After tea, I took him for a run over the Presely Hills and witnessed the birth pains of his poem *Presely*.

Joyce and I went to her brother Arthur's wedding to Anne Abbott, a floral artist who was working with Constance Spry and had arranged the flowers at the marriage of Princess Elizabeth to Prince Philip, and on other royal occasions. We stayed with Joyce's father, living by now in Hampstead. He showed me letters he had received from Herbert Morrison and Winston Churchill in appreciation of his book *Politics and Poverty*. He also spoke about his broadcast in a series called 'Britain's Crisis' in which he had taken part with Sir George Schuster, Sir Norman Kipping and George Woodcock.

I never missed an opportunity to visit Will Griffiths at his bookshop in Cecil Court and, on one occasion, when I told him that Richard Llewellyn had come to live at Newport, he asked me not to mention that name in his presence. He said that Llewellyn's original name was Lloyd and that his claim to have been born at St David's was untrue, as he had been born in London. He would never forgive him as he had not acknowledged the fact that he had obtained most of the background material for his book *How Green Was My Valley* from Griff's father, at Gilfach Goch, and had not even sent the old man a copy of the book.

Morfa Withington, who had succeeded her mother as Lady Marcher of Cemais, came and stayed with us for the Court Leet and installation of William Morgan Jermain as mayor. She was a patient at St David's Hospital, Carmarthen, at the time and when I went there to fetch her, Dr Sidney Davies, the Superintendent, asked me to sign two pieces of paper. One was for the diamond mace brooch, which she wore in her corsage during the installation ceremony, and the other was for her, to be returned to the hospital by the following Monday morning. Later, she sent me a copy of her grandmother's book, *An Epitome of the Twenty-five Lords of Kemes*, which Lady Lloyd had inscribed: 'To my darling daughter Nesta, from her ever loving mother, Katharine Lloyd.' Morfa, naughtily, had crossed out the dedication to her mother and substituted: 'To Dillwyn with many thanks. Morfa.' Inside the book were some loose papers, including a copy of the pedigree of the family attested by David Edwardes of Rhydygors, and a letter from Lady Lloyd to Nesta telling her how to behave with the chauffeur.

On the morning of the fifteenth of November 1948, as I was driving to attend a meeting of the County Welfare Committee at Haverfordwest, there were flags flying everywhere to celebrate the birth of Prince Charles. Captain Geoffrey Crawshay, chairman of the Welsh Board of Health, was present at the meeting and, when the business was done, he and I went to the Hotel Mariners for lunch. The landlord, Harold Headley, was behind the bar and when I asked for two glasses of beer he said: 'Today is special, and you will drink this!' and poured us each a bottle of Prince's Ale, which had been laid down in Burton-on-Trent in 1929 when Edward, Prince of Wales, visited that town. It drank like a rich barley wine. Headley then said: 'And now there is only one other drink that we can drink today,' and produced a bottle of Welsh whiskey. Squire Price of Rhiwlas, after his horse Bendigo had won the Cambridgeshire in 1889, conceived the idea of bringing employment to the Welsh people by establishing a distillery at Frongoch, north of Bala, that would produce 'the most wonderful whiskey that ever drove the skeleton from the feast, or painted landscapes on the brain of man . . . the mingled souls of peat and barley washed white within the waters of Tryweryn.' He sent a case to Queen Victoria and received from her private secretary an assurance that Buckingham Palace would never again be without Welsh whiskey. Wynford Vaughan Thomas related this story to Prince Philip who ordered a search in the royal cellars, but could not find any.

My brother, who had been in partnership with a local estate agent, decided to set up on his own and asked me to join him and so, at the beginning of 1949 the business firm of Messrs. Miles and Miles, Estate Agents, was established, with offices in a bow-windowed house of character in Market Street, Newport, known as Bryn Coed.

The Territorial Army was re-formed in Pembrokeshire to comprise 302nd Field Regiment, 424th and 425th Coast Regiments and 109th Transport Column RASC. I was invited to join 424, with my old rank of Captain, only a little before it was converted into 424th Heavy Anti-Aircraft Regiment RA (TA). We had our drill meetings in the Drill Hall at Fishguard on week nights, and on Sundays Bombadier Glyn Rees would bring his Army truck up to the castle to take me to firing practice at the School of Artillery at Manorbier. Sometimes I would go to Milford, which was 424's main base. One July evening, after listening to Brigadiers Phillips and Bordass addressing us, Major James Eaton-Evans asked me if I would like to join him and Lieutenant Colonel Dan Bruton for a drink. We walked down into the Docks and I was beginning to wonder where we were going to have the drink when James told me to jump into his boat and away we went across the Haven to Angle, to the Old Point Inn. The culm fire in the bar, the landlord claimed, had been kept burning for 212 years.

We held the Officers' Ball, the first to be held after the war, at the De Valence Pavilion in Tenby with the Royal Artillery Dance Band in attendance. The officers were appropriately dressed, wearing miniatures, and the ladies wore ball gowns that made the event redolent of the colour and style of pre-war balls. Joyce and I went with Graham and Patsy Johns, Manorowen, and we stayed the night at the Royal Gate House Hotel, Tenby. My connection with the military was further strengthened by my appointment to represent the Pembrokeshire County Council on the Territorial Army and Voluntary Reserve Association.

Fforddolion Ceredigion, the Cardiganshire Wayfarers' Society, composed in the main of the literati of that county, was formed under the presidency of Dewi Emrys. It held its first annual dinner at the Webley Hotel, St Dogmaels, on St David's Day 1949, and I was invited to propose the toast to the society. Dewi, during his response, admitted that he was inclined to agree with the opinion expressed by the great poet and scholar, Professor T. Gwynn Jones, that if anything immortal had come from his pen, it was the poem he had written, in the local dialect, to Pwllderi. I suggested to him that he should take us there, which he did in the following September, and it was a memorable occasion. Dewi stood above the steep cliffs, his eagle face looking out to sea, and into the wind that tossed his hair. Slowly he turned round and raised an arm towards the heather-clad slopes of Garn Fawr, towards his 'homestead among the mountain streams and health-giving air,' and began to recite the poem:

> *Fry ar y mwni mae nghartre bach*
> *Gyda'r goferydd a'r awel iach . . .*

He walked away as soon as he had spoken the last line, taking one look at the purple and gold of the heather and gorse and the wave lashed rocks below. Later that evening, at the Sailors Safety at Pwllgwaelod, he recited the poem once more, this time for me, he said.

ON THE COUNCIL

AN INVITATION TO STAND FOR THE Pembrokeshire County Council in a by-election caused by the death of the sitting member for the Nevern Division came unexpectedly. This was a vast constituency, about the largest in Wales, comprising the parishes of Nevern, Bayvil, Meline and Llanychllwydog and extending from Newport Sands almost to Moylgrove along the coast, and including the northern slopes of the Presely Hills, and the Gwaun Valley to within a few miles of Fishguard. I had been told that I would be returned unopposed but when I went to submit my nomination papers I found that I had an opponent in George Bowen of Llwyngwair. The Bowen family had resided at Llwyngwair since about 1500 and had provided leaders in the local community since Norman times. The relationship between them and the lords of Cemais at Newport Castle had not always been a happy one, and the election was immediately looked upon by the local people as a resurgence of the rivalry between the castle and the mansion house. It took me every day of three weeks to cover the ground of the division, entailing long walks to upland holdings that I thought to be no longer inhabited and, with very few exceptions, I found the people extraordinarily kind and welcoming. When the result of the poll was declared, I had a substantial majority.

At the first meeting of the new County Council the chairman, Alderman Ralph Warren, extended a welcome to three new members: Sir Charles Price, formerly Conservative Member of Parliament for the county; Captain Graham Johns, and me. I was placed on a number of committees, including those dealing with Education, Planning and Public Assistance, and membership of these led to being elected to serve on a variety of subcommittees and outside bodies, from the Cemais Board of Guardians to the Courts of the Governors of the University of Wales and of the National Library.

At lunch time, Graham and I were invited to join the senior Aldermen, J. O. Vaughan, B. G. Llewhellin, Maesgwynne, Simon Morris of Boncath, Major Hall Morgan, R. S. Kelway and Ronald Mathias of Lamphey Court, at the Lower Three Crowns, which was next door to the Shire Hall. This was a hard-drinking sanhedrin at which much of the business of the Council was planned or plotted.

Dr Dyfrig Pennant, DSO, one time surgeon at a London hospital, was chairman of the Allensbank Management Committee, of which I was a member. Allensbank was originally the Narberth Workhouse which, in an age of euphemisms, had been given a distracting name. At a meeting of the committee, one day, he announced that he wished to resign from the chair and informed the members that he wanted them to appoint me, as a young person, in his place, and this was agreed. When I visited the home on the following New Year's Day, as I moved among the patients – the deformed, the unkempt, the inelegant, all huddled together in this awful place, I felt that it was absurd to wish them a Happy New Year. Martha Francis, aged ninety-one and monoglot, smiled wearily when I spoke to her in Welsh. Young Graham, deaf, dumb, blind and incontinent, alone in his dark world, grunted as I put my hand upon him. Like Wilfred Owen, I thought . . .

> *Was it for this the clay grew?*
> *– O, what made fatuous sunbeams toil*
> *To break earth's sleep at all?*

The former Olympic runner, H. M. Abrahams, who was Secretary of the National Parks Commission, together with Lord Merthyr, a member of the Commission, came to meet the County Planning Committee in order to discuss a proposal to establish a national park in Pembrokeshire. The Committee, having listened to them sympathetically, decided in principle to do so and set up the Pembrokeshire National Park Committee, of which I was appointed a member, to explore the matter.

Hugh Dalton, when he was Minister of Town and Country Planning, used to arrange a walking tour each Whitsuntide with a select company of friends and, in 1951, they came to Pembrokeshire. Those of us who were concerned in the matter immediately thought that he would take advantage of the visit to designate the Pembrokeshire Coast National Park, or even that he might have arranged the visit for that purpose, but we were wrong. He merely proposed to walk along the coastal path and Joyce and I invited him and his friends to coffee at Newport Castle before they set off. The party included Barbara (later Baroness) Castle, Geoffrey de Freitas, Arthur Blenkinsop, all Members of Parliament, and our member, Desmond Donnelly, together with a number of Fleet Street journalists who were allowed, or invited, each year to follow the party and to report each day's happenings. Dalton invited Ronald Lockley and I to join them that first day. One of the newspapers made use of my mayoral position to give his report the heading 'Mayor takes Mr Dalton for a Walk'.

I took advantage of Dalton's presence to launch our *Festival of Britain* activities by turning on a commemorative fountain in Llysmeddyg Gardens. He turned the valve with such force that, as the *Western Mail* stated, 'he gave himself a sharp and refreshing shower before he moved hurriedly out of range.'

We started our walk at Ceibwr and, by the time we got to the collapsed blowhole at the Witches' Cauldron, Dalton was loudly deploring the custom of setting gin-traps on open ground, and he was still fulminating when he crossed a stile that stood on a low hedge bank. As he got off the hedge bank, he stepped squarely on a gin-trap. He leapt into the air and, uttering stentorian oaths, dragged the trap from its anchorage and flung it over the cliff.

We walked as far as Newport Sands, by which time the Minister complained of a thirst and I took the party to the Sailors Safety at Pwllgwaelod where he enjoyed a refreshing pint of ale. Joyce and I were invited to dine with the Minister at the Hotel Mariners that evening and, after dinner, at about eleven o'clock, Dalton said: 'Do you know where I would like to go now, Dillwyn? I'd like to go to that pub you took us to this afternoon.' I rang Monté Manson at the Sailors Safety and, in no time, we were on our way. Dalton was in his element and Barbara enjoyed an opportunity to dance.

Dalton left without making any declaration and it was not until the following year that the Pembrokeshire Coast National Park was designated. I remained a member of the National Park Authority, sometimes as a County Council representative and other times as a Minister's nominee, for the next twenty years.

I was a member of the County Libraries and Museum Committee, which appealed to me greatly, and I was soon appointed its chairman. The committee was optimistically named as it had no museum, as yet, but it had a well-stocked library at Haverfordwest. I assumed the chair with an ambitious programme in mind for, apart from wanting to have a museum and also a record office, I wanted to establish branch libraries where none existed. I remembered the Reading Room at the Memorial Hall at Newport that was also intended to be a library, in the sense that it had a bookcase that contained a few books but was permanently locked. Its primary purpose was served by a table to which the *Western Mail* was fixed by a brass rod, open at the penultimate page which contained a section headed 'Movements of Vessels', by consulting which housewives could get to know where their seafaring husbands, or sons, had docked or left port, and when to expect them home. It had been my ambition for some time to have a proper library in the town and I felt that I now had an opportunity to do so. It was with great pleasure, therefore, that on 30 June 1950, I opened the branch library at Newport, at West End House, in the presence of the Mayor and a large body of people.

I also wanted to have a mobile library service for the rural areas and I was able to preside at the inauguration of a scheme before I relinquished the chair in

February 1952, when the first purpose-built vehicle took to the road, its cost having been borne by the Welsh Church Fund in celebration of the Festival of Britain.

Thomas (Tim) Davies, the librarian, and I looked around for premises that would be suitable for conversion to a museum and record office and, having heard that Foley House was on the market, we inspected the premises and I managed to persuade the County Council to purchase the house for this purpose. Because money for the conversion of the premises and the appointment of officers could not be found at the time, the house was used temporarily for committee meetings. I resigned from the Council when I left the county in 1952 and when I returned two years later I was distressed to find that Foley House had been converted into committee rooms, and that its facade had been vandalised by the County Architect in the process.

I had hoped that it would have been possible to offer the post of County Archivist to Francis Jones who had worked on the county records at Haverfordwest Castle before the war and had continued to maintain an interest, particularly in family records. I knew that he would shortly be completing his work on the official history of the war at the Cabinet Office and that he would like to return to Pembrokeshire. I met him whenever I went to London and kept him informed of the situation. As we were having a drink in The George in Great Portland Street, one day, my colleague from Carmarthenshire, Elwyn Samuel, heard me inform Francis of the current position and intervened to say that the Carmarthenshire County Council had decided to appoint an Archivist and, as chairman of the Council's Finance Committee, he recommended Francis to apply for the post, which he did and was appointed County Archivist for Carmarthenshire, in January 1959, to the great loss of Pembrokeshire.

The museum was eventually established at the old police headquarters at Haverfordwest Castle. By this time, having returned to Pembrokeshire, I was again a member and vice-chairman of the Committee, and I suggested that the wall space in the museum be reserved for the displaying the county's art treasures, while that of the new Library Hall, that was being erected on the site of the old Grammar School, should be used for travelling exhibitions. When I called at the castle one day, I found that the County Architect had lined the walls with red brick and had introduced a diaper patter in a brick of different colour. This was not a suitable background for hanging pictures and the walls had to be given a white wash.

I became a member of the Cemaes Rural District Council the meetings of which were held alternately at Eglwyswrw and Crymych. At Eglwyswrw we met in the church hall, conveniently situated behind the Serjeant's Arms. The meetings usually ended before three o'clock, but if it did not, the back door of the

Serjeant's would always be open to thirsty Councillors. I kept constant pressure on the Cemaes RDC to provide houses for the elderly and got them to agree to build pairs of bungalows at Newport at a cost of £1,750 per pair for letting at around 5/- (25p.) per week, it being understood that the bungalows would be made available to young married couples should there be no demand from the elderly.

I was also a member of the Newport Parish Council, of which I had previously been the clerk, and soon discovered that the minutes, which I had persuaded the members to keep in Welsh in 1934, had long since reverted to English. I was appointed to represent the Council on the Pembrokeshire Association of Local Councils and attended their annual meeting, over which Lord Merthyr presided. At the meeting, I was nominated as the county's representative on the National Association of Local Councils, but as I was already heavily committed with public work I had to decline. Within five years, however, I was a member of the National Association, and Lord Merthyr was its president, and I was later to become its chairman and then vice-president.

I was appointed by the County Council to serve as its representative on the Pembrokeshire Rural Community Council and on the Pembrokeshire and Cardiganshire Rural Industries Committee and, as such, I attended an exhibition of rural crafts at which there was also a wildlife exhibition set up by the West Wales Field Society. I little thought that within a decade I would be responsible for these organisations.

It came as a shock, at the Michaelmas Court Leet, at which nominations for Mayor are made, to hear one of the Aldermen propose my name as 'a fit and proper person to be mayor of this town for the ensuing year,' and the motion was carried with acclamation before I could say anything. I was installed, the youngest mayor ever, at the Court held at the Llwyngwair Arms on 11 November 1950. The Steward gave me a Bible to hold in my right hand while I took the customary oath to 'well and truly execute and exercise the Office of Mayor for the Town and Liberties of Newport within the Barony of Cemais for the ensuing year' and to 'do equal right to the poor and to the rich. So help you God,' said the Steward, and I kissed the Bible. The Lady Marcher, Morfa Withington, granddaughter of the late Sir Marteine Lloyd, then placed the mayoral chain round my neck, and I presented her with a red rose, a thought that arose from Lady Lloyd's story about her son sending her a red rose on her birthday, until he was on the Somme, when he sent her a Flanders poppy.

My successors have repeated the gesture, and it has amused me to read reports in the local newspapers, each year, stating the new Mayor, after being installed, had presented a red rose to the Lady Marcher 'in accordance with the centuries' old tradition.'

The mayoral banquet, after the installation, was followed by toasts that demanded twenty-eight speeches and lasted until midnight. The following day, being Sunday, we attended the civic service at St Mary's Church, as I had appointed the rector as my Chaplain, and as it was also Remembrance Day, we paraded, in the usual manner, from the Llwyngwair Arms to the church and, after the service, to the Memorial Hall, where another two minutes' silence was observed. I endeavoured, year after year, to have one combined service, but the chapels would not agree.

It was one of my ambitions, as Mayor, to revive the fair. There were two fairs at Newport, granted under a thirteenth century charter, the one, *Ffair Gurig*, in June, being described by the historian George Owen as 'a great fair'. I remembered the streets full of horses, standing with their heads towards the houses on both sides of the street, with only a narrow space between their haunches, far too dangerous to walk along. In the evening, as darkness fell, the stall holders and street traders would light their naphtha flares, which would splutter and sizzle, especially in the other fair, in October, when there would be a wind and, often, rain. Some characters would get maudlin drunk, which would provide us children with a rare and entertaining spectacle, especially when PC Owen came along to deal with them.

By now, the fairs had ceased to exist, leaving a gap in the corporate life of the town. I announced that there would be a fair, and a few horses came, and a number of voluntary organisations responded to my request that they should erect stalls in the street so as to raise funds for their own causes. I also managed to persuade Messrs Studt to bring their dodgems and roundabouts and coconut shies and other stalls to the Playing Field. I declared the fair open by cutting a ribbon held across the street and exercised my duty as mayor by collecting 'the tolls for pitchings and standings', charging each stall-holder the sum of one penny. This realised the total sum of four shillings and two pence (21p) which I deposited at Lloyds Bank in a *Ffair Gurig* Account, and it attracted such attention at the bank's headquarters that it was featured in its journal *The Black Horse*. The mayors of Haverfordwest, Pembroke, Tenby and Cardigan accepted my invitation to be present at the fair and their worships readily joined me in a ride on the dodgems, which provided the local newspapers with some jolly photographs. Even the *Radio Times* showed a picture of me cutting the ribbon, with Joyce and the Bailiff and the other mayors beside me.

Having invited the mayors of the other towns to Newport, for the first time, I received invitations to be present at their functions. I attended the presentation of the Freedom of the Town and County of Haverfordwest to Alderman George Williams, Lord Mayor of Cardiff, and to the Reverend Arthur Baring Gould, who had been vicar of St. Martin's Church since 1908, and the Mayor of Haverfordwest, Councillor Eddie Jones, in his capacity as Admiral of the Port, invited me to accompany him, and the Mayors of Pembroke and Tenby, on his barge as he sailed down river to inspect his rights of fishery.

It was my good fortune to be Mayor of Newport during the Festival of Britain, our programme for which was described by the editor of the *Western Mail* as 'rich in variety and reflecting the ceaseless endeavours of a small community', while the editorial in the *County Echo* expressed the opinion that it was 'doubtful whether any district, comparable in size and population, had a greater variety of functions to celebrate the Festival than Newport.'

The mayors and provosts of cities and towns throughout Great Britain were invited to a service of thanksgiving at St Paul's Cathedral as a part of the celebration of the Festival of Britain. No such invitation arrived for the Mayor of Newport, however, and I therefore wrote to the Lord Mayor of London pointing out our common date of installation and he arranged for one to be issued, together with an unexpected invitation to the opening of the South Bank Exhibition.

After the service we got out on to the apron in front of the Cathedral in time to see the King and Queen emerge, followed by Queen Mary and the Princesses Elizabeth and Margaret, and the other members of the Royal Family. Then came the Prime Minister, Clement Attlee, and the Leader of the Opposition, Winston Churchill, who received an especially loud cheer from the gathered crowd, followed by the war leaders led by Montgomery. Alanbrooke, Cunningham, all bemedalled and in full uniform. We were again in close proximity to the Royal Family the next day when the King opened the Festival on the South Bank, a hundred years after the opening of the Great Exhibition of 1851.

When I heard that Princess Marina, Duchess of Kent, was scheduled to visit west Wales and was to call at Cardigan and Fishguard, I immediately got in touch with the Lord Lieutenant, Colonel Hugh Higgon, with a request that she should stop at Newport. This, I was told, would be out of the question as her itinerary had been arranged and approved by Buckingham Palace and it would be impossible to change. I protested that it would only be a matter of minutes which could be easily gained by careful planning and, eventually, Hugh Higgon rang me to say that he had been able to arrange for Her Royal Highness to call and to be received by me as Mayor.

The Duchess would arrive at eleven o'clock on the morning of the 12th of July 1951 and would stay for twenty minutes before proceeding to Fishguard and Haverfordwest. I was up early that morning marshalling my assistants and making the necessary preparations. We borrowed some empty beer barrels and laid planks across them to form a dais that filled the width of Market Street and which we covered with our large drawing room carpet brought down from the castle. We placed tubs of flowers on the carpet and in front to hide the beer barrel supports.

I appointed Captain Johnny Davies, Dandre, retired master mariner, in charge of flags and bunting to decorate the town and asked him to find a large Welsh flag to hang across the Square, where the royal car would stop. When I finally arrived on the scene in my robe and chain of office, ready to receive HRH, I saw a flag hanging from a rope tied to the top of the telegraph pole on one side and to the top of a lamp standard diagonally opposite, and so huge that it swept the road. One half of the flag was white and the other black. I swore at Johnny, who claimed that he had not been able to find a large Red Dragon and added that had I known anything about the Navy I would know the message of his flag. 'What is it, for God's sake?' I snapped at him in my temper. 'It means,' he said solemnly, 'stop or I fire across your bows,' and then burst out laughing.

The school children sang as the royal car pulled up on the crowded Square, and the Bailiff, in his top hat and maroon frock coat, carried the mace ahead of the Duchess and the Lord Lieutenant, and led them through a guard of honour of young ladies dressed in Welsh costume to the dais, where I bid her welcome and presented Joyce to her, along with a number of the local dignitaries. Marilyn, aged five and dressed in a Welsh costume, presented the Duchess with a bouquet of flowers.

Once the ceremony was over, Joyce and I went to Haverfordwest to a luncheon given by the Mayor. The Duchess's Private Secretary, Sir Philip Hay, wrote to convey HRH's 'very warm thanks and appreciation of the kind welcome with which she was received when she paid a brief visit to Newport' and said that she was 'delighted with the charming gift of flowers with which she was presented and was extremely touched by the kind thought which prompted the gift.' The Lord Lieutenant also wrote to thank me 'most sincerely for the excellent arrangements' and added that 'Her Royal Highness was very touched by the warm welcome given her by the people of your ancient borough.'

I had been concerned for some time at the manner in which the names of prospective burgesses were brought forward at the Court Leet. According to custom, a man's name was proposed as 'a fit and proper person to be a burgess' in open Court, without notice, and rarely would any burgess have the courage to object or give good reason, if there were any, why the person nominated should not be admitted. In consequence, there had been some embarrassing nominations, and also, there had been persons nominated who did not live in the borough. I reminded the Court that burgesses should be men resident within the borough, which was coterminous with the parish, and suggested that the names of prospective burgesses should be placed before a selection committee appointed for that purpose. This was agreed and it has worked successfully ever since. There had also been difficulties with regard to nominations for the office of mayor, as I had myself experienced when I was nominated without any warning, and I suggested that a Court of Aldermen be established that would be available to advise the mayor at any time, if called upon, and to prepare a list of three names for the approval of the Court which, if acceptable, would be submitted to the Lord Marcher who, by tradition, would select the first name. I wanted the second name on the list to be Deputy Mayor, who would then have opportunity to prepare himself for office. This, again, was agreed but it has been more difficult to implement through lack of suitable candidates.

I had noticed at mayoral gatherings that the mayoress of Newport was conspicuous in that she did not wear a badge or chain. I, therefore, arranged for a badge for the succeeding mayoress to be made, to mark the Festival of Britain.

I came close to having to relinquish my office one evening, when I called at the Castle Hotel, a little before closing time, to meet the landlord and the clerk to the Parish Council, Joe Williams, to discuss a matter relating to the town. A man came into the bar and took Joe to a corner where he offered him a salmon which Joe thought was too big for him and he asked me to share it with him. He then took the fish to the back kitchen and laid it on a slate slab so as to divide it. At that moment the back door opened and in walked PC Jones. He fixed his eye on the salmon and I immediately had a vision of the headline: 'Mayor caught in possession of poached salmon while consuming alcoholic liquor during non-permitted hours.' I would resign, of course, but the stigma would remain and visit my children and my children's children. The policeman took the knife from Joe's hand and addressed the fish by cutting off its head and its tail. He wrapped the rest in the newspaper upon which it lay and tucked it under his arm and walked out, saying 'Goodnight gentlemen'. Joe and I looked at each other and laughed, and drank to rough justice.

In May 1952, the BBC asked me to prepare and present a programme in the network series *Country Magazine*. I hesitated to accept the responsibility for such a prestigious programme, which had one of the highest listening figures and to which the whole nation would be listening, following the lunch time news each Sunday. I decided to do it from Newport Castle and to subtitle it 'The Lordship of Cemais'. I chose people with a variety of interest and skills: Idris Davies, Trewilym, dairy farmer and chairman of the county branch of the National Farmers Union; Joyce Joy, who had been blind and now could see enough to grow *helichrysum* and other 'everlasting' flowers in her market garden; Tim Davies, county librarian and naturalist; Frank Thomas, who had lost an arm as a boy but was an able seine-net fisherman and rabbit dealer, and Hamish Stewart

Peter, a Scottish flockmaster as unpredictable as any of his mountain sheep that roamed the Presely Hills. Mansel Owen, baritone monumental mason, sang a local ballad to the accompaniment of a harp.

Sometimes, when I went to London, I would meet Keidrych Rhys who was the gossip columnist with *The People* at the time and he would invariably take me to one of his Clubs. When I asked him on one occasion how he could afford to belong to so many Clubs, he said that he did not belong to any of them, but had open access to them all as a gossip journalist. One of his favourite places was the Gargoyle Club in Soho which had been opened by David Tennant and his wife, Hermione Baddeley, in 1925. They had made Augustus John president of the Club at the outset and he had remained a privileged habitué. He was present the first evening that I was taken there and took an immediate, though ephemeral, interest when he heard that I was from Haverfordwest, the scene of his boyhood which he had described in his *Chiaroscuro* as 'the home of my father's people.'

Keidrych took me to the Colony Room Club where I met Lucien Freud, Francis Bacon and Daniel Farson, and John Minton, who was soon to die. We went to Churchill's and to Eve's, in Regent Street, where a performing fire-eater took his flare to a table at which Prince Abdul-Illah of Iraq was sitting and invited the Prince to play the flame along the sole of his foot, which he did, very slowly until one could smell burning skin.

The man who came and sat next to me in the train before we left Paddington had a face that was familiar and it was only when he asked how far I was going that I recognised the voice as that of Professor Joad, the controversial philosopher on the BBC Brains Trust made famous by his expression: 'It depends what you mean.' He said that he was going to Ireland to see his daughter and would therefore be travelling all the way to Fishguard Harbour. When dinner was announced he asked 'Will you give me the pleasure of dining with me?' I told him that I proposed dining anyway and that perhaps we could share a table. He then insisted that he should buy the wine. 'Do you enjoy travelling?' he asked, as we were eating. I said that I did, but not up and down the same line all the time. 'Oh,' he said laughingly, at the top of his high pitched voice, 'that's like saying that you would like to sleep with a different woman every night!' I heard the knives and forks drop on the plates and felt that all the faces in the dining compartment were directed towards us.

Lady Petrie wrote to say that she would like to accept our invitation to stay with us and, to my surprise, she tolerated the children and even spoke to them occasionally, while they looked upon her as a resurrected Egyptian mummy. She still had the same straw hat that she wore in Jerusalem, and the skin of her face still resembled crinkled brown leather. We took her to a concert at Ebenezer Chapel

Joyce being presented to Her Majesty the Queen by the Lord Lieutenant, 1967.

Portfield House, Haverfordwest.

Best Kept Village presentation ceremony at Nevern, 1957.
Left to right: Lieut. Colonel Patrick Lort-Phillips; Air Commodore J. B. Bowen, Lord Lieutentant; the Mayor and Mayoress of Newport (Alderman and Mrs George Evans); Lady Merthyr; DM; Lord Merthyr; the Rev. E. T. Jones, Vicar; Penry Evans, Clerk to the Nevern Parish Council.

DM sworn as Mayor of Haverfordwest, 1961.

The new Mayoress and Mayor with the Very Reverend Eric Green and Mrs George Llewellin, the retiring Mayor and Mayoress.

Visit to Cork, as Sheriff of the Town and County of Haverfordwest.
On my left the Mayor of Newport, Mon., the Mayor of Merthyr Tudful,
the Lord Mayor of Cork, and the Lord Mayor of Cardiff.

Sean MacReamoinn, Alun Williams of the BBC, and DM at the Sychnant Pass Hotel.

Wynford Vaughan-Thomas presenting first copy of *A Portrait of Pembrokeshire* to Marilyn.

Presentation of the first copy of my book *The Royal National Eisteddfod of Wales* to the Prime Minister, Lord Callaghan. On either side, Sir Geraint Evans and Sir Alun Talfan Davies, 1978.

Wynford Vaughan-Thomas signing the book at the Moonrakers' Dinner at Devizes.
The President, DM and Anthony look on.

DM as Grand Swordbearer, the Archdruid (Trefin), Her Majesty the Queen, the Prince Philip (awaiting admission to the Gorsedd of Bards), and T. W. Thomas, at the Cardiff Eisteddfod, 1960.

The Herald Bard with the Archdruid Ap Llysor (W. R. P. George).

The Herald Bard, mounted.

GREN – at the EISTEDDFOD

"I didn't know they were doing the Desert Song..."

... as seen by Gren.

The Herald Bard receiving the Prince of Wales at the Flint Eisteddfod, 1969.

The Prince of Wales and his Committee on Snowdon.

The Prince of Wales' Committee meeting at Haverfordwest in 1972.

Front row: DM, Baroness White, Dr Tom Richards, HRH the Prince of Wales, the Marchioness of Anglesey, Captain H. R. H. Vaughan and, among others, Harold Naylor, S/Ldr. David Checketts, David Evans, Colonel John Williams-Wynn, Charles Quant, Professor P. F. Wareing, John Zehtmayer, Peter Schofield, E. H. Owen, John Gittins, Tom Jones, Alwyn Willliams, R. O. Hughes, and Ivor Cassam.

Seal marking by curragh – Anthony, DM and R. M. Lockley.

R. M. Lockley, DM, Sir David Attenborough.

Haverford Hunt Club, Haverford, Pennsylvania, USA.

DM sitting where Dylan Thomas sat at the bar, White Horse Tavern, New York.

DM with grandchildren, Max, Emily, Tamsin, Andrew.

DM and Judith.

Warden's Court, Gild of Freemen of Haverfordwest. Swearing in the chairman of the County Council as a Burgess by the Master, Colonel John Green, OBE, DL, TD. *Standing*: Dr Derry Bowen, John Jones, Malcolm Thomas, DM, Malcolm Green, C Thomas David Evans, Roderick Thomas, and Paul Lucas, clerk.

DM with Judith and Jenny Ogwen at The Galway Film Festival.

DM, chairman, and the Duke of Grafton, president, of the National Association of Local Councils.

Receiving award from HRH the Duke of Edinburgh.

Presentation of portrait by the Archdruid on retirement as Herald Bard, 1996.

and as we sat in our old family pew I could not help visualising the late Reverend Ben Morris looking down upon us and wishing that he had been spared to welcome the widow of the great Sir Flinders Petrie, whose name he had called so often to witness the words of God.

I managed to rescue a cross-incised stone pillar that stood as a gatepost opposite Cnwce farm when a house was being built on the site, and had it conveyed to St Mary's Churchyard, and erected outside the west door, where it could be seen from the road by passers-by.

'There has been a considerable amount of speculation as to why Wilfred Pickles's *Have A Go* programme will be broadcast from Newport,' wrote the envious editor of the *Western Telegraph*, while the editor of the *West Wales Guardian* wondered 'Why is Wilfred Pickles' famous broadcast programme *Have A Go* coming to Newport of all the towns in the county? This question has been asked several times in the last fortnight and the answer is that Captain Dillwyn Miles extended the invitation to Mr Pickles as long ago as 1950.' It pointed out that the BBC had enough invitations from places to keep the programme going for the next thousand years. That Wilfred and his team had enjoyed their visit may be gathered from the ease with which I was able to persuade them to bring the programme to Pembrokeshire three times again, to St David's, St Dogmael's and Haverfordwest.

Sir Grismond Philipps, Lord Lieutenant of Carmarthenshire, was one of a select band of officers responsible for the King's body during the war. One day, while we were conversing, he told me that he was a trustee of the estate of the late Mrs Powell of Nanteos, and I asked him what had happened to *Cwpan Nanteos*, the Nanteos Cup, 'the Holy Grail', reputed to have been brought from the Cistercian Abbey of Strata Florida after the Dissolution, and had passed eventually to the care of the Powells. It was now the subject of litigation among claimants under Mrs Powell's will and was in Sir Grismond's charge as executor. 'Don't tell anybody,' he said, 'but I've got the damned thing locked up in a bank here in Carmarthen.' It eventually passed to a branch of the family living outside Wales and no one seemed to notice that the Principality had lost one of its most famous treasures.

Towards the end of our mayoral year, Joyce was taken ill and, through the good office of her uncle, John Ord, a consultant in Harley Street, she went to see Sir Horace Evans, later Lord Evans, physician to the King, who told her that her heart was not in good condition and that she should no longer live at the Castle which, as she had described it, was 'a boxed-in staircase'. This was a sad blow to us both, as we had looked forward to living there for the rest of our lives. I had to resign from the County, District and Parish Councils and some forty committees, and was not able to carry on as Mayor for a second year. We felt that we could not bear to live in the shade of the castle, and decided to leave the area.

Recalling Sir Wyndham Deedes' advocacy of Community Centres when he was chairman of the National Council of Social Service, I applied for the vacant position of Community Centres Officer for Wales. There were more than a hundred applicants for the post and, following an interview with Sir Wynn Wheldon and The Hon. John Bruce and two others, I was offered the appointment, with an office at the headquarters of the Council of Social Service for Wales, at 2 Cathedral Road, Cardiff.

Joyce found ideal accommodation for us in Tŷ Dyfrig, a large house in Llandaff which we shared with its owner, Mrs Gould, The children were happy as there were fields at the bottom of the garden and ponies that they could ride. They were fascinated by some of my friends who came to the house. Anthony had his big blue eyes fixed on Alun Williams as he sang and played the piano with his elbows, and they both enjoyed sitting on the floor playing games with Terry Nation. Terry used to haunt the Overseas Club and was always trying to obtain some small part in a broadcast feature or play. I was told later that he had invented a talking machine but did not know what to call it until, as he sat in his chair one evening, his eyes fell on the spine of one of the volumes of *Encyclopaedia Britannica* the contents of which were indicated as DAL-EKS, and this gave him the idea to call his invention DALEKS.

I joined the Overseas League Club at Cardiff, which was conveniently situated next to the BBC in Park Place and, in addition to being a place used by BBC producers, it was also frequented by actors and other artists, many of them from London. I soon became involved in BBC work, with the result that I was on the air several times a week.

I was invited to take the chair in a series of broadcast programmes called *Voice of the People* which was a BBC Wales version of *Any Questions?* Alun Williams, who was the producer, and I, were sent to Wareham, in Dorset, to see how *Any Questions?* was done and met the team on that occasion, Anthony Crosland, Arthur Street, Dingle Foot and Mary Stocks, and the chairman, Freddie Grisewood. The first programme I chaired came from Pontypridd, and others came from Birmingham, Shotton, Colwyn Bay, and Liverpool, when the Marquess of Anglesey and Alun and I stayed at the Adelphi and sat up late while Anglesey spoke about his childhood, much of which was spent in the company of the Princesses Elizabeth and Margaret as his father was Lord Chamberlain. At Birmingham Lady Megan Lloyd George, while we were having tea at the hotel before the programme, called me to the window and said: 'That's the door of the Town Hall through which my father escaped from the mob that was ready to lynch him, during the Boer War, disguised as a policeman.'

When the new town at Cwmbran was near completion, I was asked by the

BBC to prepare a programme illustrating its growth. I went to meet Huxley Turner, chairman of the Cwmbran New Town Development, and the General Manager, Major General Wynford Rees, famously known as 'Dagger Rees of Mandalay', who was interested to hear that his ancestors had lived in Pembrokeshire, at Brithdir at Newport.

In March 1953 I was asked to present a Sunday afternoon programme called *Arolwg Wythnos* which gave a digest of the week's main events and I continued to do this for the next two years.

In the following November I started a series of monthly programmes, in Welsh, celebrating the month in story and in song which was produced by Aled Vaughan and it attracted a record audience. It was succeeded by another series which received the highest listening figure of all programmes broadcast in the Welsh language. Some time after I had finished the series, the radio critic of the *South Wales Echo* wrote that 'a new vogue in monthly programmes seems to be fashionable in broadcasting these days. It all started when Dillwyn Miles devised a series of Welsh radio programmes for each month. And last night we had a taste of another item, "May in the Welsh Countryside," this time devised by Aneirin Talfan.'

Y Bywgraffiadur Cymreig (the Dictionary of Welsh Biography) appeared in April 1953 and I felt flattered to be the only one of the 3,223 contributors 'of standing and integrity' to be referred to in the columns of the *News Chronicle*, the editor of which wrote: 'I have found endless pleasure in reading the considered judgement of men whom I have known. I couldn't find myself in disagreement with any. Captain Dillwyn Miles tells the story of the Reverend John Owen, author of the *Mochyn Du* ballad, from an unpublished autobiography. Mr Owen deplored the effect of this innocuous but immensely popular song on the youth of Wales, and was sorry he had written it in his unregenerate days.' Some years later, after Osian Ellis had referred to it as 'a nonsense song', the Reverend Jacob Davies sprang to its defence, in his column in the Welsh language weekly, *Y Cymro*. He ascribed the authorship of the article in *Y Bywgraffiadur* to Archbishop David Mathew of Mombasa, however, and heaped praise upon him. The contributors to the *Dictionary* had been identified by their initials and D.M. had been given, in error, both to Archbishop Mathew and to me, and this had escaped the notice of Jacob Davies. When I pointed out his error to Jacob, he hid his face in mock shame, but no correction was ever published. In the English version of the dictionary, that was published later, I was abbreviated as DIL.M. to avoid further confusion.

At the Overseas Club, one day, the publisher and local newspaper proprietor Rowland Harries, asked me if I would be interested in becoming the editor of the

Fishguard *County Echo* if he bought it. I told him that nothing would have appealed to me more at one time, as I had spent so much time watching it being set and printed, but regrettably not under my present circumstances. I then managed to persuade him to publish a guidebook to Newport, Pembs., which I would prepare, as apart from the guide published in 1916, and another in 1936, nothing had been published. Harries insisted on producing a more ornate publication than I had envisaged, with a drawing of an archway through which there was a view of Newport bay and the printing was done in sepia. When it appeared the *Cardigan and Tivy-Side Advertiser* reported that 'Newport now owes another debt to Captain Dillwyn Miles for the care and skill he has devoted to compiling a guide and historical sketch of the small but ancient town.'

My father-in-law, Lewis Craven Ord, died suddenly. He had been born in Toronto in 1881 and had served his apprenticeship in industry with the Canadian Pacific Railway with which, according to the *National Encyclopaedia of Canadian Biography*, his father, Craven Robert Ord, had been associated for half a century. After the war he became an industrial consultant, much in demand because of his theories, which the BBC summarised, when they stated in the *Radio Times* that 'Lewis Ord argued that the main trouble with British industry is that it has too many men playing about with bits of paper, and not enough on the production line.' This, too, was the central theme of his books, *Secrets of Industry* and *Politics an Poverty*. His *Industrial Facts and Fallacies* contained the gist of forty talks that he gave in the twelve months ending June 1949 to various institutions in all parts of Britain. He had held executive appointments in this country, France and Belgium, and had visited Australia at the invitation of the Australian Government to advise on aircraft manufacture. During the 1939-45 war he became Director of Planning to the British Air Commission in New York and Washington and was in turn consultant to the Treasury, Ministry of Works and Board of Trade and he worked with Lord Beaverbrook, when Churchill made him Minister of Aircraft Production.

Bruce Seton, the celebrated title actor in 'Fabian of the Yard', who once gave me his autograph in duplicate so that the children should have one each, died and I saw in his obituary in *The Times* that he was Sir Bruce Lovat Seton, 11th Baronet, but he died in poverty as he was typecast as Fabian and could not find another job.

I was pleased to read that Oscar Nemon, who was the most modest of men when I knew him at Palestine House, had been invited to do the statue of Churchill for the House of Commons, and had been present when it was placed where it will be for all time, one hopes, beside the Churchill Arch.

In October 1955 I represented the Gorsedd of Bards and the National Eisteddfod at the *Oireachtas*, the Irish cultural festival, in Dublin. I was met at the station by Sean MacReamoinn, of Radio Eireann, who had a horse-drawn buggy ready to convey us to the Gresham Hotel where I was to stay. We then trotted to the Tower Bar, beside the Post Office building, to meet his colleagues, Seamus Cavanagh and Seamus Kelly, and Seamus Ennis, the Irish folk singer, among others.

At the official opening ceremony that evening I was introduced to Eamonn de Valera who, when he heard that I came from Pembrokeshire, asked whether I knew 'a great Welshman by the name of D. J. Williams.' When I told him that I had sat at his feet as a student and knew him well, he reached out his hand again and grasped mine and said: 'Then you are a friend of mine, my boy!' At the official dinner I was placed to sit at a round table with De Valera, President Sean T. O'Kelly, Prime Minister Costello, Chief Justice Maguire, Monsignor Padraic Brown, President of Galway University, and John Yeats, the poet's son, together with a sprinkling of priests.

On the Sunday morning I walked in Phoenix Park, and went to the Zoo and, after a good lunch, I was escorted to the hurling match between Wexford and Kilkenny and taken to sit in the President's Box. The field was the colour one would expect in the Emerald Isle and around it sat all the Irishmen in the world, or so it seemed. Up and down the close-mown sward there marched, not so much in step, a band of uniformed musicians, but uniformed only in the sense that each one wore a uniform of sorts, each different from the others, and each man wore different headgear: one a bearskin, one a busby, one a beret, another a beaver, another a pith helmet, a pillbox, a shako, a forage cap, and tam o'shanters of various styles. Each man played a different instrument, and it sounded as though each played a different tune. The result was a cat's concert, but it visibly entertained the vast crowd, already bursting with excitement and anticipation.

As the hour approached for the arrival of the President, a group of small boys appeared and formed two rows at the foot of the steps leading to the President's Box. I enquired of my escort their significance and he explained that they were 'boys from an institution – what you might call in England a Borstal.' 'It's their privilege to greet the President,' he added. A massive limousine then drew up and out stepped President O'Kelly, all four-foot-something of him. He shook hands with the man in charge of the boys, and then with the boys, one by one, and as he did so, a voice from the gods behind us shouted: 'Oi! Why don't someone cut the grass so we can see the President!'

That night I was taken to a *ceilidh*, and then to another and another, each more hospitable than the one before, by Seamus Ennis, who had brought his flute, and his father, his fiddle. The next morning I appeared at the Tower Bar where I had promised to meet Sean and the other Seamuses. Seamus Ennis was complaining that he had 'the father and mother of all hangovers'. After he had tackled his third pint of porter, I asked him if he felt any better. 'Now that you've asked me, Dillwyn,' he replied, 'I'll tell you. I feel more like I do now than when I came in!'

Seamus came to Pembrokeshire later, with his EMI tape-recorder in search of Pembrokeshire folk singers. I took him to the Gwaun Valley to Andrew Thomas, Pencnwc, and his sister, Eliza, at their cottage, where he recorded a selection of Andrew's songs, together with songs sung by his brother Thomas Thomas and by his nephew Beni, and by Ben 'Bach' Phillips, all of which the BBC has in its archives.

THE MOST INTERESTING JOB . . .

WHEN I REPRESENTED THE Pembrokeshire County Council on the Pembrokeshire Rural Community Council (PRCC), I took considerable interest in its work and regretted having to discontinue my connection with it on going to Cardiff. It was, indeed, because of this interest that I had applied for the post of Community Centres Officer for Wales, which I now held. When I was told that the secretary of the PRCC, J. B. Perkins, was indisposed and asked whether I would like to keep an eye on the work of the Council during his absence, which I was delighted to do as it would enable me to spend more time in my native county. Within a short time, Mr Perkins died, and I looked after the office, as well as carrying out my other duties, for about three months before the post was advertised. The fifty-four applicants were reduced to a short list of seven and I was appointed.

Our search for accommodation in Haverfordwest led us to Portfield House, said to have been built as a shooting box for Picton Castle. The house appealed to us as it had large rooms and a walled garden, stood on a narrow road with stone-built hedgerows and was surrounded by fields. We purchased the house and arrived, with our furniture and belongings, on the day following the great storm of 29 November 1954, to find that the roof had been partly blown off and that the garden sheds and the garage had suffered damaged.

The Pembrokeshire Rural Community Council was an autonomous body comprising representatives of local authorities and voluntary organisations with the almost unlimited remit of 'promoting the general good of the community in the county of Pembroke.' Through its Rural Industries Department it provided technical advice and monetary loans to craftsmen and, in particular, it assisted village blacksmiths to convert themselves into agricultural engineers, and later formed the Pembrokeshire Guild of Craftsmen. It promoted the social well-being of the community by assisting in the provision and management of village halls and playing fields, and in encouraging art and drama, and the study of local history. It advanced schemes for the welfare of the elderly and operated a Citizens' Advice Bureau, and it provided the secretariat for the Pembrokeshire Association of Local Councils and other voluntary bodies.

Following my report to the first annual meeting, the local newspapers gave considerable prominence to the activities of the Council, or rather to those of its component parts, as the Council itself was largely an umbrella body that held together the various departments providing services for the community. I had been able to revive the dormant County Old People's Welfare Committee, later Age Concern, and by arranging the celebration of the first Old People's Week, established local Old People's Welfare Committees at Milford Haven, Haverfordwest, Fishguard, Tenby, Pembroke, Newport and other places. I inaugurated the Meals on Wheels scheme at Haverfordwest, which was taken up by the local committees, and introduced a chiropody service, with the aid of a County Council grant, which enabled the house bound elderly to get about.

The new County Drama Committee was hailed as 'the lifeblood of the Drama movement in the county'. While there was a great deal of interest in amateur drama, there was a perceptible absence of competent producers and so I invited Stanley Hildebrandt and other leading producers to conduct weekend courses at Llwyngwair Manor, which became known as 'Mr Miles's Dramatic Weekends.'

In my first annual report to the Pembrokeshire Association of Local Councils I pointed out that there were 150 parishes in the county, but only 74 of them had parish councils, and suggested that some parishes should be grouped so that every parish should have the advantage of parish government. Lord Merthyr, the president of the Association, used to say that Pembrokeshire had the worst system of parish government in the country, and he and I spent hours playing about with maps and population figures preparing a scheme for the grouping of parishes. When the Minister of State, Eirene (later Baroness) White, and officials from the Welsh Office, came to consider local government reorganisation, they expressed their appreciation of our pioneering work, and accepted our proposals for the reorganisation of parishes.

I wanted to improve the standard of appearance and tidiness of the villages in Pembrokeshire and Viscount Bledisloe, who ran a Best Kept Village Competition in Gloucestershire, gave me a copy of the rules and some useful advice on organising a competition. Lord Merthyr agreed to present a trophy, in the form of a gibbet sign, to be awarded to the successful village each year. This was the first county competition in Wales and, as such, it attracted considerable coverage in the local and national papers. I invited Sir Clough Williams Ellis to adjudicate a short list drawn from the forty entrants and I was particularly glad when he chose the village of Llangwm as the winner, and stated in his adjudication that 'the greater natural charm of the other finalists had no relevance to the matter being judged, which was "How well is this village tidied and maintained by those who live there?"' The following year, Dr Alwyn Lloyd awarded the trophy to Saundersfoot, and the next year's winner was the village of Nevern, with which the adjudicator, Colwyn Ffoulkes, could find no fault, except that the sign of the Trewern Arms was not very attractive. The landlady, Pan Nelson-Edwards, sought my advice and I suggested that she should erect a sign bearing the appropriate coat of arms, namely, *azure*, a lion rampant within an orle of roses *or*, and, at her request, I had an appropriate sign made for her.

The possibility of forming a film society emerged following a discussion I had with Commander Henry Offord, the lessee of the Masonic Hall. I had hoped to be able to establish a Community Centre at the hall but I was beaten to the post by Offord who was able to offer a commercial rent for the premises. We conceived the idea of showing classic, or otherwise interesting or unusual, films on Sunday evenings, so as not to compete with the cinemas. I wrote to the Federation of Film Societies and got my Council to sponsor the formation of the Pembrokeshire Film Society. A committee was formed, with the Mayor, Colonel John Green, as chairman and I was appointed honorary secretary. The object of the Society was given as the encouragement of an intelligent and discriminating attitude towards films, and the membership was restricted to persons over sixteen years of age. The membership fee was fixed at five shillings per annum. In no time, we had over four hundred members, and the Hall was packed on our opening night on 2 October 1955, when we showed films of the Queen's visit and the Royal Welsh Show, taken by Gordon Mackenzie-Bennett's and for which I had done the commentaries, followed by the British Academy Award film, *The Lavender Hill Mob*. I informed the members that it was our intention to show films of merit, some in a foreign language, like our next film, *Monsieur Hulot's Holiday*.

It did not take long for me to realise that we had stirred a hornet's nest of no small proportions. The chapels were quick to raise objections to the hallowing of the Sabbath; the fire authorities appeared and quoted the fire regulations, and the police threatened to prosecute but could not decide on a charge. My Council took fright and withdrew its sponsorship and, consequently, I had to resign from the secretaryship of the Society, which thanked me for 'doing so much to launch the Society successfully and build up a formidable membership.' I continued to act as secretary, however, in a personal capacity. The Society, having survived the threats of the police and the authorities and the censure of the interfering bodies, eventually had to discontinue when the cinema proprietors prevented the suppliers from supplying it with films.

Among the various duties of which I had not been apprised and which only came to light as time progressed was the secretaryship of the County War Memorial Committee. This was the Committee that had prepared the Book of Remembrance, bearing the names of those who had fallen in the 1939-45 war and which was deposited in St Andrew's Chapel in St David's Cathedral. On looking through the list of names I noticed that there were some incongruities, such as the description of one deceased soldier as of the 'Light Sussex Regiment', and there were omissions and, in at least one case, the improper inclusion of the name of a friend of mine, Jim Davies. A native of Boncath, he had parachuted, as a Sergeant in the Royal Air Force, from a burning Lancaster over the Netherlands where he was befriended by Dutch families who planned his escape, which failed when he was betrayed by a double agent and he spent the rest of the war in prisoner-of-war camps in Poland and Germany. On demobilisation he taught in London until he was appointed Youth Officer in Pembrokeshire, and he later became Director of Education for Montgomeryshire and, then, Principal of Bangor Normal College. I casually mentioned my discovery to Alun Williams of the BBC with the result that a series of television programmes were made depicting Jim's harrowing experiences.

I endeavoured to amend the entries in the Book, but the response was poor as, by then, widows had remarried or left the area and did not wish to disclose their present whereabouts, and the insertion of notices in the newspapers met with little success. I was able to make dozens of corrections, however, but others remain and the errors may cease to be recognised with the passage of time. Before I retired I got Colonel Hugh Higgon who, as Lord Lieutenant, was chairman of the County War Memorial Committee, to countersign a cheque for the balance of the funds in the Committee's account, which I handed to the Dean of St David's.

Our Rural Industries Department arranged a representative exhibition stand at the Royal Welsh Show when it was held at Haverfordwest in July 1955, that included saddlery, pottery, basketry, wrought iron work, wood turning, boat building, textiles, quilting, slate work, coracle making and walking stick making. There were competitions in oxyacetylene and electric welding, and in horse shoeing, in connection with which I mounted a display of various kinds of horse-shoes, some fifty in all, which Howells, the Haverfordwest blacksmith, had given me. The Minister of Agriculture, the Rt. Hon. Derek (later Viscount) Heathcoat-Amory, visited our stand and was presented with a buttonhole by my small daughter, Marilyn, dressed in Welsh costume. A photograph of her cuddling a piglet appeared in the *Daily Mail* and the caption read: 'This little piggy went to – the Show, and found its way into the arms of eight-year old Marilyn Miles of Haverfordwest in her traditional Welsh costume.'

In response to a request from beekeepers I revived the Pembrokeshire Beekeepers Association, with the assistance of the Agricultural Advisory Service, and obtained supplies of sugar for the beekeepers and the means to counteract diseases such as American Foul Brood. I invited the chairman of the South Wales Area of the Ramblers' Association to address a public meeting in the Shire Hall at which a branch was formed.

I felt that something should be done to promote tourism as an industry second to agriculture in the county and called a meeting of local authority representatives to consider establishing a Pembrokeshire Tourist Board, which was agreed. Three years later, the editor of the *Western Telegraph* wrote in his editorial that he had 'just been reading the excellent and comprehensive report of the Pembrokeshire Community Council. It contains a great many matters of interest,' he observed, 'but the one that took my eye related to the boom that Pembrokeshire enjoys from tourism where it is stated that the number of enquiries received in connection with holiday problems and accommodation exceeded all previous years, and the Welsh Tourist Board, for which the Council acts as agent, has confirmed that more enquiries are directed to Pembrokeshire than any other county in Wales. This is indeed good news.' Another report stated: 'A man who takes more than a casual interest in Pembrokeshire's holiday potential is Mr Dillwyn Miles, secretary of the Pembrokeshire Community Council, a member of the Haverfordwest Town Council and of the National Park Committee. There are a few cranks about, you know, who would be quite happy if no visitors came here at all, but Mr Miles is not one of those. He is deeply interested in the natural beauty of the county and his greatest fear is that Pembrokeshire may become too commercialised – on a par with Devon and Cornwall.'

Soon after I had revived the dormant Pembrokeshire Local History Society, I discussed with its President, Sir Frederick Rees, the feasibility of producing an authoritative history of the county. He thoroughly approved of the idea and suggested that we should begin by sending a questionnaire to the head teachers of all the primary schools in the county in order to obtain the basic information, but this met with little success. Some time later I mentioned the matter to Dr Elwyn Davies and he agreed to chair a small committee to consider the possibility of publishing a county history, in four or five volumes, on the lines of the Glamorgan County History. A grant of £5,000 was obtained from the Welsh Church Fund and the members of the committee were appointed trustees and the Pembrokeshire County History Trust was established, with me as secretary, until I resigned, when I was appointed a trustee. Professor W. F. Grimes had already promised that he would edit the first volume but he was unable to continue with the work on account of indisposition that led to his death. The Trust then decided to publish the first volume to be completed, which was the third, under the title *Early Modern Pembrokeshire, 1536-1815*. Elwyn Davies had undertaken to edit this volume but he died in 1986, and his place was taken by Brian Howells, and the volume appeared in 1987. The fourth volume, *Modern Pembrokeshire,*

1815-1974, edited by David Howell, next appeared in 1993. The editorship of second volume, was undertaken by Dr R. F. Walker.

During the time that I was honorary secretary to the Society, from 1954 to 1981, I arranged for 111 lectures to be given on topics of interest to the members, and I founded and edited a journal, *The Pembrokeshire Historian*, but could only produce seven volumes on account of shortage of funds.

John Price, the National Park Officer, in conversation one day, realised that 1957 would be the five-hundredth anniversary of the birth of Henry Tudor at Pembroke Castle, and when I suggested that it would be an occasion for a great pageant, he urged me to pursue the idea. The Pembrokeshire Local History Society agreed to back the proposal and I called a conference of local authorities and voluntary organisations in the county at which the Pembroke Pageant Committee was formed, with the Mayor of Pembroke as chairman and I as honorary secretary. Huw T. Edwards, chairman of the Festival of Wales, asked us to postpone the celebration for a year so that the pageant would become part of the Festival, and this we willingly agreed as it gave us more time to prepare and to obtain publicity. I found a lady experienced in pageant production in Mary Buckland of St David's, who travelled all over the county to produce the section parts.

As the date of the Pageant approached I felt like a man sitting in a thorn bush: whichever way I turned there were problems, and often there was no one who could help me out. There were rehearsals to arrange in several places at the same time; coteries of ladies to fashion rolls of hessian into costumes and knit string into chain mail, and tents and chairs and all the impedimenta that were required to stage a medieval production within the castle walls.

On the opening day of the Pageant one of the London papers commented that 'Henry VII, the Welsh-born King, has been haunting Mr Dillwyn Miles by night and keeping him hard at work by day,' and it went on to say that I would shortly 'see the fruits of a job' which had kept me at my desk and 'on the road for fifteen hours a day over the last months as chief organiser.' Keidrych Rhys wrote in is column in *The People* that Joyce had told him that I had worried about the Pageant for weeks, and that I had dreamt about it and used to mutter in my sleep about it. He was glad he had seen it: it had been such a success that people had been turned away. 'Now it is the talk of the county. Everyone who missed it is clamouring for a repeat,' he wrote.

Early in 1958 I was approached by members of the West Wales Field Society and asked if I would consider becoming the Honorary Secretary of the Society. The Society had begun its life twenty years earlier as the Pembrokeshire Bird Protection Society with R. M. Lockley, one of its founders, as Honorary Secretary and Chief Warden. At the end of the war, in 1945, it extended its area, in response to requests received from the counties of Carmarthen Cardigan and Merioneth, and became the West Wales Field Society with Lockley as its chairman and Colonel Harold Allen as secretary. I felt that it was an appointment that required office facilities and secretarial support, and that it was something that the Pembrokeshire Community Council should take under its wing. The Council agreed and I took over in 1958, at a time when the purchase of Skomer was being negotiated and the island was being handed over to the Nature Conservancy. The Conservancy built a house for the warden and the first full time warden was appointed in 1960, towards whose salary I obtained a grant from the Welsh Church Fund.

The Society's twenty-first annual general meeting was held at Picton Castle, and was meant to be a celebratory occasion and I was glad to see the baronial hall full of people, with an unusual number of new members. The meeting was considerably enlivened when John Barrett, warden of Dale Fort Field Centre, got to his feet and moved a vote of no confidence in the chairman, Ronald Lockley. Lockley was the founder of the Society and, above anyone else, he had brought it to its present successful position. He had, also, been instrumental in obtaining Barrett his post as warden, and had enabled Dale Fort to use Skokholm for its studies, yet Barrett did not disguise the fact that he hated him. The new members, I discovered, were his supporters, specially enrolled, for that year only, to vote the chairman out of office. Lord Merthyr, who presided, ruled Barrett out of order, however, and adjourned the meeting. At the adjourned meeting Barrett regretted that there had been disagreement and a member commented that he had changed from being 'a gnashing lion to a sucking dove.'

I had invited Ludwig Koch to address the adjourned meeting and, the following day, at his request, I took him on a tour of north Pembrokeshire. As we approached Fishguard he asked, 'Vhere can I buy a Velsh dictionary?' 'Are you thinking of learning Welsh?' I jocularly asked him. 'No,' he replied, 'but I think it's time Charles did, now that he is Prince of Vales.' He was, at the time, tutoring the royal children in bird study. 'Princess Anne, she is good at it,' he said, 'better than her mother – and much better than Charles!' I took him to Martin's book shop on Fishguard Square where he bought a copy of Caradar's *Welsh Made Easy*, to give to the Prince. We went on to Newport and called at the Golden Lion. It was a fine day and we took our ale and sandwiches into the garden and sat on a seat that was surrounded by rose bushes. The landlord's little granddaughter ran across the garden in front of us. 'Come here, *meine kinde*,' called Ludwig. She came and allowed him to lift her on to his lap, and he sang '*Roslein, roslein, roslein rot* . . .' The little girl enjoyed it, and then leapt off his lap and ran away singing her own version, never to know that one of the leading *lieder* singers in Germany before the war had sung to her.

I then took him to Roch Castle, knowing that the Kenswoods were always glad of interesting company. They were thrilled to meet him and when Koch realised that Lord Kenswood was formerly Ernest Whitfield, the concert violinist, he got up and shouted out, 'I remember you in Sydney in 1908.' 'And I was there, too,' added Madeleine. 'I sang.' 'You ver ze beautiful singer. I remember you vell.' The three of them were ecstatic. Ernest went quietly to a corner and brought out his Stradivarius and played.

When H. V. Morton called to see me, at the suggestion of Olwen Caradoc Evans, it gave me great pleasure to tell him that I had spent five years travelling in the Land of Israel with his *In the Steps of the Master* in my hand, and knew people whom he had met when he was in Jerusalem.

I stood for the County Council in a by-election in a division that comprised the Hamlet of St Martin and the Hamlet for St Thomas, together with the parishes of Boulston, Uzmaston, North Prendergast and Haroldston St Issell's and became known as 'the Member for the Hamlets'.

Not long after I had been elected, the editor of the *Tenby Observer*, when he saw that the County Council had set up a Development Committee whose job it was to explore means of attracting new industries, wrote suggesting that an 'ambassador' be appointed and, having referred to my Council's work in encouraging rural crafts and social activities and to its secretary as 'a forceful personality with a marked gift of salesmanship,' that he should 'be lent to the Development Committee for a year to use his talents in "selling Pembrokeshire" in a wider field.' This, he stated, was 'one practical suggestion I throw out to the Development Committee, if they can come to terms with he Community Council and, of course, its able secretary.'

At the National Eisteddfod held at Caernarfon in 1959, Edgar Phillips (Trefin) was appointed Archdruid. He had been Grand Sword-bearer since 1947 and I was appointed to take his place.

When the Queen and Prince Philip came to the Royal National Eisteddfod at Cardiff, the Pavilion was filled to overflowing, and there were thousands more on the Eisteddfod field unable to gain admittance, as the Queen and the Duke of Edinburgh arrived and were led to the stage. The fanfare that greeted them was sounded on the trumpets used at the Coronation which had been given to the Gorsedd in memory of Captain Geoffrey Crawshay, the former Herald Bard. The Duke wore the green robe of an ovate, as the Queen had done when she was made an honorary member of the Gorsedd of Bards at Mountain Ash in 1946. He came forward and placed his hand on the blade of the Grand Sword held by the Herald Bard and me before him, and which I then raised for him to approach the Archdruid to be admitted under the bardic name *Philip Meirionydd*, with reference to his second title, Earl of Merioneth. The audience sang a Welsh rendering of 'God Save the Queen' and the Eisteddfod President, Sir Thomas Parry-Williams, read a message of greeting and loyalty in Welsh, thanking Her Majesty for her patronage of a festival that was dedicated to preserving the language of the country of which she had made her son and heir Prince.

David Jones, of the British Travel and Holiday Association, sent the photographer, Fred Maroum to Pembrokeshire and asked if I would help him to take pictures for the American magazine *Holiday*. I took him to Solva, and called at The Ship where Maroum took a picture of my friends, Commander George Ellison and his wife, Owen and Mary Lewis and Grace Davies, and me, talking at the bar. The September issue of the magazine contained a feature article entitled 'A Journey Through Wales'. In it was a full page colour picture of the Marquess of Anglesey entitled 'The Nobility' and, facing it, also full page size and in colour, was our picture in The Ship, captioned 'The Commonalty'.

I was elected to the Borough Council in 1957 and soon found myself opposing a proposal to charge for parking cars in the car park on the grounds that this was a service the Council should provide, as it provided pavements for pedestrians, and pointing out that the overheads would leave little, if any, profit to the Council, but would create an enormous amount of bad feeling among the public, and losing shoppers to Milford where parking was free. I was more successful when I moved that the Press should be admitted to meetings of Council's committees.

The Mayor, the Very Reverend Eric Green, wished to revive the custom for the Mayor, as Admiral of the Port, to go down river to inspect his rights of fishery. I arranged with Monté Manson, who had taken over the Bristol Trader, to provide a reception at the inn for the Admiral's party on landing, and to present him with a bag of apples, as a token of the toll of 200 apples formerly paid to the Mayor out of every shipload arriving at the quay from the Forest of Dean each year, and a 'Mayor's kechyn', a kind of brawn presented to the Mayor at Christmas.

On 25 May 1961, on my forty-fifth birthday, I was installed Mayor of the Borough of the Town and County of Haverfordwest and Admiral of the Port. 'Happy Birthday for the new Mayor' was the headline in the *Western Telegraph*, and 'Guests sing "Happy Birthday"' to County Town's New Mayor' said the *South Wales Evening Post*. The papers pointed out that I had been a member of the Borough Council for only three years, that I was the Grand Sword-bearer, a member of various county and national organisations, and a radio and television contributor, both in English and in Welsh. *The West Wales Guardian's* announced that I had achieved the Double. Twice made Mayor – and this time on his Birthday' and went on to say that 'Mr Dillwyn Miles, the well known public figure, made history when he was elected Mayor of the Borough and Admiral of the Port of Haverfordwest at the Shire Hall on Thursday. He was the first Pembrokeshire man – and indeed probably the first in the Principality – to be elected Mayor of two different boroughs [in the same county] only a few years having passed since he held that office in his native Newport (Pem.).'

After the installation at the Shire Hall, we adjourned to the Masonic Hall for the Mayoral Luncheon where, the *West Wales Guardian* said, 'the speeches were probably the most entertaining of any heard at similar functions in recent years . They had no particular news value but were so witty and polished that the large number of guests went away delighted and replete.' The High Sheriff, Colonel Christopher Fothergill, proposed the toast to the Borough and, in responding, I referred lightly to the loss of my ancient offices, as Coroner, Escheator, Chief Magistrate, Judge of the Pie-Powder Court, Deputy Lieutenant and Clerk of the Market, and regretted that the Admiral of the Port, who once received ships' dues and had dealings with visiting pirates, could not collect the odd bob from the oil leviathans of the deep that came into Milford Haven these days. The Archdruid Trefin responded to the toast to the guests proposed by the retiring mayor, Father Green, and Binnie Vaughan, Bishop-elect of Mandeville, and my friend Alun Williams of the BBC also spoke. Cliff Morgan and his wife, Nula, had come from Cardiff with Alun and Peri and, on the way down, Cliff had asked his wife why she was wearing a wide-brimmed hat and she had replied: 'You said that we were going to a hay-making, didn't you!'

The civic service was held at St Mary's Church on the following Sunday. It was taken by my chaplain, Canon Bowden Thomas, and the lessons were read by me and my fellow councillor, Canon Richard Williams, while Binnie Vaughan delivered the sermon. I sat in the Mayor's Pew which is surely the most painfully uncomfortable pew in the country, apart from the Sheriff's Pew, alongside.

On the next day, I was sworn a Magistrate, though no longer the Chief Magistrate as in former days, and served only during my year of office.

I had to leave the High Sheriff's Luncheon before the speeches were over to go to the unveiling of a stone at Pwllderi in memory of Dewi Emrys, who had immortalized that place with his poem *Pwlldderi*. I deliberately appeared as I was, in my morning suit and wearing the mayoral chain, because I knew that it would have delighted old Dewi to see the Mayor of Haverfordwest at the ceremony. The stone had been erected on the roadside, near to where I had seen Dewi recite the poem. It was draped with the We;sh flag and was unveiled by Cynan, and he and the Archdruid Trefin and I were called upon to add our tributes to the dead poet.

As Admiral of the Port, I invited the Mayors of Pembroke, Tenby and Newport to accompany me on my launch, to inspect my rights of fishery and led a procession of boats down river as far as the White Stone where I was met by the

Officer Commanding HMS *Goldcrest*, Captain E. S. Carver, DSC, and received a salute of nineteen guns. I was told afterwards that two small boys watched this performance on the river bank and saw me standing before the mast, in my scarlet robe and jabot and chain of office, while the guns were firing, leaving white puffs of smoke resting on the water. After the last gun was fired, one turned to the other and said: 'Cor! With all that, they missed him!'

In the way that I had officially opened St Curig's Fair at Newport, I introduced a similar ceremony at Portfield Fair.

The Lovat Scouts (540 LAA Regiment) came with their pipes and drums to beat retreat at Haverfordwest. I took the salute and, afterwards, entertained the senior officers in the Mayor's Parlour where they expressed a wish to go to Grassholm. I arranged to do so the next day and expected to see the hardy scouts, apart from some of the older officers, streak up the cliffs. I found the reverse to be the case, and we had considerable trouble in taking the food and the Mess silver and linen tablecloths, which they had insisted on bringing, on to the island.

The Glen, a small gentleman's residence on the edge of the town, was converted into a hotel by Messrs W. H. George and Sons, the Wine and Spirits Merchants, and I was asked to perform the opening ceremony, when I had the pleasure of christening my friend Tom George 'the Monarch of the Glen'.

Christmas tide was largely devoted to the welfare of the elderly and infirm, which caused the *Western Mail* to report that 'the Mayor and Mayoress of Haverfordwest, with members of their family, had a busy time on Christmas Day. They attended Holy Communion at St Mary's at 7.30 a.m. and, later, accompanied by their son, Anthony, aged 16, and daughter, Marilyn, aged 15, visited St Thomas's Hospital, Withybush Hospital and the County Hospital . . . In the afternoon they visited the County Council Residential Home for Old People at Avallenau.' It did not mention the attendances at Darby and Joan Club Christmas parties, and the like, and the home visits, and that I had also delivered parcels from the BBC Children's Fund to poor children, as I did every Christmas morning and had been unable to return home in time for my Christmas dinner on account of being snowbound.

Senator Anthony Barry, Lord Mayor of Cork, called on me when I was Mayor, as leader of the 'Welcome to Cork' promotion, and he was interested to know that his forbears came from Manorbier, the home of William de Barri. He was accompanied by George Crosbie, president of the Cork Publicity Association and managing editor of *The Cork Examiner*, and his wife, Jean. We took them to dinner and they invited us to visit Cork for the opening of Welcome to Cork Week. We crossed from Fishguard on the MV *Innisfallen*, and rounded Roches Point on a beautiful April morning. As we passed Cobh, the Lord Mayor of

Cardiff, Alderman Charles Horwood, told me that he had worked there as a boilermaker, and he blanched when he saw his official Rolls Royce car being hoisted high from the ship's hold and deposited on the quay.

The moment the ship docked, the hunch-backed Senator Gus Healy, Deputy Lord Mayor of Cork, leapt on board shouting *Cead mille failte*, 'a hundred thousand welcomes', a phrase we were going to hear time and again. 'But,' he said, 'what a terrible, terrible t'ing it is that you should be setting foot in Ireland on such a day, for it's Easter Sunday, a day upon which all the pubs in all Ireland will be closed. Will you now please take the cars waiting for you at the foot of the landing steps and they will convey you to your hotel where I shall see you later.' The chauffeur-driven cars took us to the Hotel Metropole where we were immediately joined by Gus Healy who solemnly repeated his sermon: 'What a terrible, terrible t'ing it is . . . all the pubs in all Ireland are shut and there's not a drop to drink anywhere – but what will you have now?' and ushered us to the inviting bar. It was just gone nine o'clock in the morning and, by eleven, I was beginning to feel that it would be politic to have a break, so Joyce and I slipped out quietly and went for a walk. We had not gone far when, sitting in the window of the Imperial Hotel and looking at us with unbelieving eyes, we saw Harry and Nancy McEntee, our friends from Haverfordwest.

We had lunch that lasted until teatime and then we were taken to Blackrock Castle for tea, which appeared in the form of glasses of Guinness, unless you insisted on tea. There was a reception at Mount Vernon that evening and we returned to the Metropole by half past eleven for the official opening of Welcome Wales Week by the Lord Mayor. A little before midnight I found myself talking to a tall man until someone came and tapped him on the shoulder. He opened his waistcoat and out of it poured yards of gold chain. He was Sean McCarthy, the Lord Mayor of Cork.

We went to Llandaff Cathedral for the consecration of my cousin Binnie Vaughan, Dean of Trinidad, as Bishop of Mandeville in Jamaica. The Welsh bishops were present and so were the Bishop of Jordan, Syria and the Lebanon, and the Bishop of Bath and Wells representing the Archbishop of Canterbury.

As Age Concern Dyfed was now firmly established, I felt that similar arrangements should be made to aid the disabled and so I invited the secretary of the Wales Council for the Disabled to a meeting of interested people and the Dyfed Association for the Disabled was formed, with an area committee in each of the former three counties. I deliberately got people who were suffering from some form of disability to take the chair, both of the Association and of the area committees, and had asked Lord Kenswood, who was blind, to be its president, Having established the Association, I felt that it was necessary for them to have a journal that would keep the disabled in touch with matters, local and national, affecting their welfare. It was called *Dyfed Link* and the 3,000 copies of the first issue were soon taken up. It lasted until its fiftieth issue in 1998 when, sadly, the new Pembrokeshire County Council ceased to give it financial support.

For the International Year of the Disabled, I arranged a service at St David's Cathedral, which the Dean conducted and at which the Bishop preached a sermon. The Secretary of State, Nicholas Edwards, agreed to read the lesson, and he and I and the Bishop were entertained to tea at the Deanery afterwards, where he delighted the Dean by saying that there was a distinct possibility that the Queen would come to St David's for a Maundy Thursday, and that St David's would be included in the Prince of Wales's honeymoon tour.

When I rang Lord Kenswood to express my sympathy on the death of his wife Madeleine, whom he always called 'The Chief', he immediately asked 'Who told you?' I enquired when the funeral would be and he said: 'I'm not telling you. You're much too busy to be there,' but I found out that the funeral service would take place at Roch church on the Friday evening at eight o'clock. I asked if one could send flowers, and he replied: 'No. There'll only be one red rose from the garden from me. I don't want any competition.' I then asked if there was anything I could do and he said: 'There's nothing you can do, except think kindly of "The Chief".'

The West Wales Field Society became the West Wales Naturalists' Trust at the twenty-third annual meeting held at Hean Castle in May 1961, when the deed which I had prepared, whereby it became a company limited by guarantee and not having share capital, was adopted.

It took several years for me to get Edward Lloyd of Coedmor to sign a lease granting the West Wales Naturalists Trust a lease of the Cardigan Marshes. Each time I ran him to earth, usually at the bar of the Black Lion at Cardigan, we would have a few drinks together but when it came to putting his name to the lease agreement, which I carried with me in anticipation, he would simply say: 'Next time.' In the end, I got him to sign, which was fortunate, for he died not long afterwards.

Peter Scott and Philippa arrived at the house one day and I noticed that Peter's Harris tweed jacket, had the buttons torn off savagely, leaving jagged ends of material. When I commented on this, he explained that they were on their way back from Scotland and had called to see Gavin Maxwell where Mij, the otter, had removed the buttons.

When Roy (later Lord) Jenkins of Hindhead, and his wife, Dame Jennifer, came to stay with Desmond Donnelly, Ronald Lockley took us all to Ramsey. They wanted to see the seals and Ronald and I went ashore, on the western side of the island, where we found a baby seal that showed all the signs of having been abandoned. We took it aboard, where Joyce held it on her lap, and we placed it in our seal hostel, where it throve until it was ready to go to sea.

Among its many other activities, the Trust carried out a programme of seal-marking for which we used an Irish curragh that proved to be ideal for reaching caves and other unapproachable places. Some of the young seals were recovered on the west coasts of Ireland and of France and one on the north coast of Spain.

I found landing on the Smalls lighthouse a frightening experience. The 'front door' is twenty feet above the rock surface and it can only be reached by climbing steps, in the form of bends of brass fixed to the wall about a yard apart. On the rock surface I noticed the petrified remains of the oak pillars that supported the 'barracoon of a building' that was the original lighthouse. When the time came to leave, I stood at the door and looked down on the rocks below and the surging sea and, for a moment, I felt that I would sooner spend the rest of my life on the lighthouse rather than attempt to descend the brass bends.

I was the first person in west Wales to be appointed a lay member of the Mental Health Review Tribunal. The chairman was Major Tasker Watkins, VC, and the professional members varied according to the hospital in which we sat. Patients applied to the panel for release and when, for the best known reasons, we refused, I shuddered at the thought that we were, in effect, passing a life sentence of confinement on the applicant, especially in cases where the main reason for refusal was that the applicants did not have a home, or a caring person to look after them.

I brought Wilfred Pickles to Pembrokeshire for the fourth time, when he came to Haverfordwest for a *'Have A Go'* broadcast which we did from the Masonic Hall and arranged it as a special St David's Day edition. A lady from Liverpool wrote a letter to the paper stating that 'the boost that Wilfred Pickles gave to the scenery of Pembrokeshire must be worth thousands of pounds in publicity value.'

Some of the leading young businessmen in the county established the Pembrokeshire Junior Chamber of Commerce and invited me to be their President, to which I agreed, but found it difficult to keep up with their dynamism.

I took the chair at an exhibition of works by Ronald Lowe at the Howard Roberts Gallery in Cardiff, and when I called on Leo Abse, MP, who arrived in one of his flowery silk waistcoats, to open the exhibition, he pontificated in his customary manner, paying little regard to the works exhibited.

In view of the growing interest in art throughout the county, I called together representatives of the various art groups and established the Pembrokeshire Art Society.

When Dr Roger Webster, Director of the Arts Council in Wales, was at Haverfordwest one day, I told him that I would like to see a first-class exhibition in the town so as to give local people a taste of great art. He asked: 'Like what?' and I said: 'Like Epstein,' which was the first thought that came into my head. He laughed, and I forgot about it until, some weeks later, he rang me and said: 'I've got Epstein for you.' I was speechless. Twenty-six pieces of sculpture arrived and were placed on display at St Mary's Hall. Members of the Haverfordwest Art Exhibitions Council, of which I was president, supervised the exhibition, which was kept under strict guard. The bronze head of Victor, Epstein's West African cook's baby, which stood eight inches high, was screwed to its plinth, as several attempts had been made to steal it in the past. People came from distant places to view the exhibition. Webster then asked me what I would like next and I got Graham Sutherland and then John Piper, whom I got to open the exhibition of his works, and Stanley Spencer.

The Graham Sutherland Gallery was later located in the outbuildings of Picton Castle but, after a while, there was disagreement between Sutherland and Lady Marion Philipps and he proposed taking the pictures away from there. He would like to erect a new gallery and wondered whether I could advise him on planning procedure. I took him to see the County Planning Officer and we discussed various sites before arriving at one that appeared to be acceptable. A reconciliation was reached, however, and the gallery remained at Picton until it was later removed by the National Museum of Wales.

The Llanelli Art Society invited me to open its summer exhibition at Plas Howard, where I experienced a role reversal in that I was introduced by the Lord Lieutenant, David Mansel Lewis, in unexpectedly glowing terms, instead of me introducing him as usual at such functions.

I went to Stirling to represent the Eisteddfod at the Scottish cultural festival, the *Mod*. The landlord of the hotel at which I had been put to stay could hardly wait to tell me that he had made a signal contribution to the festival. 'I have done something for it that has never been done before,' he said. 'I've got the pubs to stay open all night,' and he suggested that I should go out and take advantage of his achievement. I called at one of the pubs and met a fine figure of a man in a kilt, who said that his name was Angus, and he had a young woman with him. We went on to another pub together and, after a while, he sang a song called '*Sheenagh vahn*'. We visited more pubs and, at one, a photographer came in and asked us to move round the corner of the bar so that the clock, showing that it was a quarter past two in the morning should be in view. I was rather horrified the following morning to find from the photograph, that appeared in the local newspapers, that Angus was none other than His Grace the Duke of Montrose.

In an amusing article in the *Sunday Times* under the headline 'Bardolatry', Robert Robinson gave his impressions of the National Eisteddfod held at Llanelli in 1962. 'The Archdruid,' he wrote, 'was in gold, and a tall man with a moustache who looked like one of nature's Flight-Lieutenants carried an enormous sword . . . "Is there Peace?" shouted the Archdruid, half drawing the sword proffered by the Flt-Lt. "Peace," roared the crowd.' The editor of the *West Wales Guardian* quoted from the article adding: 'No prizes are offered for identifying the Flight-Lieutenant.' The article was published in its entirety later by the author in his book, *Inside Robert Robinson*. When I met him, some years later, in the Savile Club, I asked him what he meant by 'nature's Flight-Lieutenant', and he replied that he had no idea, but that it was certainly not meant to be uncomplimentary, which was no answer as all I wanted was a definition of a term that I had never heard.

The Archdruid, Trefin, had lost his voice almost completely by the Llanelli Eisteddfod and, as he stood on the Logan Stone he looked at me as much as to say: 'This is it!' Some days later, he sent me an *englyn*, a stanza containing a correspondence of consonants and interchange of vowels, written in English, which he called 'Melancholy':

> Where I pass the grass will grow – and the wind
> Will wail in the willow;
> Unhallowed in a hollow,
> I will be laid well below.

He died before the month was out, and I wrote an appreciation of him for the local papers. He had died at Slough, where he lived with his wife, the author Maxwell Fraser, to whom I had introduced him at the Dolgellau Eisteddfod in 1949. He was cremated at Ruislip and the ashes were buried at Rehoboth, near Mathry, within sight of his native village, Trefin, when I was asked to deliver the oration on behalf of the Gorsedd of Bards, and found myself in a pulpit for the only time in my life. His widow, erected a large tombstone on his grave, upon which there was a small vacant panel, which I took to be meant for her name. She died eighteen years later and her ashes were interred beside his. When I attended a funeral service in the same chapel some years afterwards, I noticed that the panel was still without an inscription and, as I was given to understand that she had left all her worldly wealth to the National Library of Wales, I wrote to the Librarian, Dr Brynley Roberts, and suggested that the Library might like to have her name inscribed on the tombstone. He responded generously but asked if I would undertake to have it done, which I succeeded in doing after considerable difficulty. She did not appear to have a relative in the world, but I eventually obtained her personal particulars from the broadcaster Steve Race, who had spoken at her funeral at Slough.

R. M. Lockley and I went, one day, to the Red Wilderness, a small bay on the north Pembrokeshire coast, the location of which we kept a close secret as it was a favourite breeding place for the grey Atlantic seal. We climbed down a perilous goat path, often clinging to clumps of ling and when we reached the beach, as stealthily as we could, some of the two hundred seals that were basking on the rocks or lying on the shingle, began to make for the sea, and the rest leisurely followed. At the western end of the beach I thought I saw a large smooth rock, until it began to move and reveal itself as a bull seal, the largest I had ever seen. It was only when we got close to it that we realised that it was blind. It had been asleep and only stirred when it heard our footsteps on the pebbles. It slowly shuffled towards the water.

Twenty years later the Red Wilderness became world famous as Seal Bay, the haunt of drug smugglers. A lobster fisherman saw a wraithlike figure on the beach on a foggy day. When the police came, they found, hidden under polythene sheets, four large inflatable boats with powerful outboard motors and up-to-date navigation and other equipment, all brand new and worth a mint of money. On closer investigation it was found that a part of the beach had been excavated to provide a subterranean chamber, lined and laid with fibreglass and made waterproof for storage. It soon became apparent that here was a hide-out for drug smugglers on an international scale and, eventually, seven men and one woman were arrested and tried at the Swansea Crown Court. They were all convicted and sentenced to varying terms of imprisonment, the ringleader to ten years and fined £75,000 and made to pay £75,000 towards prosecution costs. In addition, just before he stepped into the dock to be sentenced, a tax inspector handed him a letter containing a tax bill for £1,300,000.

The West Wales Naturalists' Trust purchased Cardigan Island for £4,000, and when I came to sign the conveyance I noticed that it referred to the property as 'that piece of land surrounded by water, known as Cardigan Island', which I thought to be the perfect description of an island.

The Trust decided that it should have an emblem. Some members of the Executive Committee wanted to have the puffin, but it was realised that it was widely used elsewhere, and I suggested the Manx Shearwater and drew a rough sketch of the bird in flight, which they adopted and it became the official emblem of the Trust.

Lorant de Bastyai, the Chief Falconer of Hungary, escaped to this country and we were asked to find him a job. He seemed very pleased to be made assistant warden on Skomer, but when Joyce and I crossed to the island, we found that he had no food. or any means of obtaining any, apart from catching a rabbit or eating seagulls' eggs, and when we invited him to share our food, we did not have much left for ourselves. He wore leather breeches and woollen stockings, a tweed jacket and a Tyrolean hat with a feather, and looked, as someone said, like Jesus Christ in a Tyrolean hat. He spoke little English and when I asked him what he would do if he tore his breeches, he replied: 'I take she to saddler.' Skomer was no place for him and he was found a post as taxidermist at the Monmouth Museum, from where he went on to Rowland Ward's, which was owned by Gerald Best, one of our officers at Q in Jerusalem. I next saw him at the Royal Welsh Show taking part in a falconry display.

After I was no longer a member of the Borough Council, I was appointed Sheriff of the Town and County of Haverfordwest, being the first Sheriff to be appointed from outside the Council for many years, and the last. The duties were not onerous, except that one had to wait upon the Judge when he came to take the Assizes, which coincided with those of the county of Pembroke.

Judge Owen Temple Morris came as a special commissioner to take the case of Colonel Walter Barrett, the County Architect, who was charged with having corruptly received materials, labour and money in connection with his work, and of Cyril Rogers, a jobbing builder, who was alleged to have corruptly handed £600 to Barrett for receiving favours and to have obtained money from the County Council by falsely pretending to have carried out work. As the case had been referred to the Assizes of the Town and County of Haverfordwest, I, as Sheriff, had responsibility for the Judge and had to wait on him throughout the period of the Assize, which lasted for three weeks. In view of the fact that my offices were almost across the road from the Shire Hall, where the trial took place, and as Sir Owen Temple Morris was a kind man, I was able to go about my business once I had delivered him to the Shire Hall and until I had to collect him. After several days, he complained that his chair was uncomfortable and so I bought him a sprung cushion which is there to this day.

In contrast to the experience at my first Assize, I had the pleasure, at the next, of presenting the Judge, Mr Justice Barry, with a pair of white gloves to indicate that the Town and County of Haverfordwest was free of crime, for which the Judge was thankful and offered his congratulations to me and to the town.

Gervas Huxley came to judge the Best Kept Village competition that year, and he brought his wife, Elspeth, with him. She told me that they were recently in Australia and while flying from Alice Springs to Darwin their plane had landed in the middle of nowhere to pick up two people who turned out to be Pat Lort-Phillips and his wife, whom the Huxleys knew through Mrs Lort-Phillips' sister, Joyce Grenfell.

At the National Eisteddfod at Llandudno Alan Villiers came looking for me, having been sent by the *National Geographical Magazine*. He had sailed as

Captain of the replica of the *Mayflower*, with Dick Brennan, proprietor of the Wig and Pen Club in Fleet Street, of which I was a member, as cook. He had come to Wales to write an article, which appeared under the title 'Wales, Land of Bards' in the June 1965 issue of the *Magazine*, with photographs by Thomas Nebbia, the magazine's photographer. Villiers wrote of the Eisteddfod at Llandudno, to which he had come expecting to see a 'hill farmer, or perhaps a parson or a schoolmaster, a miner or a steel worker – for in Wales any man may be a poet – come forward' to be chaired. 'The Archdruid Cynan . . . stood up, stern and solemn Dillwyn Cemais, the sword-bearer, moved close to him. In his wonderfully strong and melodious voice, the Archdruid announced something in Welsh, very briefly. A spontaneous roar of the most intensely felt emotion arose from the whole crowd. It was a moaning roar of heartfelt disappointment, with overtones almost of despair. "No bard! No bard!" said the gentleman beside me. Dillwyn Cemais advanced, holding the great sword horizontally. Slightly unsheathing it, a few inches of steel protruding, he placed sword and sheath across the chair . . . The chair would stay empty. The lights beat upon the naked steel of the partly drawn sword. Moustachioed Dillwyn Cemais, his strong face grim and his six-feet-plus looking like eight, glared at the 8,000 in the audience. For a moment – intense silence. Then harps began to sing again as skilful fingers plucked vibrant strings . . . the bards filed slowly from the stage and up the long aisle, the archdruid and sword-bearer leading them. Doors opened, and they passed out into the gray day. But the 8,000 still sat there in the huge pavilion, as if they had been stunned. Where else, I thought, would a people feel so intensely about poetry?'

A colour picture of me carrying 'the Great Broadsword, weighing 60 pounds', appeared in the magazine, and another showing me, looking rather mournful, as the Herald Bard and I stood one each side of the empty chair across which the sword lay. Some months later, a man in Flagstaff, Arizona, wrote me a letter stating: 'I saw two women walk down the street in this town and they had a cute little dog which I discovered to have been a Welsh terrier. I read the article about Wales in the *National Geographic* and saw your photo. Do you think you could get me a Welsh terrier?' I sent him the name of a breeder I knew.

The telephone rang after lunch one day in August and the caller said that he was Ray Shields of Caroline Cottage, Pheasant Nest Lane, Weston Underwood, Olney, and that he was the leader of the British Glen Miller Band and had written some of the music for the film *Yanks*. He then asked me: 'Does the name Geraint mean anything to you? Does a red bed in which he and Enid lay mean anything?' He proceeded to assure me that he was not mad: he was naturally psychic, and not a crank, and he had been receiving messages from Geraint, who had been taking him to places and was now taking him to me, saying: 'Ask the man who holds the Sword of the Bard, who is the son of Geraint? He who gives the message of the Holy Grail. God has sent me to you, as a Knight of the Holy Grail. Do not let evil torment you. Hold your Sword to the Sun and lay a Cross in the place of evil. The man who answers the message is a Knight Bard of the Holy Grail.' And so he went on and on until he rang off with 'God bless you' to end a telephone call that had lasted forty minutes.

The Pembrokeshire branch of the Council for the Preservation of Rural Wales, as it was until it became the Council for the Protection of Rural Wales, comprised Colonel Patrick Lort-Phillips, Colonel George Jackson and me, as honorary secretary. I represented the Council at local inquiries, and sat on the Executive Committee of CPRW. Sir Herbert Griffin, secretary of CPRE, came from London to act as secretary of CPRW, and the membership was largely composed of elderly gentlemen, and one elderly lady, and the main topic of discussion was Snowdonia. The situation changed, when Major-General Lewis Pugh, CB, CBE, DSO and two bars became secretary. Pugh had had a most distinguished military career, and he and some former officers of the Calcutta Light Horse, had performed an incredibly brave task in eliminating German vessels in Marmagoa harbour, in Goa, an incident that had to be kept a secret until after the war when it was recorded in a film called *Sea Wolves* in which the part of Pugh was played by Gregory Peck. A man with such a background was not cut out to be the secretary of a voluntary rural committee and his methods, well meant though they were, did not endear him to the members. When Clough Williams-Ellis ceased being chairman, we were told, at the next meeting, that the secretary had found, and had brought along, a new chairman in Jenkin Alban Davies, a prosperous London Welshman who had never identified himself with rural matters, as far as we knew.

I attended a meeting of the CPRW Executive Committee at the Penygwryd Hotel and sat in the bar where Hillary and Hunt and other members of the expedition wrote their names on the ceiling before setting off to conquer Everest. Chris Briggs, the landlord and currently sheriff of Gwynedd, had been out all night on a mountain rescue, and his wife, Jo, who was a member of the committee, told me that they had been to Kathmandu. She took me upstairs to their living quarters and placed a piece of rock given to her by Sherpa Tensing in my hand. 'You can now say,' she said, 'that you have held the top of Everest in your hand!'

The Central Office of Information engaged me to do some commentaries on public service advertisements for commercial television and, when I got to London, I was taken to a special studio for that purpose which was located in a block of flats adjacent to where we had lived in St John's Wood.

Lord Merthyr rang to ask if I knew of any body that had lost its presidential chain. The chain had been found in a train in south London and it bore the name of Alderman J. M. Berry of Merthyr Tudful, but there were no other marks of identification. British Rail had been in touch with the Town Clerk of Merthyr and with Lord Merthyr and the chain now lay in the Lost Property Office. I told him that I would make enquiries. Shortly afterwards, I walked in to the Mariners and found the bar occupied only by the landlord, David Green, and Michael Harries, president of the London Pembrokeshire Society. He was telling David how his home had been burgled and that the thieves had taken money and his wife's jewellery and, above all, his president's chain, which was irreplaceable. When I told him where he would find the chain, he upbraided me for making light of his predicament, but he soon changed his tune and was glad to have it restored.

Anthony, who was head boy at the Grammar School, left for Bristol University to follow his chosen career as a dentist. Marilyn was caught by a press photographer one day and her photograph appeared in the *Western Telegraph*, under the heading 'Local Beauty in Focus', and the caption stated that 'raven-haired Miss Marilyn Miles' was at present working as a receptionist at the Hotel Mariners before going to St Godric's Secretarial College in Hampstead.

I revived the old custom of Beating the Bounds at Newport in 1964. In former times, the boundaries of the barony of Cemais were perambulated every seven years and took seven days, but I only instituted a perambulation of the boundary of the borough, which coincided with that of the parish. We assembled on Newport Square at eleven o'clock in the morning and, on horseback, I led a procession of over fifty people, mounted and on foot, behind the banner of the Barony. We went down East Street, to Penybont and across the Marsh to Parrog, where small boys among the followers were 'beaten' so that they would remember where the boundary was when they were old men. We went up Feidr Brenin and past Trewreiddig to Bedd Morus, where the boys were 'beaten' again before we partook of cakes and ale provided by the wives of the burgesses. We then moved across the open mountain on the southern slopes of Carn Ingli and down past Alltclydach to Llwyngwair Lodge and back to Newport. I had arranged for a special Court Leet to be held that evening which members of the public were invited to attend so that they could see what happened at the Court, and such a Court has been held ever since.

W. S. Gwynn Williams, director of the International Music Eisteddfod at Llangollen, kept on asking me to be a stage conductor at the Eisteddfod. He eventually persuaded me to do it for one day, which I enjoyed more than I expected, and I was only too ready to accept his invitation each year afterwards, which I received for until he retired. It was always a delight to arrive at Llangollen and to be greeted warmly at the Royal Hotel and find that my favourite bedroom had been reserved for me without having to ask for it.

My duties were described by Kenneth A. Wright, one of the music adjudicators at the Eisteddfod for many years, in his book, *Gentle Are its Songs*, where he stated that the stage conductor 'has a task calling for efficiency and tact. He has, and is, a personality in his own right. His title implies much more than Master of Ceremonies or Announcer, and the part he plays throughout every day's competitions and the evening concerts is vital. He must be prepared to spin out the time agreeably to the audience during an awkward pause. He must be polite but firm with over-boisterous competitors and their fans in the north transept of the tent, or with a group on the outside field that starts banging a drum in the middle of a choral contest item; to announce with equanimity a police message regarding a lost bunch of keys, an SOS for a doctor, a nervous children's choir or an equally nervous Prime Minister,' and he saw fit to recall the names of some of us who served, or had served, in that capacity. After introducing a competing choir, or folk song or dance group and ushering them on stage, I would go to the next choir, waiting backstage, to gather information about their origin, their occupations, their mode of travel to Llangollen and their pastimes and obtain a translation, often with great difficulty, of the titles of their songs or dances and learn to enunciate them correctly, whether they were Finnish or Sardinian or Icelandic, which was the most difficult, so as to give them a proper introduction. Whenever I approached a choir or group from behind the Iron Curtain, however, before I could finish a sentence, there would be a commissar at my side.

Whenever I arrived to take up duty on the stage, one of the ladies of the Floral Committee awaited me with a rose for my lapel, pink or yellow in the daytime, and for the evening concert, a red rose for my dinner jacket.

When I was at White's Hotel, in Wexford, on one occasion, the landlord, John Small, told me that the Dungeer Mummers, a group of elderly men from Camross, were in the bar and, at a word from their leader, Leo Carthy, they promptly donned their livery, consisting of peculiar headgear with ribbons, one being a mitre, and set into a routine of dances in the yard at the back of the hotel. I suggested to Carthy that he should bring the Mummers to Llangollen and, the following year, I had the pleasure, as stage conductor, to call them to the stage to perform. They won the first prize, and did so again the next year. They then did not come to Llangollen for some years and when they were next there I noticed that old Tomas, the 'father' of the group, was not with them and I enquired after him. 'Well,' said Leo solemnly, 'as you may know, Tomas was a road man and, one day, when he was working on the road, a great big lorry came along and kilt him – dead!'

Each year, something unusual happened at Llangollen. On one occasion, after the Vasili Levsky group of dancers, from Sofia, had finished their dance and I walked to the microphone ready to announce the next group, a man rushed forward towards the stage and threw a fistful of bank notes, that landed around my feet, and fell into the huge bank of flowers at the front of the stage. By the time the notes, amounting to some £300, had been picked up, he had disappeared. I got a message to say that he was a Bulgarian immigrant, now living in the Midlands, where he had made his fortune and he was so moved by the performance of his fellow-countrymen that he wanted to make a contribution towards their expenses. I handed the money to their leader but, the next morning, he returned it saying that his people would not take the money of 'a dirty expatriate'. I told him that we had no way of tracing the donor and he was eventually persuaded to take it.

Another occasion that I remember well was when I called Rostropovich back to the stage to respond to tumultuous applause. He was most reluctant to do so but I persisted and, in the end, he rushed towards me and threw his arms around me and kissed me on both cheeks, and rapidly returned to his wife in the wings.

Princess Anne visited the Llangollen Eisteddfod one year and I conducted her to the stage and called on the winners of the Youth Choirs to receive their awards from her, to each of whom she spoke, not briefly. The following evening I called all the adjudicators, from eight countries, led by Sir Thomas Armstrong, to the stage for a presentation to be made to W. S. Gwynn Williams on is retirement as co-founder of the festival and its musical director for thirty-one years. It was a sad day as the whole festival revolved around him, and for me, as it was my last appearance.

I was appointed to serve on the Nature Conservancy's Committee for Wales, the members of which were invited to attend some of the meetings of the Conservancy in Belgrave Square. At one of these meeting I was introduced to Sir Dudley Stamp, whose Geography books I used to study at school. He must have read my puzzled look for he said: 'I know what you're thinking. You're thinking that I died years ago. Lots of people do!'

Sir Julian and Lady Huxley came to stay with Ronald Lockley at Orielton and he invited us to dinner to celebrate Julian's seventy-second birthday. After dinner, Julian wanted to play one of his favourite games, 'Adding a Line'. The first player would compose the first line of a poem and the second would add the next line, in rhythm and in rhyme and so on. His great joy was to use words with which it would be difficult to find a rhyme, or better still, a line containing a *double entendre*. While we were thus engaged, Geoffrey Boswell and Tony Soper arrived and told Ronald privately that they had been with Ludwig Koch in Tenby. Ronald sent them off to fetch Ludwig without saying a word to any one.

The old man arrived and crept in quietly so as to surprise Julian, who could not believe his eyes. They had not met for years and, within moments, they plunged into conversation and were lost, like two small boys. The rest of us simply watched, for we were conscious that we were present at a historic scene. After a while, he turned towards Juliette and bowed and took her in his arms and swung her round in a waltz while he hummed the Blue Danube and then, as Lockley has described in his book *Orielton*, 'he bowed to Juliette and seated himself on the settle by the fire, next to the elegant Joyce Miles.' Lockley added that he regard this as 'one of the happiest occasions of the decade I lived in the old manor.'

The next day we took the Huxleys to Skomer and, as Julian and I were sitting in the warden's house, while Juliette and Joyce were admiring the kitchen, there was a flutter in the fire place and a puffin, having fallen down the chimney, landed on the hearth stone. It shook the soot from its feathers and walked across the white hearth rug leaving sooty foot marks and then flew on to the windowsill beside Julian, where I took a photograph of him chatting to the bird.

During discussion at a meeting of the County Council I pointed out that the armorial bearings on the wall behind the chairman's chair was an improper one and it was replaced by the coat-of-arms granted to the Council in 1937.

The BBC rang one day to ask if I could do a television programme on a country fair. I immediately had visions of the fair at Newport, as it was when I was a boy, with horses filling the streets and naphtha flares lighting the night It was only when I arrived at Newport on the morning of the fair and found not a horse in sight, or any sign of a fair, that I realised that I had suffered a severe mental blackout. The producer, Selwyn Roderick, and his assistant, Dyfed Glyn Jones, and the film crew, stood silent as I explained to them how distraught I felt. I rang the BBC in Cardiff, full of apologies and expected a frigid reception, but an understanding voice asked if I knew of anywhere else where there would be a fair and I said that I knew of no such place this side of Ireland. When I was asked if I could go there, I did not have the heart to say that I did not even know whether there would be a fair there, but in desperation agreed to go. We sailed that evening and arrived in Cork the following morning, being Sunday, and stayed at the Arbutus Lodge Hotel on Montenotte. As we were going to Ireland, the BBC asked us to do as many programmes as we could manage within a week.

On the Sunday afternoon, following some discreet inquiries, we were able to film the Ball Game. This was a strictly illegal pastime, not because of the game itself but on account of the immense amount of money that changed hands in wagers on the two competitors. The ball was of the size of a cricket ball but it was made of solid steel, and the winner was he who threw it along a *boreen* the least number of times in order to reach the end of the lane. I met a man who was the champion of all Ireland and his legs were a zigzag on account of the number of fractures sustained when hit by the ball.

We went to Buttevant fair the next day. Buttevant was a small town north of Cork with a wide street that was lined with horses and, here and there, a group of donkeys. The setting was perfect for our purposes, except that we were in Buttevant and not in Newport, Pembs., and I finished the programme sitting on a horse that felt as though it had been born for me to ride. The next day we did a programme on the first Steeplechase, when, in 1752, Mr Edmund Blake and a Mr O'Callaghan matched their horses in a cross country race, by moonlight some say, from the steepled church at Buttevant to the steepled St Leger Church four-and-a-half miles away.

For our last programme we went to Youghal, on the estuary of the Blackwater and made for Myrtle Grove, an Elizabethan castellated house once the home of Sir Walter Raleigh. where he is said to have planted the first potato, and tasted its berry, which is disgusting, and so he ordered it to be rooted out, but the gardener tried the tuber, and all potato lovers should be grateful to him. Another tradition maintains that he first tried tobacco here. We met Claud Cockburn, who wrote an article each week for the *Sunday Times* under the heading 'Here in Youghal . . .'

I attended the first meeting of the Sports Council for Wales and asked that there should be a representative of the Playing Fields Association on the Council's Executive Committee, but the chairman said that could not be done as there was no corporate body for Wales. I called a meeting of representatives of the County Playing Field Committees of the Welsh counties and we formed the Wales Playing Fields Association, as the required corporate body, of which I was made chairman.

When none of the burgesses was prepared to be Mayor of Newport in 1966, the Steward of the Barony asked me if I would take on the office again and I said that I would do so nominally as, otherwise, the ancient office could disappear for ever. This, however, was kept from the newspapers which simply reported that I had been installed for the second time and that, having been Mayor of Haverfordwest in 1961, I was the first person to be mayor of two boroughs in the county of Pembroke. When I was installed by the Lady Marcher, Mrs Gregson-Ellis, I handed her a red rose, as I had first done when I was made mayor in 1950, and as my successors in office had continued to do. The local papers insisted on referring to it as 'a centuries old custom', except for one that stated that I had done so as a token of my 'allegiance to the House of Lancaster.'

I called on Sir Robert Bellinger, the Lord Mayor of London, who said that he was pleased to see me, not only because we were the only two civic heads in the country now installed in November, but also because his forbears came from Cardiganshire.

The National Parks Commission asked me to produce 'the official guide on the Pembrokeshire National Park, to be published by Her Majesty's Stationery Office'. I decided that I would seek persons, preferably with a Pembrokeshire connection, who were recognised authorities in their subjects, to contribute chapters on their specialities. The book was published in 1973 by the Countryside Commission under the title *Pembrokeshire Coast National Park*, and subtitled *National Park Guide No. 10*. I soon gathered that it was in heavy demand, at 75p, which seemed to be a low price for a 150 page authoritative book. Before reprinting they sent me an amended copy, and as the reorganisation of local government had taken place and Pembrokeshire had been merged in the new county of Dyfed, they had deleted the word 'Pembrokeshire' throughout the book and replaced it with phrases like 'west Dyfed' or the 'south-west peninsula' and any other variation they could find to avoid using the name of the old county. I returned the book stating that I was ignoring all their amendments and pointed out that the park was still known as the Pembrokeshire National Park and insisted that the name Pembrokeshire should remain throughout the book. They agreed.

Meetings of the Royal Society for Nature Conservation, were held at the British Museum (Natural History) in Cromwell Road and one had to walk past the elephants and the hippopotami and the rhinoceroses to get to the foot of the stairs that led to the Board Room. Christopher Cadbury was the chairman and among the members were Helen Brotherton, who looked after the red squirrels on Brownsea Island, and Sir Thomas Barlow, Bart. Then, there was the lady dressed in black, with a black lace scarf over her head, next to whom I sat for a while without knowing that she was Miriam Rothschild, granddaughter of the first Baron Rothschild and the world's authority on the sexual life of the flea.

I strongly suspected that Gipsy Jones had taken some young peregrines, although he swore: 'On my mother's grave, Mr Miles, I haven't.' I called at Pelcomb Common, early one Sunday morning, when I was on my way to Skomer, having advised the police who provided hidden cover. When I got to his caravan, I was told by his wife that he had gone to shoot wood pigeon 'for 'is 'awks.' I told her that I had come for the 'hawks', and she produced a parrot cage in which there were three eyasses, which I transferred into a box that I had brought with me and took them to Skomer where they were hacked back by the warden. The matter received publicity when Roy Saunders, author turned falconer, wrote an article in the *Western*

Mail under the heading 'Hacked to Freedom' in which he described the story of the rescue.

The agent for the Dale Castle estate, which owned Skokholm, came to see me and stated that his landlord, Hugh Lloyd-Philipps of Dale Castle, had heard that John Barrett, warden of Dale Fort Field Centre, proposed to erect a building on the island. The West Wales Naturalists' Trust, was tenant of the island, and it had allowed the Field Studies Council its use by students who came to Dale Fort to study, and for the ringing of birds. Despite my warnings, Barrett erected the building and, in consequence, I received notice to quit and Barrett had to take down the building and remove it, together with all Field Studies Council property, off the island. It took some time before I was able to persuade Lloyd-Philipps to renew the lease, and when I did so it was at a rental of £500 per annum, instead of the £75 we paid previously, and on condition that there should be no more bird-ringing, which deprived the island of its value as a bird ringing station.

Ronald Lockley and I visited Cardigan Island, now that it had been purchased by the Trust, and found the place overrun by rats, which appeared to be unafraid of humans as they stood and gazed at us. The rats had come ashore, it was believed, when the SS *Herefordshire* was wrecked on the island in 1933 and we got the Ministry of Agriculture's pest officers to get rid of them so that not a rat remained.

I invited Sir Hugh Casson to speak to the Pembrokeshire Art Society on his chosen subject, 'The Future of the Past'. He was very amusing, saying things like 'One shouldn't lose one's sense of values – like the sign at the reception desk in a Cairo hotel which said: "Leave all you values with the porter!" . . . One must be alive. Not like those people who live in London hotels and stay in bed until *The Times* arrives, if they don't find their names in the obituary column, they get up!'

There was a good deal of discussion throughout Wales regarding the wisdom of sending the Prince of Wales to the University of Wales at Aberystwyth for a couple of terms to learn Welsh, but even so, it had an unexpected effect on the non-Welsh-speaking community who felt, for a variety of reasons, that they should follow his example. Eighty-year old Alderman L. J. Meyler of Milford told me one day that he was rushing home from County Council meetings to follow the BBC lessons in Welsh, and he was of the opinion that, as the Prince was learning the language, there were thousands like him who felt they ought to do the same. When the Prince attended the Urdd National Eisteddfod, however, and addressed the young audience in Welsh, some of their leaders walked out. This was, of course, an ill-mannered exhibition, and one that revealed that such people had no vision beyond their blind dedication to narrow nationalism. However much they disagreed with everything that the Prince stood for, they should have made use of him to promote the language.

The Nature Conservancy set out from Bangor to inspect its property, newly acquired from the Vaynol estate on Snowdon. I was travelling with Dr Tom Richards, the Director of the Nature Conservancy in Wales, who was anxious to set up a Countryside in 1970 Committee for Wales but had failed to find a suitable chairman, and we were discussing possible names as we were driving along the Pass of Llanberis, with Snowdom glowering above our heads. 'He who bears the title of this magnificent mountain,' I said to Tom, 'has a lot to live up to.' And then it struck me. 'What about asking Lord Snowdon?' 'What a brilliant idea,' said Tom. 'Why didn't we think of him before?' When we joined the others at the Pen-y-gwryd Hotel, Tom immediately got hold of Bob Boote, the Director-General of the Nature Conservancy, who simply said 'I shall go to the Palace tomorrow.' The Duke of Edinburgh was the chairman of the Countryside in 1970 Committee for England and Bob thought that it would be courteous to inform him of our proposal. When he went to see him the next day, the Duke asked: 'What's wrong with Charles?' And so it was that Prince Charles became the chairman of his first committee.

The first meeting of the Countryside in 1970 Committee for Wales, with Prince Charles in the chair, took place at the Board Room in the Welsh Office. The members were mostly chairmen of national undertakings, the editors of the *Western Mail* and the *Liverpool Daily Post*, Eirene (later Baroness) White, who had been Minister of State for Wales, and the Marchioness of Anglesey. When the meeting was over, and we were due to go to the Mansion House to have lunch with the Lord Mayor, I nipped across to the gents' toilet which I knew to be across the corridor. I realised that there was someone else there and said, as I had said many times before for the sake of saying something: 'Never miss an opportunity, as the Duke of Windsor used to say,' and I heard a deep voice saying: 'Yes, I heard that my great-uncle used to say something like that!' and we both laughed.

It was a fork lunch at the Mansion House so that people could move round. At one stage, the Prince came to me, holding his plate in one hand and a fork in the other and asked what I thought of the morning's meeting. I told him that I thought that it had gone remarkably well and that I felt for him, as I would have done for my own son, having been thrust into the chair at such an early age and congratulated him on the way he had conducted the meeting. 'I am so glad that my first chairmanship has to do with something in which I am really interested. You see,' he said, pointing his fork perilously near my nose, 'it is so much easier to do something in which you've got your heart.'

To celebrate the coming of age of the National Association of Parish Councils, I arranged with the Dean to have a service of dedication at St David's Cathedral which was attended by Parish Councillors from all parts of the county, and a dinner at the Masonic Hall that evening was equally well-attended.

Anthony was married at Spittal Church, to Kathleen Howes, whose father was a fighter pilot killed during the last days of the war. Her mother had then married the Reverend David Aylwin Rees who had served in Burma but, by now, was the vicar of Spittal. She had five young ladies in attendance, and Anthony's friend from Bristol University was best man, while four other friends acted as ushers. My friend, Alun Williams of the BBC, entertainingly proposed the toast to the bride and bridegroom at the wedding feast attended by 150 guests at the Masonic Hall afterwards. They set up home at Westbury Park, Bristol, while Anthony completed his studies as a dental surgeon. He set up his practice at Fishguard but then moved to Devizes where he was for a number of years before returning to Pembrokeshire.

Robert Mason, Marilyn's boy friend, came to supper and we sat late talking mainly about his life on sea and, more latterly, as master of one of the tugs in Milford Haven before he asked me the question he had been wanting to ask all evening. He asked for the hand of my daughter in marriage. I told him that I was concerned about his ability to keep her in comfort, but he is such a pleasant fellow and his family are such nice people that I could only give them my blessing, which I have never regretted.

Joyce and I now felt that Portfield House was too big for the two of us and we talked about moving to a smaller house. One day, she came home and said that she wanted to show me a little place that she had seen that morning, but she would not tell me where it was. I went with her to see the house which turned out to be Castle Hill, a house tucked away in a secret garden beside the old town wall, which I had long fancied. We bought it there and then, for £5,000. The house had been built in 1937 in the grounds of Court House, which had been demolished to make way for the new telephone exchange. The terraced garden was on two levels, with apple trees and a pear tree, and there was a greenhouse in which there was an ancient vine.

As Ronald Lockley and I were coming away from Martin's Haven one day, having been to Skomer, we called at the wooden bungalow that Ronald had built for himself when he lived on Skokholm and he told me that he intended to leave it to the Trust in his will. I suggested that it would be better if he handed it over now, reserving the right to use it on the rare occasions that he might want to use it. I then discovered that he held the property on lease for life and that on his death the building would have to be removed and when I reminded him of this he said that he would transfer the lease and allow the Trust to have the contents for £500. The offer was received with alacrity by the Trust and my suggestion that the bungalow should henceforth be known as Lockley Lodge was warmly received.

The editor of the *Western Mail* wrote to invite me to write four articles, on subjects of my choice, for the new 'Personal Column' feature in his paper, stating that 'from our point of view we would very much like to welcome you as a sort of "Mr Pembrokeshire".' In the first article I wrote about disappearing species in our area, such as the partridge and the nightjar, and in the second I recounted my experience of local government, from the time I was the youngest clerk to a Parish Council in the country. I dealt with gastronomy in the third, and suggested that the editor, instead of telling his readers about eating places in the Cotswolds or the quality of the vintage in Bordeaux, should inform them where to eat in Wales. In the fourth article I rejoiced in being alive and living in the most interesting time in the history of man, and in Wales.

My gastronomic references led to an invitation from the editor to contribute a monthly article on good food and where it was to be found in Wales, which entailed visiting unsuspecting restaurants and giving a fair description of the fare they provided for the next twenty years. I started my 'Good Food' column with Chez Gilbert, the restaurant at the Pembroke House Hotel at Haverfordwest and, as I expected, I could write nothing but praise for one of the high quality meals that the *patron*, Gilbert la Croix, provided. The sub-editor gave it the title 'Paradise for Gourmets'.

At a meeting of the Royal Society for the Conservation of Nature held at the British Museum (Natural History), I was elected to serve on the Council of the Royal Society for the Promotion of Nature Reserves. Christopher Cadbury and Richard Fitter and I went to lunch at the Victoria and Albert Museum where Fitter told me that one of his life's ambitions was to see the Newport Centaury, *Centaurium portense*.

An invitation came from the Lord Mayor of London, Sir Charles Trinder, to a reception at Guildhall in celebration of the fiftieth anniversary of the National Council of Social Service, at which the Queen arrived in a glittering tiara and Garter sash, and the Duke of Edinburgh was in the uniform of an Admiral of the Fleet.

Dr Brenda Swann, of the Central Registration of Commons Committee, asked me if I would act on behalf of the Committee and register common lands in Pembrokeshire in my name. I agreed and, the day before the closing date for registration, a huge consignment of maps and papers arrived from London. I could only take them to the County Office and say to the Clerk of the County Council: 'I hereby register these as common lands.' When the registrations were published, I was bombarded by people who said that I had registered their private land.

Despite inquires made over many years, I failed to get any news of my fellow student and co-digger, Bernard Garel-Jones. I was pleased, therefore, when the manager of Lloyds Bank, across the road from my office, came over to say that he brought greetings from Spain, from his cousin, Bernard. Not long afterwards, Bernard called at the office, with his wife, formerly Meriel Williams of the Welsh National Theatre. After the war, he had gone to Spain to establish an English-speaking academy and now he owned eighteen such academies in various parts of that country. He had recently made way for his son, Tristan, who later was to become a prominent cabinet minister in this country, and a life peer.

The Prince of Wales came to Bangor for the second meeting of the Countryside in 1970 Committee and, afterwards, we climbed Snowdon along the miners' track, taking with us our lunch packs, which we ate at Llyn Llydaw. I took photographs of the group and only learned afterwards that it was not permitted to take pictures of royalty while they are at their food, but the Prince did not seem to mind.

The Lord Mayor of London, Sir Ian Bowater, gave a dinner at Guildhall to announce European Conservation Year 1970. At the call of the State Trumpeters, James Fisher and I walked forward between phalanges of Pikemen to be presented to the Lord Mayor and Lady Bowater and when we were all in our places at the tables, the Duke of Edinburgh and Prince Charles, whose first visit it was to Guildhall, arrived in procession with the representatives of the twenty-one states taking part in ECY70.

At the Rural Conference held at the Beaufort Hotel at Tintern, I found myself sitting next to my colleague from Merioneth, William Jones. He got up to speak and, as he sat down, I got to my feet for the same purpose. In supporting what he had said, I turned towards him and expected to see him nod in approval, but he appeared to be asleep. I turned to him again, feeling that he could not possibly have gone to sleep so suddenly. I stopped and bent down and caught hold of his arm. He was dead. We rushed him to the front door of the hotel, and Major-General Battye gave him the kiss of life, but to no avail.

THE HERALD BARD

UNDER THE HEADLINE 'Herald Bard of Wales' the *Western Mail* reported my appointment to 'the post once held by Captain Geoffrey Crawshay'. The *Daily Express*, reported that 'Mr Dillwyn Miles – the Druid with the magnificent moustache – has been promoted Herald Bard, and the *Western Telegraph* noted that my first duty, as Herald Bard, would be to arrange for the celebration of the Eisteddfod held at Caerwys in 1568 and added that 'it is understood that he will be involved in the arrangements for the investiture of the Prince of Wales.'

For the quatercentenary commemoration of the Eisteddfod commissioned by Queen Elizabeth I at Caerwys, Cynan wanted me to lead the procession mounted and he devised a riding outfit comprising a white surcoat and a cloak of blue lined with green, so as to include the three colours of the Gorsedd robes, together with a sort of chapeau that looked like a Saracen's hat, and thigh boots which I wore over blue tights. This was the first time for the Gorsedd procession to be led by the Herald Bard on horseback since the time of Geoffrey Crawshay, who was similarly attired except that his was a grey outfit. I was given a horse of fourteen hands and was accompanied by mounted outriders in medieval costume. 'The Herald Bard will ride at the head of the Gorsedd procession through the town of Caerwys tomorrow,' reported the *Liverpool Daily Post*, stating that the local agricultural merchant, Mr John Rees, had 'bought a horse, called Barry, to carry the bulky frame of Captain Dillwyn Miles who will be a central figure in the crowning and chairing ceremonies.' I suffered some ribald remarks as when I spoke in a debate at the Celtic Society at the University College of Wales, Aberystwyth, on a motion relating to the Gorsedd of Bards. The motion was couched in a derogatory manner but I treated it lightly. The proposer of the motion, Jennie Eirian Davies, also spoke in a humorous vein and, at one stage, she invited her audience to direct their eyes towards me. 'Look at him,' she said, 'he has all the appearance of a decent sort of fellow, but have you seen him on the Eisteddfod field – leading a batch of Bedouin who have lost their camels?' Thus was born a phrase that was repeated time and again over the years.

I felt that the Prince of Wales, as he woke up on the morning of Tuesday, 1 July 1969, might have reflected that, behind the pomp and circumstance, and danger, of the day ahead, there had been dark clouds. He had been made to live among fellow students who felt that being Welsh necessitating hating him and all that he stood for. Dafydd Iwan's song *'Carlo'*, mocking the Prince who could make no reply, had reached the top of the Welsh charts, and his former tutor, Edward Millward, had offered his congratulations to four students who had gone on hunger strike in protest against the Investiture. The nationalists, who represented less than ten per cent of the population, paid no regard to the fact that eighty per cent of the people of Wales were in favour of the Investiture. The enmity and the threats of violence were such that George Thomas, the Secretary of State for Wales, who had himself received threatening letters, called a meeting, at one stage, to consider cancellation of the ceremony, and Jack de Manio, and others, had recorded a programme suitable for transmission should the Prince be assassinated, and obituary notices were prepared. The Free Wales Army, albeit a Fred Karno outfit, had claimed a close relationship with the IRA.

The royal train, carrying Her Majesty and members of the Royal Family, was delayed on its way to Caernarfon because the signalling wires were cut, in one place, and a hoax bomb had been found under a railway bridge across the river Dee. Two men, laying a live bomb at Abergele, blew themselves up.

The Gorsedd of Bards had taken part in the Investiture of the Prince of Wales, later Edward VIII, in 1911 and an invitation was received for it to be represented again in 1969. The Archduid, Gwyndaf, and the Recorder, Cynan, who was also president of the Eisteddfod Court that year, were invited to become members of the Earl Marshal's Committee and they attended the first meeting, held at Buckingham Place, towards the end of 1967. They were informed that the Gorsedd would be invited to be represented by a deputation of sixteen of its members, but Cynan succeed in increasing this number to thirty, comprising seven officers of the Eisteddfod Court, eleven Gorsedd officers and four members each from the white, blue and green orders.

I had to be at Caernarfon on the Friday before the ceremony so as to see that the Gorsedd regalia was securely stored at Segontium Lodge Masonic Hall, which we were to use as robing rooms. Joyce and I, while taking a walk before dinner, met Dilys Cadwaladr, the only woman to have won the Crown since 1883, and her German husband who, she said, always referred to me as the 'autocrat' of the Gorsedd, but quickly added: 'He means aristocrat, of course!'

We had a rehearsal on the Monday evening, when I led the Gorsedd procession, which was the largest of the many processions of dignitaries of various sorts, through the Water Gate into the Eagle Tower and up a flight of steps into the castle ward. When I reached the top of the steps I found the Duke of Norfolk, Earl Marshal, standing over me, stopwatch in hand. 'Herald Bard,' he barked, 'you are six seconds late!' I apologised and assured him that I would be on time on the morrow.

We were astir early the following morning and when I got to Segontium Lodge I was greeted by a squad of police, with their dogs. They had realised that the place had been left unguarded overnight and they were conducting a search for any bombs that they have been placed by the Welsh extremists, for even the Bards, whose motto was peace, were possible targets because they were taking part in the ceremony. Secretly, I felt that the threat of outrage gave the occasion added excitement, but I also feared the consequences to human life. The townspeople, and the thousands of people who had come to see the ceremony, already lined the streets when I went to a jeweller to have my medals polished. The jeweller refused to take any money, saying: 'I am honoured to do it for our Prince!'

Caernarfon Castle was open to ticket holders from ten o'clock that morning until noon, after which no one was admitted except those taking part in the Investiture. At a quarter past one, the Kings, Heralds and Pursuivants of Arms proceeded from the building next to ours and entered the Water Gate, and they were followed, at five minute intervals, by the Peers and Gentlemen taking part in the Prince's procession, the Mayor of the Royal Borough of Caernarfon, Ifor Bowen Griffith, and the members of his Council. Then, as the Order of ceremonial stated, 'at 1.35 o'clock the Officers and Members of the Gorsedd of Bards and of the National Eisteddfod Court will leave Shire Hall Street and proceed to the Water Gate. They will leave the Eagle Tower at 1.40 o'clock and proceed thence to their places near the Dais.' The Archdruid, Gwyndaf, and the president of the National Eisteddfod Court, Cynan, were to remain at the Eagle Tower whence they were to join the Prince's procession. Each procession was escorted by a Green Staff Officer, and ours was Sir Jeremy Mostyn, Bart., who walked ahead of me as I led the Gorsedd procession.

I led the procession down Castle Ditch and through the Water Gate and arrived at the Eagle Tower in such good time that we had to wait a few moments for the Earl Marshal to give me a nod. Standing with him were Garter King of Arms and the Peers nearest to the Prince, and Francis Jones, Wales Herald of Arms Extraordinary. Francis was in the habit, from time to time, of greeting me in the Pencaer third-person Doric and, when I appeared, he shouted: *'Odi e' wedi lladd gwair, lawr 'na?'* (Has he cut the hay down there yet?). Some laughed, some seemed amazed to hear the Wales Herald address the Herald Bard in a strange dialect. At the appointed time, we processed along the Processional Way, and I spotted Joyce sitting within touching distance in the front row along the route. We took our seats, each side of the gangway, behind the Dais, thus providing contrasting colours to the ranks of Mayors and Sheriffs and Lords Lieutenant. I looked up at the battlements and saw them lined with television cameras that were to take the historic scene that was about to be unfolded to five hundred million people all over the world. I heard a loud bang and hoped that it would not have done the damage it was intended to do. The Prince, in his coach moving along the streets, heard it too, and asked the Secretary of State, George Thomas, what it was. 'A royal salute, Sir,' replied George. 'Peculiar sort of salute,' observed the Prince. 'Peculiar sort of people up here,' said George jocularly. The Gentlemen-at-Arms before me remained motionless as statues, except for the white feathers in their helmets that wafted in the gentle breeze.

We were followed in the procession by the Mayor of Chester, as Prince Charles was to be invested Earl of Chester as well as Prince of Wales that day. Then came the Mayors of the Welsh Boroughs, followed by the Lord Mayor of Cardiff, Sir Lincoln Hallinan, and the Recorder, Sir Alun Talfan Davies.. After them came the Chairmen and Clerks of County Councils, followed by Members of Parliament, High Sheriffs, and Peers. The Royal Family began arriving at half past two, and when Prince Charles's procession, with an escort of Household Cavalry, arrived at the Water Gate, his personal banner was broken over the Eagle Tower. The State Trumpeters sounded a fanfare as he appeared in the castle ward, the crowd sang 'God Bless the Prince of Wales'. I wondered how many of the people present knew that it was in a book shop in the town that the poet Ceiriog suggested to the composer Brinley Richards that he should provide music for his poem, 'Ar D'wysog Gwlad y Bryniau', that was later translated into 'God Bless the Prince of Wales', and that it very nearly became the Welsh national anthem.

The Prince's Procession, led by two Gentlemen-at-Arms, comprised the Archdruid and Cynan, and leaders of the major Welsh institutions. Sir Hugo Boothby, Bart., carried the Banner of the Red Dragon of Cadwaladr, and Sir Watkin Williams-Wynn, Bart., bore the Banner of Llywelyn ap Gruffydd; Earl Lloyd-George carried the Prince's Sword, Lord Ogmore the Coronet, Lord Heycock the Golden Rod, Lord Maelor the Gold Ring, and Lord Harlech the Mantle. Wales Herald of Arms, Chester Herald, the Secretary of State for Wales and Garter King of Arms preceded the Prince, and he was followed by Lord Davies of Llandinam and Lord Dynevor.

A salute of guns signified the arrival of the Queen, the Duke of Edinburgh, Princess Anne, the Queen Mother and Princess Margaret. in their carriages, with a Sovereign's Escort, to be received by the Mayor of Caernarfon. The Equerry in Waiting then beat upon the door of the Water Gate and demanded admission in the name of the Queen. When the door was opened, Lord Snowdon, Constable of the Castle, surrendered his key to the Queen, who returned it to him for his keeping. As the Queen entered the castle, the banner of the Prince of Wales was struck and the Royal Standard broken over the Eagle Tower. The Queen's Procession was led by the Mayor, the Chiefs of Staff, the Lords Lieutenant, the Pursuivants and Heralds of Arms, Government Ministers, the Kings of Arms, the Earl Marshal, the Lord Great Chamberlain, and the Sword of State borne by the Marquess of Anglesey before the Queen and the Duke of Edinburgh. There followed the Mistress of the Robes, Earl Mountbatten as ADC to the Queen, the Lord Steward, the Lord Chamberlain, Gold Stick in Waiting, the Master of the Horse, Captain of the Yeomen of the Guard, Captain of the Gentlemen-at-Arms, Equerry in Waiting, Field Officer in Brigade and Silver Stick in Waiting.

They advanced towards the Dais made of Caernarfon slate and over it was a huge transparent pent-roof covering the throne and a chair for the Duke. The Queen sat on the throne and commanded the Earl Marshal to direct Garter King of Arms to summon the Prince to her presence, and he was brought, with his escort, from the Chamberlain Tower before the Queen.

Garter delivered the Letters Patent to the Lord Great Chamberlain who presented them to the Queen who handed the English version to the Home Secretary, Jim Callaghan, and the Welsh text to the Secretary of State for Wales, George Thomas, to read as the Prince knelt before the Queen. The Queen then invested the Prince with the Insignia of the Principality of Wales and the earldom of Chester. He did homage and placed his hands between those of the Queen declaring: 'I Charles, Prince of Wales, do become your liege man of life and limb and of earthly worship, and faith and truth I will bear unto you to live and die against all manner of folks.' She kissed him and gave him to his people.

Sir Ben Bowen Thomas, President of the University College of Wales, Aberystwyth, read the Loyal Address from the people of Wales, and the Prince, sceptre in hand and coronet uncertainly balanced on his head, got up to make reply, and realised that he had been sitting on his speech and had to fumble to find it, and beamed when he did.

The Queen, accompanied by the Duke of Edinburgh and the Prince of Wales, were escorted to Queen Eleanor's Gate where, to the sound of trumpets, she made the First Presentation of the Prince to the people of Wales assembled outside the walls. They proceeded to the King's Gate for the Second Presentation and, then, from the steps facing the Lower Ward, she made the Third Presentation to those assembled within the castle walls. The Royal Procession took its departure through the Water Gate to fanfares of trumpets and royal salutes and a fly past by the Royal Air Force. The Queen's Carriage Procession, now carrying the Prince as well, moved away and was greeted by the people with great rejoicing.

That evening, we went to the Investiture Ball at Glynllifon Park, once the home of the Lords Newborough. The first Lord had married, as his second wife, Maria Stella, said to have been a daughter of the Duke of Orleans, which, it was claimed, made the Newboroughs heirs to the throne of France. I recalled this when I found that we shared a table with Stella Mair, the National Hostess of Wales, and her husband, Iwan Thomas, of the BBC, Geraint Evans and Harry Secombe (both later Sir) and their wives. Rather late in the evening, the Marquess of Anglesey appeared leading Princess Margaret and her party, and it was soon obvious that they had been to another party.

On our journey homeward, the next day, we saw that the villages of Cardiganshire had vied with each other in street decoration and, as we were by now travelling a little before the Prince, on the first leg of his tour through Wales, the people were lining the road and we received a series of rousing receptions from people waiting for the Prince. At Fishguard, we could see *Britannia,* having already arrived from Caernarfon, at anchor in the bay ready for the Prince to spend the night on board.

We attended an ecumenical service at St David's Cathedral, the next morning, at which the Prince was present together with the Lords Lieutenant, Sheriffs and Mayors from the three counties of west Wales, and Garter King of Arms and Wales Herald. After the service we were invited by the chairman of the County Council to drinks at Warpool Court where Garter, Sir Anthony Wagner, told me about his Welsh connections.

The British Petroleum Company, which had its headquarters at Llandarcy and a Terminal at Angle Bay, had wanted to do something to celebrate the Investiture and their Public Relations Officer, Major Michael Wharton, asked me if I would help them to produce a film to represent the history of Wales by writing the script and do the commentary, but Equity would not permit this and, therefore, the commentary for the English version was done by William Squire and for the Welsh one by Meredith Edwards. The film was, first of all, called *The Sleeping Dragon* but this was changed to *The Proud Dragon* and it was translated into five other languages and given the titles *Draig o Dras, Der stolze Drache, Fier Dragon, L'orgoglioso Dragone* and *Den Stolta Dragon.* The director, Shirley Cobham, and the producer, Christopher Tracy, came to the Investiture and filmed some of the ceremony and, after I had led the procession back to Segontium Lodge, I had to return to the castle for opening close-up shots of me, as Herald Bard, which appeared over my opening line: 'Every Welshman is a prince . . .' As the cameras rolled, Lord Snowdon, in his Constable's uniform which Joyce said made him look like 'Buttons', walked in front of the camera and we had to retake. When the filming was done, we went to the Trident Theatre in Wardour Street to see the rough cut before going to lunch at Bianchi's where we ate in the room in which James Logie Baird had first demonstrated his television in 1926. There was a premiere of the film in Cardiff and 'first nights' in various parts of Wales, but it was not hailed as a success. The producer had an obsession with taking pictures a little out of focus, presumably intending to convey the misty past of much of Welsh history, but it only served to make fine scenes indiscernible and lost in a mist.

There was great excitement on the Eisteddfod field at Flint as the Prince of Wales was expected, though a few stood near the gate carrying placards bearing the words *Brad 1282*, referring to the slaying of Llywelyn the Last in that year. It was my duty to greet him at the entrance to the Pavilion, carrying my staff of office, and to lead him and the Lord Lieutenant down the centre aisle to the stage. There were police around, as the behaviour of the extremists was unpredictable, and there were detectives and police officers in mufti in close proximity to me and to the Prince. All of a sudden, one of them leapt at a figure in the audience, to my right, and brought down a young man who appeared as though he was going to throw something, and took him out.

The Prince was loudly cheered by the vast audience that filled the pavilion and, when I led him away, I found that I had to take him across the Eisteddfod field to his car. The crowd immediately surged around us, with everybody wanting to touch the Prince, but they were all well-behaved and made way at my request, and stood back to allow an old lady to shake hands with him. We were then carried along by the crowd until we reached his car. About a dozen youngsters displayed posters and scowled at us, but the crowd kept on singing 'God Bless the Prince of Wales'.

Cynan received the honour of knighthood following the Investiture and I suggested to the Gorsedd Board that we should give a dinner to celebrate the honour, to which they agreed, as long as I would arrange it. I did so at the Queen Hotel at Chester. where we had a splendid dinner at which warm tributes were paid to him. In responding, Cynan said that he attributed his success as Recorder to having 'three splendid Herald Bards' in Geoffrey Crawshay, Erfyl Fychan and me, as fellow officers.

I was appointed to represent the Gorsedd of Bards and the National Eisteddfod, the *Mod*, the Scottish cultural festival, held at Aviemore. Joyce and I spent the first night at the Old England Hotel at Windermere, and went over the Kirkstone Pass and along Ullswater, where the autumnal colours were at their loveliest. We called at Bannockburn and went to Stirling Castle and to the Wallace Monument. We stayed the next night at the Dunblane Hydro which had recently been renovated by a Greek named Stakis, who was to become a leading hotel proprietor.

We drove through Aberdeen, and along the Royal Dee and made a slight detour to Easter Ord, because of the Ord connection. We caught a glimpse of Balmoral across the river, and Braemar, full of empty hotels, had closed down for the winter. We then took the high road to Tomintoul, arguably the highest village in Britain. I switched on the car radio and heard *Bryn Calfaria* being sung in some chapel in Wales as the red grouse ran over the road crossing the wine red moors.

We stayed at the Strathspey, the leading new hotel at Aviemore. We had preprandial drinks with the Provost of Oban and Fyfe Robertson, of the BBC, and his wife, and after dinner we were taken to a *ceilidh* at which the master of ceremonies was the TV personality Calum Kennedy, in full Highland costume as we had seen him scores of times on posters that appeared in every town along the Spey, advertising the *Mod*.

The next day, we were shown the Aviemore Sports Centre, of which the promoters were extremely proud, and went for a drive along narrow country roads and when we came to a right-angle bend, a huge bird flew up from the other side of a stone hedge, which I recognised as capercaillie, the first I had ever seen. That evening, at dinner, prominent on the menu card was capercaillie, which we enjoyed.

After attending some of the competitions the following day, we made a tour of the Grant countryside and went to Rothiemurchus and wondered if we might see a wild cat. John Peter Grant, whom I had met at the Nature Conservancy meetings, was no longer at Rothiemurchus but now lived at Drumintoul Lodge, where he invited us to dinner. Shaggy Highland cattle stood in a stream of water that ran across the road as we approached the house and would not move until we almost pushed them out of our way. Lady Grant, heiress to her sister, the 11th Countess of Dysart, had just returned from Brecon, where their daughter lived, and John had been rounding his deer. I asked John why the Grant's wedge-shaped bottle was called *Standfast* and he reminded me of the motto of the Grants, *Standfast Craigellaichie*, Craigellaichie being the rugged rock that stood not far from our hotel.

We went to Loch Garten looking for ospreys, and to Loch an Eileann, where we saw a skein of wild geese flying honking towards the island in the Loch, with its mysterious castle. We went on to Coylum Bridge and then past Loch Morlich, and took chair lifts up the Cairgorms hoping to see the reindeer that had been naturalised there, but there was no sign of them. That evening we went to a broadcast *ceilidh,* and to another *ceilidh* with Wullie Neil, the crowned bard, and his friends. Before dawn broke, we were awakened by a regimental piper whom Wullie had got to play outside our window.

The final concert of the *Mod* was held on the ice rink of the Aviemore Leisure Centre, and we were escorted there by the Provost of Oban and Sir Robert Grieve, chairman of the Highlands and Islands Development Board. The highlight of the evening was the crowning of the bard, which everybody knew was going to be Wullie Neil. Sir Robert, who presided over the concert, placed a massive aluminium crown on Wullie's head.

We left Aviemore and crossed the Pass of Drumochter and the Pass of Killiecrankie and stayed the night at Ainstable. The following evening, we arrived at the Lion Hotel at Shrewsbury, determined to have an early night as I had a meeting at Newtown the next morning. We found, however, that the hotel was now managed by the MacElliotts who used to manage the Royal at Llangollen, and who were surprised and pleased to see us.

I accompanied the Archdruid Tilsli to the Cornish Gorsedd ceremony that was held in the Circle of the Merry Maidens near Lamorna. It was a historic occasion as it was the first time for the Archdruid and the Grand Druid of Brittany and the Grand Bard of Cornwall to be there together. On my way back from Cornwall I called to see John Fursdon of Fursdon, who was warden of Skokholm after the war, at Fursdon, where I met his wife, Christine, who was formerly married to Henry Williamson, the author of *Salar the Salmon*.

I went to the *Oireachtas* in Dublin that year, to represent the National Eisteddfod and the Gorsedd of Bards., and flew from Rhoose, with Professor Stephen J. Williams. The festival opened with a reception in the library of the Royal Dublin Society at Ballsbridge, which a monk, I was told by one of the many priests present, used to translate as *Pons testiculorum*.

I wanted to get better staffs of office for my marshals to carry during Gorsedd ceremonies and I mentioned this to Sir Alun Talfan Davies, who arranged for me to meet Anthony Windeler, the managing director of Alcoa, at Swansea, and he kindly produced mounts for the staffs to a design which I provided, showing the Gorsedd emblem on each facet.

The sun shone, contrary to expectation, on the day of the Proclamation of the National Eisteddfod at Haverfordwest and, as I led one of the longest processions ever seen, through the streets of the town, I felt rather conscious of the eyes of the people, whose mayor I had been, as I strode along, wearing my riding outfit for the last time.

Over a lunch time drink with Wynford Vaughan-Thomas, Sir Thomas Parry Williams and Sir Alun Talfan Davies, someone pointed out that there was no book written in English on the history and growth of the National Eisteddfod and Alun suggested that I should write one and he would have it published by his son, Christopher Davies. The next morning, a Sunday, I resisted an opportunity to visit Grassholm and began writing, which I continued doing for the next sixteen hours. I finished the book, *The Royal National Eisteddfod of Wales*, in about three months, having included in it appendices explaining the meaning and nature of *cynghanedd*, the strict metre in which classic Welsh poetry is written, and the Twenty-Four Metres used by the bards from medieval times.

I had greatly looked forward to the coming of the Eisteddfod to Haverfordwest, but I soon felt regret and shame when I saw the behaviour of the young hooligans it had brought with it. The local newspapers, who had no love for the Eisteddfod because of its all-Welsh rule, were quick to comment. The editor of the *Western Telegraph* expressed the view of the vast majority of the local people, many of whom had been working hard for the Eisteddfod, when he wrote that 'the fringe elements who thought they had made such a splash with incidents like the tearing down and burning of the Union Jack, and the destruction of road signs, must surely know now that they have severely damaged not only the goodwill of the people of a host county, but the status and prospects of the Royal National Eisteddfod itself,' and he went on, justifiably, to blame 'the Eisteddfod hierarchy', not only for failing to condemn the disgraceful conduct but also for allowing the Eisteddfod platform to be used for fiery political speeches. A flood of letters appeared in the local papers condemning 'the loutish and uncouth' behaviour, and referring to drunken young men vomiting in the streets and lying on the pavements, and using abusive language towards the townspeople. I, who had written no end of articles and features, under such headings as 'The Eisteddfod is Coming' and 'Outstanding Event in Welsh Calendar', was greatly embarrassed and I wrote a letter unreservedly reproving the hooliganism, but pointing out that the vast majority of young people had behaved in an exemplary fashion. I expressed regret that the editorials had decided only to report the worst side of our efforts, without referring to the quality of the music, in competition or in concert, or to the high standard of some of the literary work, or to the fact that the four great prizes – the chair and the crown, the prose medal and the drama medal – had all been considered worthy of award for the first time for several years, or to the art and other exhibitions, or to the eminent individuals who were visiting the eisteddfod, or to what they thought of it. Neither the Eisteddfod Council, nor any spokesman on its behalf, made any apology for the behaviour of the louts or for the inflammatory speeches from the platform. They ignored it as though nothing had happened, and seemed unaware that by so doing, they had permanently damaged their own image, as well as that of the Eisteddfod.

The author Jilly Cooper, who had been sent to report on the Eisteddfod by the *Sunday Times*, wrote: 'Whilst I understand and sympathise utterly with the Welsh in their passionate wish to keep their language alive, I was nevertheless appalled by the almost criminal irresponsibility of those in authority, those elder statesmen on the platform, praising the young for their militancy, urging them to shed blood for the cause . . . The polemic from the stage made the whole message of the Eisteddfod – "Is there Peace?" with the reassuring answering cry of "Peace" – a mockery.' She had earlier in her article struck a lighter note when she wrote that the Archdruid Brinli 'looked conspicuously like Arthur Lowe' and referred to me as 'Snudge the Herald Bard'. After the ceremony, Mervyn Jones and I took her for a drink that she said she badly needed and which fortified her for the evening concert. Some years later, when I met her at the Café Royal, I asked her why she had called me Snudge and she just looked at me with her bright blue eyes and said: 'Can I give you a kiss?'

News of the death of Cynan (Sir Cynan Evans-Jones) made me realise that things would never be the same again insofar as the Gorsedd of Bards and the Royal National Eisteddfod of Wales are concerned and, sadly, I was right. As I travelled homeward through Penrhyndeudraeth, after the memorial service, I was not to know that Bertrand Russell was breathing his last, at Plas Penrhyndeudraeth, at the age of ninety seven. *The Times* had a four column obituary to him the next morning, and a full page headed 'The World pays tribute to Bertrand Russell'.

The Pembrokeshire National Park Authority decided to establish an Editorial Committee and I was appointed its chairman. I arranged for the preparation and publication of a series of leaflets dealing with matters relevant to the Park, from geology to butterflies, and got the appropriate people to write them, without charge. I began with a leaflet on Welsh place-name and another on the castles of Pembrokeshire, which developed into a booklet that was published several times.

The lease of the foreshore obtained by the Pembrokeshire Coast National Park Authority from the Crown Agents specified that motor vehicles should not be allowed on Traeth Mawr, Newport, but this was not enforced because there was some local opposition on the spurious grounds that it might affect the trade of Newport. When the sand was visibly disappearing, I got Professor Kidson, of the Geography Department at the University College of Wales, Aberystwyth, and an authority on coastal erosion to visit Traeth Mawr, where John Price, the National Park officer, and I met him. He explained that the wheels of the vehicles broke the crisp surface of the sand, which was then blown away, and gave advice on means to prevent erosion of the sand dunes. The blown sand was not being replaced as the sea was running out of sand along the west coast of Britain, he said. Miss Margaret Patterson, a prominent comservationist, appeared from nowhere and invited herself to join us, but when she heard Kidson say that the beach should be closed to all wheeled traffic, she excitedly interrupted with: 'Then how shall we be able to tow our sailing boats to the sea?' Mrs Kidson, who had accompanied her husband but had taken no part in the proceedings, was moved to say: 'By hand, as we do.' On receiving the report the Authority agreed to prohibit vehicular traffic on Newport Sands, as required in their leae with the Crown Commissioners, but the matter was referred back for further consideration by the County Council and a compromise was reached.

The Authority had considerable difficulty in completing the footpath around the Pembrokeshire coast, but it was eventually opened, on 16 May 1970, by Wynford Vaughan-Thomas at a spot above Monkstone Point, following which Lord Merthyr, John Cripps, John Price and about a dozen of us walked along the path as far as Saundersfoot, passing golden sands, a hanging oakwood and a woodland carpeted with bluebells, on a perfect day.

The *Wesern Mail* described Viscount Simon, Lord Merthyr and I, the guest speakers at the London Pembrokeshire Society's dinner at the House of Lords, as 'three sons of Pembrokeshire'. In my speech I urged the Society to support, and participate in, the Eisteddfod at Haverfordwest and got them to offer a prize for an essay on Pembrokeshire's contribution to London life. The president, Michael Harries, said that the Society would be eternally grateful to Lord Merthyr and to me for having retrieved the president's chain of office, which had been stolen.

Sir Cennydd Traherne was made a Knight of the Garter and was probably the first Welshman, on Welsh soil, to receive that honour since it was bestowed on Sir Rhys ap Thomas in 1507. Sir Rhys had celebrated with a magnificent tournament at Carew Castle, and when I wrote to congratulate Cennydd, I jokingly suggested that he might hold a similar celebration at Coedarhydyglyn.

At the High Sheriff's Luncheon I suggested to Lord Merthyr that, with the disappearance of Pembrokeshire with local government reorganisation, Dean Allen's *Sheriffs of Pembrokeshire* of 1900, which gave the holders of the office from 1541 to 1895, should be updated. He asked me to undertake the task which, I discovered, entailed more research than I had anticipated. The sheriff of 1900, John Evans of Welston Court, Pembroke, gave me great trouble to trace, although his brother had been Lord Mayor of London, but I ran him to earth, eventually, in Thunder Bay, Ontario. The difficulty probably arose because he ended his life by cutting his throat, 'in a quarry or soak hole near Milton,' according to Colonel Hugh Higgon. Sadly, the last of the sheriffs of the county of Pembroke also committed suicide during his tenure of office. The one who caused me the greatest problem of all was Daniel Daniel of Ffynnone, the sheriff of 1939, who was a household name in my youth. He had died unmarried in 1952 and his beneficiaries, who were still living, knew nothing about him. It took me some time to find that he was a native of Crynant and that he and his brother had opened coal mines there, which they sold out to the Amalgamated Anthracite Company. I asked Francis Jones, Wales Herald, to write a foreword to the book, which he did in a comprehensive manner.

The closing Countryside in 1970 Conference was held in Guildhall, with the Duke of Edinburgh in the chair. Colonel Johnnie Johnson, the Assistant Comptroller, came to greet me as I arrived at St James's Palace for a reception that evening and introduced me to some of his colleagues at the Lord Chamberlain's office. Peter Thomas, the Secretary of State, took me to meet 'Jones the Palace', the Queen's Press Attaché, and introduced me as 'the most striking figure in Wales.' The Queen and the Duke and the Prince of Wales mingled freely with the guests.

The Duke presided again on the third day of the conference, when the Prince Charles reported on his committee's work in Wales. Among the speakers were Lords Redcliff-Maud, Hurcomb, Howick, and Kennet, who was followed by his half-brother, Peter Scott. The Secretary-General of the Council of Europe, Lujo Tonāi-Sorinj, gave an address and the conference was brought to a close with an uninspiring speech by the Prime Minister, Edward Heath.

A personal letter from Prince Charles came to thank me for having served on the Countryside in 1970 Committee for Wales and to invite me to serve on the reconstituted committee which was to be known as the Prince of Wales Committee, and also on the Welsh Environment Panel, with Sir William Crawshay, Colonel Morrey Salmon, Colonel John Williams-Wynne of Peniarth, and Fred Cartwright, managing director of the Steel Company of Wales. The Panel would handle the finances of the new Committee, as it was not considered desirable that a committee of which the Prince was chairman should be concerned with finance.

Prince Charles came to open the Wales Countryside Conference at Llandudno, during which a meeting of the Prince of Wales Committee was held. I invited the committee to hold its next meeting in Pembrokeshire, saying that Pembrokeshire was very pleasant in April. 'So is Paris,' said the Prince, 'but we'll come to Pembrokeshire.'

The meeting of the Prince of Wales Committee at Haverfordwest took place earlier than expected, on St David's Day, and I got the owner of the Glasnevin nursery at Tenby to provide a bowl of growing Tenby daffodils to place before the Prince, and Peter Perkins, of Longhouse, brought six hundred blooms in bunches, some of which I had made into buttonholes and corsages for the members, and the rest were used to decorate the Library Hall. D. C. Evans, the St David's baker, who was known, from his initials as 'Dai the Crust', offered to provide the bread rolls and he was known thereafter as 'Dai Upper Crust'. Some visitor to St David's, who heard this, sent the story to *Readers' Digest* and received £40 for the story.

When the day arrived, the members assembled at the Library Hall in advance of the Prince, whom I greeted with *'Croeso i Hwlffordd'* to which he replied *'Diolch yn fawr'*. We've made it at last,' and grasped my hand. Marilyn, dressed in

Welsh costume, was ready with a daffodil which she placed in his buttonhole at his request, and I conducted him to his chair and the meeting began. After the meeting I invited him to walk down to the Mariners. Great crowds had gathered outside the hall and he spoke to a number of people before we moved off. He showed an interest in St Mary's Church and, as we walked down Tower Hill, I drew his attention to a group of mentally handicapped children to whom he turned to speak. There was a drizzle and I held my umbrella over him as he stopped to speak to the bakers leaning out of Fowles the baker's upstairs window.

The Prince had expressed a desire to see the developments in Milford Haven and the Lord Lieutenant was somewhat horrified when I told him that we would take him to Milford by coach. The coach driver, waiting outside the Mariners, had thoughtfully heated the coach for us but as it was cold outside, the windows had misted over. The Prince and I sat in the front seat and in order that he could wave to the crowds along the road, he cleaned the window with his left hand and waved with the other, for which he kept apologising to me.

He complained about the rush of everyday life and said that he would have preferred to have arrived the previous evening and to have taken things easy, instead of having to travel by helicopter and, when he left us, rush back to London for a dinner. I suggested that he might have liked to take my place that evening as guest speaker at a St David's Day dinner where, I was told, they had not held one before. He asked where that was and when I told him St David's, he said: 'Oh yes, I would have loved that.'

Later, he came to launch a project at Kete airfield, near Dale. The Pembrokeshire Coast National Park Authority had cleared most of the wartime airfields but there were still some left for which we gathered an international force of volunteers. He arrived in his helicopter and was received by Lieut-Colonel Bobbie Howell, Deputy Lieutenant, who handed him to me, as chairman of the Dyfed Projects Group. Seeing a large JCB, he asked the foreman in charge of the works if he could 'have a go' on it and leapt into the driving seat and handled the machine as if he drove it daily and, with the mechanical grab, he knocked down a pine end that was all that remained of a building.

Marilyn and Robert Mason decided to get married, also at Spittal Church. I took Marilyn on my arm, looking radiant and more beautiful than ever, and I had great difficulty to hold back the tears as we walked up the aisle and I handed her to Robbie to be his wife. The church was full to overflowing and, after the ceremony, a hundred and fifty people came to the wedding breakfast at the Masonic Hall where Ivor Rees, the town clerk, splendidly proposed the health of the bride and bridegroom in the absence of the High Sheriff, Colonel John Green, who had wanted to do it. Anthony, as best man, proposed a toast to the bridesmaid, Susie Dixon, Marilyn's favourite niece, and read the telegrams, and the happy couple left for their honeymoon. When they returned they made their home in a delightful riverside house at Underwood, Hook.

Joyce and I went to see our first grandchild, two-day old Andrew, and I thought that he was the loveliest baby in the world, even though he was asleep, with dark hair and 'sun-tanned' skin. I placed in his hand the gold half-sovereign that my grandmother had given me on my eighth birthday.

My old English master, D. J. Williams, had the death of his dreams. He had gone back to his old 'square mile' to preside over a concert held in the chapel at Rhydcymerau, where he sat as a boy. He was standing in the *sêt fawr*, where the deacons sat, telling the people how they should love Wales, their country, when he dropped dead. He was eighty four years of age and I had known him for half his life. Regrettably, I was unable to attend his funeral. Francis Jones and I went to Waldo's funeral, held at Blaenconin Baptist Chapel even though he had been a Quaker for a number of years. We observed silence, and sang a hymn and listened to an oration of a high standard by James Nicholas, who was later to write Waldo's biography.

The first Viscount St David's married, as his second wife, Elizabeth (Betty) Rawdon-Hastings, in her own right Baroness Strange of Knokin, Baroness Botreaux, Baroness Hungerford, Baroness de Moleyns, Baroness Hastings, and Baroness Stanley. When peeresses in their own right were allowed to sit in the House of Lords, she asked me if I would help her to prepare her maiden speech, and I wrote her a speech on the welfare of the elderly. As it happened, she was the first lady to speak in the House and, when she had finished, peers leapt up everywhere to congratulate her, but her son Jestyn's booming voice silenced them all when he claimed the right to be the first peer ever to congratulate his mother in the Lords. She gave me a copy of Hansard to mark the occasion.

I was asked to be editor of *Nature in Wales* in succession to R. M. Lockley or, more precisely, managing-editor, as I was already had post-publication responsibility for the journal. Lockley was preparing to leave for New Zealand and, to mark his services to the conservation of nature, as one of the founders of the Pembrokeshire Bird Society in 1938 and an officer of the West Wales Field Society, that developed from it, and then the West Wales Naturalists' Trust, I asked Charles Tunnicliffe to do a painting of his favourite bird flying over his favourite bay on his favourite island – a peregrine over Mad Bay on Skokholm. I arranged a dinner at the Hotel Mariners on the night before his departure at which Lord Merthyr, as president of the Trust, presented him with the painting. Ronald and I had worked closely together for a number of years and I was immensely sorry to see him go. I could not understand how he could leave his native land and the work to which he had devoted his life. Our parting that evening, therefore, was a quick handshake, believing that we would never meet again. Four days later, as I was walking past the British Museum, I met Ronald walking towards me. We both stopped dead, and laughed.

I was touched when William Condry sent me a copy of his *Exploring Wales* inscribed 'To Dillwyn Miles in sincere appreciation of his great services to Wales and conservation.'

When *The Plants of Pembrokeshire* appeared, its author, T. A. Warren Davis, wrote in his Preface: 'Mr Dillwyn Miles persuaded me to compile the list and relieved me of most of the work in piloting it through production.'

I went to Skomer every Sunday from around Whitsun onward, as visits to the island enabled me to keep an eye on all that was happening there and it also acted as a break from the daily chore. When I set foot on the island I felt the weight and worries of the week fall off my shoulders and, after calling at the Warden's house, I would find myself a quiet corner among the bracken and relax with a book and a bottle of wine. In the late 1960s parties of skin-divers began to arrive at Martin's Haven and, with time, it became apparent that they were removing sea urchins, scallops, spiny starfish, and spider crab and taking them away in vans and other vehicles, that blocked access to Martin's Haven and to the islands. The sea urchins' shells were sold for use as little lampshades which, I was told, adorned the bars in the pubs in the Llanelli or Swansea areas, and the scallop shells as ashtrays. I became increasingly concerned about the depredation and brought it to the notice of the Nature Conservancy. The Conservancy considered means of tackling the matter to the extent of promoting a Private Bill in Parliament, which Robert Boote, the Director General of the Conservancy, referred to as 'Dillwyn's Bill'.

The Natural Environment Research Council (NERC), by now the Conservancy's parent body, then set up a working party under the chairmanship of Professor Clarke of Newcastle University, and when I appeared before it and tried to describe the depredations at Martin's Haven, the learned professor asked me whether I had made a count of the sea urchins before the plundering began. I told him, as politely as I could, that I had not been down to the sea floor with that in mind but that I hoped that members of the panel would understand that the skin-divers had denuded the sea floor in the vicinity of Martin's Haven to the extent that they now had to risk going out to dangerous waters around Skomer, an area that should be a marine reserve.

David Wood, the Nature Conservancy's Land Agent, and I went to see the Crown Estates Commissioners and found them sympathetic saying that they would grant a lease if we could find some way of obtaining the necessary statutory powers. I got tired of waiting for the Conservancy and NERC to take action and so I wrote to the Commissioners stating that the Trust had it in mind to establish a marine nature reserve around Skomer on account of the depredations, and asked them to lease the sea bed around the island, and in Jack Sound and adjoining Martin's Haven to the Trust for that purpose. The Commissioners replied to say that the Crown's ownership of the foreshore and seabed were subject to the public rights of navigation and fishing and that these could not be curtailed except under statutory powers, and that they were consulting the Nature Conservancy on the matter. The Conservancy, in turn, asked the Trust not to pursue its plans for establishing a marine nature reserve pending consultation.

We formed a Skomer Marine Reserve Steering Committee for which a management plan was prepared by Peter Hunnam of the Dale Fort Field Centre, Dr Roger Crump of the Orielton Field Centre, Stephen Evans of the Nature Conservancy Council and I, on behalf of the West Wales Naturalists' Trust, but when I ceased being Honorary Secretary of the Trust, I took no further part in the promotion of the reserve.

For more than twenty years, along with my other duties, I ran the Citizens' Advice Bureau from the office at Haverfordwest. Each week, people came with queries or problems and if I were unable to satisfy their needs myself, or by contacting a solicitor or the relevant officer at one of the local authorities, all known to me personally, I would arrange for them to see a solicitor without charge, and I also acted as the agent for Legal Aid, then in its early days. When the National Association of Citizens' Advice Bureaux received a Government grant, it decided that it should be spent on improving accommodation, and I was told by its officer for Wales that our office was unsuitable in that we did not have a special waiting room for clients. The bureau, which provided the service free of charge, and had been in existence since 4 September 1939, was closed. The officer made an application to the Preseli District Council for a grant of £4,000 a year to open a new bureau but the Council, knowing the circumstances, refused and for the next twenty years there was no Citizens' Advice Bureau in Haverfordwest

I had known Monté Manson from the day she moved to the Sailors Safety at Pwllgwaelod in May 1949, and afterwards to the Bristol Trader at Haverfordwest. When she retired, she became steward of the Haverfordwest Golf Club and one Sunday in February 1972, when I was told that her friends could not get a reply from her quarters at the Club, I decided to go there myself. When I arrived, I found that the door to her quarters was locked and that the key was in the lock on the inside of the door, I knocked and called her name, but got no reply. I went outside and looked through the window of her bedroom and I could see that she was in bed, but she made no response when I knocked at the window. I broke down the door to her quarters, and then the door into her bedroom, where I found her dead.

At a reception held at the United Services and Royal Aero Club in Pall Mall to launch the 'Fair Play for Children' scheme, by the Duke of Edinburgh, Sir Hugh Wontner, the Lord Mayor of London told me that he had received a letter that morning from someone in America addressed to 'His Workship the Lord Mayor'. Afterwards he wrote to me regarding the mayoralty of Newport and expressed the hope that it may long continue in its present form.

Joyce and I travelled to Derby where I had been invited to be the guest speaker and to propose the toast to 'the Immortal Memory of St David' at the St David's Day dinner of the Derby Welsh Society. The next day, we bought some tarts at Bakewell, and called at the Peacock Inn, a Wuthering Heights sort of place, on the Peak, on our way to Sheffield, where I had a similar pleasant duty to perform at the dinner of the Sheffield and District Cambrian Society dinner. We stayed at the Hatton Towers Hotel, where the president of the Society came to collect us and take us to the Cutlers' Hall for the dinner. There we were received by the Lord Mayor of Sheffield, the Master Cutler and the Presidents of the Caledonian, Cornish, Irish and Ulster Societies, and of the Royal Society of St George. I responded to the toast to 'the Principality of Wales' and was then presented with a pocket knife of Sheffield steel, inscribed with my name, by the Master Cutler, for which I insisted on giving him a half-penny to ward off ill-luck. I opened the blade, to show my appreciation of it, and it snapped shut on my finger causing the blood to shoot out over the tablecloth. I apologised to the Lord Mayor and congratulated the Master Cutler on the efficiency of his steel.

The National Association of Local Councils (NALC) decided to have a Committee for Wales and I was appointed its first chairman, an office which I held until I was, later, appointed chairman of its Policy Committee.

I led a deputation to the Welsh Office to discuss the future of parish councils in Wales, and to object to the proposal to rename them 'community councils', pointing out that there were Community Councils in each county already. Some of the councils in the urban and industrial areas objected to being termed 'parish', under reorganisation, and had persuaded George Thomas, the Secretary of State for Wales, to introduce the word 'community'. I suggested to him that if they must get rid of the term Parish Council, he might change it to 'Common Council', but he had already made up his mind, under pressure from the urban MPs.

I was appointed to represent the Association at the Twenty-first Congress of the International Union of Local Authorities at Lausanne and. Joyce came with me. We drove to Heathrow and when we boarded the Trident, I found a copy of the *Daily Mail* on my seat. I opened it at the centre page and my eye fell on an article written by its star journalist John Edwards about peregrine falcons which, he acknowledged, was based on information that I had given him some months previously. It was already getting dark when we landed at Geneva, and we were taken by coach to Lausanne and stayed at the Hotel d'Angleterre, where Byron wrote 'The Prisoner of Chillon'. One evening, we dined at the Chateau d'Ouchy and as we returned in the funicular railway, I found that we were among members of the Welsh Opera Group, on their way to Zurich. I wanted them to sing the hymn tune *Lausanne* but, sadly, they did not know it, and they gave us *Myfanwy* instead.

We went on a tour of the Swiss vineyards at Lavaux, and Vevey, and then on Lake Leman in a paddle steamer. We were taken to the foot of Les Diablerets where we were placed in a small cable car and carried over pine trees and fields of alpine roses and globe flowers until we were transferred to a larger car that climbed a sheer cliff face, and finally to a still larger car that crossed a vast void and eventually landed us on the summit of Les Diablerets. I had particularly wanted to see the Alpine Chough, several of which made their appearance.

People remarked on our 'secret garden' at Castle Hill which, although it adjoined the car park, was completely cut off by the row of Leylandii which I had planted and which grew at an incredible rate so that they became tall trees of thirty feet and more. We had as many birds as a country garden, including wren, dunnock, chaffinch, thrush, blackbird, blue tit, great tit, collared dove and wood pigeon nesting, and we were visited by bullfinch, goldfinch, greenfinch, coal tit, willow warbler, blackcap, tree-creeper and nuthatch. I planted a peach tree in the greenhouse, which had been built against a remnant of the old town wall but it failed to produce mature fruit. An old vine gave forth huge quantities of black grapes, and the morning glory and the passion flower that I had planted flourished. The rose garden had a wide variety of roses, among them the Omar Khayyam which I was given with an assurance that it had been grown from a cutting off a cutting off the rose that grew on old Omar's grave!

I was appointed chairman of the Prince of Wales's Committee's Dyfed Projects Group and one of the first tasks I undertook was a visit to Mr Ingle, the managing director of the Bolton Hill Quarries, to ask him to improve the appearance of the Treffgarne Quarry and to remove a derelict bridge across the road, which was removed within days.

When the Mayor of Haverfordwest, as Admiral of the Port, went down river to exercise his right of fishery that year, it was thought that this would be for the last time, as the mayoralty had been abolished under the Local Government Act of 1972. During the drafting of that Act, however, while the secretary of NALC, Charles Arnold-Baker, was discussing the future of Parish Councils with Clifford

Pearce, who was drafting the relevant parts of the Bill and was concerned what to do with rural boroughs, they settled between them on the idea of allowing such councils to call themselves Town Councils and for their chairmen to be known as Town Mayors. This was included in the Act with far greater generosity than we had envisaged, inasmuch as it was laid down that, not only former boroughs, but any parish or community council, could resolve to grant itself such status and, in consequence there grew a whole crop of Town Mayors, where there were only a few mayors of boroughs before.

I was invited to be the guest speaker at the annual dinner of the London Welsh Association, at its headquarters in Gray's Inn Road. I found myself sitting with the President, Sir Michael Williams, and Lord and Lady Edmund-Davies, but I felt that I may have spoken too generously of the Associastion in my toast when I discovered that I had not been offered overnight accommodation, or even my train fare, and had to rely on friends to drive me to Paddington to catch the night sleeper.

The Prince of Wales' Committee met at Buckingham Palace one day, in a room overlooking the Palace Gardens, adjoining the Music Room. The Prince was a little late arriving, for which he apologised, saying: that he had been made an Elder Brother of Trinity House that morning, of which his father was Master, He said: 'My father has just told me that he has grown accustomed to calling my mother 'Sir', as she is Duke of Lancaster, but he was damned if he was going to call me Brother!'

For nine years I endeavoured to bring the six naturalists' trusts in Wales together, and it was with a sense of achievement that I got them, at a meeting held at the Hotel Metropole at Llandrindod Wells, to come to an unanimous decision to establish a co-ordinating body. They later adopted my draft constitution and agreed to be known as the Association of Trusts for Nature Conservation in Wales.

T. W. Thomas, the Gorsedd Treasurer, and I were appointed to attend the Breton Gorsedd at Guingamp, and we took our wives with us. As I took up my customary position within the Gorsedd Circle, against the Stone of Covenant, in the grounds of the Chateau des Salles, I could see Joyce making frantic gestures at me and it took me some time to understand that she was warning me not to lean against the stone, as I sometimes did, as it was made of *papier maché* and when I touched it with my finger, it moved. The next morning we left Guingamp and travelled along the Circuit de L'Argoat to Pontivy and then to Josselin, to stay at the Hotel de Chateau The hotel stood on the other side of the river Oust from the faery Chateau de Josselin, that constantly looked at itself reflected in the placid water. Its beauty was even enhanced at night when its illumined towers were mirrored so perfectly that castle and reflection were as one: a sight that one was loathe to leave at bedtime.

We set off the next morning to Carnac where we looked in wonder at Kermanio, with its 982 menhirs and dolmens, at Kerlescant with another 579, and at Menec with 1,169 more, making a total of 2,730 megaliths: a petrified battalion of soldiers pursuing St Cornely, the legend said.

Our visit to Brittany was a joyous occasion, and it bore no hint of the darkness that lay ahead. In those days, one went to the office on Saturday mornings and on the last Saturday in October, as I came home for lunch, I met our cleaner, Miss Callaghan, who told me that Joyce was not well. I found her lying on the bed believing that she had had a heart attack and, within minutes, Dr Perry arrived and then an ambulance to take her to hospital. The men wheeled her on their trolley to the garden gate. She appeared to be cheerful and never more beautiful, I thought. I told her that I would visit her about teatime as I had a meeting of the Local Councils Association that afternoon at which I wanted to discuss some matters with Lord Merthyr. When I returned home, earlier than I expected, Marilyn and Robbie came with the unbearable news. My darling had died. She had rallied and then had a massive attack in the presence of the doctors, who had done everything they could. My world had come to an end.

Her death was announced on the BBC in the evening news. Letters came by the hundred, and friends called, but I wanted nothing, but to die.

St Mary's Church, where her body had lain overnight, was full for the funeral service. Binnie came, and all the canons and clergy deferred to him as Bishop. I was pleasantly surprised to see the Roman Catholic priest present, as we had no connection with the Catholic Church, except that Joyce had helped with some associated charities, and even more surprised when the Sisters of St Mary Immaculate Convent wrote to say that 'the Holy Sacrifice of the Mass will be offered for the repose of the soul of Mrs Miles' and a warm letter from Sister Mary Anthony said: 'We have arranged to have Mass offered for her eternal repose: that is the best expression of our sympathy.' Then came a letter from the Convent of Mercy in Cork, from Sister Bosco, in which she promised to pray for me and said: 'Don't be too brave – tears are God's gift in grief.' My grief could not be more complete, and I craved only death.

At meeting after meeting, there were votes of sympathy, and words of appreciation of all that Joyce had done for others, and although one understood that they all arose from good intentions, they opened the wounds anew each time.

My life was saved by my little granddaughter Emily, aged three, who insisted on staying with me from time to time.

Not long afterwards, while I was attending a meeting of the Sports Projects

Committee at the National Sports Centre at Cardiff, I received a telephone call from my secretary at the Carmarthen office to say that Joyce's brother, Kenneth, had died at Coomb Cheshire Home. After his mother's death, he had been brought to Coomb so as to be near Joyce and, once he heard of her death, he no longer had the wish to live. Mercifully, the end had been sudden: he appeared to be his normal self at 7.30 that morning but when they took him his breakfast he was dead, I was told by the secretary, Group Captain Pinnington. I made the same arrangements for his funeral as I had for Joyce. Marilyn, Robbie and I were the only members of the family able to attend, and Lady Meyrick and Major Fisher-Hoch came to represent Coomb.

The National Eisteddfod held at Cardigan celebrated the eight hundredth anniversary of the first recorded eisteddfod, held by The Lord Rhys at Cardigan Castle in 1176. To mark the occasion, I received an invitation to Broadcasting House to take part in the Pete Murray morning programme 'Open House'. I was ushered into a subterranean studio and we had a few words of greeting while a record that was being played was coming to its end, and then, without any formality, we went straight into a lengthy discussion.

When Carmarthen was getting ready to stage the Royal National Eisteddfod of Wales in 1978, I suggested to Ken Kaminski, the proprietor of the Ivy Bush Hotel, that he should place a circle of gold roundels on a window overlooking the garden where the Gorsedd ceremony had been held within a stone circle for the first time in connection with the Eisteddfod, in 1819. Without telling me, he commissioned the artist John Petts, and kept the whole thing a great secret until Petts had made and installed a great stained glass window, upon which, Kaminski light-heartedly told me, I had made him spend £2,000. Lord Chalfont unveiled the window and he later asked me to open a circle of stones he had erected in the garden.

While the Eisteddfod was at Carmarthen Wynford Vaughan-Thomas and I dined at the Ivy Bush with Neil Sheridan, great grandson of Richard Brinsley Sheridan, and the talk was of Irish writers. He said that when the Anglo-Irish writer George Moore died in London in 1933, there were those who wanted to have his cremated remains taken to Ireland, but it proved impossible to obtain the necessary import licence, until someone had the idea to label the contents 'fertilizer'. His friends wanted to scatter his ashes on Lough Carra, near Moore's birthplace and, true to style, they marked the occasion with a day-long wake. That evening, they defectively rowed a boat out on the lake and, with much noisy argument, decided on the spot where the ashes were to be scattered. When the great moment came, he who had been selected to do the honours, managed to stand on his feet long enough to open the casket and empty it of its contents, but he had not allowed for the direction of the breeze, which blew the ashes into the faces of the mourners. Wynford immediately capped the story with that of the death of Yeats at Roquebrune, in the south of France, in 1939, and his burial in the local cemetery. During the war there were many more burials in the cemetery and John Ormond, when he worked for *Picture Post*, claimed to have discovered that the body sent back to Ireland in 1948 and now lying in the churchyard at Drumcliff was not that of Yeats, but of a British soldier, whose brother lived in Hertfordshire.

The Archdruid Bryn and I were appointed to represent the Gorsedd at the *Oireachtas* in Gweedore, in Donegal. The opening ceremony was held at *Ostan Radharc* where we met my old friend Sean MacReamoin, who immediately insisted on taking us to *Ostan Derrybeg* where there was a great *ceilidh* that lasted far into the night.

We walked, the next morning, to Mount Errigal, the quartzite cone rising strangely to nearly 2,500 feet, and had lunch at the Errigal Hotel with Sean and Donal O'Morain, former chairman of RTE, and his wife, who was a Senator.

We went to Drumcliff and stood at the grave of W. B. Yeats and read the stern epitaph: *Cast a cold eye on life, on death. Horseman, pass by!* taken from his poem 'Under Ben Bulben', and said to have been inspired by his annoyance at reading Rilke's ideas on death. I recalled John Ormond's story and told it to Bryn as we rested over a glass of Guinness at Yeats's Tavern nearby. We went on to Sligo and to Lough Gill, said to be the inspiration for Yeats's 'Lake Isle of Innisfree' which, in fact, he had written when he was homesick in London and saw a fountain in a shop window in Fleet Street, and remembered some passage that his father had read to him out of Thoreau's *Walden*, which had made him want to live 'in imitation of Thoreau on Innisfree, a little island in Lough Gill.' I thought how Thoreau had similarly made R M Lockley go to Skokholm, and had inspired Gandhi.

My book, *The Royal National Eisteddfod of Wales*, appeared in time for the National Eisteddfod at Cardiff and received more publicity than I had expected as among those who were present at a dinner that I attended at the Post House was James (now Lord) Callaghan, the Prime Minister, and Merlyn Rees (later Lord Merlyn-Rees), the Home Secetary, and John Morris, the Secretary of State for Wales. Sir Alun Talfan Davies, president of the Eisteddfod, who had originally suggested that I should write the book, presided at the dinner, and he called on me to present a copy to the Prime Minister, who made reference to it in his speech. At Sir Alun's behest, I sent a copy to the Queen, and received the usual letter of thanks.

After dinner, I introduced Sean MacReamoinn of *Radio Telefis Eireann*, to the

Prime Minister. Sean, described as 'the quintessential Irishman', had been admitted an honorary member of the Gorsedd for his mastery of the Welsh language, and he came to the Eisteddfod every year. In addition to his other duties as an author and broadcaster, he made frequent visits to Rome on Papal matters. While he as speaking to the Prime Minister, a waiter came and said that he was required urgently. He soon returned and said: 'I must go to Rome. The Pope is dead.' Pope Paul VI was succeeded by Pope John Paul I, but he died within a month and Sean was back again in Rome.

The Gorsedd robing rooms, during the Eisteddfod at Cardiff, were at the Cyncoed College and I was waiting to get ready to proceed to the Chairing ceremony in the Eisteddfod pavilion when an American lady arrived by taxi. She said that she was Dr Evelyn B. Byrne and that she had read about the Eisteddfod in the *New York Times* and had arranged to meet a Mrs Evans on the Eisteddfod field. I told her that there would be many Mrs Evanses on the field and gave her a ticket for the ceremony and put her on one of our coaches in the care of a lady who would direct her to her seat. Evelyn then came to Haverfordwest and I took her to St David's for Sunday morning service and to parts of the county that I thought would interest her, and to tea at Marilyn's, where she was delighted to meet the children.

Before Christmas, Anthony helped me to dress as Santa Claus and drove me to Underwood where Marilyn had a party for my grandchildren, Emily and Max, Andrew and Tamsin and a dozen or more of their tiny friends. When I entered the room, they all froze and looked at me in wonder, obviously believing that I was the real thing. I gave them each a present from my sack, and they all thanked me and one or two of them gave me a sweet or a toffee. Their little faces made it one of the most joyous memories of my life.

Evelyn had invited me to New York for Christmas and met me at Kennedy Airport and drove me to her home. She, a Doctor of Philosophy and an Olympic swimmer, had chosen to live, and to teach in a rather unruly school with mostly black children, in The Bronx. As she was teaching the next morning, I took a Gray Line coach tour, which I found a splendid way of seeing New York for the first time. It started on 8th Avenue 53rd Street, and travelled through Times Square and along Broadway to Madison Square, through Greenwich Village and down The Bowery, where Peter Stuyvesant established his *bouverie*, or his farm. In Chinatown we called at a Chinese shop which had a Buddhist temple in a back room and then went to the Battery, facing the Statue of Liberty. Along FDR Drive and under Brooklyn Bridge we came to the United Nations building, which we briefly visited, and then along East 47th Street to the Rockefeller Center. After a slight break there, we set off for the Lincoln Center and along

Central Park West to Harlem, past Columbia University and Mornington Heights. In the evening Evelyn drove me Downtown and across Brooklyn Bridge and along Wall Street to the Fraunces Tavern Museum, the scene of Washington's farewell to his officers.

The Channel Gardens at the Rockefeller Centre were spectacularly decorated for Christmas, with a huge Christmas tree on the Lower Plaza, and scores of people skating on the nearby ice rink. We had a drink at the Waldorf-Astoria before going to the Evening Dinner Theatre at Elmsford where people dined on terraces and watched a performance of *The Music Man* while doing so.

We went to the White Horse Tavern, 'The Horse', as Dylan Thomas called it, where he had had two beers before returning 'to the Hotel Chelsea, delirium tremens and the ambulance'. Evelyn took a photograph of me sitting on Dylan's stool, at the end of the bar. A room adjoining the bar is known as the Dylan Thomas Room, and in it a large portrait of him, bedecked with tinsel, was hanging beside a notice board upon which are pinned the latest newspaper cuttings and any bits of information that appeared anywhere in the world about him. We followed his last steps to the Hotel Chelsea and stood before St Vincent Hospital, where he died.

We had Sunday lunch with Evelyn's Jewish friends, Norrie and Ellie Rosenbaum, at their home in Tarrytown, who had also invited their friends Art and Minnie Borgesson. They were eager to know about Israel, and about England, as though they were countries in another world, and when Evelyn said that I had met the Queen, they became delirious and Minnie kept on saying 'He has shaken hands with the Queen!' over and over. It was Christmas Eve and we returned through a forest that lay under snow, and went to Midnight Mass at St Brendan's in The Bronx.

On Christmas morning we visited the New York Botanical Gardens, where there were poinsettias of every colour, and a cathedral-size conservatory in which palm trees and oaks grew tall. From there we went to see Edgar Allen Poe's cottage and to General Grant's tomb which had on it a bust of General Ord. We went to Downtown Manhattan in a howling gale that seemed to challenge our ascent to the 107th floor of the World Trade Center where we had a drink in the Windows on the World Bar. The bar looked like a well-stocked library, but with bottles in place of books, and when I ordered a gin and tonic, the barman asked: 'Which gin, sir? What about a House of Lords?' of which I could see a row of bottles, each with a different coloured label all marked *House of Lords*, one of the blends of which I chose. The view over New York was as from an aeroplane: we looked down on the Empire State Building and realised that this was the second tallest building in the world, next to the Sears Roebuck Building in Chicago. I went on a pilgrimage to the Algonquin Hotel where Alexander Woollcott had established his Round Table, of which Dorothy Parker was a shining member.

When Evelyn had written to tell me that she had reserved Christmas dinner for us at Lu Chow's, I did not have the heart to say that I did not care for Chinese food. I was pleasantly surprised, therefore, to discover that Lu Chow's was 'the Ionic temple of German gastronomy', New York's oldest restaurant and renowned for its Christmas-goose dinners. Despite the early booking, we had to wait for two hours in a crowded bar before we were bidden to our table. My plate, when it came, was piled high with too much goose and no sage and onion stuffing, and the Christmas pudding was spiced with spices I did not recognise or relish, but it was an experience.

On Boxing Day we took the New Jersey Turnpike and the J. F. Kennedy Memorial Highway to Baltimore and on to Washington, where I was much taken by the Air and Space Museum with its display of every flying thing, from the Wright Brothers' *Kitty Hawk Flyer* of 1903 and Lindbergh's *Spirit of St Louis* to the *Apollo II* command nodule, together with bits of rock off the moon. We went along the National Mall to the Natural History Museum and called at the Smithsonian Institution, with whose secretary I had been in communication for some years, and who received copies of *Nature in Wales*. We drove round the Capitol and passed the Library of Congress, along Pennsylvania Avenue to the White House, and on to the Lincoln Memorial and the Jefferson Monument, to the JFK Centre, Watergate, the Pentagon and to Arlington Cemetery. I bought a guidebook which had on its cover a panoramic view of Washington at sunset and noticed that it had been taken by Fred J. Maroum whom I had taken to Solva to take a picture for the magazine *Holiday*.

A lone eagle hovered over the battlefield at Gettysburg, and as I stood where five thousand soldiers had fallen, I could hear Lincoln's words spoken there: 'Fourscore and seven years ago . . .'

We called at York and crossed the Susquehanna to Lancaster to visit the country of the Amish, the extreme Mennonites, descended from Anabaptists in Switzerland. They reminded one of orthodox Jews in that the men wore black clothing and their women covered their heads and wore black to the floor. They drove round in horse-drawn carriages and ploughed with oxen and would have nothing to do with the internal combustion engine. I wanted to stay at Intercourse, one of their main settlements, so that I could send cards to my friends stating: 'I spent last night in Intercourse . . .', but the town's only hotel was closed for the season and we went on to Bird-in-Hand and then took the Newport road to Ephrata where we stayed at the Pennsylvania Hotel, but dined at the Angus Steakhouse, and had breakfast next morning at Zinn's Diner.

At a sign marked *Uwchland*, we turned off the Pennsylvania Turnpike and I realised that we were approaching the Welsh settlement, which I had come to see. We passed fingerposts pointing towards Berwyn and Tredyffryn and Brynmawr before we came to the one that I sought: Haverford. All I could see, however, was a signboard indicating that a rather uninviting and obviously closed building was the Haverford Hunt Club, before which I had my photograph taken, and a lichen covered arch that was faintly inscribed *Haverford College*. We then set off to look for Narberth, but had no success until I saw a car, pale blue in colour except for the front door that was painted white and bore the words *Narberth Cabs*. We eventually came upon Narberth Post Office where I bought some stamps to send cards to my friends, Hywel and Betty Davies, in the original Narberth. We went through Merion and Bala Cynwyd to rejoin the Pennsylvanian Turnpike, and crossed the Delaware and followed the New Jersey Turnpike back to New York, and then went to a dinner-dance at the Tarrytown Hilton, where we stayed overnight.

After breakfast at the hotel, we drove to Sunnyside, the home of Washington Irving, and visited the location of his *Legend of Sleepy Hollow*, and then through the forest until we came to the banks of the Hudson and saw the Ossining Correction Facility, which was none other than the old Sing-Sing Gaol, with armed guards mounted on watchtowers at every corner, with rifles at the ready.

A review of my little book, *The West Wales Naturalists Trust and its Nature Reserves*, which gave a brief history of the Trust from the time of its foundation as the Pembrokeshire Bird Protection Society in 1938 and its transition to the West Wales Field Society in 1945 until it was reconstituted as The West Wales Naturalists' Trust, appeared in the *Western Mail*.

I felt that R. M. Lockley deserved a mark of recognition for the pioneering work that he had done from the time he went to live on Skokholm in 1927 and, as I believed that he would value honorary academic recognition more than a political honour, I approached the University College of Wales at Aberystwyth with a request that he be granted a doctorate, but they could do no better that an Hon. M.Sc. which he was greatly pleased to receive from the hands of the Pro-Chancellor, the Prince of Wales.

At the National Parks Conference held at Malvern I suggested that the Pembrokeshire Coastal National Park should be extended to include the adjoining sea-floor so as to protect underwater habitats, and received an ovation, and when the session was over, I was approached by officers from the Welsh Office and the Department of the Environment who asked me to prepare a memorandum on the subject. The official dinner provided a fund of good stories. After Sir Jack Longland, had delivered an entertaining speech, Sir Meredith Whittaker got up saying that anything that he had to say after Sir Jack would be an anticlimax, adding: 'And you all know what an anticlimax is? It's when you lift a fig leaf and find a fig!'

While judging entries for the Prince of Wales Award in Ceredigion, we called at Tyndomen, near Tregaron, to inspect a particular type of calves' cot, which had certain environmental qualities, built by the lady owning the farm. When we arrived we were met by an elderly gentleman wearing knickerbockers and carrying a walking stick, who said that his niece, the lady in question, had been called away and had asked him to show us the cot, which he did and afterwards invited us to take coffee at his bungalow standing near the farm entrance. He stated that he was now engaged in editing the diaries of a great-uncle who had emigrated to Australia leaving his family behind him at Tregaron and took us into a small back room where they lay, in a battered tin trunk. They were published, not long afterwards, as *The Diary of a Welsh Swagman*.

Before we left the back room, I noticed a row of thick volumes resting on a shelf and I could see that they all seemed to be about diseases of the heart, and that they were all by William Evans. In my shameful ignorance I asked: 'And who is the William Evans who's written these weighty tomes?' 'It's me,' he replied and led us out of the room. It was difficult to believe that, in that ill-lit, ill-kept little room we were in the presence of one of the country's leading cardiologists who had pioneered the use of the electro-cardiograph.

Lady Anglesey, who was vice-chairman of the Prince of Wales Committee, invited the chairmen of Projects Groups to a meeting at Plas Newydd. We dined in the dining room, with its famous Rex Whistler mural, and family portraits from the first Baron Paget, born in 1505, onward. I stayed the night and slept in a four-poster in a bedroom hanging with paintings and prints, as was its adjoining bathroom, with its huge marble bath and closed-stool type lavatory seat.

Among the tasks I gave the Dyfed Projects Group was the clearance of the Friends' Burial Ground at Sutton which had completely grown over and which revealed tombstones of some well known citizens of Haverfordwest, that had long been hidden. Another was performed by the Army Cadet Force who rebuilt the quay walls at Newport, and another was the saving of the old oak tree at Picton Ferry.

As I went to a meeting in Whitehall, I found the streets packed with people waiting for the Queen to go by on her way to the State Opening of Parliament. She was preceded by a carriage carrying the Imperial State Crown, placed on a cushion behind which sat two officers, whom I assumed to be Crown Equerries, and they appeared to be waving at someone as they went by. That evening I went to the London Welsh Association where Prince Charles was launching Youth

Action 1976, and David Checketts came up to me and said: 'You were a bit snooty in Whitehall this morning, when Johnnie Johnston and I waved at you.'

The Gild of Freemen of Haverfordwest, in addition to admitting hereditary Freemen, appointed a small number of Burgesses, being 'persons of repute who have rendered outstanding service to the town.' I saw in the local paper that I had been so appointed and I was duly sworn at a suitable ceremony by the Master of the Gild, Colonel Jack Higgon. I was also made a member of the Wardens' Court and made to wear a scarlet gown bearing the Gild's badge on its shoulder, and an academic velvet cap with yellow tassle. The badge had been designed by Francis Jones, Wales Herald Extraordinary of Wales, who was the Gild's Honorary Archivist, in which office I succeeded him when he died. I had previously held the distinction of being the only person to have been Mayor of Newport and of Haverfordwest, and I now found myself as the only one who had ever been a Burgess of the two towns.

The Freemen benefit from the Portfield Inclosure Act of 1838, the income from which is divided equally among the Freemen and, to celebrate the hundred-and-fiftieth anniversary of the award, I was asked to write a booklet which I called *The Town and County of Haverfordwest: its Freemen and its Charities*.

When the old storehouse at Parrog came on the market, I was determined that it should be acquired as premises for the boating fraternity, I met the mayor, Dr Bignall, the commodore of the local sailing club, Tony Marchington and its secretary, Morton Tucker, to discuss the idea and the possibility of forming a constituted body that could apply for financial assistance towards the purchase and adaptation of the building. I obtained an assurance from the Director of the Sports Council for Wales that the acquisition would be favourably considered for grant-aid and I had also approached the National Playing Fields Association and the County and District Councils for additional support. The National Park Officer had indicated that planning consent could not be reasonably withheld from the envisaged development. There remained one matter which concerned me and that was title to the property. The storehouse was the only survivor of several buildings of the kind, erected on the Parrog when the port was in its heyday and I knew that, for many years, attempts had been made to dispose of it, but the sale could not be completed because the title deeds could not be found. A sale was eventually concluded and deeds produced describing the premises simply as 'a storehouse situate on the Parrog'. We had several meetings of the committee to devise ways and means of achieving our aims but I left each with a feeling approaching despondency. I accompanied Dr Bignall, Marchington, and Morton Tucker to the sale, held at the Church Hall at Fishguard. We sat together and Marchington did the bidding and hesitated when he figure of £12,500 was reached.

From there on I had to press him, almost to the point of screaming, until it was knocked down to the Newport Boat Club at £14,300. The anticipated grants were obtained, all except the National Playing Fields Association, for which I was not sure until I happened to see Major Walker, from the Association, at a Garden Party at Buckingham Palace, and he came up to me and said that he had sent me a cheque that morning.

The Boat Club did me the honour of making me Life Member Number One.

I was taken by surprise, at an NALC Council meeting, to hear my name proposed, seconded and carried, as chairman. The local papers noted that I had begun as clerk to the Newport Parish Council at the age of sixteen and had now achieved the topmost position as chairman of the National Association of Local Councils.

The Times column, on the Court page, under 'Latest Appointments' read 'Dillwyn Miles, Herald Bard of Wales, to be chairman of the of the National Association of Local Councils.' The *Municipal and Public Services Journal* had 'New chairman of NALC is Welsh bard'. John Osmond, the *Western Mail* under the headline 'Herald Bard heads Councils'.

Charles Arnold-Baker, the secretary of NALC, and I, went to Hamburg to a meeting of the World Congress of Local Authorities The British delegation was first entertained to lunch at Bremen by the Burgomaster, Herr Francke, in the Kaiser's panelled room at the Rathaus. I was called upon to express thanks and, as I sat down, Frau Francke told me that she and her husband had recently returned from a holiday near Cardigan.

The Congress, the twenty third, was opened by the President of West Germany, Walter Scheel, who arrived cocooned in a phalanx of soldiery. When he got on the stage, the soldiers lined up each side of him and surveyed the audience with fingers on triggers: one felt that anyone who made a sudden movement or lifted an arm would be riddled with bullets. He left encased in his storm troopers amid sighs of relief. Visconnt Ridley, who sat next to me, as bored as I was with the Congress sessions and especially at the prospect of listening to the Mayor of Nairobi telling us how to run social services, suggested that we should go to Hagenback's Zoo, and Dame Elizabeth Coker, who sat the other side, said she would like to join us.

After the morning session the next day, we left by coach for Lübeck, which we entered by the fifteenth century Holsten Gate. We drank a stein of beer at the Schiffergeselltschaft, where we sat at long tables, and a glass of wine at the Ratweinkellar. I was particularly interested to be shown Buddenbrookhaus, the home of Thomas Mann, whose great novel, *Buddenbrooks*, banned and burned by Hitler, I had recently read. We were taken round the city and as we went through the Turkish quarter our guide, Frau Haas, made it clear that the Germans had no love for the Turkish immigrants. We were then entertained to a Hanseatic Tafeley as given in 1502 in the Holsten Hall. The servants were in medieval costume and so were the heralds who greeted us with trumpets. After a word of welcome from the Stadtpresident, we were served the first of the twenty-seven courses of the medieval meal which included venison, sturgeon, starlings, pike and swan, all served on birch platters, with generous quantities of Rhenish wine, followed by marzipan and buckwheat pancakes and Lübeck cake. Each delegate was presented with a pewter wine mug as we left.

The Congress ended with a resolution embodying its views on the matters considered but, to our minds, it appeared flawed and Arnold-Baker proposed an amendment that was accepted, which we considered an achievement.

Lord Merthyr resigned as president of NALC in 1974 and his place was taken by the Duke of Grafton, to the envy of the other local authority associations. When the Duke and I were invited to have dinner at the Savoy with Michael Heseltine, Secretary of State for the Environment, and Patrick Jenkin, Secretary of State for Health and Social Security, the Earl of Gainsborough, president of the Association of District Councils, whose leg I pulled over being stuck a lift when he came to open the Haverfordwest Rural District Councils' new headquarters, Cambria House, asked: 'How did you manage to get hold of him as your president?' To which I replied:'Just knowing the right people.'

I took the chairman and secretary of the Association of District Councils to lunch at *The George and Vulture*, between Cornhill and Lombard Street, in which Mr Pickwick was arrested by the sheriff's men and to which he returned after his release from the Fleet. It appeared to have changed little since Dickens' time.

A meeting of the International Union of Local Authorities (IULA) held at York, was opened by Guido Brunner, one of the EEC Commissioners, who spoke brilliantly without a note, and he was followed by Geoffrey (later Lord) Rippon on 'Direct Elections to the European Parliament'. We were invited to luncheon by the Lord Mayor of York who received us in the State Room at the Mansion House He showed me his unique chain, which has no medallion, and his butler gave us a talk on the city regalia. The dining table was laid with gold and silver vessels and candelabra, and as it was below the level of the street, passers by could look down upon us.

I attended the Council for Europe Symposium on Historic Towns at Munich. Snow was falling steadily as we were driven from the airport to the hotel, *Der Königshof*, on the Karlsplatz. The meetings were held in Cuvillé's Theatre, built by François Cuvillé's in about 1740, that had been mercifully saved from war damage and remains the most beautiful Rococo theatre in all the world. I had breakfast with Lord Duncan-Sandys the next day and we left the hotel by taxi at eight o'clock to join a coach at the Residentz that would take us to Landshut. The countryside was flat and uninteresting, under a blanket of snow, but we all turned our heads when we saw a sign inscribed 'Dachau 15km'. We held our final meeting in the stateroom in the Town Hall, the walls of which were painted with scenes depicting the wedding of Duke Georg the Rich and Princess Jadowska of Poland in 1475. We were then taken to Trausnitz Castle where we were greeted by trumpeters in period costume on the castle walls. The feast we had been led to anticipate turned out to be fish soup, boiled beef and carrots, while minstrels entertained us with deafening bagpipes.

It was a privilege to represent NALC at the Service of Thanksgiving on the occasion of the eightieth birthday of the Queen Mother at St Paul's Cathedral, where I sat in the north transept with Lord Ridley and Sir Gervas Walker and other local government representatives. On a television screen set on a nearby pillar, we watched the Royal Family leave Buckingham Palace and their progress until they arrived at the cathedral, where they were received by the Dean and the Archbishop of Canterbury. The Yeomen of the Guard and the Gentlemen at Arms were in attendance and the band of the Coldstream Guards played soft music.

I was invited to address the weekend conference of the Cumbria Association of Local Councils held at Shap Wells. I took my friend Phyllis Clifton with me and we stayed at the Clifton Arms Hotel, at Lytham. The Cliftons, from whom her late husband was descended, had held the manor of Clifton from the time it was part of the Amounderness fee of Earl Tostig, and had possessed the manor of Lytham since 1606. Lytham Hall had long been the home of the Clifton family ending with the eccentric Talbot Clifton whose life and travels have been documented by his widow, Violet Clifton, in *The Book of Talbot*, from the time 'he suckled his mother so fiercely that she had a wound in her breast.' We went over the house, with which Phyllis was familiar, and was now the Guardian Assurance Company's head office, and visited the dovecot, which had 850 nesting ledges.

I attended the first meeting of Rural Voice, a small body of representatives of the leading organisations concerned with the countryside, on behalf of NALC, and proposed Michael Dower, whom I had known as a bright young man, as its chairman.

I went to Brussels to discuss a role for the NALC in European affairs with the chairman of the Economic and Social Committee of the EEC, and to Luxembourg, with the British delegation, for a meeting of IULA We were taken to dinner at Poële D'Or and, from the window one could see the Royal Luxembourg Guard on duty outside the royal palace across the road. The next morning, Illtyd Harrington and I walked to the European Parliament for our meeting.

Professor Bryan Keith-Lucas took me to lunch at the National Liberal Club, which is heavily populated with statues and bust of his kinsman, W. E. Gladstone, to discuss the future of the chairmanship of NALC. The Council of the Association had re-appointed me chairman and there were requests that I should stay on for 'at least a couple more years.' Blunt Councillor Stotesbury, the Isle of Wight representative, said: 'We are more than content with the present chairman and do not want to get rid of him yet.' I was to remain chairman for ten years.

I found it difficult to convince the British Section of the International Union of Local Authorities (IULA) that our Association deserved better representation. I eventually found an ally in Roderick Doble who was the officer dealing with relations between IULA and the European Parliament. He arranged for me to visit Brussels, and I took advantage of the occasion to go to Waterloo where I saw Le Haye Sainte and Hougomont, with its walls still battle pockmarked, and stood where General Sir Thomas Picton had been fatally wounded.

I received a letter from Lord Merthyr one morning, at my Carmarthen office, and I noticed that his signature revealed a shaky hand. As I drove home later that day, I heard on the car radio that he had died. I rang his son and heir, Trevor, to express my condolence, which he greatly appreciated as he knew that his father and I were close friends. He then said: 'You get around and see a lot of people. I would like you to make it known that I have disclaimed the title to the barony.' I told him that this would come as deep-felt disappointment to the community in general and asked whether there was any hope that he would reconsider his decision, but he said that he had already decided and the disclaimer was irrevocable. I remembered that Merthyr was also a baronet and I asked Trevor what he was going to do about that, as he could not renounce a baronetcy, and he said that he could only hope that people would respect his wishes and call him 'Mr Lewis' rather than 'Sir Trevor'. I represented the National Association at the memorial service held at St Issell's Church, and I wrote an appreciation which appeared in the *Western Telegraph*.

At the NALC biennial conference held at Harrogate, Lord Greenwood delivered the first 'Lord Merthyr Memorial Lecture', which I had persuaded the Association to inaugurate with the money that Merthyr had left the Association in his will. In the absence of the the Duke of Grafton, I presided over the conference at which there were over eight hundred delegates present from all parts of England and Wales, as well as carrying out my duties as chairman.

I went to the University of Aston at Birmingham to preside over the national conference of County Association Secretaries, and to York to meet the Public Affairs Manager and the Chief Passenger Manager of British Rail, Eastern Region, to discuss proposed rail cuts in their area. I went to Devizes to speak to the Wiltshire Association, and to Gloucester to speak to the Gloucestershire Association, and to

Newcastle-on-Tyne to attend a testing meeting at the Civic Centre when representatives of the Town Councils in Tyne and Wear wanted to form their own county association rather than stay with the Nortumberland Association, and to Goole to make peace between the Lincolnshire and Humberside Associations. I met the chairman of the Development Commission, Nigel (later Lord) Vinson, and Tom King, the Minister for the Environment, to discuss rural housing and to ask for better grants for County Associations.

I went to Liverpool to preside over a panel comprising Gordon Oakes, MP, Peter Price, MEP, Shirley (later Baroness) Williams, MP and Lord Evans of Claughton, to whom members of the Merseyside Local Councils Association addressed their questions. There was a good deal of banter during which Shirley Williams referred to me as one of the Taffia.

John Horrell, the chairman of the Association of County Councils, gave a dinner at the Goring Hotel at which the other guests included Dr Gerard Vaughan, Minister for Consumer Affairs; Gerald Kaufman, Opposition Spokesman on the Environment, Lord Duncan-Sandys, Lord Shepherd; Sir Gordon (later Lord) Barrie, Director-General of Fair Trading, and Jennifer Jenkins, chairman of the Historic Buildings Council for England, who recalled warmly the time we had taken her and Roy to Ramsey Island to see the seals.

The British Section of IULA held one of its sessions at Swansea, where the Mayor gave a rather frugal reception at the Glyn Vivian Art Gallery, but we had a fine dinner that evening at the Orangery at Margam, where the chairman, Lord Pargiter, called on me to express our thanks. I find that once you tell a joke or two at such a gathering, you become a target for such tasks.

I represented the Association at a joint IULA and Council of European Municipalities Conference at Edinburgh at which the Lord Provost, Tom Morgan, told me that he had no Welsh connection and was 'a Scottish Morgan'. I went to see Edinburgh Castle and Holyrood House and St Giles Cathedral, which was rather dreary except for the Chapel of the Order of the Thistle. The conference was opened by Dr Gordon Adam, MEP, in the absence of Piet Dankert, the president of the European Parliament, and the main speakers were Ivor (later Lord) Richard, and the former Prime Minister, Edward Heath. The Convention of Scottish Authorities gave a dinner at the Royal Commonwealth Pool which was attended by three hundred delegates and I was asked to propose the vote of thanks. I started by stating that I need only say: *Ni bu mor gyfor/O Eidyn ysgor*, which were the words written in the sixth century in praise of a feast given at Edinburgh, when Edinburgh was Din Eidyn, the capital of a Welsh tribe called the Gododdin, or Votadini. This surprised them somewhat, and pleased W. R. P. George and Ioan Bowen Rees, who were the Welsh delegates.

I was invited to a dinner at the Mansion House to celebrate the twenty-fifth anniversary of the Civic Trust, and was received by the Lord Mayor, Sir Christopher Leaver, and the Sheriffs. Afterwards I was taken to the Oxford and Cambridge Club where I met David Thomson, a descendant of the Herberts, who wanted to start a Sir Richard Colt Hoare Society.

I attended the World Congress of Local Authorities at Columbus, Ohio, as a member of the British delegation and was greeted at the City Hall by the mayor, Tom Moody, whom I had met at Strasbourg. We were taken on a tour of the town and shown the house where James Thurber was born, and the State Capitol, Frank Lloyd Wright's 'most honest of all American structures'. We were entertained to lunch at the Academy for Contemporary Problems at the Ohio State University, following which Ralph Widner, the president of the Academy, took me in a vain search for a Cardinal, the State bird. We were then driven across the flatlands, with prairie dogs popping up all around us, to the foothills of the Appalachians, and along the Scioto river, to Chillicote, to see a Hopwellian mica-lined burial site, of about 1000 BC.

The Malaysian Minister of Housing told me that he had been educated at the University College of Wales, Aberystwyth, and the Mayor of Mandeville, Jamaica, said that she could not speak highly enough of my cousin, Binnie Vaughan when he was Bishop there.

We were invited to Darby Dan Farm, the home of John D. Galbreath who was the only man to have won the Derby, with Roberto ridden by Lester Piggott in 1972, and the Kentucky Derby, which he had won twice. The Saudi delegation at the Congress had arrived there earlier in the day to see some of his 150 race horses go through their paces and had, we were told, purchased a few to take home with them. Ralph Widner and his wife took me to the safari park with its bison and zebra and antelopes and elephants and rhinoceros and exotic birds: Ralph said that when I inquired about the State bird he felt that I was a man after his own heart, but when I asked him about the Buckeye, the State emblem, he did not know the answer and asked Galbreath to show me one. 'Jump in,' said Galbreath, 'I'll show you,' and we drove around in his vast Chevrolet for quite a while before he stopped suddenly and said: 'That's it,' and I was rather disappointed to find that the buckeye was a horse chestnut. Galbreath told me that his estate covering 4,300 acres, required 57 miles of paling that was painted white in a five year cycle, using 3,000 gallons of paint each year. The Guest House, which was a palatial secondary building away from the house, stood by a large lake upon which there floated a massive 'Tugboat Annie'.

I flew from Columbus to La Guardia airport where Evelyn waited for me and took me to her home in The Bronx. She had planned to take me on a tour of the eastern states and Canada and we left New York after breakfast the next day and travelled along the New England Turnpike 95 through places with familiar names like Greenwich, Stamford, Stratford, Milford and New Haven where we called at Yale University, that was founded by Elihu Yale from Wrexham in 1718. We passed through New London, which had 'ye ancientest burial ground', and Mystic Seaport where the square-rigged schooner *Joseph Conrad* lay among many ships in the largest maritime museum in the USA. We left the Turnpike and crossed Newport Bridge to Newport, Rhode Island, with the mayor of which I had corresponded when I wrote to all the Newports in the world when I was first mayor of Newport, in 1951, but it was a Saturday afternoon and all the offices were closed. We drove along Belle Vue Avenue and Ochre Point to view the fine mansion houses designed after Chateau d'Asnieres or Versailles or Louis XIII's palace or Marie Antoinette's Grand Trianon, for the Vanderbilts and the like in a splendid spirit of one-upmanship.

We drove to Plymouth and stood beside Plymouth Rock, where the Pilgrim Fathers landed, and went on board the *Mayflower* which Alan Villiers, as captain, and Dick Brennan, of the Wig and Pen Club, as cook, had sailed across the Atlantic in 1957.

At Boston, we had been recommended to dine at Anthony's Pier 4 but we had difficulty in finding our way there and went through the Callaghan Tunnel and under Boston Harbour twice before we came across the restaurant at the end of one of the piers. I ordered rib of beef and was taken aback when the waiter laid before me a huge platter bearing a whole rib. Next day, we made a Gray Line Tour of Boston and its environs beginning with Harvard University, at Cambridge. We then followed the route of Paul Revere's ride to Lexington and saw the houses in which Nathaniel Hawthorne, Ralph W. Emerson, Oliver Wendell Holmes, Louisa M. Alcott, and Henry Thoreau had lived. I was disappointed that we were unable to go to Walden Pond about which Thoreau wrote his book, *Walden*.

We called at Salem to see the Witch House, where those who were accused of witchcraft were examined before they were hanged on Gallows Hill, and stopped at The House of Seven Gables that inspired Hawthorne's book of that name, and at the house where he was born.

At Portsmouth, New Hampshire we visited the birthplace of John Paul Jones and, after crossing into Maine, we went through Ogunquit and Kennebunk until we got to Portland where I wanted to see Longfellow's home. As a small boy I had learned his poem, 'The Village Blacksmith', and had a vision of the smithy, 'under the spreading chestnut tree', but I was disappointed to find that it was situated in Congress Street, Portland, Maine. We passed by Bowdoin College in

Brunswick at which Longfellow and Hawthorne had graduated, and called at Stowe House where Harriet Beecher Stowe wrote *Uncle Tom's Cabin*.

We turned inland at Waterville and came to Skowhegan, where a sixty foot high totem-pole, weighing twelve tons, stood in the town square. We then followed the Kennebec River to The Forks, and went through Bingham and followed the Benedict Arnold Trail to Jackman. Evelyn, being a good Catholic, wanted to make a pilgrimage to St Anne-de-Beaupré where thousands of pilgrims had already gathered, most of them elderly ladies, at the shrine of St Anne, the mother of Mary, whose arm was allegedly displayed in a gold case on the altar of the ornate church. At Quebec, which takes its name from the Indian *kebec* meaning 'the narrowing of the waters', we had lunch at the Chateau Frontenac Hotel, where my father-in-law, Lewis Craven Ord, normally stayed.

We found Montreal much more friendly than Quebec although our evening there was ruined by torrential rain. As we passed MacGill University I thought of John Hughes, a native of Fishguard, who was Professor of English there. The following morning we went to Mount Royal cemetery, where Joyce's grandfather, Colonel Lacey Johnson, commander of the Heavy Armoured Brigade, was buried with full military honours in 1915.

We made the obligatory visit to the CN Tower at Toronto before proceeding to Niagara Falls, where we were clad in oilskins and taken behind the Falls, in preference to boarding the *Maid of the Mist*. We then sat in the Panasonic Tower watching the illumination of the Falls at dusk. Toronto was *en fête*, having celebrated Dominion Day the previous day and expecting a visit by the Queen Mother the next. We went to Eaton's, claimed to be the world's largest shopping centre, with three hundred shops and eighteen cinemas under one roof, and a flight of stuffed Canada geese suspended high in the entrance hall, that itself looked like Crystal Palace. I bought a book on Muskoka where Joyce's family owned several islands in the lake and where she had spent part of her childhood. I then went in search of Rosedale, the house where her ancestor, Colonel Jarvis lived, that was commemorated and illustrated in the book *Mary's Little Rosedale*, but there was no sign of the house or of the parkland around it, as it all lay under Toronto's suburbia.

At Toronto we got news of a possible air-crew strike and as I wanted to get home, we left immediately and drove through Buffalo and Pembroke and Rochester, and by the Finger Lakes to Syracuse and Oneida and Utica and Schenectady and, in the rain after dark, through Catskill and Tarrytown reaching The Bronx at half past two in the morning. The next morning I rang J. F. Kennedy Airport and was able to bring forward my departure to ten o'clock that evening.

I was invited to Brecon for Binnie's enthronement as Bishop of Swansea and

Brecon. The cathedral presented a colourful scene, with the medieval pageantry of the church provided by more than a hundred robed clergy, along with the Canons and the Dean, in their brightest copes, and the Chancellor, Judge Rowe Harding, in his full-bottom wing. The Lords Lieutenant of Glamorgan and of Powys, Sir Cennydd Traherne, KG, and Colonel John Corbett-Winder, brought greetings from their people, and the black Bishop of Belize, who had succeed Binnie, was there, along with a deputation of natives from Jamaica, where he had also been Bishop of Mandeville, who had come over for the ceremony.

I went to a Rural Life Conference held at the Badock Hall, at Bristol University, where Sir Gervas Walker, chairman of the Association of County Councils, spoke and after dinner he and I got into a corner with our drinks to discuss the future relationship between his Association and NALC. The next day, I had lunch with Judith Graham-Jones, the representative of the Essex Association of Local Councils and, that evening, we had a drink at The George at Norton St Philip, one of the oldest inns in England, and dinner at The Old Rectory at Woolverton. The following day, being Sunday, I took her to catch her train at Bath and then went on to Devizes where Anthony and family took me to a picnic lunch at Savernake Forest.

IN ANECDOTAGE

> *When a man fell into his anecdotage it was a sign for him to retire from the world.*
>
> Benjamin Disraeli in *Lothario*.

I WOKE IN A WELTER OF THOUGHTS, on the first morning of 1981, as the year ahead was to be the year of my retirement. Throughout my life I had endeavoured to fill 'the unforgiving minute' and I had no relish for a life of leisure. I could not envisage myself whiling away the hours on the golf course, or cruising round the world, or being involved in the good works from which I would have retired. I was under pressure to continue as chairman of the National Association of Local Councils, and there was no good reason why I should not continue as Herald Bard for as long as I would be required. My one ambition was to be free to pursue my interest in the past of my surroundings.

My reverie was short lived, however, as Emily and Max, who had stayed the night so that their parents could enjoy a New Year's Eve party, came to my bed and made me read *The Wind in the Willows* to them. It was like being a father again. When I paused to turn a page, Emily whispered in my ear: 'Max can be such a nice little boy, but he makes me feel naughty at times.' She was full of wise saws and colourful expressions at that stage. When I went to see her after she had been unwell and asked her how she was, she replied: 'I feel now as I always do,' and when she was selected to read the prayers at school she told me: 'I have to do the hands-together-and-eyes-closed tomorrow morning,' and she told me that she had 'a good memory-box'. When the vicar called one day, she rushed to show him her book of Bible stories 'which my Bumpa gave me.' The vicar thumbed through the book and said 'What a nice book!' at which Max asked him: 'Would you like to borrow it?'

One morning, when Emily was staying with me and we walked past St Mary's Church she said she would like to go inside. I took her in to the church and showed her the Philipps of Picton memorials and the amusing grotesques on the pillars, and the carved mayor's stall and the sheriff's, and read her the memorial to 'the lovely Hesse Jones'. She then asked 'Where is Glannie's tomb?' I showed her where Joyce's coffin had rested and as we went down the aisle, she went back and bent down and then rushed up to me saying: 'I kissed my hand and put it on the floor where Glannie's coffin was.'

My book, *The Sheriffs of the County of Pembroke:1541-1974*, appeared, in a white dust jacket bearing the county's coat-of-arms in colour. and it was favourably reviewed in the local papers, and in *Archaeologia Cambrensis*, *The Welsh History Review*, *The Antiquaries Journal*, the Heraldry Society's journal *Coats of Arms*, and, later on, in *Shrievalty News*, the journal of the Shrievalty Association.

On the day of the Queen's Jubilee, I watched Her Majesty leave Buckingham Palace in the state coach and heard Alun Williams's commentary from the Victoria Monument and saw Francis Jones, Wales Herald Extraordinary, with the Kings of Arms and Heralds in their tabards greeting her at St Paul's Cathedral, and then I went to Fishguard to interview Wynford Vaughan-Thomas. This was a change for him, as he would normally have been on the royal route, but he was now a director of Harlech TV and no longer with the BBC. That evening I took part in broadcast programme on 'Royalty and Monarchy' with Godfrey Talbot.

A registered package that came by post contained the Queen's Silver Jubilee Medal, and a certificate which said that it was 'to be worn in commemoration of Her Majesty's Silver Jubilee.' A report in the local papers revealed that four other men in the county had received one, but no one seemed to know why.

The Queen came to Haverfordwest a fortnight later and the Wardens of the Gild of Freemen stood robed at the Shire Hall gate where she was to sign the visitors' book, in fact two books, one for the District Council and one for the Town Council. She could not get the pen to write, however, and scribbled on the back page of one of them until the ink came. She signed the two and nudged Prince Philip to sign. He then turned to us and asked if we were the Town Council and John Green, as Master, was quick to say that we were the Gild of Freemen, which seemed to puzzle the Prince.

Having been asked to open the Castle Hotel and the Glen Hotel at Haverfordwest during the year of my mayoralty, it was as secretary and founder of the Pembrokeshire Tourist Association that Maureen Dytor invited me to open the Sir Benfro Hotel at Herbrandston.

Auntie Bess died in her hundred-and-third year, the last of her generation. I took a wreath to Hendre on the day of her funeral and, for the private service, I stood beside the couch where she always made Joyce sit beside her and hold her hand as she and I lived the past together times over. She, like me, had always wanted to be buried in Nevern churchyard, but the churchyard was full and a special dispensation had to be obtained for her to be interred in the family tomb, with her parents and her bachelor brothers, T. Y. and John Lewis. Binnie, in his bishop's raiment, conducted the service and, at the committal, movingly referred to her as 'our sister and mother, Elizabeth'.

Not long afterwards, her son, Evan, died, at the age of sixty-four, having narrowly missed fulfilling his mother's prophecy that he would become Director General of Lloyds Bank by retiring as Deputy as the holder of that office was too young for Evan to succeed him. His brother Binnie, Bishop of Swansea and Brecon, officiated, assisted by the Bishop of St David's, and the rector. After the funeral we returned to Hendre, where we were told that Binnie had hurried back to Brecon as his wife, Nesta, was seriously ill. Within a week I was at Brecon Cathedral attending her funeral in the presence of eighty clergy, the Dean and the Archdeacons and four bishops, whom Binnie followed in the procession in his mitre and robes. He stopped and bowed to us, his relatives and mourners as he went by. Her body was laid in the plot reserved for bishops of the diocese, behind the cathedral. We retired to Ely Tower, the Bishop's Palace, after the committal.

The telephone rang and the voice the other end said: 'Lord Pembroke here.' For a moment I thought it was some friend pulling my leg until the voice said: 'As you may know, I have never been to Pembroke and I thought it was about time I came, and Lord Cawdor suggested that I should contact you.' He was the Earl of Pembroke and he had brought with him Edward Adeane, son of Sir Michael (later Lord) Adeane, the Private Secretary to the Queen, with whom I had been in touch about the connection between the Adeanes and the Ords. I took them to the islands and to Pembroke, having arranged for the mayor to receive us. We were met at Pembroke Castle by Major Ivor Ramsden who pointed to the renovations made by his grandfather, General Sir Ivor Philipps, which the Ministry of Works wished to remove, and Lord Pembroke and Adeane and I climbed to the top of the donjohn. At the National Park Information Centre, at the castle gate, the girl attendant drew our attention to the Park's booklet, *The Castles of Pembrokeshire*, and turned to me saying: 'This booklet will tell you everything about castles.' I could not resist saying: 'I'm glad to hear: I wrote it.'

When, once more, all efforts to find a mayor of Newport had failed, the Steward of the Barony turned to me and said: 'You'll have to take it on again!' I reluctantly agreed to do so, but only in a titular capacity so that the office should not become extinct. I had great difficulty in persuading Marilyn to be my mayoress, as she did not want to do it in name only, but she eventually agreed when I explained to her that she would be doing a great favour to me and to the ancient borough. At my installation I nominated her to take the place her mother had occupied on three occasions. At the mayoral banquet that followed, the toast of the barony was proposed by Colonel Jack Higgon, Master of the Gild of Freemen of Haverfordwest, and other speakers were Sir Goronwy Daniel, Her Majesty's Vice-Lieutenant, and Wynford Vaughan-Thomas. I read the first lesson at the civic service the next morning, and laid a wreath on behalf of the town on the war memorial at the Memorial Hall. At the Aldermen's Luncheon I thanked everyone, but Robbie in particular for allowing Marilyn to be my Mayoress. Emily and Max had lunch at Manora, my brother's house, where Emily had occupied her time writing an essay on the church service, with a drawing of me reading the lesson.

Marilyn accompanied me to a Garden Party at Buckingham Palace where Johnnie Johnston was prominent, in the uniform of a Colonel in the Grenadier Guards, as Queen's Equerry. A few days later there was a picture of him in *The Times*, again in uniform, holding the Queen's handbag while she presented new colours to the 1st and 2nd Battalions of he Grenadiers.

Before I left office as mayor of Newport, I arranged to have the mayor's chain re-gilded. This had not been done since it had been presented to the town in 1896 by Kemes Lloyd. The shield on the medallion, bearing the Martin coat of arms, had been wrongly emblazoned, with two blue, instead of red, bars, and I had this corrected.

One Sunday, at nut gathering time, I took Marilyn and the children to Aber Rhigian. We went into the hazel wood where Emily clung to my hand with the joy of adventure. To share one's happiness with a little child is happiness indeed, were it not for one's ever present grief. We called at Islwyn where Peggy, in the tradition of her grandmother, laid the table without asking whether we would take tea.

I took Wynford Vaughan-Thomas to Devizes where he gave an entertaining talk to the Moonrakers, a fund raising body named after a legend concerning a man who had seen his shadow, or his ghost, in the pond at Devizes. The dinner was held at the Bear Hotel, at which Anthony presided over a boisterous gathering of young men.

The Cardiff architect, Idris Lewis, whom I had first met in charge of a Mule Company in the hills above Hebron during the war and now had a holiday home at Newport, rang to say that he and his wife had spent the weekend at the Bay Tree at Burford where they had got into conversation with two ladies who were also staying there. When he said that they had a house at Newport one of the ladies said: 'I once knew a chap at Newport, Dillwyn Miles.' She was Dodie Crowther, now the widowed Mrs Tuppen, and still living at Rugby. She was delighted when I telephoned her that evening, and invited me to stay when next in that area. She had lost her husband and her son had died of cancer in his twenties, and she now devoted her life to raising funds for cancer research. She asked if I could help her by getting a celebrity to appear at a fund-raising dinner that she arranged annually. Max Boyce willingly agreed to fit such an engagement in with his busy programme, on his way from a performance at Birmingham to one at Belfast. He gave an after-dinner speech that lasted an hour, which the guests found highly entertaining and, at the end, loudly clamoured for more.

The Earl of Cranbrook used to say that the arrangement whereby the Pembrokeshire Rural Community Council provided secretarial services for the West Wales Naturalists' Trust, in return for a contribution, was the ideal one and openly advocated that it should be followed in the other counties of England and Wales.

Following the amalgamation of the counties of Pembroke, Cardigan and Carmarthen as the new county of Dyfed, it was decided that the three Rural Community Councils be joined together to form the Dyfed Rural Council, of which I was appointed Director. This saddened me, but I had the satisfaction of knowing that some provision had been made in Pembrokeshire for the elderly, with 34 local Old Peoples Welfare Committees established in the county; that 37 new village halls and 114 playing field schemes had been assisted with grant-aid; that the social life of the people had been improved through the promotion of drama and art and local history; that the West Wales Field Society had become the West Wales Naturalists' Trust and had acquired Skomer and 25 nature reserves; that the Pembrokeshire Local Councils Association had been placed on a firm foundation, and that its president and secretary had been elected president and chairman of the National Association of Local Councils.

In my new post I had to endeavour to combine the work of the three former RCCs as a county unit, which was difficult as there was little community of interest between the people of Llanelli and Llanilar, or of Brynaman and Martletwy. I, therefore, quietly retained the former system as much as possible in an effort to save the old community spirit.

I continued as managing-editor of *Nature in Wales* until John Barrett persuaded the Executive Committee of the Dyfed Rural Council, of which he was a member, that I should not do so. I had to resign and, in my last issue, Volume 16 No. 4, September 1979, I wrote a brief history of the journal since the publication of the first quarterly issue by the West Wales Field Society in 1955. William Condry, in his 'Country Diary' in *The Guardian*, had envisaged the difficulties one had to encounter when he wrote that 'it cannot be easy to have to edit a local natural history journal whose field may be the whole world of biology,' and he went on to distinguish between the few who revelled in the 'severely scientific and the many who wanted to read easy articles about birds and butterflies and wild flowers.' Such journals had been going for well over a century, and many had failed but others kept steadily on and looked like continuing. He was 'moved to these ruminations by the receipt of the current number of *Nature in Wales*, a journal always full of good things about all aspects of Welsh wild life and conservation.'

Nature in Wales Volume 17, No. 1, contained a 'Profile' of me written by Jack Donovan which began: 'Surprisingly, and perhaps, sadly, it is not often that one can meet a Welshman who is fluent – indeed scholarly – in both his native tongue and the English language, who also includes natural history and wildlife conservation in his main interests and who, in addition, can blend these attributes with great administrative ability. Such a man is Dillwyn Miles.'

The new editor, Dr Brian John, had two assistant editors, a business manager and a secretary, as well as scientific advisers, with an editorial board comprising a chairman and eight members, in order, said Dr John in his first editorial, 'to maintain the very high scientific reputation of the journal which has been built up patiently and skilfully by Dillwyn Miles during his years as Managing Editor.' Regrettably, the journal did not live long under the new regime. In his fourth issue the editor reported that 'quite suddenly we have to recognise that the future of *Nature in Wales* is under threat' and rehearsed the problems that I, and those before me, had encountered, and had to overcome. The business manager had resigned and as Dr John's request to be paid £1,000 a year was not granted, he could 'no longer afford to spend two months of each year entirely on unpaid work.'

In 1982 *Nature in Wales* appeared in a new guise, now published by the National Museum of Wales under the editorship of Dr Douglas Bassett, Professor of Geology at the University of Wales, Cardiff, with John Barrett as chairman of the editorial board. In his foreword, Barrett gave scant credit to the West Wales Naturalists' Trust, but said that he had been a member of it since 1946 and admitted that he had 'contributed minimally to *Nature in Wales*.' In truth, he had told me that he would not contribute to the journal as long as Lockley was editor, and he did not do so afterwards either. Dr Bassett, in his editorial, referred to my 'story of the journal over the first twenty-five years', quoting my description of the cover designs. The original one had a figurative drawing of a fiery dragon emblazoned with wild life scenes by Charles Tunnicliffe, RA, and when we felt that the design should change, he willingly did a drawing of a polecat.

John Barrett wrote, as chairman, stating that it was planned to issue the journal twice yearly, but it only appeared annually, and two years went by before a volume appeared for 1987-88 and, despite an assurance given by the Director of the National Museum that *Nature in Wales* would continue as a Museum publication, this was the last issue. Had I been allowed to continue, it would not have been.

Mrs M. J. Morgan, a long-standing member of the North Wales Naturalists'

Trust, wrote referring to the meeting I had called at Aberystwyth in September 1963 to invite the other Trusts to participate in the production of the journal, and recalled the idea of publishing a special number of the journal to celebrate European Conservation Year which developed, instead, into a book, *Welsh Wildlife in Trust*, to which I contributed a chapter giving 'A Short History of the Naturalists' Trust Movement in Wales'. The book received a Prince of Wales Award and the Prince contributed a brief foreword. She also recalled that, towards the end of 1974, after several years of endeavour, I had 'succeeded in getting together representatives of all the County Trusts in Wales to consider the setting up of a national body', which became the Association of Trusts for Nature Conservation in Wales.

A letter from *Who's Who* asking for personal particulars so that my name should appear within its covers came with the same post as another from the Savile Club to say that I had been elected a member of the Club. As I arrived there for the first time, the BBC rang and I had to do two telephone interviews, one in English and the other in Welsh, on the content of my speech at the National Conference of Local Councils at Central Hall the following morning. I dined at the long table with Huw Wheldon, Michael Forman, Sir James (Hamish) Blair-Cunnynghame and Professor G. P. Wells. Hamish had once told a guest dining at the long table how his sore throat had been miraculously cured by some magical stuff extracted from mouldy cheese, or old socks, or something, which he considered to be a major breakthrough, but 'not many people knew about it yet', without being aware that he was speaking to Sir Alexander Fleming. 'Gip' Wells, who was Professor of Zoology at University College, London, asked me about Ronald Lockley and said that he was busy studying lugworms but was still involved in sorting out his father, HG's, papers and affairs.

Another evening I sat at the long table between Donald Baverstock who now held a responsible position with Yorkshire TV, but would have liked to return to Wales, and Ben Lucien Burman, 'the new Mark Twain'. Ben said that Disney was making a film based on his Catfish Bend books, and that he was on his way to Sri Lanka, to see an old sweetheart. When I wished him well and hoped that she would be as beautiful as ever, he said: 'She will. She's an elephant.'

Wynford Vaughan-Thomas invited me to join him and Kingsley Amis at dinner at a private table at the Savile when Amis would talk about nothing but his wife, Elizabeth Jane Howard, who had refused to come back to him. Another time when he came to dinner, he spoke mainly about the Garrick, a place not mentioned in the Savile, except to mock its 'cassata of pistachio and strawberry ice-cream' tie.

Marilyn told me one day that she had received a letter from the Lord Chancellor stating that he proposed to appoint her a magistrate, but she was disinclined to agree as she felt that she was too young and should wait until she was older. I impressed upon her that if she did not accept now, she would probably not be asked again and that she should give it due consideration. She was sworn at the Crown Court by Judge Charles Pitchford who agreed that I should bring Emily and Max into court to witness the ceremony.

John Green, Master of the Gild of Freemen of Haverfordwest, and I, went to Leicester to attend the annual meeting of the Freemen of England, which we eventually had reconstituted 'Freemen of England and Wales'. The Lady Marcher, Mrs John Hawkesworth, who had invited us to stay the night at her home at Knossington, came with us to the banquet.

The Prince and Princess of Wales visited Haverfordwest on their honeymoon tour of Wales. As Wardens of the Court of the Gild of Freemen, we stood in our scarlet robes at the steps of the Shire Hall where the royal couple were to sign the visitors' book. As the Prince came forward he turned to me and said: 'Good heavens, what are you doing here – but you live here, of course? You're no longer on the Prince of Wales' Committee.' I said that I was now retired and too old, which he pooh-poohed and then said 'I haven't seen you wear those medals before.'

I received an invitation to go to Buckingham Palace to receive the President's Certificate from the Duke of Edinburgh, president of the National Playing Fields Association. There were ten of us, one fellow from Scotland, me from Wales: and the other men were from the English counties. We were ushered into the Chinese Room and the Duke came and shook hands and had a chat with each of us as he handed us the certificate, and then we had our photograph taken with him. He complained about the deteriorating quality of the certificate itself, that was once on vellum. 'Will shortly be on lavatory paper,' he added.

Judith invited me to her home in Great Baddow, near Chelmsford, and took me on a most enjoyable and instructive tour of Essex. I was particularly glad to be taken to the Saxon church at Greensted-juxta-Ongar to see the box marble tomb of my children's ancestor, Craven Ord the Antiquary who died in 1832, and to read a tablet in memory of his wife, Mary Redman in the church, and the tomb of their son, Robert Hutchison Ord, Knight of the Guelphic Order. We called at Greenstead Hall, the home of the Redmans into which family Craven Ord had married.

Judith picked me up at the Savile Club to go to dinner at the Speaker's House. As we were a little early, we popped in to St Stephen's Tavern, which turned out to be for the last time before it was demolished to make offices for Members of Parliament. The Speaker, George Thomas, greeted us with his usual warmth. 'Knowing that you had spent some time in Palestine, Dillwyn,' he said, 'I have invited the Chief Rabbi,' and on looking at the list of thirty guests it struck me that, wittingly or otherwise, he had done more than that as most of the guests were either Welsh or Jewish. Among the Welsh were the Archdruid, James Nicholas, W. Emrys Evans, G. V. Wynne Jones and their wives, while apart from the Chief Rabbi and Lady Jacobovitz, there were Sir Sigmund Sternberg, Grenville (later Lord) Janner, MP, and his mother, Lady Janner, Leonard Goss, Dr Schonveld, Henry Nyman and Max Reinhardt. The menu was simple and comprised Crême Forestière: Darne de Saumon Hollandaise, Pomme Duchesses, Carottes Clamart: Poire de Comice Alma, followed by coffee and petit fours, and the wine was Liebfraumilch Silver Goblet 1979 and Armagnac. The State Dining Room was hung with portraits of past Speakers, among which I noticed that of an earlier Welsh Speaker, John Williams.

The Savile had reciprocal arrangements with the Garrick Club, and so I took Judith there for lunch one Saturday, the only day when ladies were permitted. We then went to the National Portait Gallery, and visited the remains of the Mithras Temple which Peter Grimes had discovered.

Judith arrived at Castle Hill one evening, after being interviewed at Bristol for the post of Director of the Avon Community Council. Ten minutes after she arrived, the chairman of the Council rang to offer her the post.

By now I was busily engaged in catching up with the years when I wanted, but could not find time, to commit words to paper. I had edited, *The Pembrokeshire Coast National Park* for the Countryside Commission, published by the HMSO in 1973 and republished in 1978; had written *The Writers of the West/ Llenorion Gorllewin Cymru* (1974) jointly with Rhys Nicholas, and had published *The West Wales Naturalists' Trust and its Reserves* (1975); *The Sheriffs of Pembrokeshire* (1976); *The Royal National Eisteddfod of Wales* (1978), and *The Castles of Pembrokeshire* (1979, republished in 1983 and in 1988). I had for a long time been collecting the words of others about Pembrokeshire and these were published in *A Pembrokeshire Anthology* which was launched with a flourish by Wynford Vaughan-Thomas, who had written a Foreword to the book, at a ceremony held at the County Library Hall in March 1983.

I was commissioned by Robert Hale Ltd., to write *Portrait of Pembrokeshire* in their Portrait Books series and when I had almost completed the book they wrote to say that they had just realised that Pembrokeshire had been subsumed in the new county of Dyfed and that they could not well publish a book about a county that did not exist. I told them that although Pembrokeshire no longer existed as an administrative unit or as a county, its division into two districts, one of which, South Pembrokeshire, preserved its name, which also survived in institutions such as the Pembrokeshire Health Authority, the Pembrokeshire Agricultural Society, the Pembrokeshire Cricket Club, the Pembrokeshire National Park, and I hoped that for a long time to come Her Majesty the Queen would have her favourite Pembrokeshire corgis around her. They agreed.

John Llewelyn Jones, my classmate at school, who won the first *Western Mail* essay competition, and now wrote for *Country Life* and was the author of *Schoolin's Log* and other books, telephoned late one evening to say that he had read *Portrait of Pembrokeshire* at a sitting, 'unable to put it down', and considered that it was 'the first synthesis of history done to Pembrokeshire'.

I had no sooner finished the *Portrait* than a request came from Lynn Hughes, general editor of the Welsh Classics Series, to write an edited, modernised version, with introduction and notes, of *The Description of Penbrokshire* by George Owen of Henllys for the series. Though written in 1603, *The Description* had not been published as a book until it appeared in the Cymmrodorion Record Series published by The Honourable Society of Cymmrodorion in 1892, and it was my hope that another century would not go by before it appeared again. It appeared in 1994.

In an article in the *Transactions of the Honourable Society of Cymmrodorion*, Kathleen Loesch wrote that, while seeking particulars of Dylan Thomas, she had found a letter addressed by Dylan to Hamish Miles and added in a footnote that 'Hamish Miles, the Scot and a scout for the publisher Jonathan Cape was the addressee suggested to me by David Higham – after I had eliminated the two outstanding Mr Mileses of Wales – Mr Dillwyn Miles of Haverfordwest and Mr David Miles of Aberystwyth.'

The Countess of Strathmore called with her daughter, Lady Elizabeth Bowes Lyon, after she had been reading the *Pembrokeshire Anthology* saying that she had never been to Pembrokeshire and adding: 'We are only here because of you.' She then wrote, with a pressing invitation for me to call at Glamis, and enclosed an autographed booklet on the castle.

My friend John Green invited me to accompany him to Spain and we flew from Cardiff and landed in Alicante where his kinsman, Neville George, met us and drove us through showers of snow that mingled with the almond blossom, to his house at Altea. We then undertook a few days' tour across Spain to Conil de la Frontera, to visit friends, and on to Cadiz and Granada, and returned along winding roads on the lower slopes of the Sierra Nevada, calling at Guadix, where the cave dwellings were now equipped with television aerials.

I attended the IULA World Congress at Stockholm as part of the British delegation and stayed at the Sheraton Hotel which was in the centre of the city and enabled us to walk through the old town, Gama Stan, where buskers and entertainers enlivened the narrow, cobbled Västerlånggatan. We walked by the Stortorget where the noblemen were massacred in 1520, and visited the Bourse where the Swedish Academy meets to elect the Nobel Prize winner for literature. We took a 'Stockholm in a Nutshell' tour the following morning and had pike and asparagus for lunch at the restaurant of the Opera House before attending the opening session at the Folkets Hus Congress Centre with a speech of welcome by the King of Sweden. I spoke at the Local Councils Working Party, which was chaired by Alfred Loessner from the USA, the next morning and recommended an international study of such councils, which met with universal approval and after the meeting I was approached by delegates from the Netherlands and Zimbabwe and other countries for my plans for such a survey, which embarrassed me as I had not thought about it until I had mentioned it at the Working Party. We were taken to Vaxholm, one of the 24,000 islands in the archipelago, and we went to see the *Vasa*. That evening we dined on Lapland elk in a reconstructed Scandinavian manor house at the Skansen Rural Museum which, I recalled, had inspired Iorwerth Peate to establish the Welsh Folk Museum at St Fagan's. The final session ended with a highly political and ill-advised speech by the Prime Minister of Sweden, Olaf Palme, who was assassinated on his way home from a visit to the cinema three years later.

I went to Westminster Abbey to see the recently installed memorial to Dylan Thomas, which was a slab of green Penrhyn stone set in the floor below the tomb of Geoffrey Chaucer, to whom Poet's Corner owes its origin. I also went to the South Choir aisle to see the memorial to George Stepney, of the Stepneys of Prendergast, diplomat and poet whose pall was carried to the Abbey by two barons, two earls and two dukes.

I was invited to take part in the launching of the Council of Europe's Water's Edge Campaign on the canal behind King's Cross Station, where I met William Wilkinson, the chairman of the Nature Conservancy Council, together with the chairman of the British Waterways Board and Lords Skelmersdale, Melchett and Craigton. We were ushered aboard a gaily painted barge that chugged along until we got to a basin where we stopped and Skelmersdale spoke and called on me to speak on behalf of the local authorities. Before I could say a word, however, a booming voice from the other end of the crowded barge shouted 'Good old Dillwyn!' It was Lord St David's who, afterwards, invited me aboard his barge that was moored alongside and upon which was painted the black lion, ducally gorged and chained, the crest of the Philipps family. He was a great barge enthusiast, and had pioneered a method of running a barge on batteries so as to avoid the use of fuel.

I was speaking to the Duke of Grafton as we gathered for the seventy-fifth anniversary dinner of the Association of Councillors at the Connaught Rooms, when Lord Vinson took upon himself to introduce the Duke to the Prince of Wales. The Duke turned and asked the Prince if he knew me and the Prince, with a smile, said: 'Yes, of course. He is an important figure in Wales!'

The first of a series of the Development Commission's Rural Development Programme Seminars was held at Birmingham. The representatives of the Associations of County Councils and of District Councils both spoke in a pessimistic mood. When I got to my feet and asked whether I could be heard in the back and someone answered 'Yes!', I referred to the occasion when Lloyd George had asked that question and drew the reply: 'I can hear you, but I'm willing to change with someone who can't,' to which the audience responded quickly. Lord Vinson, chairman of the Commission, maintained that my speech had changed the mood of the meeting, and asked me if I would attend the seminars that were to be held in the other regions. The next was held at Darlington, at the Blackwell Grange Moat Hotel, a house built by George Allen in 1693. On the wall was a framed notice stating that Craven Ord the Antiquary, Joyce's great great grandfather, had visited the house. I also went with Vinson to similar meetings at Kendal and Plymouth.

At the Savile one evening, Robert Clark, the yacht designer, and I were invited to have a post-prandial drink with members of the Sublime Society of Beef Steaks, founded in 1735, who were having their dinner in the Ballroom. They seemed a strange lot, dressed in Dickensian garb, and among those to whom we were introduced were the Baron von Brisson, and Count Nicolai Tolstoi, grandson of the great writer, whom Lord Aldington had taken to court and had been awarded damages of a million pounds for defamation of character, but Tolstoi had no money.

The Lord Mayor of Sheffield, Councillor Munns, gave us a civic welcome at the opening of the Conference of Local Councils in Metropolitan Counties, held in the Sheffield Town Hall, before handing over his massive 'throne', as he called it, to me to preside over the proceedings. He was a metallurgist, on sabbatical leave for his mayoral year, and he reminded us that 'England was born in Sheffield, when the treaty between Northumbria and Mercia was made,' which was an interpretation of history that was new to me.

Mr Jones of Trelech rang to thank me for having got £17,000 for his Council by way of damages from their solicitors, who had advised them badly. He had come to me some years before I retired to complain that his Council could not find a solicitor who was prepared to take their solicitors to court for failure to act in the interests of the Council in connection with land that belonged to the council. I got Ivor Rees, the principal of Messrs Price and Son, Haverfordwest, to do so and the money for which Mr Jones thanked me turned out to be only a fraction of the total amount eventually received, which approached £200,000. Jones told me that the clerk of the Council had consulted the breakaway Wales Association of Town and Community Councils which had advised them that there was no hope of obtaining any compensation.

Scan Films came to film the story of my life in a these-you-have-loved kind of series called *Mwynhau'r Pethe*. Apart from shooting at the house, we went to Newport, where they filmed my brother and I together, and I was shown having lunch with Wynford Vaughan-Thomas and his wife, Charlotte, at the Hotel Mariners, when we ostentatiously drank a bottle of Chateau Bauduc, from the vineyard in Bordeaux owned by a local boy, David Thomas. We went to Hook where they filmed my grandson, Max at home at Underdown, playing chess with me, and Emily and I walking hand in hand down a sun dappled lane.

I took Emily to London, as I had promised her. We went to the Tower and the Houses of Parliament and Westminster Abbey. We then walked up Whitehall and saw the changing of the guard at Horseguards, and she had her photograph taken feeding the pigeons on Trafalgar Square. We walked through St James's Park and along The Mall to Buckingham Palace, and all the time her eyes were filled with wonder. As we crossed Green Park I asked her what she thought of London. 'I think London's lovely,' she said, 'but not as nice as Hook!' Hook, a mining village in the former Pembrokeshire coal field and now a scattered dormitory settlement, had never been so honoured.

I watched my friend Sean McReamoin being interviewed on HTV by Emyr Daniel, who referred to him as 'the quintessential Irishman'. Sean rang from Dublin later in the year to invite us to the Golden Harp Film Festival dinner at Galway, as he knew that we would be in Ireland at the time, taking Judith's mother, Elizabeth, who was staying with us. We stayed the first night at the Oranmore Lodge at Oranmorw, where the Festival dinner was held. Sean arrived and ordered champagne and introduced me to his RTE colleague Kieran MacMahoun, who told me that a death mask of the handsome Seamus Ennis had been taken. We then met Euryn and Jenny Ogwen Williams who were covering the event for HTV, and Arwel Ellis Owen, who had done his first radio interview with me at Little Haven in 1967, when he was extremely nervous, and who was now the head of BBC Belfast.

Under the headline 'Mr Pembrokeshire's Lifetime of Service' the *County Echo* devoted more than half a page, with a picture of me sitting by my desk at Castle Hill, to an article by Kim Kirby in which she gave a brief account of my life.

Judith and I went to Scotland to stay with Winifred Bowman at Dhivach Lodge, Drumnadrochit, where Ronald Lockley was on a visit from New Zealand.

Winnie told us that among Dhivach Lodge's previous occupants were Trollope, J. M. Barrie and the Llewelyn-Davieses, Henry Irving, and Ellen Terry with her sister Kate, who married Arthur Lewis, of Regent Street, and her daughter Kate, who became the mother of John Gielgud. I remembered that Aunt Bess always maintained that we were related to the Terry Lewises and so I wrote to Gielgud to ask him about his grandfather, Arthur Lewis, but he wrote back to say that he knew nothing about him. Ronald was in the process of writing a book, in collaboration with Winnie, about Dhivach, which they called *The House above the Waterfall*.

We went to Inverness and to Cawdor Castle but found that Earl Cawdor, whom I knew as Viscount Emlyn, was away from home. The first thing that caught my eye in the entrance hall was a great spread of muskets arranged fanwise on the wall, which I recognised as those surrendered by the French on Goodwick beach in 1797 and which, I thought, should have been left in Pembrokeshire when Emlyn had demolished Stackpole Court. We went to Beauly and Cromarty and Kirkmichael, and to Cilicudden where the cemetery had tombs like Greek temples. We crossed the Moray Firth to Muir of Ord and called at the Ord Arms Hotel. We passed Lord Lovat's Beaufort Castle and returned through Glenurquhart. After dinner we listened to a recording of Ronald being interviewed by Roy Plomley in *Desert Island Discs,* and played Scrabble, at which both Ronald and Winnie were expert by long practice. Winnie lent me a copy of her book, *I'll Sing No More*, from which I learned that she had come to London from the United States in 1926, to study music, as a singer, under Sir George Henschel. I had heard about her efforts to teach the Americans to speak English properly by taking companies of English actors to New York to perform Shakespearean plays, and I knew that she had served as a voluntary cook on Skokholm and, when we purchased Skomer, she gave us the furniture for the Warden's House. Like so many women, she had fallen for Ronald, and when he married, for the third time, she expressed her displeasure to me and said: 'Why didn't he tell me that he wanted another wife. I would have married him!'

We left Dhivach after a chanterelle breakfast and arrived at Bristol that evening ready to go to London the next day for a meeting of the NALC Council and then on to Witham to address the annual meeting of the Essex Association of Local Councils, with Lord Alport, presiding.

I went to a meeting of Rural Voice at Berwick-on-Tweed and stayed at the King's Arms whence I was taken to have supper with the Lord Lieutenant, Willie Swan, at is home, Blackhouse, near Reston, where I had an opportunity to discuss with some Scots the position of Scottish Community Councils.

I was surprised to be invited to write the foreword for *The Local Government*

Administrators Official Source Book, and to provide a photograph, as I did not know anyone connected with its publication.

The Duke of Grafton told me, one day, that he would have to give up the presidency, which he had held for seven years, owing to his other commitments, but he agreed to stay another year so that we could find a suitable replacement. I remembered that when I visited the Yorkshire Association, I had been impressed by their president, Lord Feversham and when I suggested his name, it met with general approval. Before he succeeded to the peerage, Peter Duncombe was a journalist and I recalled that his uncle, the Earl of Feversham, had come abroad with the 1st Cavalry Division in 1939 but I had no account of him after we landed in Haifa. He had died leaving no male issue and the earldom had become extinct, but a barony remained which Peter had inherited as the sixth baron.

I went to Ipswich to address the annual meeting of the Suffolk Association, at which Lord Tollemache took the chair. I took Arthur Ord's daughter, Shirley, to dinner at my hotel, the Great White Horse, where Mr Pickwick had encountered the lady in yellow curl-papers. She gave me an account of her father's funeral, which had taken place when I was abroad. Some of his surviving friends from the Chindits were present, together with a strong Masonic presence, as he had been Master of both the Arlington Lodge, in London, and of the Brightlingsea Lodge at the same time.

Professor Bryan Keith-Lucas and I attended a memorial service for Baroness Sharp at St Margaret's, Westminster. From where I was sitting I could see the tomb of Sir Walter Raleigh, buried beneath the altar, and tablets in memory of Erskine May and Dingle Foot. There were readings by Dame Alice Meynell and Lord Allen of Abbeydale and an address by Sir James Jones.

In an endeavour to promote the Breton Gorsedd, which continued to be divided against itself, a party of about a hundred members of the Gorsedd of Bards visited Rennes for a joint meeting, and afterwards to attend the Breton Gorsedd ceremony. Judith and I decided to combine the visit with a tour of Brittany. We made for Paimpont hoping to find accommodation at the Relais de Brocéliande, but it was full and we were offered a room in The Abbey, originally a monastery built in the seventh century that was now an extension to the hotel. The Gorsedd, and the Breton Gorsedd, met at eleven the next morning and I led the procession through an archway and along the Bourg to the lakeside, where the ceremony was held. There were more Welsh than Bretons present, and some of the latter were slovenly dressed.

We went on to Carnac, to marvel once again at the massive alignments of 'petrified soldiers', and to Guérande and Angers where dappled fallow deer grazed among the floral beds in the moat of the great chateau. We called at the chateaux at Saumur and Azay-le-Rideau, and at Chinon, Chenonceaux and Chateau d'Amboise. We stayed at Le Chartre-sur-le-Loir, and then toured Normandy, through countryside that often reminded one of the Pembrokeshire landscape. We came to Falaise, with its castle defending a rocky spur with precipitous cliff, or *falaise*. At the fountain below the castle Robert le Diable saw the tanner's daughter, Arlette, washing linen, and violated her, and the result was the bastard William, Duke of Normandy, whom history knows as William the Conqueror.

I attended the Breton Gorsedd again, at Kerantorec, for which we sailed from Plymouth to Roscoff, and from there we went to Quimperlé where we had been put up at the Hotel d'Europe. This was a typically Breton hotel where Madame Hervé, in her *coif*, and aged ninety, presided over the bar. When she heard of my mission, she produced photographs of the joint Gorsedd ceremony held at Riec-sur-Belon in 1927 and gave me one, which I published in my book, *The Secret of the Bards of the Isle of Britain*. The French poet Bertrand Borne called for us early the next morning and took us to Kerantorec, to a thatched building in the forest, which had been a ciderie and now was a creperie. Here we found the Grand Druid Gwenc'hlann and his wife, Mme Scouzec, and Professor Michel Raoult, of the University of Nigeria, who had used my book *The Royal National Eisteddfod of Wales* while writing a history of the Breton Gorsedd.

The Association of District Councils gave a reception at the Banqueting House, which is all that remains of the old Palace of Whitehall. Tony Prendergast, former Lord Mayor of Westminster and High Sheriff of London, drew my attention to the Rubens ceiling commissioned by Charles I, and the window through which he had walked out to the scaffold.

Judith, as the representative of the Avon Association of Local Councils, and I, set off for the biennial conference of NALC held at Llandudno and had lunch at Bodysgallen, a former home of the Mostyn family and now claiming to be the top hotel in Wales. Sir John Banham, Director of the Audit Commission, delivered the Lord Merthyr Memorial Lecture.

Two days later, I was on my way to Berlin to the Assembly of European Municipalities and Regions held at the International Congress Centre, a hideous colossus that looked like a set for a space film. We, the British delegates, were given a pep-talk on Berlin and Berliners by an officer of the British Military Government before the official opening at which there were delegates present from twenty-one countries. We were welcomed by the Lord Mayor of Berlin, Herr Diepgen, and there were interminable speeches by the President of the European Parliament and an ex-Premier of France and others.

We were taken on a tour of East Berlin and at Checkpoint Charlie our passports were closely scrutinised and mirrors were used to inspect the under parts of the coach, and we picked up an official East Berliner courier. Before we left Berlin I went to the Egyptian Museum to see the bust of Nefertiti, and stood outside Spandau Gaol and pondered over the waste of money and man power involved in confining the no-longer-sane Rudilf Hess behind the red brick walls of this gaol.

Judith and I left Littleton-on-Severn, where she was now living, to go to the Isle of Man where I was to represent the National Eisteddfod at *Yn Chruinnaght*, the Manx cultural festival that is more like the *Mod* in Scotland and the *Oireachtas* in Ireland than the Eisteddfod. We drove to Speke Airport and flew to Ronaldsway. We then set off, in a hired car, on a tour of the island and called on my friend, Reg Thomas, former owner of the *Western Telegraph* and his wife Phyllis, whose house was near the Tynwald. Reg then conducted us to Douglas to see his half-brother, Herbert Thomas and his wife Barbara, where we were greeted with champagne. We went to the opening of an arts and crafts exhibition by Sir Charles Kerruish, the Speaker of the House of Keys, and, following his address, I was called upon to convey my greetings.

On my seventieth birthday, Anne Cromwell invited Judith and I to dinner at the Hotel Mariners, where I was guided to the residents' lounge and when I opened the door I found the room in darkness. The lights were suddenly switched on and I saw that it was full of my friends and family. Judith had arranged a surprise party, with a first class buffet and wine and champagne, all of which overwhelmed me. It was such a kind thought, and I was so glad when my grandchildren came forward with a beautiful bouquet which they gave to her, and they gave me a red rose.

The BBC invited me to do a programme in their 'Celebrity Choice' series, which I opened with the *Introduction and Rondo Capriccioso* by Saint-Saens because, to me, who could not sing or play a note, it represented the marvel of music, and as I know so little about it, the enjoyment is enhanced by a sense of wonder.

Judith decided to retire from her post as Director of the Avon Rural Community Council and wanted to buy a house in Haverfordwest. She bought No. 9 St Anthony's Way and I sold Castle Hill and moved in with her. It was a bungalow set in the most select part of the town, with extensive lawns, though they were on a gradient, and mature trees which had formed part of the grounds of The Glen, a small gentleman's seat before the house became a hotel, which I had opened when I was mayor. It had eight rooms which enabled us to have a study each.

A quantity of cannabis valued at £4 million was found by the police at Aberbach, stored in the cottage where John Harries used to brew beer and distil spirits. I called at the Shire Hall and saw the nine accused persons, one of them a woman, in the dock as they were remanded to Swansea Prison. The skipper of the boat would not speak or give his name, beyond Bob, and he wore a T-shirt across the breast of which was written THE END.

At the launch of his book *Wales: A History*, Wynford Vaughan-Thomas gave me a copy in which he wrote: 'To Dillwyn in admiration and friendship'.

When I heard that Wynford had been admitted to Withybush Hospital I went to see him but I was told by the Hospital Secretary that he had received instructions from Charlotte that he was to receive no visitors. I managed to see him, however, almost daily and watched him getting weaker and less coherent until, eventually, he was almost unable to finish his sentences. He was then taken home, to Pentower, and a day or two later, Charlotte rang to say that he would like to see me. It was agreed that I should call the next morning, but when I got there I was told that he had suffered a severe haemorrhage and could not see anybody. He died the next day. There were generous obituaries in *The Times* and in the *Western Mail*, but the family notices stated that the funeral would be private and 'No flowers, no letters, no memorial service, please.' This surprised, and saddened, his friends, and his admirers, whose numbers were legion.

I spoke at the annual meetings of many of the County Associations of Local Councils, including the Isle of Wight where I was entertained to dinner by Lord Mottistone. During dinner, a large sailing ship sailed up The Solent, to Mottistone's great delight, as it was the *Lord Nelson* built specially for disabled persons and he had been involved in its construction.

As I was going to a meeting of IULA at Strasbourg, Judith arranged to combine the visit with a holiday. We flew from Heathrow to Basle and took a train to Zurich and then along the Zurichsee and the Churfirsten Mountains to Chur, and we then took the Glacier Express. The Rhine, full of melting snow, was the colour of La Lique glass. We crossed the Oberalp Pass and looked down on Andermatt where the trains looked like toy trains. We changed trains at Brig and climbed to Tasch, beyond which no cars were allowed, and got to Zermatt, at the foot of the Matterhorn, where we were taken to our hotel by troika. We returned to Brig and went through the Simplon Tunnel to Domodossol and Locarno, and eventually arrived at Lugano. The journey by the Lorelei Express must have been one of the loveliest train journeys in the world we thought. We then took a train from Basle to Strasbourg and, the following morning, I went to Le Palais de l'Europe to attend a meeting of IULA in the European Parliament chamber where I sat next to Signor Martini, the leader of the Italian delegation, while Judith was taken to the visitors' gallery.

I felt that the time had come for me to retire from the chair of NALC, after ten years, and I was made a Vice-President of the Association. I was entertained to lunch at the Kenilworth Hotel when Lord (Patrick) Jenkin presented me with a cheque on behalf of the National and County Associations and paid me fulsome tributes.

David and Charles decided to publish a series of books on National Parks in which they invited William Condry to do the one on *Snowdonia,* and me to write the one on the Pembrokeshire National Park.

Colonel Chaldecott rang and said that the Lord Lieutenant had advised him that I might be able to suggest someone who would help to organise a Pembrokeshire branch of the Trust for Sick Children in Hospital in Wales and would I call on him at his home, Vrynylan, near Nantgaredig, to see his daffodils, but when he said that he had invited the Dalai Lama to call on him I wondered whether it was some joke. Remembering that Judith had been chairman of the National Association for the Welfare of Children in Hospital, I mentioned her name, with her consent. He invited us to lunch and asked whether we would prefer duck or pheasant and I said that we would be happy with either. He rang again to ask the same question and I gave him the same answer. We had salmon, with a fine Gewurtztraminer and a very smooth 1983 Coteaux du Tricastin.

A man called John Keith Jones rang from north Wales and came to see me to discuss a plan for community radio for Pembrokeshire of which he wanted me to be chairman. I met him off the train and brought him home and listened to him. I then heard from him saying that he wanted to have a meeting with Members of Parliament and others in London and he would fix it to suit my convenience. The meeting took place in the Norman Shaw Building, which was the former New Scotland Yard and the eight MPs who were present seemed to wonder why they were there. I heard no more from him but when I opened the newspaper one morning, I saw that he had murdered his father and his mother.

We joined the plane watchers on the viewpoint on the roof at Heathrow as we waited for our plane to Italy. We stayed a few days in Rome, visiting the Coliseum and St Peter's, the Sistine Chapel and all the traditional sites before taking the Milan Express to Florence. We went to Pisa and to Siena, and then took a train to Venice where we spent seven blissful days.

After attending a Garden Party at Buckingham Palace, John and Marlene Green took us to Wyndham Lewis's flat, which was formerly Stanley Baker's, below Lord Archer's much publicised penthouse flat, on the Victoria Embankment, where we drank champagne while we enjoyed the splendidly panoramic views up the Thames.

I went to represent the Eisteddfod and the Gorsedd, at the Mod at Stornoway. Judith and I first crossed to Skye from Kyle of Lochalsh to Kyleakin and toured the island. We then took the ferry boat from Uig to Tarbert and stayed at the Harris Hotel where the landlord, John Morrison, taught me some Gaelic phrases to use in my speech at the *Mod*. As I had forgotten to bring any headgear I bought a deer-stalker hat at Tarbert, and also a Harris tweed jacket. We toured the bleak landscape of South Harris, before taking the lonely road to Stornoway. The official opening ceremony was held at the Seaforth Hotel, after which Simon Mackenzie of BBC Scotland, congratulated me on my 'perfect Gaelic'. On the Sunday we went to see the Broch of Carloway and the ruins of *tigh dubh*, the 'black houses', at Gavinin, and the great stone circle at Callanish. We went to the kirk in the evening for the official *Mod* service and I was fascinated by the 'mouth singing', a primitive unaccompanied humming led by the precentor.

When we got to Fort William I rang Humphrey Drummond of Megginch and he immediately insisted that we go to the castle to stay the night. His wife, Cherry (Baroness Strange) was away, sitting in the House of Lords, and much as I tried to get him to come out to eat, he would cook a supper, with Judith's help, which we ate in the candlelit glow of the dining room. The baronial drawing room was comfortably lived-in, but it was cold despite the huge log fire.

Humphrey took us round the gardens the following morning, where there were pheasant and peacocks and a dovecote that looked like a pagoda, built by a Drummond who had been to the Far East. The Bird Room had 649 specimens, from Robin to Griffon Vulture, all shot by Captain H. M. Drummond who had died in 1852 but about 70 had been lost in a fire that took place at the castle in 1969.

We called at Gleneagles where Judith bought a golfing hat, and went on to stay at the Sharrow Bay Hotel which was, of course, very comfortable though overstocked with Victoriana in every room, and the dinner was excellent, though over-rich. We had breakfast with a view of Helvellyn and walked in th garden before we set off for Pooley Bridge and travelled along Ullswater and over the Kirkstone Pass to Troutbeck and Ambleside. We had lunch at Hawkshead and called at Beatrix Potter's cottage at Sawney.

We were invited, as guests of British Telecomm, to a Bach Festival Concert at St David's Cathedral followed by a reception at the Warpool Court Hotel where the chairman of the St David's Community Council asked me whether I thought that St David's could invite the Royal National Eisteddfod of Wales to be held there in the year 2000. A couple of years later, I received a request to meet the Community Council and I gave members an idea of the commitment, financial and otherwise. I heard no more until I saw an application by St David's before the Eisteddfod Council but, by then, it was rather late and it was decided that the festival should be held at Llanelli in 2000. St David's was chosen as the venue for 2002.

On the evening prior to the Proclamation ceremony at Mold, we dined at Sychtyn Hall, built by Bishop Wynne of St Asaph in about 1720, and rebuilt in 1868 by the Bankes family. The ceremony was held on the motte of the old Norman Castle. We left Mold for London and called at Llwyn Eglwys at Gresford to see my best man, John Gwilym Jones and his wife, Bethan, who made us stay the night.

We called at the *Spreadeagle* at Thame where I found the name of the former landlord, John Fothergill, prominent about the place, and the receptionist was impressed when I told her that I knew him. We visited the Meeting House at Jordans and stood at the grave of William Penn, and went to Stoke Poges Church where we saw Thomas Gray's tomb.

We sailed from Portsmouth to Cherbourg on our way to Brasparts to attend at the Breton Gorsedd ceremony once more. We stayed the first night at St Vaast-le-Hougue and, the next morning, we called at Dol-de-Bretagne Cathedral to see the figure of Samson of Caldey in the stained glass window. We stayed at Dinan and spent the following morning at Dinard and Guingamp, and went on to Belle Isle-en-Terre, where the village was *en fête* in celebration of Bastille Day, ending in a bonfire and fireworks. We arrived early at Brasparts and were greeted by the Grand Druid and Bertrand Borne. After the ceremony we had a pleasant pastoral lunch under the oak trees at an old mill at Skourick when Borne told me all about their problems.

Geoffrey George, who had been steward of the barony of Cemais for almost as long as I had been a burgess, died while on holiday in Cyprus and the Lady Marcher asked me to attend his funeral as her representative. Judith and I sat in the choir stalls of the little church of Llangoedmor, immediately beside the lead-lined coffin, while the new vicar began by saying that he had not known Mr George and went on to extol his virtues by hearsay. We were invited to the house after the funeral, where Judge Lewis Bowen spoke highly of Marilyn as a magistrate.

Anne Cromwell invited John and Marlene, Judith and I to her villa in Mojacar. We flew from Birmingham and were met at Almeria, and driven a hundred kilometres to Mojacar, except that when we were within sight of the place, we found the road blocked by a landslide and we had to return almost to Almeria and take another route. We stopped at Cariboneras, at the Hotel del Palmas, as the only place where we were likely to have something to eat, and went through Los Molinos and Turre, reaching Mojacar just before midnight. We hired a car and travelled around and went to Granada, where we stayed at the Melia Granada Hotel and spent the following day visiting the Alhambra and the Generalife, which John and I had visited before.

In a bundle of books that I had bought for sixpence at an auction sale at the Memorial Hall at Newport before the war, there was a small volume, covered in hessian, which I might have cast aside rather than carry it home had I not seen, on opening it, that it was called *The Whole Art of Leger-de-main: or Hocus Pocus*, published in 1772. More than half a century later it was still among my books and I feared that, one day, someone might pick it up and, on account of its condition, throw it into the rubbish bin. I mentioned the book during conversation with Dr Feisenberger at the Savile one evening, and he suggested that I should take it to Sotheby's. There I was met by a tall young man, named Michael Heseltine, who said that it might fetch £500. I left it with him and, a few days after the sale, I was informed that it had been bought by a buyer in Europe for £3,275.

At an Eisteddfod Council meeting held at Mold, Dr Eirwen Gwynn gave notice of a motion to delete the word 'Royal' from the title of the Royal National Eisteddfod of Wales. I appealed to her to withdraw the motion on the grounds that it would be hurtful to loyal Eisteddfod followers, and would provide an opportunity for the Eisteddfod's enemies to withdraw financial support provided by local authorities. At the following meeting of the Council, the Director stated that he had received letters from local authorities warning against the financial consequences of renouncing royal patronage and the matter was quickly dropped.

When the Eisteddfod was at Mold, we stayed at The Tower, a fortified tower house built by Rheinallt Gruffydd ap Bleddyn in the fifteenth century, where we were greeted by Charles and Wendy Wynne-Eyton. Charles showed us round the house and and pointed to a large hook protruding from the ceiling above the long oak table in the dining room from which, he said, his ancestor had hanged the Mayor of Chester.

The Cambrian Archaeological Association asked me to arrange their summer meeting in Pembrokeshire, as I had done previously in 1956. Judith and I carried out a reconnaissance of the routes and made the necessary arrangements at St Non's Hotel at St David's, which we had made our headquarters, and I gave the opening address.

We travelled through the Mersey Tunnel, for the first time for me, on our way to attend the NALC biennial conference at Southport. I found that the house where I had been so well entertained in 1947, No. 20, The Promenade, by Dr Clements who had murdered two wives and was in the process of poisoning the third, was now Bailey's Hotel. The walls of the bar were covered in press cuttings referring to the celebrated doctor.

Judith arranged for us to take another holiday in Italy. We flew to Naples, whence we were taken by coach to Sorrento to stay at the Grand Hotel di Capodimonte, an architectural achievement fitted into the face of the rock. We went by jet foil to the Isle of Capri, where it was a joy to visit the Villa San Michele, in which Axel Munthe had been inspired to write his much loved book, *The Story of San Michele*.

We went to Pompeii where we were taken on a conducted tour along the chariot-rutted streets of that once buried city and to the Forum and the Basilica, and the many brothels and wine bars, the House of the Faun and the House of the Tragic Poet, with its mosaic of a chained dog, with its warning *Cave Canem*. We then went to Vesuvius and were taken by coach to within a thousand feet of the edge of the volcano, after which we had to clamber up the steep slope of littered charcoal. When we got back to the hotel I read the contemporary account of the destruction of Pompeii, 'on the 24th of August 79 BC', by the Younger Pliny, who had survived because he had declined the invitation of his uncle, Pliny, to investigate the eruption with him.

The next day we took a bus along 'the most romantic drive in Italy', to Amalfi. We had the front seats which made the journey an exciting one as the driver had had a violent quarrel with a colleague as we left, and drove with fury, mumbling foul oaths, and skimming the precipitous bends so that it seemed as though we were about to be hurled over the side of the cliff on to Positano, John Steinbeck's 'dream place'. Beautiful Amalfi was dominated by a statue of Flavio Gioia, the inventor of the marine compass. The Villa Rufio was about to close for the two-hour lunch period when we arrived at Ravello but the keeper allowed Judith to take a picture of the gardens in which Wagner found inspiration for his magic garden in 'Parsifal'. The return journey was more enjoyable as the driver's fury had subsided.

The Gorsedd of Bards made preparations for the celebration of the bicentenary of its foundation by Iolo Morganwg (Edward Williams) in 1792. After making inquiries in various parts of England and Wales, I managed to get hold of Iolo's great-great-great-grandson, also named Edward Williams, living in Bath, and invited him and his wife to attend a celebratory dinner. The former Archdruid Geraint Bowen, assisted by his wife, Zonia, wrote a history of the Gorsedd, *Hanes Gorsedd y Beirdd*, to mark the occasion, and I was asked to write one in English, which I called *The Secret of the Bards of the Isle of Britain*, being a translation of Iolo's *Cyfrinach Beirdd Ynys Prydain*.

The Archdruid's robe, of heavy satin, was becoming frayed at the edges and I set out to find material to replace it. I tried the shops in Oxford Street and Regent Street and stalls at the back of Soho, Ede and Ravenscroft and the factory at Sudbury that had made Princess Diana's wedding dress, the mills of Lancashire and the shops of Paris, Brussels, Zurich, among other places, but to no avail. I mentioned the matter during conversation to Tom Hughes, of Messrs T. P.

Hughes, the Haverfordwest drapers, and the next day he rang to say that he had found a bolt in a dark corner in his store, which was within an arrow shot of my house. The cost of the material, close on £1,000, and of making the robe, was paid by my friend Towyn Jones.

One of my problems, as Herald Bard, had always been the prolixity of Archdruids once they got on the Logan Stone, and this was especially so when the weather was unpredictable, as it so often was. I, therefore, prepared a handbook, *Llawlyfr Cyfarwyddyd y Swyddogaeth a'r Seremonïau*, in which I gave the order of procedure in each of the ceremonies, and included a schedule of the duties of all the officers.

Judith planned a holiday for us in Vienna, where we stayed at the Hotel Pertschy in Habsburgstrasse, which was said to have been built as a palace for one of the Habsburg Emperor's officers. The hotel was famous for 'the blue stove in room 220', a bedroom adjacent to ours, but we were not able to discover the reason as it seemed rather ordinary. We immediately made for the Stephansdom, St Stephen's Cathedral, which, though severely damaged during the war, had been reconstructed and restored to its former glory, and its 450 foot spire was visible from everywhere. We saw the pulpit carved in 1515 by Master Pilgram, decorated with the figures of saints, and of himself as a Peeping Tom. We went to the State Opera House, and the Hofburg, the castle from which the Emperors ruled, and to the Kunsthistorisches Museum, the Museum of Art History, which would take a week to appreciate its fine collections of treasures and of paintings by Rembrandt, Rubens, Vermeer, Veronese, Holbein, Dürer and Peter Breughel, a third of whose works were there. We visited the Schönbrunn Palace, which has 1,441 rooms and was the residence of Maria Theresa, whose favourite rooms Napoleon occupied. We went to Grinzing and drank wine at the Reinprecht Heurige, and to Gumpoldskirchen where wine has been made for a thousand years, or even twice as long, its people will tell you; to Baden, a spa since Roman times, and to the house where Mozart lived and wrote his *Ave Verum*, and to Kahlenberg to look over the city. We travelled through the Vienna Woods and sang the song, 'Tales from the Vienna Woods' and visited the Belvedere-Schlösser Palaces, which now house the Austrian Gallery Museums. We saw the Anker clock in the Hoher Markt strike twelve, with its parade of twelve people, from Marcus Aurelius to Joseph Haydn, and called at the Griechenbeisl, the historic inn where Wagner and Strauss and Brahms drank and where Mark Twain wrote his 'Million Pound Note'. We visited the Karlskirche and the Schottenkirche built by Irish monks at a time when Ireland was known as 'New Scotland', and Peterskirche, modelled on St Peter's, Rome, and the Votive Church, built after the failure of an attempt to assassinate Franz Joseph, and the Capuchin Church where he, and other Emperors lie buried in the Imperial vault. The Empress Maria Theresa is commemorated by one of the most impressive monuments in Vienna, as her sarcophagus takes the form of a bed of state upon which she lies with her husband, Francis I.

A high point for me was a visit to the Spanish Riding School which dates back to 1572 and is the only place in the world where the Classical style of riding is still practised. The Lippizzaner stallions do not begin their training until they are four years old and at the age of seven they learn the ground exercises, from which they graduate. The riders wear buckskin breeches, high black boots, brown jackets and bicorn hats trimmed with gold. The Baroque Riding School in which they perform was built in about 1730 by Charles VI whose portrait, hanging on the wall, they salute before each display.

We visited the great Benedictine abbey of Melk, standing fortress-like above the Danube. We dined at the Ofenloch, one of Vienna's leading restaurants, which boasted Franz Joseph's favourite dish, *tafelspitz* – boiled beef with horse radish sauce and potatoes. We had coffee and *sachertorte* at the Hotel Sacher and, most afternoons we had tea on the Graben, an open half-street half square, which is the hub of Vienna. Most evenings ended at the famous Café Hawelka, the haunt of the great literary figures of the past, that was full of atmosphere and smoke and students.

Not long after we got home, we went to the *Oireachtas* at Dungarvan and on our way there we called on the Marquis of Waterford at Curraghmore. Judith had difficulty in negotiating the long drive as it was thickly populated by pheasant: I asked the Marquis how many he had and he said that he did not know but that ten thousand had been released that week. He showed us the house, and the Shell House built by the mother of the first Marquis, and the tallest Douglas fir tree in the British Isles. He explained the difficulties in keeping the estate afloat and feared that he would not be able to pass it on to his son, the Earl of Tyrone.

The official opening of the *Oireachtas* at Dungarvan took place at the Park Hotel and, after I had made my speech conveying greetings, I was presented with a Mullingar silver pewter. The President for the year, Kieran Mac Mahoun, whom I had met previously at Galway and whose soft voice one heard on Sunday mornings at eight on *Radio Eireann* presenting a programme which, he said, was 'designed for those suffering from hangovers'. He told me that he had a message for me from Sean MacReamoinn and took me to his room to telephone him. Sean apologised for being unable to some to the festival and invited us to go to Dublin when it was over. A lively lady who said that she was working on St Patrick's connection with Wales, proved to be a nun, Sister Declan, and she maintained that I was descended from the Deisi who had occupied west Wales from the fourth to the tenth centuries.

We drove to Dublin to stay with Sean and his wife, Pat. The next day we visited Trinity College for Judith to see the Book of Kells, and the College Library. We had coffee at the Kildare Street and University Club, which has a reciprocal arrangement with the Savile, and lunch at the Shelburne, and in the afternoon we visited the National Gallery.

Leaving Dublin we took the road through Dun Laoghaire and Dalkey and down the Vale of Clara, in its autumn glory. At the 'Meeting of the Waters' I took a picture of the memorial plaque to Tom Moore, and we then drove along the 'Sweet Vale of Avoca' to Rosslare.

At a meeting of the Wardens' Court of the Gild of Freemen of Haverfordwest, I suggested that the Marquis of Waterford, as he sat in the House of Lords by virtue of his Imperial title, Baron Tyrone of Haverfordwest, be invited to become a Burgess, which he regarded as a great honour.

On our way to Lichfield to attend the annual meeting of the National Association of City and Town Sheriffs in England and Wales, we stayed at Bredwardine Hall, and visited the churchyard to see Kilvert's tomb, inscribed: 'He being dead yet speaketh.' We called at Whipsnade and at Woburn Abbey, and also at Shugborough Hall, where I was reminded that the first Lord Lichfield had married a daughter of Nathaniel Phillips of Slebech. At the meeting, held at the Guildhall, the President, Andrew Gravells, accepted my notice of a motion to remove the name of the Town Reeve of Bungay, who had been improperly admitted as his office was more like that a mayor rather than that of a sheriff. The meeting also accepted my amendments to the constitution without discussion. We were taken on a conducted tour of the city and, at Dr Johnson's birthplace, I was particularly interested to see a picture of his *protégé* Anna Williams of Rosemarket. Following the Sheriffs' Service, held at Lichfield Cathedral, I told the Dean that I was thinking of raiding his cathedral library so as to retrieve the eighth century *Book of Teilo*, otherwise known as the *Book of St Chad*, misappropriated from Llandeilo, a thousand years ago.

The following year the Association held its annual meeting at Haverfordwest and we, as the Shrievalty Association of Haverfordwest, played host to them. The first delegate to arrive at the reception on the Friday evening was a large, black, man, who was a former Sheriff of Nottingham. He confirmed the strange reports that I had seen in the papers that Nottingham had been unable to find anyone to be Sheriff in recent years and said that he, as a former sheriff, had come to represent the city. Following the annual meeting, held on the next morning, I took a coach-load of delegates to St David's where we were met at the Cathedral by the Dean, and afterwards along the coast to Fishguard. The President asked me if I would contact London with a view to holding the annual meeting there in the year 2000 and I wrote to Group Captain John Constable, the Secondary of London, the relevant officer, but when they realised the commitment, they abandoned the idea.

At the annual meeting of the Pembrokeshire Historical Society I was appointed President to succeed the late Francis Jones, Wales Herald of Arms.

I went to see Bryn Parry-Jones, the Chief Executive of the new Pembrokeshire County Council and suggested that he should get his Council to register the coat-of-arms of the old Pembrokeshire County Council, the blazoning of which I gave him, as its own, which it did at an expenditure of £7,000. Parry-Jones did not appear to have a knowledge of its purpose, however, as he allowed, or even encouraged, the Council to use a 'logo' comprising the cross-head of the Nevern Cross to be used on Council property and note paper, and even on the road signs standing at the approaches to the county, where the coat-of-arms normally appears.

The County Librarian, Mary John, asked me to launch the publication of a facsimile copy of Richard Fenton's *Historical Tour through Pembrokeshire*. There followed requests to lecture on Fenton to the Pembrokeshire Historical Society and to the Fishguard and the St David's Societies, and a request for an article for the *Journal of the Pembrokeshire Historical Society*.

I presented the Newport Golf Club with an old hickory-shaft putter which had been made for me by the former professional, R. E. Nurse, in about 1930.

Chipperfields' Circus came to town, or rather to the Pembrokeshire County Show ground, and David George, as a director of the Show, was given ringside seat tickets and invited me to join him. The performing animals included eight perfect Arab stallions, two African elephants, zebras, sea lions and eight tigers. The artistes were hair-raisingly magnificent and the clowns were all that clowns should be. It was a most enjoyable event and probably the last of its kind that will ever come this way.

We took Anthony to Newport to celebrate his fiftieth birthday. Harry and Juliette Holt invited us to the castle for pre-prandial drinks and took us over the place to remind Anthony of his haunts as a boy. We then went to Cnapan, where he had spent some of his pre-natal time as we frequently visited our friends Dai and Iris Havard, and Dai, as our doctor, did all in his power to persuade him to arrive in this world.

My book *The Ancient Borough of Newport in Pembrokeshire*, published by the Cultural Services Department of the Dyfed County Council, was launched at a ceremony held at the Library Hall where Mary John, the Librarian, had arranged for Lady Lloyd's paintings, which I remember hanging in Newport Castle, were displayed at my request. The Mayors of Newport and of Haverfordwest, and the Chairmen of the Preseli District Council and of the Pembrokeshire County Council,

Councillor John Thomas, were present when Dr Geoffrey Wainwright, Director of English Heritage, launched the book in generous terms.

I wrote to Sir Cennydd Traherne, KG, as a fellow member of the Gorsedd, to acquaint him of a proposal to remove the picture of the Queen, in Gorsedd robes, that appeared in the Gorsedd programme each year. Sir Cennydd, in his reply, wrote that 'those of us who are loyal to the Crown will have to examine our consciences if this break with tradition comes to pass.' The next day he went to London to represent the Queen at the memorial service to Lord Shackleton at Westminster Abbey, which was his last duty. He died the day following.

A centenary dinner to commemorate the birth of Cynan was held at Pwllheli. where he was born, together with a special Gorsedd ceremony. A symposium to mark the occasion was published, to which I contributed a chapter which I called 'Pendefig Pasiant' (the Master of Pageantry).

We travelled to the Eisteddfod at Colwyn Bay and stayed at Y Faenol Fawr, a house built in 1597 by John Lloyd, diocesan registrar of St Asaph, whose arms were carved over the fireplace in the dining room. On the Sunday morning we went to see St Margaret's, the marble church built by Margaret, Lady Willoughby de Broke, daughter of Sir John Williams of Bodelwyddan Castle, in 1860, and the graves of the Canadian soldiers who had been shot in the mutiny at Kinmel Park Camp in 1919.

It was an emotional moment for the Archdruid when, on the Monday afternoon, as Herald Bard, I led his brother to him to be invested Crown Bard, and even more so on the Friday, as I handed his son to him to be installed the Chaired Bard. This had never happened before and it will be a long time before, if ever, it happens again.

When we were staying at Y Faenol Fawr, Juliette Holt had run us to earth and rang to ask us to lunch at Newport Castle the following week. She also invited us to stay there the night of the mayoral installation, when I had the slightly traumatic experience of sleeping there again after close on half a century.

The Gorsedd Banner needed renewal and I decided that I would have it replaced as my final contribution to the Gorsedd. As with the material for a new robe for the Archdruid, I had no small amount of difficulty. I tried all known embroidery bodies in Wales and then sent it to the Royal School of Needlework at Hampton Court who said that they would undertake the work for £20,000. I finally got a firm in Swansea, that normally made Masonic regalia, to do it at a cost of less than £2,000 and my friend Simon Davies, of London, generously met the cost.

Marilyn was appointed chairman of the Dyfed Magistrates Association in succession to the late formidable Auriol Watkin.

The demand for membership of the Haverfordwest Probus Club made it necessary to establish another, to be known as Haverfordwest Probus Club No. 2, with Douglas Imrie-Brown as President. The president, John Green, and I, as incoming President, joined the new club for its first year so as to establish a relationship between the two clubs, and at my installation, I invited Imrie-Brown to be present.

While I was writing *A Book on Nevern*, we went to Nevern Church where Judith read out the inscriptions on the memorials and gravestones in her melodious voice, which made listening to them afterwards a pleasure. She said that she wanted my ashes to be buried in Nevern churchyard.

The Pembrokeshire Coast National Park Committee held a reception for past and present members at which the chairman pointed out that I was the only surviving member of the original committee formed in 1952.

The Prince of Wales Committee held its last meeting at the Park Hotel, Cardiff and past and present members were invited to a luncheon after the meeting. I went to Bala to select the matron and the maiden for the forthcoming Eisteddfod and we stayed at the Wild Pheasant, Llangollen, as we were on our way to Scarborough to attend the biennial NALC conference. We stopped for lunch, the next day, at T'Racecourses Hotel at Kettlewell and halted at the pretty village of East Witton. We had tea at Jervaulx, near the abbey ruins, where a peacock in moult vainly endeavoured to be in pride. We stayed at Middleham, at the Miller's House Hotel, where Judith had ostrich for dinner. The following morning the town resounded as scores of racehorses clattered past Middleham Castle.

We called at Fountains Abbey, and at Rievaulx Abbey, which had mementoes of the Duncombes, Lord Feversham's family. We had lunch at the Feversham Arms at Helmsley and walked round the market where there were statues of two former Feversham barons. We called at Duncombe Park and found Peter mending a tractor, prior to leaving for the conference at Scarborouigh, where we stayed at the Royal Hotel.

We left Scarborough after the conference, which was the poorest I had yet attended as it was dominated by the new chairman, Anthony Hayward of Essex, and made for Lincoln to see my grandson Andrew, who was a chiropractor there, and took him and his girl friend, Ruth, to dinner at the twelfth century Wig and Mitre Inn. On our homeward journey we had lunch at the George at Stamford which claimed to be the oldest coaching house in the kingdom, with twenty coaches calling daily in its heyday.

I gave an address on George Owen of Henllys to the Honourable Society of Cymmrodorion, meeting at the British Academy and at the reception that followed I met a number of old friends. The editor of *The Transactions of the Honourable Society*, Dr Peter Roberts, of Canterbury, asked me to write an article on George Owen for the journal, which appeared in the 1998 edition.

The *Daily Telegraph* rang and a voice asked: 'Is that the College of Arms?' When I said that it was not, a young lady said that she wanted to speak to the Herald Bard. It was the *Telegraph's* way of checking to see whether I was still alive to go into their Birthdays List. *The Times* always rang and tactfully asked 'Are you still the Herald Bard?' I found it strange, however, to receive a request from the *Glasgow Herald* for permission to include my name in its Birthday List, in the manner of *The Times* and *The Daily Telegraph* and *The Independent*.

Having been a Burgess of the ancient borough of Newport for sixty years, I was presented with a whisky decanter inscribed with the arms of the barony and my name and a suitable legend.

I was invited to speak to the members of the Newport Community Council at a dinner held at the Golden Lion, during which I referred to the Council as it was when I was appointed Clerk sixty-six years previously.

To celebrate my eightieth birthday, my family took me to dinner at Stone Hall, where we were warmly welcomed by Dr Watson and his wife. The gardens were lovely with azaleas and rhododendrons, magnolias and bluebells, and the echoing song of a thrush. My brother and Janet brought a Staffordshire plate which they had had specially made and inscribed. We had a party at the house, and John Green arranged a luncheon party at the Mariners for fifteen of my men friends, and my brother.

I went with Anthony and Di to Andrew's graduation ceremony at Bournemouth, and to Tamsin's at Cardiff, and with Marilyn and Robbie to Swansea to Emily's at the Brangwyn Hall, Swansea, but failed to get to Max's at Southampton. We were able to attend his Passing Out Parade at the Royal Naval College at Dartmouth, however, and I took him and his parents and Emily to dinner at the Royal Castle Hotel the previous evening. We arrived early at the College and were given seats from which to watch the Parade at which the Queen, as Lord High Admiral of the United Kingdom, took the salute. Max and the family had lunch with Her Majesty while Judith and I had our meal in the Gunners' Room. The Queen planted a tree in the grounds of the College and, in the evening, we attended a service in the College Church, which was followed by a cocktail party on the Quarter-deck. On our homeward journey we stayed at the Royal and Fortescue Hotel at Barnstaple, where Emily joined us for dinner. We called, the following day, at Holnicote, where Richard Fenton had stayed with the Fortescues, according to his *Tour in Quest of Genealogy*, and went to Selworthy, and had a garden tea at Kitnog's in Bossington.

Prior to the Proclamation of the National Eisteddfod at Bala, I wrote to James Nicholas, the Gorsedd Recorder, giving twelve months' notice of my intention to retire from the office of Herald Bard. I had been a member of the Gorsedd for sixty years, a member of its Board for fifty years, and Herald Bard for thirty years and I reckoned that this would be a good time to call it a day. Furthermore, my health was beginning to give concern. He wrote to say that he received my letter with great regret and asked whether I would consider changing my mind. The Board, at first, refused to accept my notice, and offered to appoint a deputy or assistant to assist me to carry out the duties, but I declined the offer.

Some days after I had submitted the notice, I received a telephone call from the journal *Golwg* referring to my refusal to accept mail from a Gorsedd member, a girl from Bala, requesting the loan of a robe, upon which the postage stamp had been deliberately placed upside-down, intending it to be an insult to the Queen. I had returned the envelope, which also contained a reply-paid envelope with the stamp placed upside-down, stating that I was not prepared to accept it and that I would be glad to reply to a communication addressed to me in the conventional manner. I had experienced a case of the kind, some years earlier, when an extremist vicar had sent me a letter stamped in this manner, and I had written to him in the same vein and he had apologised but this girl took the matter to the media. The call from *Golwg* was followed by requests for radio and television interviews, and the matter was taken up by the *Liverpool Post* and the *Western Mail*, and *The Guardian*, which had a report headed 'Druids banned by the high-ranking Herald Bard'. A friend rang from London to say that it had been featured in the *Evening Standard*.

The Eisteddfod at Llandeilo proved to be an exciting one, on the one hand with plaudits for providing a new Gorsedd banner and regrets at my departure and congratulations on the stand that I had taken with regard to the stamp. The Archdruid and members paid their tributes at the Board meeting and when the Archdruid asked if I would like to say something, I said: 'Yes. Next business, please.' There was more appreciation at the annual general meeting and, in the Gorsedd Circle, the Archdruid spoke kind words from the Logan Stone. By now I was suffering from a heart complaint and, at the Chairing ceremony on the Friday afternoon I was not feeling well and, at the end of the ceremony, I was glad to feel that I was walking off the stage for the last time.

At my last meeting of the Gorsedd Board, held at the National Library, there was some discussion with regard to my action regarding the stamp and some of the nationalist members felt that I should have accepted it and moved that the Gorsedd officials should receive letters so stamped in future. The motion, despite its disrespect to the Queen, a fellow member of the Gorsedd, was supported by the Eisteddfod's Honorary Secretary who had recently been appointed a Commander of the British Empire by Her Majesty. I left as soon as my successor was appointed, relieved that I did not have to cause a stir by resigning from a Board that behaved in that way and I thought how different things would have been had Cynan been alive.

I had previously been asked by the Board to record my recollections of the past sixty years which I did in my book, *Atgofion Hen Arwyddfardd* (The Reminiscences of an Old Herald Bard), that was published by Gwasg Gee of Denbigh so that it was available in time for the Bala Eisteddfod. I handed the first copy to the Archdruid at a reception at which he presented me with a portrait of myself in the robes of the Herald Bard, which was to be handed to the National Library of Wales after my time.

I completed *The Lords of Cemais*, giving the history of the lords of the barony in greater detail than I was able to do in *The Ancient Borough of Newport*.

I relinquished the chair of the Shrievalty Association of the Town and County of Haverfordwest, to become its President for the next three years, at each of which I attended the Sheriff's service, and read the First Lesson, at St Mary's Church and entertained the current High Sheriff and the chairman of the Pembrokehsire County Council and their wives at our Sheriff's Breakfast at the Hotel Mariners. As President I received from the hands of the Mayor a medallion to be worn by former sheriffs on a ribbon on appropriate occasions.

We sailed from Dover in the *Saga Rose*, on a Baltic cruise which Judith had arranged for us. We went ashore at Stockholm and took a Royal Canal Tour, past Skansen where I had dined on elk during a previous visit, and Prince Eugen's Waldemariudde, and the Royal Palace, and the *Vasa* Museum. The ship called at Helsinki the next day, and Judith went ashore. When we arrived at St Petersburg we were greeted by a Russian band which made a bold effort at a rendering of 'God Save the Queen'. Everything we saw at St Petersburg was more fabulous than anything that one had expected. We saw the Peter and Paul Fortress, stood beside the fine equestrian statue of Peter the Great and visited the Cathedral with the incredibly thin spire of gold where he lies buried; stood on Neva Bridge with its twin lighthouses, and went to an art gallery where we were served with vodka, and to St Isaac's Cathedral, which is now a museum. We stood on the Nevsky Prospect and watched old women sweep the streets with besoms.

The Hermitage is the place of all places. To go round and see everything there, we were told, would take seven years. We had but a day. Leonardos and Rembrandts and all the great artists covered the walls; a State Coach to rival our own Queen's stood in a state room, and the Golden Peacock clock. Palaces everywhere, many in need of restoration, but that they, and all their magnificent contents, should have survived the Bolsheviks, the Communists and two wars, is a miracle of our time.

At Tallinn we went ashore but I returned to the ship after a while and lay on a bed-chair on deck reading *The Man Behind the Smile: Tony Blair and the Politics of Persuasion* by Leo Abse I found this a frightening book as it reveals sides of Blair's character which present a grave danger to this country, once he gets his way, which he always insists on getting, and he will not be satisfied until he runs the country in a presidential manner, treating the Queen as his poodle.

We sailed on a lake-like sea to Gdansk where, on docking, we nearly ran into an Indian ship after a rope had snapped with the crack of a gun. We were shown the shipyard and Waleska's house, where he entertained Margaret Thatcher, and taken to Sopot, the seaside resort, with its memorial to Joseph Conrad, near which the three-masted frigate *Dar Pomorza* lay at anchor, and then to Gdynia, the youngest of the tri-cities. The old city had interesting buildings, many of which had been rebuilt.

We anchored off the island of Ronne and those who so wished, which included Judith, were taken off by boat to Bornholm. At Copenhagen we sat in the Tivoli Gardens and, the next morning we sailed through the Oslo Fjord and tied up under Akershus Castle, alongside a sinister looking modern French warship. We had stormy weather going through the Skaggerrat and across the North Sea and were glad to dock at Dover. We got off as soon as possible as I had to attend a meeting of the NALC Council in London. Judith drove magnificently and we arrived on time at the Kenilworth Hotel, where we were booked for the night. That evening the Council held its annual reception at Barclay's Bank, Gracechurch Street, after which Major John Turner, and his wife, Jane, took us to dinner at Rules.

Soon after one o'clock one morning, while listening to the BBC World Service, I heard the announcer say that Princess Diana had been involved in a car accident in Paris. It was later reported that her companion, Dodi el Fayed, and the driver had been killed and that she suffered a broken arm and thigh and had concussion. Updated reports were given throughout the night until five o'clock when it was announced that she had died. Her body was brought home and the world went into mourning, and mad with grief. The BBC interviewed Lord Elis-Thomas and I on her death, the tragedy of our time: she who would have been Queen had ended her life in a car smash with the son of an disreputable Egyptian. One could not resist thinking, however, of the awful alternative, whereby she might have married him and borne his children.

A congratulatory card from the Marquess of Anglesey was the first indication I received that I had been elected a Fellow of the Society of Antiquaries, and then came a letter from Geoffrey Wainwright, a Vice-President of the Society, who had put my name forward. I went to the Society's headquarters in Burlington House to be installed and was greeted, to my surprise, by Eve, Keidrych Rhys's widow, and by the secretary, David Morgan Evans, who took me to his office where he had the original of Tongue's painting of Pentre Ifan hanging on the wall. I took the oath and signed the book of members, first signed by George IV, and by Royal Fellows up to the Queen, and was admitted by the President, Simon Swynfen, holding a silver mace on his shoulder.

When I had returned to the Savile that evening, Piers Pottinger arrived in great form as his horse had won at Wincanton and he invited Dr Joe Loudon and I to help him celebrate with a bottle of Verve Clicquot. This was my last night at the Club, which was jolly but sad without my great friends, such as Wynford Vaughan-Thomas and Huw Wheldon and others who had died, and Tony Garrett Anderson, who was not expected to be there again.

We went for a holiday to the west coast of Ireland and stayed at the Westport Woods Hotel, set in the grounds of Westport House, home of the Marquess of Sligo, which was most comfortable, and at the Yeats Country Hotel, Rosses Point where Yeats spent his summer holidays. While we were there, we visited Donegal and took another pilgrimage to Drumcliff where we found Yeats's grave surrounded by large American ladies. In the hotel bedroom I watched President Clinton being interviewed regarding his relationship with Monica Lewinsky, which he made even more undignified by drinking quantities of coke out of tins.

Arriving at Renvyle House, 'a sea-grey house', was, for me, a dream fulfilled. Here Oliver St John Gogarty played host to Bernard Shaw, Shane Leslie, Lady Lavery, Augustus John and Yeats, who was said to be disliked by the house's dormant spirits. I felt their ghosts around me in the lounge, where so much wit had once gathered.

We called at the Alcock and Brown Hotel at Clifden and had lunch at Ballynahinch Castle, once the home of the Irish Martins. The hotel manager, Desmond Lally, was interested to hear about the Martin Lords of Cemais and gave me a copy of a booklet he had written about the hotel and its Martin connection. He was a devotee of Dylan Thomas and was excited to meet someone who had known him. As we came away we saw a sign which stated: 'Deserted Village for Sale'.

On our journey homeward we were invited to take tea with Lord and Lady Waterford at Curraghmore, which was so good that it rather spoilt our appetite for the dinner that I had ordered at the Lobster Pot at Carne, where Judith had to face a huge platter of sea food and I a fine fillet steak.

I was taken by surprise once more on my birthday, on my eighty-third, and this time by my grandchildren who had cleverly conspired to arrange a large luncheon party at the Beggars Reach Hotel to which they had invited the other members of my family and a dozen of my closest friends.

Anthony showed me the Internet on his computer and asked me to suggest a word to the computer. I frivolously suggested 'Eisteddfod' and, to my amazement, the word appeared on the desktop together with the name of my book, *The Royal National Eisteddfod of Wales*, as obtainable from Amazon Ltd., of Seattle, the biggest book shop in the world. I later discovered that most of my books were listed on Amazon Books and Barnes and Noble of Dayton, New Jersey, Blackwells, The Bookpl@ce and others. A few weeks later I bought my own computer, for use as a word processor, which Anthony set up for me, and my world changed.

The Oxford University Press invited me to contribute the entries on George Owen of Henllys, on his father, William Owen, and on his illegitimate son, George Owen, York Herald, for the *New Dictionary of National Biography*, which is due to appear during the first decade of the new millennium.

The editor of the journal *Llafar Gwlad* asked me to write some articles and I sent him *Storïau Daniel y Pant* and *Storïau Gwir Tydrath*, dealing with Newport characters, and I also wrote an article based on the manuscript autobiography of the Reverend John Owen, author of the popular ballad *Y Mochyn Du* (The Black Pig) for the journal.

As I had been involved in the promotion of the study of local history in Pembrokeshire for close on half a century, it was suggested that I should write its history for the Historical Society's *Journal*.

People kept asking me to write a book on Haverfordwest but I told them that I had neither the time nor the competence. In the end, I approached a number of authors who were authorities on their subject and invited them to contribute to the book. They all responded willingly and with great expertise to produce an authoritative work, *The History of the Town and County of Haverfordwest*, which was launched at a ceremony held at the Haverfordwest Castle Gallery.

The County Archivist came to collect some more papers for the 'Dillwyn Miles Collection' at the County Record Office, and to be told what was to be taken eventually.

The writing of books gave me great pleasure and I felt privileged to be included in the *New Companion to the Literature of Wales* as 'writer, historian and Herald Bard'.

ENVOI

I HAVE LIVED IN A SPELL OF TIME unrivalled in human history. My grandfather who died when I was five, had experienced an age not much changed since medieval days. And then, like Noah's Flood, there came a thousand things that are now commonplace, but each, to us, was a new wonder. Never before had man's inventiveness made such a leap in discovery. The one thing that remained unchanged was 'man's inhumanity to man'.

I was born in one war, and came of age in time for another. War gave my life a new shape, and all but took it away, and its aftermath, following five years of warfare in a foreign clime, found one restless and indecisive. I was offered opportunities to study to become a barrister or an academic, but I had a wife and the expectation of a family to care for. The Army, and working for Sir Wyndham Deedes, who was also chairman of the National Council for Social Service, steered me towards social service, and public service as a sideline.

These memoirs are a heavily abridged version, hence their brevity in places. The original lies at the Pembrokeshire Record Office should anyone for some inexplicable reason wish to consult them.

I, too, had 'intimations of immortality in early childhood', soon dispelled by the death of my grandfather. My Sunday School heresy in questioning eternal life remained with me, even in the Holy Land, and was articulated by my old professor, Sir Thomas Parry-Williams, in the closing couplet of his great sonnet, in which he maintains that in fleeing from our fatuous toil, we shall do no more than steal back silently into the stillness whence we came.

Ni wnawn wrth ffoi am byth o'n ffwdan ffôl
Ond llithro i'r llonyddwch mawr yn ôl.

CHRONOLOGY

1916	Born at Newport, Pembrokeshire.
1920-36	Educated at Newport Council School, Fishguard High School, University College of Wales, Aberystwyth.
1932-35	Clerk to the Newport Parish Council.
1935-	Burgess of the Town and Corporation of Newport.
1936-	Member, Gorsedd of Bards of the Isle of Britain.
1936-39	School teacher.
1939-45	World War II: Middle East, Army Captain.
1942	Founded Jerusalem Welsh Society.
1944	Married Sub-Lieutenant Joyce Ord, ATS, St George's Cathedral, Jerusalem.
1945	Anthony born.
1945-47	National Organiser, Palestine House, London.
1945-96	Board of the Gorsedd of Bards.
1946	Marilyn born.
1946-	Fellow of the Royal Geographical Society.
1947-52	Extra-Mural Lecturer, University of Wales.
1946-52	Newport Parish Council.
1947-52	Cemaes Rural District Council.
1947-63	Pembrokeshire County Council.
1947-64	Executive Committee, Council for the Protection of Rural Wales.
1950-51	Mayor of Newport. Established Court of Aldermen and Selection Committee, Revived Perambulation of the Boundaries of Newport.
1951-	Alderman.
1951-75	Member and Vice-Chairman, Pembrokeshire Coast National Park Authority. Chairman, Editorial Committee.
1952-54	Community Centres Officer for Wales.
1954-75	General Secretary, Pembrokeshire Rural Community Council. Founded Old People's Week, Meals on Wheels & Chiropody for the Elderly.

Established Pembrokeshire Guild of Craftsmen.
Introduced Pembrokeshire Best Kept Village Competition.
Inaugurated Pembrokeshire Tourism Association.
Created County Drama Festival and Gŵyl Ddrama Penfro.
Initiated and administered Pageant of Pembroke 1958.
Established Pembrokeshire Art Society.
Founded Pembrokeshire Film Society.
Revived Pembrokeshire Local History Society, arranged 111 lectures, founded and edited *The Pembrokeshire Historian* and promoted publication of the *Pembrokeshire County History*.

1954-	National Association of Local Councils.
1956-59	Executive Committee, Pembrokeshire Territorial Association.
1957-66	Court of Governors, University of Wales.
1957-63	Haverfordwest Borough Council.
1959-66	Grand Sword Bearer, Gorsedd of Bards.
1958-75	Honorary Secretary, West Wales Field Society/Naturalists' Trust.
1959-71	Mental Health Review Tribunal for Wales.
1961-62	Mayor of Haverfordwest and Admiral of the Port.
1961-64	Court of Governors, National Library of Wales
1961-73	Council of the Society for the Promotion of Nature Reserves.
1962	West Wales Tourist Association, founder.
1963-64	Sheriff of the Town and County of Haverfordwest.
1965-69	Sports Council for Wales.
1966-73	Nature Conservancy Council for Wales.
1966-67	Mayor of Newport.
1966-96	Herald Bard.
1966-87	Rent Review Tribunal for Wales.
1967-96	Council, Royal National Eisteddfod of Wales.
1967-68	Mayor of Newport.
1968-72	Council for Small Industries in Wales.
1969-70	Council, Countryside in 1970, Wales.
1971-81	Prince of Wales Committee for Wales.
1971-81	Welsh Environment Foundation.
1972-77	Executive Committee, Age Concern, Wales.
1973	Association of Trusts for Nature Conservation in Wales, founder.
1974-81	Member, Heraldry Society.
1974-	Burgess Warden, Gild of Freemen of Haverfordwest.
1975-81	Director, Dyfed Rural Council.
	Established Dyfed Association of Local Councils.

          Inaugurated Age Concern, Dyfed.
          Founded Dyfed Association for the Disabled.
1977-81   Executive Committee, National Playing Fields Association.
1978-81   Executive Committee, National Council of Social Service.
1979-80   Mayor of Newport.
1980-86   Rural Voice.
1980   Duke of Edinburgh Award.
1993-   Hon. Archivist, Gild of Freemen of Haverfordwest.
1998   Fellow of the Society of Antiquaries.
1999   Member of the Welsh Academy.
2000   Fellow of the Royal Historical Society.

CHAIRMAN:

1950-52   Libraries and Museums Committee, Pembrokeshire County Council.
1950-52   Further Education Committee, Pembrokeshire County Council.
1961-65   Pembrokeshire Arthritis and Rheumatism Council.
1965-81   Wales Committee, National Playing Fields Association.
1971-74   Policy Committee, National Association of Local Councils.
1972-80   Dyfed Projects Group, Prince of Wales Committee.
1974-76   Wales Committee, National Association of Local Councils.
1975-80   Pembrokeshire Community Health Council.
1976-86   National Association of Local Councils.
1984-94   Pembrokeshire Post Office and Telecommunications Advisory Committee.
1988-89   Pembrokeshire Wildlife Appeal Committee.
1992-95   Shrievalty Association of the Town and County of Haverfordwest.

VICE-PRESIDENT:

1975-   Wales Wildlife Trust, West Wales.
1976-   National Association of Local Councils.

PRESIDENT:

1971-75   Pembrokeshire Junior Chamber of Commerce.
1995-98   Shrievalty Association of the Town and County of Haverfordwest.
1994-   Pembrokeshire Historical Society.

Editor:

1955-81 *The Pembrokeshire Historian.*
1971-80 *Nature in Wales.*

Publications:

1973 *Pembrokeshire Coast National Park*: (ed.) 2nd, edn, 1978: Countryside Commission, HMSO, London.
1974 *Writers of West Wales/Llenorion y Gorllewin*: West Wales Association for the Arts, Carmarthen.
1975 *The West Wales Naturalists' Trust and its Nature Reserves*: Haverfordwest.
1976 *The Sheriffs of the County of Pembroke 1541-1974*: Haverfordwest.
1979 *The Castles of Pembrokeshire*: republ. 1983 and 1988: Pembrokeshire Coast National Park.
1982 *The Royal National Eisteddfod of Wales*: Christopher Davies, Swansea.
1983 *A Pembrokeshire Anthology*: Hughes & Son (Publishers) Ltd.; republ. 2000, Dinefwr Press.
1984 *Portrait of Pembrokeshire*: Robert Hale.
1987 *The Pembrokeshire Coast National Park*: David and Charles.
1988 *The Town and County of Haverfordwest: its Freemen and its Charities*: Haverfordwest.
1992 *The Secret of the Bards of the Isle of Breitain*: Dinefwr Press.
1994 *The Description of Pembrokeshire: George Owen* (ed.): Gomer Press.
1995 *The Ancient Borough of Newport in Pembrokeshire*: Haverfordwest Library; 2nd edn. 1998: Cemais Publications Haverfordwest.
1997 *Atgofion Hen Arwyddfardd*: Gwasg Gee.
1997 *The Lords of Cemais*: Dinefwr Press.
1998 *A Book on Nevern*: Gomer Press.
1999 *A History of the Town and County of Haverfordwest*: Gomer Press.

Broadcast features, articles for journals, etc.
Contributor to *The Dictionary of Welsh Biography, The New Dictionary of National Biography, The Encyclopaedia of Wales*, etc.